The
Everyday
Writer
and Researcher

The Everyday Writer

and Researcher

Andrea A. Lunsford

STANFORD UNIVERSITY

Mike Palmquist

COLORADO STATE UNIVERSITY

Coverage for multilingual writers with

Paul Kei Matsuda

ARIZONA STATE UNIVERSITY

Christine M. Tardy

UNIVERSITY OF ARIZONA

macmillan learning
curriculum solutions

bedford/st.martin's ▪ hayden-mcneil ▪ w.h. freeman ▪ worth publishers

Additional content taken from:

The Everyday Writer, Sixth Edition
by Andrea A. Lunsford
© 2016 by Bedford/St. Martin's

The Bedford Researcher, Fifth Edition
by Mike Palmquist
© 2015 by Bedford/St. Martin's

1   0   9   8   7   6
f   e   d   c   b   a

For information, write: Macmillan Learning Curriculum Solutions,
14903 Pilot Dr, Plymouth, MI 48170, www.macmillanlearning.com

ISBN 978-1-319-09827-8 (University of La Verne Edition)

Acknowledgments

Contents

The Writing Program at the
University of La Verne   *ULV-1*

Part 1: The Everyday Writer

Writing Processes
1   The Top Twenty: A Quick Guide to Troubleshooting Your Writing   *4*
4   Exploring Ideas   *32*
5   Planning and Drafting   *39*
6   Developing Paragraphs   *51*
7   Reviewing, Revising, and Editing   *65*
8   Reflecting   *82*

Critical Thinking and Argument
9   Critical Reading   *91*
10   Analyzing Arguments   *107*
11   Constructing Arguments   *122*

Style
30   Coordination, Subordination, and Emphasis   *305*
31   Consistency and Completeness   *311*
32   Parallelism   *314*
33   Shifts   *317*
34   Conciseness   *320*
35   Sentence Variety   *323*

Sentence Grammar
36   Parts of Speech   *331*
37   Parts of Sentences   *338*
38   Verbs and Verb Phrases   *352*
39   Nouns and Noun Phrases   *369*
40   Subject-Verb Agreement   *374*
41   Pronouns   *380*

42 Adjectives and Adverbs *390*
43 Modifier Placement *398*
44 Prepositions and Prepositional Phrases *401*
45 Comma Splices and Fused Sentences *404*
46 Sentence Fragments *410*

Punctuation and Mechanics

47 Commas *416*
48 Semi Colons *426*
49 End Punctuation *428*
50 Apostrophes *431*
51 Quotation Marks *434*
52 Other Punctuation Marks *439*
53 Capital Letters *444*
54 Abbreviations and Numbers *449*
55 Italics *454*
56 Hyphens *455*

MLA Documentation

57 The Basics of MLA Style *461*
58 MLA Style for In-Text Citations *468*
59 MLA Style for a List of Works Cited *475*
60 A Student Research Essay, MLA Style *508*

APA Documentation

61 The Basics of APA Style *521*
62 APA Style for In-Text Citations *525*
63 APA Style for a List of References *530*
64 A Student Research Essay, APA Style *555*

Part 2: The Bedford Researcher

Joining the Conversation

3 Developing Your Research Question and Proposal *45*

Working with Sources

7 Managing Information *113*

Creating Your Document

15 Using Sources Effectively *257*

Courtesy of the University of La Verne

The Writing Program at the University of La Verne

The Writing Program at the University of La Verne

A Few Words of Welcome from the Director of the Writing Program *ULV-3*

ULV Writing Program Mission *ULV-5*
a Learning Outcomes for WRT 110 College Writing A (LVWA) *ULV-5*
b Learning Outcomes for WRT 111 College Writing B Research Writing (LVWB) *ULV-5*

Writing Program Information *ULV-6*
a Campus Resources for Writers *ULV-6*

UNIVERSITY OF LA VERNE

A Few Words of Welcome from the
Director of the Writing Program

Dear Leo Writers:

On behalf of the Writing Program faculty, I welcome you to a foundational course in your academic career: college writing and/or research writing. In your hands is a resource to guide you through your courses. Whether you are enrolled in WRT 109, WRT 110S Writing Studio, WRT 110 or 111, you will need this handy reference as you learn the genres, strategies, and processes of academic writing. WRT 110 and 111 fulfill the Written Communication A and B general education (GE) requirements, which are pre-requisites to many courses in your majors, and are required courses for your undergraduate degree.

Some of you may be thinking, "I got to just get through these GE courses so I can take courses I *want* to take in my major!" Along the same lines, you may be tempted to rent or resell this textbook at the end of the semester. If that is what is running through your mind, please STOP! Take a moment to consider the following:

- Writing Program faculty have worked closely with the publisher to bring you the most informative, yet affordable, college writing textbook that is required for both WRT 110 and 111. One reasonably priced textbook for two semesters!

- *The Everyday Writer and Researcher* covers material that you will use beyond your GE writing courses, including up-to-date references for MLA and APA styles, the two major academic style conventions used by arts & humanities majors, STEM majors, and social sciences majors. This textbook will be a helpful reference for any GE or major course that assigns writing. And I'm going to break it to you gently: most college courses assign some type of writing assignment.

- Part of our mission is to ensure that when you graduate with a La Verne degree, you will be able to "communicate clearly, ethically, and purposefully to a variety of audiences in the structured written genres relevant to [your] academic and/or professional contexts" (Baccalaureate Learning Outcomes). This textbook will help you reach this important goal.

These are just some of the reasons why writing faculty believe that your writing course is the gateway to a productive and fulfilling college experience. And that begins this semester, by reaching the course learning outcomes. Writing Program faculty are here to help you reach these goals every step of the way.

Warmly,
Dr. Jolivette Mecenas,
Writing Program Director and Associate Professor of Writing

ULV Writing Program Mission

The Writing Program fosters the study and practice of writing as a life-long method of inquiry and learning foundational to ethical and reflective communication in academic, professional, and civic life.

Learning Outcomes for WRT 110 College Writing A (LVWA)

Students are able to do the following:

- State explicitly a claim or thesis and develop this assertion using a logical organization appropriate for the writer's argument or other rhetorical purpose.
- Summarize, analyze, and synthesize a variety of sources for various rhetorical purposes.
- Develop facility in use of language that reflects awareness of audience and purpose through appropriate vocabulary, and through varied sentence structure and style.
- Demonstrate writing as a recursive process, using multiple drafts to plan, organize, edit, revise, and proofread work.
- Develop facility in use of standard written edited English conventions, and in use of academic citation conventions.

Learning Outcomes for WRT 111 College Writing B Research Writing (LVWB)

Students are able to do the following:

- Develop and respond to a research question with a controlling idea, using a logical organization appropriate for the writer's argument or other rhetorical purpose.
- Demonstrate facility in use of language that reflects awareness of audience, purpose, and genre through appropriate vocabulary and sentence style.
- Summarize, evaluate, and synthesize a variety of primary and secondary research materials for the purpose of making explicit links between one's own ideas and those of others.
- Demonstrate control and application of standard written edited English conventions, and of academic citation conventions.

Writing Program Information

Faculty offices are located in Miller Hall
Faculty mailboxes are located in Miller 115
To reach administrative staff for the Writing Program, contact:
Melanie Brown: mbrown@laverne.edu
Phone: (909) 448-4361
Writing Program Web site: http://sites.laverne.edu/writing-program/
Dr. Jolivette Mecenas, Writing Program Director: jmecenas@laverne.edu

Full-time Faculty
Claire Angelici, Full-time Instructor of Writing: cangelici@laverne.edu
Sean Bernard, Associate Professor of Creative Writing: sbernard@laverne.edu
Dr. Judy Holiday, Assistant Professor of Writing: jholiday@laverne.edu
Dr. Jennifer Jared, Full-time Instructor of Writing: jjared@laverne.edu
Dr. Joshua Jensen, Full-time Instructor of Writing: jjensen@laverne.edu

Part-Time Faculty
Jeffery Anderson, Adjunct instructor: janderson2@laverne.edu
Bryanna Bynum, Adjunct Instructor: bbynum@laverne.edu
Dr. Caroline Carpenter, Adjunct Professor: ccarpenter@laverne.edu
Megan Gallagher, Adjunct Instructor: mgallagher@laverne.edu
Ashley Hamilton, Adjunct Instructor: ahamilton@laverne.edu
Kristen Macias, Adjunct Instructor: kmacias@laverne.edu
Dr. Rachel Morrison, Adjunct Professor: rmorrison@laverne.edu
Emily Schuck, Adjunct Instructor: eschuck@laverne.edu
Katrina Sire, Adjunct Instructor: ksire@laverne.edu
Joshua Wagenhoffer, Adjunct Instructor: jwagenhoffer@laverne.edu
Dr. Gary Westfahl, Senior Adjunct Professor: gwestfahl@laverne.edu

Campus Resources for Writers

Here are other important resources on the main La Verne campus and online.

Academic Success Center
ASC Mission Statement
The Academic Success Center is committed to helping all ULV students become the most confident, curious, and engaged learners they can be.
Location: The Sarah & Michael Abraham Campus Center, second floor
Email: asc@laverne.edu
Phone Number: (909) 448-4342
Web site: http://sites.laverne.edu/academic-success-center/
Tweet to: @laverneasc

Wilson Library
Location: La Verne Main Campus and online
Email: ask@laverne.libanswers.com
Phone Number: (909) 593-3511
Web site: http://library.laverne.edu/
Tweet to: @Leo_Librarian

The Everyday Writer

Andrea A. Lunsford
STANFORD UNIVERSITY

Coverage tor multilingual writers with

Paul Kei Matsuda
ARIZONA STATE UNIVERSITY

Christine M. Tardy
UNIVERSITY OF ARIZONA

1 The Top Twenty: A Quick Guide to Troubleshooting Your Writing

Surface errors — grammar, punctuation, word choice, and other small-scale matters — don't always disturb readers. Whether your instructor marks an error in any particular assignment will depend on personal judgments about how serious and distracting it is and about what you should be focusing on in the draft. In addition, not all surface errors are consistently viewed as errors: some of the patterns identified in the research for this book are considered errors by some instructors but as stylistic options by others. Such differing opinions don't mean that there is no such thing as correctness in writing — only that *correctness always depends on some context,* on whether the choices a writer makes seem appropriate to readers.

Research for this book reveals a number of changes that have occurred in student writing over the past thirty years. First, writing assignments in first-year composition classes now focus less on personal narrative and much more on research essays and argument. As a result, students are now writing longer essays than they did twenty years ago and working much more often with sources, both print and digital. Thus it's no surprise that students today are struggling with the conventions for using and citing sources, a problem that did not show up in most earlier studies of student writing.

What else has changed? For starters, wrong-word errors are *by far the most common* errors among first-year student writers today. Thirty years ago, spelling errors were most common by a factor of more than three to one. The use of spell checkers has reduced the number of spelling errors in student writing — but spell checkers' suggestions may also be responsible for some (or many) of the wrong words students are using.

All writers want to be considered competent and careful. You know that your readers judge you by your control of the conventions you have agreed to use, even if the conventions change from time to time. To help you in producing writing that is conventionally correct, you should become familiar with the twenty most common error patterns among U.S. college students today, listed here in order of frequency. A brief explanation and examples of each error are provided in the following sections, and each error pattern is cross-referenced to other places in this book where you can find more detailed information and additional examples.

QUICK HELP

The Top Twenty

1. Wrong word
2. Missing comma after an introductory element
3. Incomplete or missing documentation
4. Vague pronoun reference
5. Spelling (including homonyms)
6. Mechanical error with a quotation
7. Unnecessary comma
8. Unnecessary or missing capitalization
9. Missing word
10. Faulty sentence structure
11. Missing comma with a nonrestrictive element
12. Unnecessary shift in verb tense
13. Missing comma in a compound sentence
14. Unnecessary or missing apostrophe (including *its/it's*)
15. Fused (run-on) sentence
16. Comma splice
17. Lack of pronoun-antecedent agreement
18. Poorly integrated quotation
19. Unnecessary or missing hyphen
20. Sentence fragment

---

1 Wrong word

▶ Religious texts, for them, take ~~prescience~~ *precedence* over other kinds of sources.

Prescience means "foresight," and *precedence* means "priority."

▶ The child suffered from a severe ~~allegory~~ to peanuts.
   _{allergy}

Allegory is a spell checker's replacement for a misspelling of *allergy*.

▶ The panel discussed the ethical implications ~~on~~ the situation.
   _{of}

Wrong-word errors can involve using a word with the wrong shade of meaning, using a word with a completely wrong meaning, or using a wrong preposition or another wrong word in an idiom. Selecting a word from a thesaurus without knowing its meaning, or allowing a spell checker to correct spelling automatically, can lead to wrong-word errors, so use these tools with care. If you have trouble with prepositions and idioms, memorize the standard usage. (See Chapter 29 on word choice and spelling and Chapter 44 on prepositions and idioms.)

2 Missing comma after an introductory element

▶ Determined to get the job done, we worked all weekend.

▶ Although the study was flawed, the results may still be useful.

Readers usually need a small pause—signaled by a comma—between an introductory word, phrase, or clause and the main part of the sentence. Use a comma after every introductory element. When the introductory element is very short, you don't always need a comma, but including it is never wrong. (See 47a.)

3 Incomplete or missing documentation

▶ Satrapi says, "When we're afraid, we lose all sense of analysis and reflection." (263).

This quotation comes from a print source, so a page number is needed.

▶ Some experts agree that James Joyce wrote two of the five best novels of all time. ("100 Best Novels").

The source of this information should be identified (this online source has no page numbers).

Cite each source you refer to in the text, following the guidelines of the documentation style you are using. (The preceding examples follow MLA style—see Chapters 57–60; for other styles, see Chapters 61–67.) Omitting documentation can result in charges of plagiarism (see Chapter 15).

4 Vague pronoun reference

POSSIBLE REFERENCE TO MORE THAN ONE WORD

▶ Transmitting radio signals by satellite is a way of overcoming the

problem of scarce airwaves and limiting how ~~they~~ *the airwaves* are used.

In the original sentence, *they* could refer to the signals or to the airwaves.

REFERENCE IMPLIED BUT NOT STATED

▶ The company prohibited smoking, ~~which~~ *a policy* many employees

resented.

What does *which* refer to? The editing clarifies what employees resented.

A pronoun should refer clearly to the word or words it replaces (called the *antecedent*) elsewhere in the sentence or in a previous sentence. If more than one word could be the antecedent, or if no specific antecedent is present, edit to make the meaning clear. (See Chapter 41.)

5 Spelling (including homonyms)

▶ Ronald ~~Regan~~ *Reagan* won the election in a landslide.

▶ ~~Every where~~ *Everywhere* we went, we saw crowds of tourists.

The most common misspellings today are those that spell checkers cannot identify. The categories that spell checkers are most likely to miss include homonyms, compound words incorrectly spelled as separate words, and proper nouns, particularly names. After you run the spell checker, proofread carefully for errors such as these—and be sure to run the spell checker to catch other kinds of spelling mistakes. (See 29f.)

6 Mechanical error with a quotation

▶ "I grew up the victim of a disconcerting confusion,"/Rodriguez says
(249).

The comma should be placed *inside* the quotation marks.

Follow conventions when using quotation marks with commas (47h),
colons (52d), and other punctuation (51f). Always use quotation marks
in pairs, and follow the guidelines of your documentation style for
block quotations (51b). Use quotation marks for titles of short works
(51c), but use italics for titles of long works (55a).

7 Unnecessary comma

BEFORE CONJUNCTIONS IN COMPOUND CONSTRUCTIONS THAT ARE NOT
COMPOUND SENTENCES

▶ This conclusion applies to the United States/and to the rest of the world.

No comma is needed before *and* because it is joining two phrases that
modify the same verb, *applies*.

WITH RESTRICTIVE ELEMENTS

▶ Many parents/of gifted children/do not want them to skip a grade.

No comma is needed to set off the restrictive phrase *of gifted children*,
which is necessary to indicate which parents the sentence is talking about.

Do not use commas to set off restrictive elements that are necessary
to the meaning of the words they modify. Do not use a comma before
a coordinating conjunction (*and, but, for, nor, or, so, yet*) when the conjunction does not join parts of a compound sentence. Do not use a
comma before the first or after the last item in a series, between a
subject and verb, between a verb and its object or complement, or
between a preposition and its object. (See 47j.)

8 Unnecessary or missing capitalization

▶ Some ~~Traditional~~ *traditional* Chinese ~~Medicines~~ *medicines* containing ~~Ephedra~~ *ephedra* remain

legal.

Capitalize proper nouns and proper adjectives, the first words of
sentences, and important words in titles, along with certain words

indicating directions and family relationships. Do not capitalize most other words. When in doubt, check a dictionary. (See Chapter 53.)

9 Missing word

▶ The site foreman discriminated *against* women and promoted men with less experience.

Proofread carefully for omitted words, including prepositions (44a), parts of two-part verbs (44b), and correlative conjunctions (36g). Be particularly careful not to omit words from quotations.

10 Faulty sentence structure

▶ ~~The information which high~~ *High* school athletes are presented with ~~mainly includes~~ information on what credits *they* needed to graduate, ~~and~~ ~~thinking about the~~ college which *colleges to try* ~~athletes are trying~~ to play for, and apply. *how to*

A sentence that starts out with one kind of structure and then changes to another kind can confuse readers. Make sure that each sentence contains a subject and a verb (37a), that subjects and predicates make sense together (31b), and that comparisons have clear meanings (31c). When you join elements (such as subjects or verb phrases) with a coordinating conjunction, make sure that the elements have parallel structures (see Chapter 32).

11 Missing comma with a nonrestrictive element

▶ Marina, who was the president of the club, was first to speak.

The clause *who was the president of the club* does not affect the basic meaning of the sentence: Marina was first to speak.

A nonrestrictive element gives information not essential to the basic meaning of the sentence. Use commas to set off a nonrestrictive element (47c).

12 Unnecessary shift in verb tense

> *slipped* *fell*
> Priya was watching the great blue heron. Then she ~~slips~~ and ~~falls~~ into
> the swamp.

Verbs that shift from one tense to another with no clear reason can confuse readers (33a).

13 Missing comma in a compound sentence

> Meredith waited for Samir, and her sister grew impatient.
>
> Without the comma, a reader may think at first that Meredith waited for both Samir and her sister.

A compound sentence consists of two or more parts that could each stand alone as a sentence. When the parts are joined by a coordinating conjunction, use a comma before the conjunction to indicate a pause between the two thoughts (47b).

14 Unnecessary or missing apostrophe (including *its/it's*)

> *child's*
> Overambitious parents can be very harmful to a ~~childs~~ well-being.

> *its* *It's*
> The car is lying on ~~it's~~ side in the ditch. ~~Its~~ a white 2004 Passat.

To make a noun possessive, add either an apostrophe and an *-s* (*Ed's book*) or an apostrophe alone (*the boys' gym*). Do not use an apostrophe in the possessive pronouns *ours, yours,* and *hers*. Use *its* to mean *belonging to it*; use *it's* only when you mean *it is* or *it has*. (See Chapter 50.)

15 Fused (run-on) sentence

> *but*
> Klee's paintings seem simple, they are very sophisticated.

> *Although she*
> ~~She~~ doubted the value of meditation, she decided to try it once.

A fused sentence (also called a *run-on*) joins clauses that could each stand alone as a sentence with no punctuation or words to link them. Fused sentences must either be divided into separate sentences or joined by adding words or punctuation. (See Chapter 45.)

16 Comma splice

> *for*
> ▶ I was strongly attracted to her, she was beautiful and funny.
> ^

> *that*
> ▶ We hated the meat loaf/the cafeteria served it every Friday.
> ^

A comma splice occurs when only a comma separates clauses that could each stand alone as a sentence. To correct a comma splice, you can insert a semicolon or period, connect the clauses with a word such as *and* or *because,* or restructure the sentence. (See Chapter 45.)

17 Lack of pronoun-antecedent agreement

> *All students* *uniforms.*
> ▶ Every student must provide their own uniform.
> ^ ^

> *its*
> ▶ Each of the puppies thrived in their new home.
> ^

Pronouns must agree with their antecedents both in gender (male or female) and in number (singular or plural). Many indefinite pronouns, such as *everyone* and *each,* are always singular. When a singular antecedent can refer to a man or a woman, either rewrite the sentence to make the antecedent plural or to eliminate the pronoun, or use *his or her, he or she,* and so on. When antecedents are joined by *or* or *nor,* the pronoun should always agree with the closer antecedent. A collective noun such as *team* can be either singular or plural, depending on whether the members are seen as a group or as individuals. (See 41f.)

18 Poorly integrated quotation

> *showed how color affects taste:*
> ▶ Schlosser cites a 1970s study that "Once it became apparent that the
> ^
>
> steak was actually blue and the fries were green, some people became
>
> ill" (565).

> *According to Lars Eighner,*
> ▶ "Dumpster diving has serious drawbacks as a way of life" (Eighner
> ^
>
> 383). Finding edible food is especially tricky.

Quotations should fit smoothly into the surrounding sentence structure. They should be linked clearly to the writing around them (usually with a signal phrase) rather than dropped abruptly into the writing. (See 15b.)

Taking a Writing Inventory

One way to learn from your mistakes is to take a writing inventory. It can help you think critically and analytically about how to improve your writing skills.

1. Collect two or three pieces of your writing to which either your instructor or other students have responded.

2. Read through these writings, adding your own comments about their strengths and weaknesses. How do your comments compare with those of others?

3. Group all the comments into three categories — *broad content issues* (use of evidence and sources, attention to purpose and audience, and overall impression), *organization and presentation* (overall and paragraph-level organization, sentence structure and style, and formatting), and *surface errors* (problems with wrong words, spelling, grammar, punctuation, and mechanics).

4. Make an inventory of your own strengths in each category.

5. Study your errors. Mark every instructor and peer comment that suggests or calls for an improvement, and put all these comments in a list. Consult the relevant part of this book or speak with your instructor if you don't understand a comment.

6. Make a list of the top problem areas you need to work on. How can you make improvements? Then note at least two strengths that you can build on in your writing. Reflect on your findings in a writing log that you can add to as the class proceeds.

19 Unnecessary or missing hyphen

▶ This paper looks at fictional and real-life examples.

A compound adjective modifying a noun that follows it requires a hyphen.

▶ The buyers want to fix up the house and resell it.

A two-word verb should not be hyphenated.

A compound adjective that appears before a noun needs a hyphen. However, be careful not to hyphenate two-word verbs or word groups that serve as subject complements. (See Chapter 56.)

20 Sentence fragment

NO SUBJECT

▶ Marie Antoinette spent huge sums of money on herself and her

favorites. ~~And~~ helped bring on the French Revolution.
      Her extravagance

NO COMPLETE VERB

▶ The old aluminum boat sitting on its trailer.
            was

BEGINNING WITH A SUBORDINATING WORD

▶ We returned to the drugstore/, ~~Where~~ we waited for our buddies.
                       where

A sentence fragment is part of a sentence that is written as if it were a complete sentence. Reading your draft out loud, backwards, sentence by sentence, will help you spot sentence fragments. (See Chapter 46.)

4 Exploring Ideas

The point is so simple that we often forget it: we write best about topics we know well. So among the most important parts of the entire writing process are choosing a topic that will engage

your interest, exploring that topic by surveying what you know about it, and determining what you need to find out. You can explore a topic in many ways; the goal is to find strategies that work well for you.

4a   Try brainstorming.

Used widely in business and industry, brainstorming involves tossing out your ideas—either orally or in writing—to discover new ways to approach a topic. You can brainstorm with others or by yourself.

1. Within a time limit of five or ten minutes, list every word or phrase that comes to mind about the topic. Jot down key words and phrases, not sentences. No one has to understand the list but you. Don't worry about whether or not something will be useful—just list as much as you can in this brief span of time.
2. If little occurs to you, try coming up with thoughts about the opposite side of your topic. If you are trying, for instance, to think of reasons to raise tuition and are coming up blank, try concentrating on reasons to lower tuition. Once you start generating ideas in one direction, you'll find that you can usually move back to the other side fairly easily.
3. When the time is up, stop and read over the lists you have made. If anything else comes to mind, add it to your list. Then reread the list, looking for patterns of interesting ideas or one central idea.

4b   Try freewriting or looping.

Freewriting is a method of exploring a topic by writing about it for a period of time *without stopping*.

1. Write for ten minutes or so. Think about your topic, and let your mind wander; write down whatever occurs to you. Don't worry about grammar or spelling. If you get stuck, write anything—just don't stop.
2. When the time is up, look at what you have written. You may discover some important insights and ideas.

If you like, you can continue the process by looping: find the central or most intriguing thought from your freewriting, and then

---

CONSIDERING DISABILITIES

Freespeaking

If you are better at talking out than writing out your ideas, try freespeaking, which is basically the talking version of freewriting. Speak into a tape recorder or into a computer with voice-recognition software, and keep talking about your topic for at least seven to ten minutes. Say whatever comes to your mind — don't stop talking. You can then listen to or read the results of your freespeaking and look for an idea to pursue at greater length.

---

summarize it in a single sentence. Freewrite for five more minutes on the summary sentence, and then find and summarize the central thought from the second "loop." Keep this process going until you discover a clear angle or something about the topic that you can pursue.

4c Try drawing or creating word pictures.

If you're someone who prefers visual thinking, you might either create a drawing about the topic or use figurative language — such as similes and metaphors — to describe what the topic resembles. Working with pictures or verbal imagery can sometimes also help illuminate the topic or uncover some of your unconscious ideas or preconceptions about it.

1. If you like to draw, try sketching your topic. What images do you come up with? What details of the drawing attract you most? What would you most like to expand on? Even abstract doodling can lead you to important insights about the topic and to focus your topic productively.
2. Look for figurative language — metaphors and similes — that your topic resembles. Try jotting down three or four possibilities, beginning with "My subject is _____" or "My subject is like _____." A student working on the subject of genetically modified crops came up with this: "Genetically modified foods are like empty calories: they do more harm than good." This exercise made one thing clear to this student writer: she already had a very strong bias that she would need to watch out for while developing her topic.

Play around a bit with your topic. Ask, for instance, "If my topic were a food (or a song or a movie or a video game), what would it be, and why?" Or write a Facebook status update about your topic, or send a tweet about why this topic appeals to you. Such exercises can get you out of the rut of everyday thinking and help you see your topic in a new light.

4d   Try clustering.

Clustering is a way of generating ideas using a visual scheme or chart. It is especially helpful for understanding the relationships among the parts of a broad topic and for developing subtopics. You may have a software program for clustering. If not, follow these steps:

1. Write down your topic in the middle of a blank piece of paper or screen and circle it.
2. In a ring around the topic circle, write what you see as the main parts of the topic. Circle each part, and then draw a line from it to the topic.
3. Think of more ideas, examples, facts, or other details relating to each main part. Write each of these near the appropriate part, circle each one, and draw a line from it to the part.
4. Repeat this process with each new circle until you can't think of any more details. Some trails may lead to dead ends, but you will still have many useful connections among ideas.

Here is an example of the clustering Emily Lesk did for her essay about Coca-Cola and American identity:

EMILY LESK'S CLUSTERING

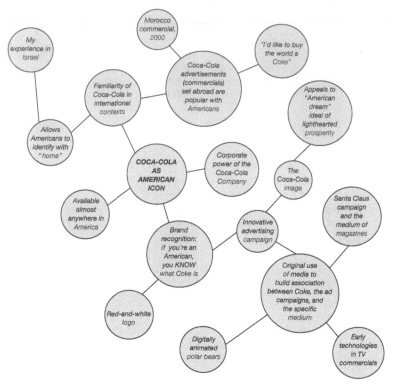

4e Look at images and videos.

Searching images or browsing videos may spark topic ideas or inspire questions that you want to explore. If you plan to create a highly visual project—a video essay or slide presentation, for instance—you will probably need to decide what you want to show your audience before you plan the words that will accompany the images.

4f Keep a reflective journal or private blog.

Writers often get their best ideas by jotting down or recording thoughts that come to them randomly. You can write in a notebook, record audio notes on a phone, store pictures and video files on a private blog—some writers even keep a marker and writing board on the shower wall so that they can write down the ideas that come to them while bathing! As you begin thinking about your assignment, taking time to record what you know about your topic and what still puzzles you may lead you to a breakthrough or help you articulate your main idea.

4g Ask questions.

Another basic strategy for exploring a topic and generating ideas is simply to ask and answer questions. Here are several widely used sets of questions to get you started, either on your own or with one or two others.

Questions to describe a topic

Originally developed by Aristotle, the following questions can help you explore a topic by carefully and systematically describing it:

- *What is it?* What are its characteristics, dimensions, features, and parts? What do your senses tell you about it?
- *What caused it?* What changes occurred to create your topic? How is it changing? How will it change?
- *What is it like or unlike?* What features differentiate your topic from others? What analogies can you make about your topic?
- *What larger system is the topic a part of?* How does your topic relate to this system?
- *What do people say about it?* What reactions does your topic arouse? What about the topic causes those reactions?

Questions to explain a topic

The well-known questions *who, what, when, where, why,* and *how,* widely used by news reporters, are especially helpful for explaining a topic.

- *Who* is doing it?
- *What* is at issue?
- *When* does it take place?
- *Where* is it taking place?
- *Why* does it occur?
- *How* is it done?

Prewriting > Video Prompt: Getting ideas from social media

Questions to persuade

When your purpose is to persuade or convince, the following questions, developed by philosopher Stephen Toulmin, can help you think analytically about your topic (10d and 11j):

- What *claim* are you making about your topic?
- What *good reasons* support your claim?
- What valid *underlying assumptions* support the reasons for your claim?
- What *backup evidence* can you find for your claim?
- What *refutations* of your claim should you anticipate?
- In what ways should you *qualify* your claim?

4h Browse sources.

At the library and on the Internet, browse for a topic you want to learn more about. If you have a short list of ideas, follow links from one interesting article to another to see what you can find, or do a quick check of reference works to get overviews of the topics. You can begin with a general encyclopedia or a specialized reference work that focuses on a specific area, such as music or psychology. You can also use Wikipedia as a starting point: take a look at entries that relate to your topic, especially noting the sources they list. While you should not rely on Wikipedia alone, it is a highly accessible way to begin your research.

4i Collaborate.

As you explore your topic, remember that you can gain valuable insights from others. Many writers say that they get their best ideas in conversation with other people. If you talk with friends or roommates about your topic, at the very least you will hear yourself describe the topic and your interest in it; this practice will almost certainly sharpen your understanding of what you are doing. If those you talk to are not familiar with the topic, their questions will help you see what you need to explain. You can also use conversation with others to analyze your own assumptions. In addition, you can seek out online discussions on social media as places to share your thinking on a topic and find inspiration.

Planning and Drafting **5**

S ome writers just plunge right into their work and develop it as they go along. Others find that they work more effectively by making detailed blueprints before they begin drafting. Your planning and drafting may fall anywhere along this spectrum. As you plan and draft, you narrow your topic, decide on your thesis, organize materials to support that central idea, and sketch out a plan for your writing. As one student said, this is the time in the writing process "when the rubber meets the road."

5a Narrow your topic.

After exploring ideas, you may have found a topic that interests you and that you think would also be interesting to your readers. The topic, however, may be too large to be manageable. If that is the case, narrow your topic using any exploring technique that works for you (see Chapter 4).

WORKING THESIS: Plan Your Approach

Survey what you know about the topic.

ASK:

What is your **connection** *to the topic?*

What does your audience need to know?

How can you make your topic **manageable?**

Remember that there are many possible paths to approaching a topic.

Emily Lesk planned to discuss how advertising affects American identity, but she knew that such a topic was far too broad. After thinking about products that are pitched as particularly "American" in their advertising, she posted a Facebook status update asking friends to "name products that seem super-American." She quickly got seventeen responses ranging from Hummers and Winchester rifles to "soft toilet paper," Spam, Wheaties, and apple pie. One friend identified Coca-Cola and Pepsi-Cola, two products that Emily associated with many memorable and well-documented advertising campaigns.

5b Craft a working thesis.

Academic and professional writing in the United States often contains an explicit thesis statement. The thesis functions as a promise to readers, letting them know what the writer will discuss. Your readers may (or may not) expect you to craft the thesis as a single sentence near the beginning of the text. If you want to suggest a thesis implicitly rather than stating one explicitly, if you plan to convey your main argument somewhere other than in your introduction, or if you prefer to make your thesis longer than a single sentence, consider

WORKING THESIS: Refine Your Topic

Match your approach to the requirements of the topic.

SCENIC DETOURS!

SHORTCUT TO TOP

ASK:

How will your audience connect to your topic?

How can you help them see your perspective?

What is the most persuasive message for this context?

Remember that you are creating a *working thesis* that you can change as you go.

whether the rhetorical situation allows such flexibility. For an academic project, also consult with your instructor about how to meet expectations.

Whether you plan to use an implicit or explicit thesis statement in your text, you should establish a tentative working thesis early in your writing process. The word *working* is important here because your thesis may well change as you write—your final thesis may be very different from the working thesis you begin with. Even so, a working thesis focuses your thinking and research, and helps keep you on track.

A working thesis should have two parts: a topic, which indicates the subject matter the writing is about, and a comment, which makes an important point about the topic.

> ▶ In the graphic novel *Fun Home*, illustrations and words combine to make meanings that are more subtle than either words alone or images alone could convey.

A successful working thesis has three characteristics:

1. It is potentially *interesting* to the intended audience.
2. It is as *specific* as possible.
3. It limits the topic enough to make it *manageable*.

WORKING THESIS: Craft Your Message

Draft a working thesis.

ASK:

Should your thesis be implicit or explicit for this context and audience?

Are you conveying your own message—not just facts?

Does your working thesis help you understand where to go next?

Consider this a starting point for organizing and planning your draft.

FOR MULTILINGUAL WRITERS

Multilingual **Stating a Thesis Explicitly**

In some cultures, stating the main point explicitly may be considered rude or inelegant. In U.S. academic and business practices, however, readers often expect the writer to make key points and positions explicit. Unless your main point is highly controversial or hard for the reader to accept (such as a rejection letter), state your main point early — before presenting the supporting details.

You can evaluate a working thesis by checking it against each of these characteristics, as in the following examples:

▶ **Graphic novels combine words and images.**

INTERESTING? The topic of graphic novels could be interesting, but this draft of a working thesis has no real comment attached to it—instead, it states a bare fact, and the only place to go from here is to more bare facts.

▶ **In graphic novels, words and images convey interesting meanings.**

SPECIFIC? This thesis is not specific. What are "interesting meanings," exactly? How are they conveyed?

▶ **Graphic novels have evolved in recent decades to become an important literary genre.**

MANAGEABLE? This thesis would not be manageable for a short-term project because it would require research on several decades of history and on hundreds of texts from all over the world.

5c Gather information.

Writing often calls for research. Your curiosity may be triggered by a found object or image that you want to learn more about. An assignment may specify that you conduct research on your topic and cite your sources. Even if you're writing about a topic on which you're an expert, you may still find that you don't know enough about some aspect of the topic to write about it effectively without doing research.

You may need to do research at various stages of the writing process—early on, to help you understand or define your topic,

---

and later on, to find additional examples and illustrations to support your thesis. Once you have developed a working thesis, consider what additional information, opinions, visuals, and media you might need.

Basically, you can do three kinds of research to support your thesis: library research, which includes books, periodicals, and databases (and perhaps archives of other kinds of sources, such as music, films, posters, photographs, and so on); online research, which gives you access to texts, visuals, media, and people on the Internet; and field research, which includes personal observation, interviews, surveys, and other means of gathering information directly. (For more information on conducting research, see Chapter 13.)

5d Organize information.

While you're finding information on your topic, think about how you will group or organize that information to make it accessible and persuasive to readers. At the simplest level, writers most often group information in their writing projects according to four principles—space, time, logic, and association.

Spatial organization

Spatial organization of texts allows the reader to "walk through" your material, beginning at one point and moving around in an organized manner—say, from near to far, left to right, or top to bottom. It can be especially useful when you want the audience to understand the layout of a structure or the placement of elements and people in a scene: texts such as a museum visitors' audio guide, a written-word description of a historic battlefield, or a video tour of a new apartment might all call for spatial organization. Remember that maps, diagrams, and other graphics may help readers visualize your descriptions more effectively.

Chronological organization

Organization can also indicate *when* events occur, usually chronologically from first to last. Chronological organization is the basic method used in cookbooks, lab reports, instruction manuals, and many stories and narrative films. You may find it useful to organize information by describing or showing the sequence of events or the steps in a process.

Logical organization

Organizing according to logic means relating pieces of information in ways that make sense. Following is an overview of some of the most commonly used logical patterns: *illustration, definition, division and classification, comparison and contrast, cause and effect, problem and solution, analogy,* and *narration.* For examples of paragraphs organized according to these logical patterns, see 6c.

ILLUSTRATION

You will often gather examples to illustrate a point. If you write an essay discussing how one novelist influenced another, you might cite examples from the second writer's books that echo themes or characters from the first writer's works. For a pamphlet appealing for donations to the Red Cross, you might use photographs showing situations in which donations helped people in trouble, along with appropriate descriptions. For maximum effect, you may want to arrange examples in order of increasing importance unless your genre calls for an attention-grabbing initial illustration.

DEFINITION

Often a topic can be developed by definition—by saying what something is (or is not) and perhaps by identifying the characteristics that distinguish it from things that are similar or in the same general category. If you write about poverty in your community, for example, you would have to define very carefully what level of income, assets, or other measure defines a person, family, or household as "poor." In an essay about Pentecostalism, you might explain what characteristics separate Pentecostalism from related religious movements.

DIVISION AND CLASSIFICATION

Division means breaking a single topic into separate parts; classification means grouping many separate items of information about a topic according to their similarities. An essay about military recruiting policies might divide the military into different branches—army, navy, air force, and so on—and examine how each recruits volunteers. For a project on women's roles in the eighteenth century, you could organize your notes by classification: information related to women's education, occupations, legal status, and so on.

COMPARISON AND CONTRAST

Comparison focuses on the similarities between two things, whereas contrast highlights their differences, but the two are often used together.

If you were asked to analyze two case studies in an advertising text (one on Budweiser ads and the other on ads for the latest iPhone), you might well organize the response by presenting all the information on Budweiser advertising in one section and all the information on iPhone ads in another (block comparison) or by alternating between Budweiser and iPhone ads as you look at particular characteristics of each (alternating comparison).

CAUSE AND EFFECT

Cause-effect analysis may deal with causes, effects, or both. If you examine why something happens or happened, you are investigating causes. If you explain what has occurred or is likely to occur from a set of conditions, you are discussing effects. An environmental impact study of the probable consequences of building a proposed dam, for instance, would focus on effects. On the other hand, a video essay on the breakdown of authority in inner-city schools might begin with the effects of the breakdown and trace them back to their causes.

PROBLEM AND SOLUTION

Moving from a problem to a solution is a natural way to organize certain kinds of information. For example, a student studying motorcycle parking on campus decided to organize his writing in just this way: he identified a problem (the need for more parking) and then offered two possible solutions, along with visuals to help readers imagine the solutions (his outline appears on p. 47). Many assignments in engineering, business, and economics call for a similar organizational strategy.

ANALOGY

An analogy establishes connections between two things or ideas. Analogies are particularly helpful in explaining something new in terms of something very familiar. Likening the human genome to a map, for example, helps explain the complicated concept of the genome to those unfamiliar with it.

NARRATION

Narration involves telling a story of some kind. You might, for example, tell the story of how deer ravaged your mother's garden as a way of showing why you support population control measures for wildlife. Narrating calls on the writer to set the story in a context readers can understand, providing any necessary background and descriptive details as well as chronological markers and transitions (*later that day*, *the following morning*, and so on) to guide readers through the story.

Association

Some writers organize information through a series of associations that grow directly out of their own experiences and memories. In doing so, they may rely on a sensory memory, such as an aroma, a sound, or a scene. Thus, associational organization is common in personal narrative, where the writer follows a chain of associations to render an experience vividly for readers, as in this description:

> Flying from San Francisco to Atlanta, I looked down to see the gentle roll of the Smoky Mountains begin to appear. Almost at once, I was transported back to my granny's porch, sitting next to her drinking iced tea and eating peaches. Those fresh-picked peaches were delicious — ripened on the tree, skinned, and eaten with no regard for the sticky juice trickling everywhere. And on special occasions, we'd make ice cream, and Granny would empty a bowl brimming with chopped peaches into the creamy dish. Now — that was the life!

QUICK HELP

Organizing Visuals and Media in Academic Writing

- Use video and still images to capture your readers' attention and interest in a vivid way, to emphasize a point you make in words, to present information that is difficult to convey in words, or to communicate with audiences with different language skills.

- Consider whether you want to use images alone to convey your message, or whether words are also needed to help readers understand.

- For presentations, consider what your audience should look at as they listen to you. Make sure that the visuals enhance rather than compete with what you say. (Chapter 23)

- If you are using visuals and words together, consider both the way each image or video works on its own and the way it works in combination with the words you use.

- If you are using visuals to illustrate a written-word text, place each visual as near as possible to the words it illustrates. Introduce each visual clearly (*As the map to the right depicts . . .*). Comment on the significance or effect of the visual (*Figure 1 corroborates the firefighters' statements . . .*). Label each visual appropriately, and cite the source.

Combined organizational patterns

In much of your writing, you will want to use two or more principles of organization. You might, for example, combine several passages of narration with vivid examples to make a striking comparison, as one student did in an essay about the dramatic differences between her life in her Zuñi community and her life as a teacher in Seattle. In addition, you may want to include not only visuals but sound and other multimedia effects as well.

5e Make a plan.

At this point, you will find it helpful to write out an organizational plan, outline, or storyboard. To do so, simply begin with your thesis; review your exploratory notes, research materials, and visual or multimedia sources; and then list all the examples and other good reasons you have to support the thesis. (For more information on paragraph-level organization, see Chapter 6.)

An informal plan

One informal way to organize your ideas is to figure out what belongs in your introduction, body paragraphs, and conclusion. A student who was writing about solutions to a problem used the following plan:

WORKING THESIS

▶ **Increased motorcycle use demands the reorganization of campus parking lots.**

INTRODUCTION

give background and overview (motorcycle use up dramatically), and include photograph of overcrowded lot

state purpose — to fulfill promise of thesis by offering solutions

BODY

describe current situation (tell of my research at area parking lots)

describe problem in detail (report on statistics; cars vs. cycles), and graph my findings

present two possible solutions (enlarge lots or reallocate space)

CONCLUSION

recommend against first solution because of cost and space

recommend second solution, and summarize advantages

A formal outline

Even if you have created an informal written plan before drafting, you may wish (or be required) to prepare a more formal outline, which can help you see exactly how the parts of your writing will fit together—how your ideas relate, where you need examples, and what the overall structure of your work will be. Even if your instructor doesn't ask you to make an outline or you prefer to use some other method of sketching out your plans, you may want to come back to an outline later: doing a retrospective outline—one you do after you've already drafted your project—is a great way to see whether you have any big logical gaps or whether parts of the essay are in the wrong place.

Most formal outlines follow a conventional format of numbered and lettered headings and subheadings, using roman numerals, capital letters, arabic numerals, and lowercase letters to show the levels of importance of the various ideas and their relationships. Each new level is indented to show its subordination to the preceding level.

> Thesis statement
> I. First main idea
>   A. First subordinate idea
>   1. First supporting detail or idea
>   2. Second supporting detail or idea
>   3. Third supporting detail
>   B. Second subordinate idea
>   1. First supporting detail or idea
>   2. Second supporting detail or idea
> II. Second main idea
>   A. (continues as above)

Note that each level contains at least two parts, so there is no A without a B, no 1 without a 2. Comparable items are placed on the same level—the level marked by capital letters, for instance, or arabic numerals. Keep in mind that headings should be stated in parallel form—either all sentences or all grammatically parallel topics.

A storyboard

The technique of storyboarding—working out a narrative or argument in visual form—can be a good way to come up with an organizational plan, especially if you are developing a video essay, website, or other media project. You can find storyboard templates online to help you get started, or you can create your own storyboard by using note cards or sticky notes. Even if you're writing a more traditional word-based college essay, however, you may find storyboarding helpful; take advantage of different colors to keep track of threads of argument, subtopics, and so on. Flexibility is a strong feature of storyboarding: you can move the cards and notes around, trying out different arrangements, until you find an organization that works well for your writing situation.

Use linear organization when you want readers to move in a particular order through your material. An online report might use the following linear organization:

LINEAR ORGANIZATION

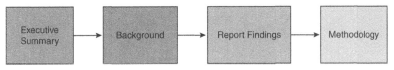

A hierarchy puts the most important material first, with subtopics branching out from the main idea. A website on dog bite prevention might be arranged like this:

HIERARCHICAL ORGANIZATION

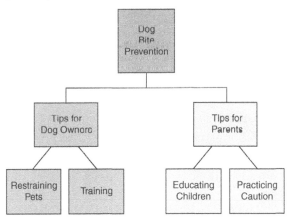

A spoke-and-hub organization allows readers to move from place to place in no particular order. Many portfolio websites are arranged this way:

SPOKE-AND-HUB ORGANIZATION

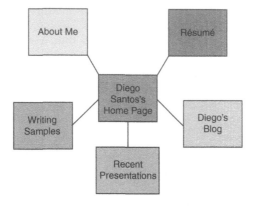

Whatever form your plan takes, you may want or need to change it along the way. Writing has a way of stimulating thought, and the process of drafting may generate new ideas. Or you may find that you need to reexamine some data or information or gather more material.

5f Create a draft.

No matter how good your planning, investigating, and organizing have been, chances are you will need to return to these activities as you draft. This fact of life leads to the first principle of successful drafting: be flexible. If you see that your organizational plan is not working, do not hesitate to alter it. If some information or medium now seems irrelevant, leave it out, even if you went to great lengths to obtain it. Throughout the drafting process, you may need to refer to points you have already written about. You may learn that you need to do more research, that your whole thesis must be reshaped, or that your topic is still too broad and should be narrowed further.

macmillanhighered.com/everyday6e
🄴 Reviewing and Revising > Student Writing: Early draft, Emily Lesk
🄲 Drafting > Tutorial: Word processing
　Drafting > Video Prompt: It's hard to delete things
　Drafting > Video Prompt: You just have to start

QUICK HELP

Guidelines for Drafting

- *Set up a computer folder or file for your essay.* Give the file a clear and relevant name, and save to it often. Name your files to distinguish among drafts. Since you will likely change your text over time, save a copy of each version. If you are sending a copy to classmates for review, give the file a new but related name.

- *Track changes within a document file to try out new versions.* This function is useful when you are working on a piece of writing with another writer or when you aren't sure which version of your draft you like best.

- *Have all your information close at hand and arranged according to your organizational plan.* Stopping to search for a piece of information can break your concentration or distract you.

- *Try to write in stretches of at least thirty minutes.* Writing can provide momentum, and once you get going, the task becomes easier.

- *Don't let small questions bog you down.* Just make a note of them in brackets — or in all caps — or make a tentative decision and move on.

- *Remember that first drafts aren't perfect.* Concentrate on getting all your ideas written down, and don't worry about anything else.

- *Stop writing at a place where you know exactly what will come next.* Doing so will help you start easily when you return to the draft.

Developing Paragraphs

Paragraphs serve as signposts — pointers that help guide readers through a piece of writing. A look through a popular magazine will show paragraphs working this way: the first paragraph of an article almost always aims to get our attention and to persuade us to read on, and subsequent ones often indicate a new point or a shift in focus or tone.

Put most simply, a paragraph is a group of sentences or a single sentence set off as a unit. All the sentences in a paragraph usually revolve around one main idea.

> QUICK HELP
>
> **Editing Paragraphs**
>
> - What is the topic sentence of each paragraph? Is it stated or implied? Is the main idea of the paragraph clear? (6a)
> - Does the first sentence of each paragraph let readers know what that paragraph is about? Does the last sentence in some way conclude that paragraph's discussion? If not, does it need to?
> - Within each paragraph, how does each sentence relate to the main idea? Revise or eliminate any that do not. (6a)
> - How completely does each paragraph develop its main idea? What details and images are included? Are they effective? Do any paragraphs need more detail? (6b)
> - What other methods of development might make the paragraph more effective? (6c)
> - Is each paragraph organized in a way that is easy to follow? Are sentences within each paragraph clearly linked? Do any of the transitions try to create links between ideas that do not really exist? (6e)
> - Are the paragraphs clearly linked? Do any links need to be added? Are any of the transitions from one paragraph to another artificial? (6e)
> - How does the introductory paragraph catch readers' interest? How does the last paragraph draw the piece to a conclusion? (6f)

6a Focus on a main idea.

An effective paragraph often focuses on one main idea. A good way to achieve such paragraph unity is to state the main idea clearly in one sentence and then relate all the other sentences in the paragraph to that idea. The sentence that presents the main idea is called the topic sentence.

Topic sentence

The following paragraph opens with a clear topic sentence, and the rest of the paragraph builds on the idea stated in that sentence:

> *Our friendship was the source of much happiness and many memories.* We grooved on every new recording from Jay-Z. We sweated together in the sweltering summer sun, trying to win the championship for our softball team. I recall the taste of pepperoni pizza as we discussed the highlights of our team's victory. Once we even became attracted to the same person, but luckily we were able to share his friendship.

FOR MULTILINGUAL WRITERS

Multilingual **Being Explicit**

Native readers of English generally expect that paragraphs will have an explicitly stated main idea and that the connections between points in a paragraph will also be stated explicitly. Such step-by-step explicitness may strike you as unnecessary or ineffective, but it follows the traditional paragraph conventions of English.

A topic sentence does not always come at the beginning of a paragraph; it may come at the end. Occasionally a paragraph's main idea is so obvious that it need not be stated explicitly in a topic sentence.

Other related sentences

Whether the main idea of a paragraph is stated in a topic sentence or is implied, make sure that all other sentences in the paragraph contribute to the main idea. In the preceding example about friendship, all of the sentences clearly relate to the point that is made in the first sentence. The result is a unified paragraph.

6b **Provide details.**

An effective paragraph develops its main idea by providing enough details—including visual details—to hold the reader's interest. Without such development, a paragraph may seem lifeless and abstract.

A POORLY DEVELOPED PARAGRAPH

No such thing as human nature compels people to behave, think, or react in certain ways. Rather, from our infancy to our death, we are constantly being taught, by the society that surrounds us, the customs, norms, and mores of a distinct culture. Everything in culture is learned, not genetically transmitted.

This paragraph is boring. Although its main idea is clear and its sentences hold together, it fails to gain our interest or hold our attention because it lacks any specific examples or details. Now look at the paragraph revised to include needed specifics.

THE SAME PARAGRAPH, REVISED

A child in Los Angeles decorates a Christmas tree with shiny red ornaments and sparkling tinsel. A few weeks later, a child in Beijing celebrates the Chinese New Year with feasting, firecrackers, and gift money in lucky red envelopes. It is not by instinct that one child knows how to

TALKING THE TALK

Paragraph Length

"How long should a paragraph be?" In college writing, paragraphs should address a specific topic or idea and develop that idea with examples and evidence. There is no set rule about how many sentences are required to make a complete paragraph. So write as many sentences as you need — and no more.

decorate the tree while the other knows how to celebrate the New Year. No such thing as human nature compels people to behave, think, or react in certain ways. Rather, from the time of our infancy to our death, we are constantly being taught, by the society that surrounds us, the customs, norms, and mores of one or more distinct cultures. Everything in culture is learned, not genetically transmitted.

Though both paragraphs present the same point, only the second one comes to life. It does so by bringing in specific details *from* life, including images that show readers what the paragraph describes. We want to read this paragraph because it appeals to our senses and our curiosity (why are red envelopes considered lucky?).

Details in visual texts

Details are important in both written and visual texts. If you decide to use an image because of a particular detail, make sure your readers will notice what you want them to see. Crop out any unnecessary information, and clarify what's important about the image in your text or with a caption. If you are taking a photo to illustrate a blog post on street food, for example, you will need to decide whether you should frame (or crop) the image to focus on the food or whether your discussion calls for the photo to include more of the surroundings.

6c   Use effective methods of development.

The patterns discussed in 5d for organizing essays can also help you develop paragraphs.

Narrative

A narrative paragraph uses the chronological elements of a story to develop a main idea. The following is one student's narrative paragraph that tells a personal story to support a point about the dangers of racing bicycles with flimsy alloy frames:

> People who have been exposed to the risk of dangerously designed bicycle frames have paid too high a price. I saw this danger myself in last year's Putney Race. An expensive graphite frame failed, and the rider was catapulted onto Vermont pavement at fifty miles per hour. The pack of riders behind him was so dense that other racers crashed into a tangled, sliding heap. The aftermath: four hospitalizations. I got off with some stitches, a bad road rash, and severely pulled tendons. My Italian racing bike was pretzeled, and my racing was over for that summer. Others were not so lucky. An Olympic hopeful, Brian Stone of the Northstar team, woke up in a hospital bed to find that his cycling was over — and not just for that summer. His kneecap had been surgically removed. He couldn't even walk.

Description

A descriptive paragraph uses specific details to create a clear impression. Notice how the following paragraph includes details to describe the appearance of the skyscraper and its effect on those who see it.

> The Chrysler Building, completed in 1930, still attracts the eyes of tourists and New Yorkers alike with its shiny steel exterior. The Chrysler cars of the era are incorporated into the design: the eagle-head gargoyles on the upper vertices of the building are shaped like the automobiles' hood ornaments, and winged details imitate Chrysler radiator caps. At night, an elaborate lighting scheme spotlights the sleek, powerful eagles from below — turning them into striking silhouettes — and picks out each of the upper stories' famed triangular windows, arching up into the darkness like the rays of a stylized sun.

Definition

You may often need to write an entire paragraph in order to define a word or concept, as in the following example:

> Economics is the study of how people choose among the alternatives available to them. It's the study of little choices ("Should I take the chocolate or the strawberry?") and big choices ("Should we require a reduction in energy consumption in order to protect the environment?"). It's the study of individual choices, choices by firms, and choices by governments. Life presents each of us with a wide range of alternative uses of our time and other resources; economists examine how we choose among those alternatives.
>
> — TIMOTHY TREGARTHEN, *Economics*

Example

One of the most common ways of developing a paragraph is by illustrating a point with one or more examples.

> The Indians made names for us children in their teasing way. Because our very busy mother kept my hair cut short, like my brothers', they called me Short Furred One, pointing to their hair and making the sign for short, the right hand with fingers pressed close together, held upward, back out, at the height intended. With me this was about two feet tall, the Indians laughing gently at my abashed face. I am told that I was given a pair of small moccasins that first time, to clear up my unhappiness at being picked out from the dusk behind the fire and my two unhappy shortcomings made conspicuous.
>
> — MARI SANDOZ, "The Go-Along Ones"

Division and classification

Division breaks a single item into parts. Classification groups many separate items according to their similarities. A paragraph evaluating a history course might divide the course into several segments — textbooks, lectures, assignments — and examine each one in turn. A paragraph giving an overview of many history courses might classify the courses in a number of ways — by time periods, by geographic areas, by the kinds of assignments demanded, by the number of students enrolled, or by some other principle.

DIVISION

> We all listen to music according to our separate capacities. But, for the sake of analysis, the whole listening process may become clearer if we break it up into its component parts, so to speak. In a certain sense, we all listen to music on three separate planes. For lack of a better terminology, one might name these: (1) the sensuous plane, (2) the expressive plane, (3) the sheerly musical plane. The only advantage to be gained from mechanically splitting up the listening process into these hypothetical planes is the clearer view to be had of the way in which we listen.
>
> — AARON COPLAND, *What to Listen For in Music*

CLASSIFICATION

> Two types of people are seduced by fad diets. Those who have always been overweight turn to them out of despair; they have tried everything, and yet nothing seems to work. A second group of people to succumb appear perfectly healthy but are baited by slogans such as "look good, feel good." These slogans prompt self-questioning and insecurity — do I really look good and feel good? — and as a direct result, many healthy people fall prey to fad diets. With both types of

people, however, the problems surrounding such diets are numerous and dangerous. In fact, these diets provide neither intelligent nor effective answers to weight control.

Comparison and contrast

When you compare two things, you look at their similarities; when you contrast two things, you focus on their differences. You can structure paragraphs that compare or contrast in two basic ways. One way is to present all the information about one item and then all the information about the other item, as in the following paragraph:

> You could tell the veterans from the rookies by the way they were dressed. The knowledgeable ones had their heads covered by kerchiefs, so that if they were hired, tobacco dust wouldn't get in their hair; they had on clean dresses that by now were faded and shapeless, so that if they were hired they wouldn't get tobacco dust and grime on their best clothes. Those who were trying for the first time had their hair freshly done and wore attractive dresses; they wanted to make a good impression. But the dresses couldn't be seen at the distance that many were standing from the employment office, and they were crumpled in the crush.
> – MARY MEBANE, "Summer Job"

Or you can switch back and forth between the two items, focusing on particular characteristics of each in turn.

> Malcolm X emphasized the use of violence in his movement and employed the biblical principle of "an eye for an eye and a tooth for a tooth." King, on the other hand, felt that blacks should use nonviolent civil disobedience and employed the theme "turning the other cheek," which Malcolm X rejected as "beggarly" and "feeble." The philosophy of Malcolm X was one of revenge, and often it broke the unity of black Americans. More radical blacks supported him, while more conservative ones supported King. King thought that blacks should transcend their humanity. In contrast, Malcolm X thought they should embrace it and reserve their love for one another, regarding whites as "devils" and the "enemy." The distance between Martin Luther King Jr.'s thinking and Malcolm X's was the distance between growing up in the seminary and growing up on the streets, between the American dream and the American reality.

Analogy

Analogies (comparisons that explain an unfamiliar thing in terms of a familiar one) can also help develop paragraphs.

> Since the advent of Hollywood editing, back in the earliest days of cinema, the goal of filmmakers has been for us to feel the movement of the camera but not to be aware of it, to look past the construction of the

media, to ignore the seams in the material. Just as an Olympic diver smiles and hides the effort as she catapults skyward and manages to pull off multiple flips while seemingly twisting in both directions, good storytelling—whether oral, in print, or visual—typically hides the construction and the hard work that go into making it. Both the medal-winning dives and the best stories are more intricate than they appear.

– STEPHEN APKON, *The Age of the Image: Redefining Literacy in a World of Screens*

Cause and effect

You can often develop paragraphs by explaining the causes of something or the effects that something brings about. The following paragraph discusses the causes that led pediatrician Phil Offit to study science and become a physician:

To understand exactly why Offit became a scientist, you must go back more than half a century, to 1956. That was when doctors in Offit's hometown of Baltimore operated on one of his legs to correct a club foot, requiring him to spend three weeks recovering in a chronic care facility with 20 other children, all of whom had polio. Parents were allowed to visit just one hour a week, on Sundays. His father, a shirt salesman, came when he could. His mother, who was pregnant with his brother and hospitalized with appendicitis, was unable to visit at all. He was five years old. "It was a pretty lonely, isolating experience," Offit says. "But what was even worse was looking at these other children who were just horribly crippled and disfigured by polio." That memory, he says, was the first thing that drove him toward a career in pediatric infectious diseases.   – AMY WALLACE, "An Epidemic of Fear"

Process

Paragraphs that explain a process often use the principle of time or chronology to order the stages in the process.

In July of 1877, Eadweard Muybridge photographed a horse in motion with a camera fast enough to capture clearly the split second when the horse's hooves were all off the ground—a moment never before caught on film. His next goal was to photograph a sequence of such rapid images. In June of 1878, he set up twelve cameras along a track, each connected to a tripwire. Then, as a crowd watched, a trotting horse raced down the track pulling a two-wheeled carriage. The carriage wheels tripped each camera in quick succession, snapping a dozen photographs. Muybridge developed the negatives and displayed them to an admiring public that same morning. His technical achievement helped to pave the way for the first motion pictures a decade later.

Problem and solution

Another way to develop a paragraph is to open with a topic sentence that states a problem or asks a question about a problem and then to offer a solution or answers in the sentences that follow—a technique used in this paragraph from a review of Ted Nordhaus and Michael Shellenberger's book *Break Through: From the Death of Environmentalism to the Politics of Possibility*:

> Unfortunately, at the moment growth means burning more fossil fuel. . . . How can that fact be faced? How to have growth that Americans want, but without limits that they instinctively oppose, and still reduce carbon emissions? [Nordhaus and Shellenberger's] answer is: investments in new technology. Acknowledge that America "is great at imagining, experimenting, and inventing the future," and then start spending. They cite examples ranging from the nuclear weapons program to the invention of the Internet to show what government money can do, and argue that too many clean-energy advocates focus on caps instead.
> – Bill McKibben, "Can Anyone Stop It?"

Reiteration

Reiteration is a method of development you may recognize from political speeches or some styles of preaching. In this pattern, the writer states the main point of a paragraph and then restates it, hammering home the point and often building in intensity as well. In the following passage from Barack Obama's 2004 speech at the Democratic National Convention, Obama contrasts what he identifies as the ideas of "those who are preparing to divide us" with memorable references to common ground and unity, including repeated references to the United States as he builds to his climactic point:

> Now even as we speak, there are those who are preparing to divide us—the spin masters, the negative ad peddlers who embrace the politics of anything goes. Well, I say to them tonight, there is not a liberal America and a conservative America—there is the United States of America. There is not a black America and a white America and Latino America and an Asian America—there's the United States of America. The pundits like to slice and dice our country into Red States and Blue States: Red States for Republicans, Blue States for Democrats. But I've got news for them, too. We worship an awesome God in the Blue States, and we don't like federal agents poking around in our libraries in the Red States. We coach Little League in the Blue States and yes, we've got some gay friends in the Red States. There are patriots who opposed the war in Iraq and there are patriots who supported the war in Iraq. We are one people, all of us pledging allegiance to the stars and stripes, all of us defending the United States of America. – Barack Obama

6d Consider paragraph length.

Paragraph length is determined by content and purpose. Paragraphs should develop an idea, create any desired effects (such as suspense or humor), and advance the larger piece of writing. Fulfilling these aims will sometimes require short paragraphs, sometimes long ones. For example, if you are writing a persuasive piece, you may put all your evidence into one long paragraph to create the impression of a solid, overwhelmingly convincing argument. In a story about an exciting event, on the other hand, you may use a series of short paragraphs to create suspense, to keep the reader rushing to each new paragraph to find out what happens next.

REASONS TO START A NEW PARAGRAPH

- to turn to a new idea
- to emphasize something (such as an idea or an example)
- to change speakers (in dialogue)
- to get readers to pause
- to take up a subtopic
- to start the conclusion

6e Make paragraphs flow.

A paragraph has coherence—or flows—if its details all fit together clearly in a way that readers can easily follow. When you arrange information in a particular order (as described in 5d and 6c), you help readers move from one point to another. Regardless of your organization, however, be aware of several other ways to achieve paragraph coherence.

Repetition of key words and phrases

Weaving in repeated key words and phrases—or pronouns pointing to them—not only links sentences but also alerts readers to the importance of those words or phrases in the larger piece of writing. Notice in the following example how the repetition of the italicized key words and the use of pronouns that refer to those words help hold the paragraph together:

> Over the centuries, *shopping* has changed in function as well as in style. Before the Industrial Revolution, most consumer goods were sold in open-air *markets*, *customers* who went into an actual *shop* were expected to *buy* something, and *shoppers* were always expected to *bargain* for the

best possible *price.* In the nineteenth century, however, the development of the department *store* changed the relationship between buyers and sellers. Instead of visiting several *market* stalls or small *shops, customers* could now *buy* a variety of merchandise under the same roof; instead of feeling expected to *buy,* they were welcome just to look; and instead of *bargaining* with several merchants, they paid a fixed *price* for each *item.* In addition, *they* could return an *item* to the *store* and exchange *it* for a different one or get their money back. All of these changes helped transform *shopping* from serious requirement to psychological recreation.

Parallelism

Parallel structures can help connect the sentences within a paragraph. As readers, we feel pulled along by the force of the parallel structures in the following example:

> William Faulkner's "Barn Burning" tells the story of a young boy trapped in a no-win situation. If he betrays his father, he loses his family. If he betrays justice, he becomes a fugitive. In trying to free himself from his trap, he does both.

Transitions

Transitions are words such as *so, however,* and *thus* that signal relationships between sentences and paragraphs. Transitions help guide the reader from one idea to another. To understand how important transitions are in directing readers, try reading the following paragraph, from which all transitions have been removed.

A PARAGRAPH WITH NO TRANSITIONS

> In "The Fly," Katherine Mansfield tries to show us the real personality of the boss beneath his exterior. The fly helps her to portray this real self. The boss goes through a range of emotions and feelings. He expresses these feelings to a small but determined fly, whom the reader realizes he unconsciously relates to his son. The author basically splits up the story into three parts, with the boss's emotions and actions changing quite measurably. With old Woodifield, with himself, and with the fly, we see the boss's manipulativeness. Our understanding of him as a hard and cruel man grows.

If we work at it, we can figure out the relationship of these sentences to one another, for this paragraph is essentially unified by one major idea. But the lack of transitions results in an abrupt, choppy rhythm; the paragraph lurches from one detail to the next, dragging the confused reader behind. See how much easier the passage is to read and understand with transitions added.

Making Connections with Transitions

Writers use transitions to show a variety of relationships between ideas: to show contrast (*on the other hand*); to put ideas in sequence (*first, next, finally*); to counter an idea (*however, nevertheless*); to show a causal relationship (*due to, as a result*); to compare (*in the same way, likewise, similarly*); to add an idea (*also, in addition*); or to illustrate a point (*for example*). Professor Laura Aull's research shows that expert academic writers use a wider range and variety of transitions than student writers do and that the transitions are closely tied to their purpose. Experts are most likely to use transitional markers to show contrast, sequence, addition, comparison, and illustration. Look closely at the transitional words and phrases in your writing. Is their purpose clear and appropriate? Overusing causal transitions can make your writing seem to jump to conclusions too quickly, while overusing countering transitions can make your writing seem more aggressive than you intend. Take a tip from expert writers and take particular care with transitions that show cause and effect and countering.

THE SAME PARAGRAPH WITH TRANSITIONS

In "The Fly," Katherine Mansfield tries to show us the real personality of the boss beneath his exterior. The fly in the story's title helps her to portray this real self. In the course of the story, the boss goes through a range of emotions. At the end, he finally expresses these feelings to a small but determined fly, whom the reader realizes he unconsciously relates to his son. To accomplish her goal, the author basically splits up the story into three parts, with the boss's emotions and actions changing measurably throughout. First with old Woodifield, then with himself, and last with the fly, we see the boss's manipulativeness. With each part, our understanding of him as a hard and cruel man grows.

Commonly used transitions

TO SIGNAL SEQUENCE AND TIME

after a while, afterward, again, and then, as long as, as soon as, at last, at that time, before, besides, earlier, finally, first . . . second . . . third, immediately, in the meantime, in the past, last, lately, later, meanwhile, next, now, presently, simultaneously, since, so far, soon, still, then, thereafter, until, when

TO ADD IDEAS

again, also, furthermore, in the same way, likewise, moreover, similarly, too

TO SHOW CONTRAST OR COUNTERARGUMENT

although, but, despite, even though, however, in contrast, indeed, in spite of, instead, nevertheless, nonetheless, on one hand . . . on the other hand, on the contrary, regardless, still, though, while, yet

TO SIGNAL EXAMPLES AND ILLUSTRATIONS

for example, for instance, in fact, of course, specifically, such as, the following example, to illustrate

TO SIGNAL CAUSE AND EFFECT

accordingly, as a result, because, consequently, due to, hence, so, then, therefore, thereupon, thus, to this end

TO SIGNAL PLACE

above, adjacent to, below, beyond, closer to, elsewhere, far, farther on, here, near, nearby, opposite to, there, to the left, to the right

TO SIGNAL SUMMARY, REPETITION, OR CONCLUSION

as a result, as has been noted, as I have said, as mentioned earlier, as we have seen, in any event, in conclusion, in other words, in short, on the whole, therefore, to summarize

6f Work on opening and closing paragraphs.

Opening paragraphs

Even a good piece of writing may remain unread if it has a weak opening paragraph. In addition to announcing your topic, an introductory paragraph must engage readers' interest and focus their attention on what is to follow. One common kind of opening paragraph follows a general-to-specific sequence, in which the writer opens with a general statement and then gets more and more specific, concluding with the thesis. The following paragraph illustrates such an opening:

> The human organism is adapted to function in face-to-face encounters. We know that face-to-face is the most effective way to pitch woo. And face-to-face is obviously the best way to transact an intimate relationship long term. But while we know this, there's much more to face-to-face interaction than meets the naked eye. And it is of grave importance. We risk losing a great deal in any heavy shift of social traffic onto exclusively electronic media. — MARIAM THALOS, "Why I Am Not a Friend"

In this paragraph, the opening sentence introduces a general subject, and the last sentence presents the thesis, which the rest of the essay will develop.

OTHER EFFECTIVE WAYS OF OPENING

- with a quotation: *There is a bumper sticker that reads, "Too bad ignorance isn't painful."* – NIKKI GIOVANNI, "Racism 101"
- with an anecdote: *Social networking pioneer Howard Rheingold begins his digital journalism course each year with a participatory experiment. Shut off your cell phones, he tells his students. Shut your laptop. Now, shut your eyes.* – CATHY DAVIDSON, *Now You See It*
- with a question: *Why are Americans terrified of using nuclear power as a source of energy?*
- with a strong opinion: *Men need a men's movement about as much as women need chest hair.* – JOHN RUSZKIEWICZ, *The Presence of Others*

Concluding paragraphs

A good conclusion wraps up a piece of writing in a satisfying and memorable way. A common and effective strategy for concluding is to restate the central idea (but not word for word), perhaps specifying it in several sentences, and then ending with a much more general statement.

> Lastly, and perhaps greatest of all, there was the ability, at the end, to turn quickly from war to peace once the fighting was over. Out of the way these two men [Generals Grant and Lee] behaved at Appomattox came the possibility of a peace of reconciliation. It was a possibility not wholly realized, in the years to come, but which did, in the end, help the two sections to become one nation again . . . after a war whose bitterness might have seemed to make such a reunion wholly impossible. No part of either man's life became him more than the part he played in this brief meeting in the McLean house at Appomattox. Their behavior there put all succeeding generations of Americans in their debt. Two great Americans, Grant and Lee—very different, yet under everything very much alike. Their encounter at Appomattox was one of the great moments of American history.
> – BRUCE CATTON, "Grant and Lee: A Study in Contrasts"

OTHER EFFECTIVE WAYS OF CONCLUDING

- with a quotation
- with a question
- with a vivid image
- with a call for action
- with a warning

Reviewing, Revising, and Editing **7**

The ancient Roman poet Horace once advised aspiring writers to get distance from their work by putting it away for *nine years*. Although impractical for college writers, to say the least, Horace's advice holds a nugget of truth: putting your draft aside even for a short while will help clear your mind and give you more objectivity about your writing.

Make time to review your work (by yourself or with others) and to revise, edit, and proofread. Reviewing calls for reading your draft with a critical eye and asking others to look over your work. Revising involves reworking your draft on the basis of the review, making sure that the draft is clear, effective, complete, and well organized. Editing involves fine-tuning, attending to all the details.

7a Reread.

After giving yourself and your draft a rest, review the draft by rereading it carefully for meaning; recalling your purpose and audience; reconsidering your stance; and evaluating your organization and use of visuals.

Meaning

When you pick up the draft again, don't sweat the small stuff. Instead, concentrate on your message and on whether you have expressed it clearly. Note any places where the meaning seems unclear.

Purpose

If you responded to an assignment, make sure that you have produced what was asked for. If you set out to prove something, have you succeeded? If you intended to propose a solution to a problem, have you set forth a well-supported solution rather than just an analysis of the problem?

Audience

How appropriately do you address your audience members, given their experiences and expectations? Will you catch their interest, and will they be able to follow your discussion?

Stance

Ask yourself one central question: where are you coming from in this draft? Consider whether your stance appropriately matches the stance you started out with, or whether your stance has legitimately evolved.

Organization

One way to check the organization of your draft is to outline it. After numbering the paragraphs, read through each one, jotting down its main idea. Do the main ideas clearly relate to the thesis and to one another? Can you identify any confusing leaps from point to point? Have you left out any important points?

Genre and media

You decided to write in a particular genre, so think again about why you made that choice. Is writing in this genre the best way to achieve your purpose and reach your audience? Does the draft fulfill the requirements of the genre? Would any content in your draft be more effective presented in another medium—for example, as a print handout instead of a PowerPoint slide? Should you consider "translating" your work into another medium (see Chapters 5 and 24)? Do you need to take any additional steps to make your work as effective as it can be in this medium?

Look closely at any images, audio, and video you have chosen to use. How do they contribute to your draft? Make sure that all visuals and media files are labeled with captions and sources, and remember to refer to visuals and media and to comment on their significance to the rest of your text. Would any information in your draft work better in visual than in verbal form?

■■ FOR MULTILINGUAL WRITERS

Multilingual **Asking an Experienced Writer to Review Your Draft**

One good way to make sure that your writing is easy to follow is to have someone else read it. You might ask someone who is experienced in the kind of writing you are working on to read over your draft and to point out any words or patterns that are unclear or ineffective.

7b Get the most from peer review.

In addition to your own critical appraisal and that of your instructor (7c), you will probably want to get responses to your draft from friends, classmates, or colleagues. In a writing course, you may be asked to respond to the work of your peers as well as to seek responses from them.

The role of peer reviewers

One of the main goals of a peer reviewer is to help a writer see a draft differently. When you review a draft, you want to *show* the writer

---

QUICK HELP

Guidelines for Peer Response

- *Initial thoughts.* What are the main strengths and weaknesses of the draft? What might confuse readers? What is the most important thing the writer says in the draft? What will readers want to know more about?
- *Assignment.* Does the draft carry out the assignment?
- *Title and introduction.* Do the title and introduction tell what the draft is about and catch readers' interest? How else might the draft begin?
- *Thesis and purpose.* Paraphrase the thesis: *In this paper, the writer will . . .* Does the draft fulfill that promise?
- *Audience.* How does the draft interest and appeal to its audience?
- *Rhetorical stance.* Where does the writer stand? What words indicate the stance?
- *Supporting points.* List the main points, and review them one by one. How well does each point support the thesis? Do any need more explanation? Do any seem confusing or boring?
- *Visuals, media, and design.* Do visuals, if any, add to the key points? Do media files play properly and serve their intended purpose? Is the design clear and effective?
- *Organization and flow.* Is the writing easy to follow? How effective are transitions within sentences, between sentences, and between paragraphs?
- *Conclusion.* Does the draft conclude memorably? Is there another way it might end?

FOR MULTILINGUAL WRITERS
Multilingual Understanding Peer Review

If you are not used to giving or receiving criticisms directly, you may be uneasy with a classmate's challenges to your work. However, constructive criticism is appropriate to peer review. Your peers will also expect you to offer your questions, suggestions, and insights.

---

what does and doesn't work about particular aspects of the draft. Visually marking the draft can help the writer absorb at a glance the revisions you suggest.

REVIEWING A PRINT DRAFT

When working with a hard copy of a draft, write compliments in the left margin and critiques, questions, and suggestions in the right margin. As long as you explain what your symbols mean, you can also use boxes, circles, single and double underlining, highlighting, or other visual annotations as shorthand for what you have to say about the draft.

PEER REVIEW: Work with a Writer

Give your full attention to offering as much help as you can.

ASK:

What does the writer want you to **focus** on for this stage of the draft?

Can you restate the **main points** as you see them?

What **specific** suggestions do you think will improve the draft?

Make sure that the writer can move forward when you're finished.

macmillanhighered.com/everyday6e

e Reviewing and Revising > Storyboard Activity: Being a peer reviewer

▶ Reviewing and Revising > Video Prompt: Lessons from being a peer reviewer

REVIEWING A DIGITAL DRAFT

If the draft is a digital file, the reviewer should save the document in a peer-review folder under an easy-to-recognize name. It's wise to include the writer's name, the assignment, the number of the draft, and the reviewer's initials. For example, the reviewer Ann G. Smith might name the file for the first draft of Javier Jabari's first essay *jabari.essay1.d1.ags*.

The reviewer can then use the word-processing program to add comments, questions, and suggestions to the text. Most such programs have a TRACK CHANGES tool that can show changes to the document in a different color and a COMMENT function that allows you to type a note in the margin. If your word processor doesn't have a COMMENT function, you can comment in footnotes instead.

You should also consider using highlighting in written-word texts. If you explain to the writer what the colors mean and use only a few colors, highlighting can make a powerful visual statement about what needs to be revised.

For media drafts that are difficult to annotate visually, ask the writer about preferred ways to offer suggestions. Can you include audio annotations? If not, try written notes that indicate the time stamp, so the writer will know which part of the file you are commenting on. Does the writer prefer written notes? Can you comment privately on a posted file? Should you discuss the draft in person?

BASING RESPONSES ON THE STAGE OF THE DRAFT

Different stages in the writing process call for different strategies and areas of focus on the part of the peer reviewer.

- Writers of early-stage drafts need direction and options, not editing that focuses on grammar or punctuation. Pointing out surface errors such as misspellings and missing commas will not be a good use of either your time or the writer's if the writer later decides to delete the whole sentence. Your goal as a peer reviewer of an early draft is to help the writer think of ways to expand on the ideas. Pose questions and offer examples that will help the writer think of new ways to approach the topic. Try to help the writer imagine what the final draft might be like.

- Writers of intermediate-stage drafts need to know where their claims lack sufficient evidence, what ideas confuse readers, and how their approach misses its target audience. They also need to know which parts of their drafts are clear and well written, so remember to praise as well as to criticize.

- Writers of late-stage drafts need help with first and last impressions, sentence construction, word choice, tone, and format.

Your job as a peer reviewer is to call attention to the sorts of problems writers need to solve before submitting their final work. Identify the overall strengths of the draft as well as one or two weaknesses that the writer can reasonably improve in a short amount of time.

Reviews of Emily Lesk's draft

On the following pages are the first paragraphs of Emily Lesk's draft, as reviewed by two students, Beatrice Kim and Nastassia Lopez. Beatrice and Nastassia reviewed the draft separately and combined their comments on the draft they returned to Emily. As this review shows, Nastassia and Bea agreed on some of the major problems—and good points—in Emily's draft. Their comments on the draft, however, revealed some different responses. You, too, will find that different readers do not always agree on what is effective or ineffective. In addition, you may find that you simply do not agree with their advice. In examining responses to your writing, you can often proceed efficiently by looking first for areas of agreement (*everyone was confused by this sentence—I'd better revise it*) or strong disagreement (*one person said my conclusion was "perfect," and someone else said it "didn't conclude"—better look carefully at that paragraph again*).

All-Powerful Coke

Comment (NL): I'm not sure the title says enough about your argument.

I don't drink Coke. Call me picky for disliking the soda's saccharine aftertaste. Call me cheap for choosing a water fountain over a twelve-ounce aluminum can that costs a dollar from a vending machine but only pennies to produce. Even call me unpatriotic for rejecting the potable god that over the last century has come to represent all the enjoyment and ease to be found in our American way of life. But don't call me a hypocrite when I admit that I still identify with Coke and the Coca-Cola culture.

Comment (NL): The first sentence is a good attention-getter.

Comment (BK): The beginning seems kind of abrupt.

Comment (BK): What does this mean? Will other members of your audience know?

Comment (NL): The style of repeating "call me" is good, but I'm not sure the first three have much to do with the rest of the essay.

I have a favorite T-shirt that says "Drink Coca-Cola Classic" in Hebrew. It's Israel's standard tourist fare, like little nested dolls in Russia or painted horses in Scandinavia, and before setting foot in the Promised

Comment (NL): Do you need these details? Will any of this be important later?

Land three years ago, I knew where I could find one.
The T-shirt shop in the central block of a Jerusalem
shopping center did offer other shirt designs ("Maccabee
Beer" was a favorite), but that Coca-Cola shirt was what
drew in most of the dollar-carrying tourists. I waited
almost twenty minutes for mine, and I watched nearly
everyone ahead of me say "the Coke shirt" (and "thanks"
in Hebrew).

> **Comment (NL):** One of what? A doll or a horse?

> **Comment (BK):** Saying it in Hebrew would be cool here.

At the time, I never asked why I wanted the shirt. I
do know, though, that the reason I wear it often, despite
a hole in the right sleeve, has to do with its power as
a conversation piece. Few people notice it without asking
something like, "Does that say Coke?" I usually smile
and nod. They mumble a compliment and we go our
separate ways. But rarely does anyone want to know what
language the world's most famous logo is written in. And
why should they? Perhaps because Coca-Cola is a cultural
icon that shapes American identity.

> **Comment (NL):** This transition works really well. I wasn't sure where this was going, but here you are starting to clue the reader in.

> **Comment (NL):** Good detail! Lots of people can relate to a "conversation piece" shirt.

> **Comment (NL):** Good question! But I don't think the next sentence really answers it.

> **Comment (BK):** Is this the thesis? It kind of comes out of nowhere.

Throughout the company's history, marketing
strategies have centered on putting Coca-Cola in scenes
of the happy, carefree American life we never stop
striving for. What 1950s teenage girl wouldn't long to
see herself in the soda shop pictured in a Coca-Cola ad
appearing in a 1958 issue of *Seventeen* magazine? A
clean-cut, handsome man flirts with a pair of smiling
girls as they laugh and drink Coca-Colas. And any girls
who couldn't put themselves in that perfect, happy
scene could at least buy a Coke for consolation. The
malt shop — complete with a soda jerk in a white jacket
and paper hat — is a theme that, even today, remains a
symbol of Americana.

> **Comment (BK):** OK, here I am beginning to understand where your argument is going.

> **Comment (NL):** Maybe this is a little too broad?

> **Comment (BK):** *Any* girls? Really?

PEER REVIEW: Work with Reviewers

The writer's role in peer review

Remember that your reviewers should be acting as coaches, not judges, and that their job is to help you improve your essay as much as possible. Listen to and read their comments carefully. If you don't understand a particular suggestion, ask for clarification, examples, and so on. Remember, too, that reviewers are commenting on your writing, not on *you*, so be open and responsive to what they recommend. But you are the final authority on your essay; you will decide which suggestions to follow and which to disregard.

7c Consult instructor comments.

Instructor comments on any work that you have done can help you identify mistakes, particularly ones that you make repeatedly, and can point you toward larger issues that prevent your writing from being as effective as it could be. Whether or not you will have an opportunity to revise a particular piece of writing, you should look closely at the comments from your instructor.

macmillanhighered.com/everyday6e

e Reviewing and Revising > Storyboard Activity: Getting help from peer reviewers

◉ Reviewing and Revising > Video Prompt: Lessons from peer review

In responding to student writing, however, instructors sometimes use phrases or comments that are a kind of shorthand—comments that are perfectly clear to the instructor but may be less clear to the students reading them. The instructor comments in the following chart, culled from over a thousand first-year student essays, are among those that you may find most puzzling. Alongside each comment you'll find information intended to allow you to revise as your instructor recommends. If your paper includes a puzzling comment that is not listed here, be sure to ask your instructor what the comment means and how you can fix the problem.

Instructor Comment	Actions to Take in Response
thesis not clear	Make sure that you have a main point, and state it directly. The rest of the paper will need to support the main point, too—this problem cannot be corrected by adding a sentence or two.
trying to do too much covers too much ground	Focus your main point more narrowly (5a) so that you can explain your topic fully in a project of the assigned length. You may need to cut back on some material and then provide evidence and details to expand what remains.
hard to follow not logical incoherent jumps around parts not connected transition	If overall organization is unclear, try mapping or outlining and rearranging your work. (5d) See if transitions and signals or additional explanation will solve the problem.
too general vague	Use concrete language and details, and make sure that you have something specific and interesting to say. (29c) If not, reconsider your topic.
underdeveloped thin sparse	Add examples and details, and be as specific as possible. (29c) You may need to do more research. (Chapters 12–14)
what about the opposition? one-sided condescending overbearing	Add information on why some people disagree with you, and represent their views fairly and completely before you refute them. Recognize that reasonable people may hold views that differ from yours. (11f)

continued

Instructor Comment	Actions to Take in Response
repetitive *you've already said this*	Revise any parts of your writing that repeat an argument, point, word, or phrase; avoid using the same evidence over and over.
awk *awkward*	Ask a peer or your instructor for suggestions about revising awkward sentences. (Chapters 30–35)
syntax *awkward syntax* *convoluted*	Read the sentence aloud to identify the problem; revise or replace the sentence. (Chapters 30–35)
unclear	Find another way to explain what you mean; add any background information or examples that your audience may need to follow your reasoning.
tone too conversational *not an academic voice* *too informal* *colloquial*	Consider your audience and genre, and revise material that may suggest that you are not serious about the topic, audience, or assignment. (Chapter 29)
pompous *stilted* *stiff*	Make sure you understand the connotations of the words that you use. Revise material that adds nothing to your meaning, no matter how impressive it sounds. (29a and b)
set up quotation *integrate quotation*	Read the sentence containing the quotation aloud; revise it if it does not make sense as a sentence. Introduce every quotation with information about the source. Explain each quotation's importance to your work. (Chapter 15)
your words? *source?* *cite*	Mark all quotations clearly. Cite paraphrases and summaries of others' ideas. Give credit for help from others, and remember that you are responsible for your own work. (Chapters 14 and 15)
doc	Check the citations to be sure that you include all of the required information, that you punctuate correctly, and that you omit information not required by the documentation style. (Chapters 57–67)

7d Revise.

Approach comments from peer reviewers or from your instructor in several stages. First, read straight through the comments. Take a few minutes to digest the feedback and get some distance from your work. Then make a revision plan—as elaborate or as simple as you want—that prioritizes the changes needed in your next draft.

If you have comments from more than one reviewer, you may want to begin by making two lists: (1) areas in which reviewers agree on needed changes, and (2) areas in which they disagree. You will then have to make choices about which advice to heed and which to ignore from both lists. Next, rank the suggestions you've chosen to address.

Focus on comments about your purpose, audience, stance, thesis, and support. Leave any changes to sentences, words, punctuation, and format for later in the process; your revision of bigger-picture issues comes first.

Prepare a file for your revised draft. Use your previous draft as a starting point, renaming it to indicate that it is a revision. (For example, Javier Jabari might rename his file *jabari essay1 d2*, using his name, assignment number, and draft number.)

REVISING AND EDITING: Read All Comments Carefully

Analyze feedback from your instructor and other readers.

ASK:

What additional questions do you have about the feedback?

Which comments are most important and useful?

Which comments will point you toward the most improved next draft?

Remember: how you respond to suggestions is up to you.

REVISING AND EDITING: Plan Your Next Draft

In the new file, make the changes you identified in your revision plan. Be prepared to revise heavily, if necessary; if comments suggest that your thesis isn't working, for example, you may need to change the topic or the entire direction of your text. Heavy revision is not a sign that there's something wrong with your writing; on the contrary, major revision is a common feature of serious, goal-oriented writing.

Once you are satisfied that the revisions adequately address your major concerns, make corrections to sentences, words, and punctuation.

TALKING THE TALK

Revision

"I thought I had revised my assignment, but my instructor said I'd just corrected the typos." It's always a good idea to clarify what *revision* means with a particular instructor. Generally, though, when a writing teacher asks for a revision, minor corrections will not be enough. Plan to review your entire draft, and be prepared to make major changes if necessary. Look for sentence-level errors and typos later, during the editing stage, since these may disappear or change as you revise.

Thesis

Make sure that your thesis states the topic clearly and comments on what is particularly significant about the topic (5b). In addition, ask yourself whether the thesis is narrowed and focused enough to be thoroughly supported. If not, take time now to refine or limit your thesis further.

When you revise your thesis, remember also to revise the rest of the draft accordingly.

Support

Make sure that each paragraph relates to or supports the thesis and that each paragraph has sufficient detail to support the point it is making. Eliminate unnecessary material, and identify sections that need further details or examples.

Organization

Should any sections or paragraphs be moved to clarify your point or support your thesis more logically? Are there any paragraphs or parts of paragraphs that don't fit with the essay now or that are unnecessary? Look for confusing leaps or omissions, and identify places where transitions would make the writing easier to follow.

Title, introduction, and conclusion

Does the title give information and draw readers in? Does the introduction attract their interest and present the topic in a way that makes them want to keep reading? Does the conclusion leave readers satisfied or fired up and ready to take action? Because readers notice beginnings and endings more than other parts of a piece of writing, pay special attention to how you introduce and conclude your work.

Visuals, media, and design

As you check what you've written about your topic, you also need to take a close look at the way your text looks and works. Do your visuals, audio, and video (if any) help you make your points? How can you make this content more effective? Do you use design effectively for your genre and medium? Is your text readable and inviting?

7e Edit.

Once you have revised a draft for content and organization, look closely at your sentences and words. Turning a "blah" sentence into a memorable one—or finding exactly the right word to express a thought—can result in writing that is really worth reading. As with life, variety is the spice of sentences. You can add variety to your sentences by looking closely at their length, structure, and opening patterns.

Sentence length

Too many short sentences, especially one following another, can sound like a series of blasts on a car horn, whereas a steady stream of long sentences may tire or confuse readers. Most writers aim for some variety in the length of their sentences.

Sentence structure

Using only simple sentences can make your writing sound choppy, but overusing compound sentences can result in a singsong rhythm, and strings of long complex sentences may sound—well, overly complex. Try to vary your sentence structure!

REVISING AND EDITING: Polish Your Draft

Don't forget the details.

ASK:

What does each **sentence** contribute to your purpose?

How can you choose **words** more effectively?

How can you improve your **tone** or **style**?

Follow appropriate conventions for your genre and audience.

Sentence openings

Most sentences in English follow subject-predicate order and hence open with the subject of an independent clause, as does the sentence you are now reading. But opening sentence after sentence this way results in a jerky, abrupt, or choppy rhythm. You can vary sentence openings by beginning with a dependent clause, a phrase, an adverb, a conjunctive adverb, or a coordinating conjunction (35b).

Emily Lesk's second paragraph (see pp. 70–71) tells the story of how she got her Coke T-shirt in Israel. Before she revised her draft, every sentence in this paragraph opened with the subject: *I have a favorite T-shirt, It's Israel's standard tourist fare, I waited. . . .* In her revision, Emily deleted some examples and varied her sentence openings for a dramatic and easy-to-read paragraph:

> *Even before* setting foot in Israel three years ago, I knew exactly where I could find the Coke T-shirt. The tiny shop in the central block of Jerusalem's Ben Yehuda Street did offer other designs, but the one with a bright white "Drink Coca-Cola Classic" written in Hebrew cursive across the chest was what drew in most of the dollar-carrying tourists. *While waiting* almost twenty minutes for my shirt, I watched nearly every customer ahead of me ask for "the Coke shirt, *todah rabah* [thank you very much]."

Sentences beginning with *it* and *there*

As you go over the opening sentences of your draft, look especially at those beginning with *it* or *there*. Sometimes these words can create a special emphasis, as in *It was a dark and stormy night*. But they can also appear too often. Another, more subtle problem with these openings is that they may be used to avoid taking responsibility for a statement. The following sentence can be improved by editing:

▶ *The university must*
  ~~It is necessary to~~ raise student fees.
  ^

Tone

Tone refers to the attitude that a writer's language conveys toward the topic and the audience. In examining the tone of your draft, think about the nature of the topic, your own attitude toward it, and that of your intended audience. Does your language create the tone you want to achieve (humorous, serious, impassioned, and so on), and is that tone an appropriate one, given your audience and topic?

Word choice

Word choice—or diction—offers writers an opportunity to put their personal stamp on a piece of writing. Becoming aware of the kinds of words you use should help you get the most mileage out of each word. Check for connotations, or associations, of words and make sure you consider how any use of slang, jargon, or emotional language may affect your audience (see 29a and b).

Spell checkers

While these software tools won't catch every spelling error or identify all problems of style, they can be very useful. Most professional writers use their spell checkers religiously. Remember, however, that spell checkers are limited; they don't recognize most proper names, foreign words, or specialized language, and they do not recognize homonym errors (misspelling *there* as *their*, for example). (See 29f.)

Document design

Before you produce a copy for final proofreading, reconsider one last time the format and the "look" you want your text to have. This is one last opportunity to think carefully about the visual appearance of your final draft. (For more on document design, see Chapter 22. For more on the design conventions of different disciplines, see Chapters 17–23.)

QUICK HELP

Word Choice

- Are the nouns primarily abstract and general or *concrete* and *specific*? Too many abstract and general nouns can result in boring prose.
- Are there too many nouns in relation to the number of verbs? This sentence is heavy and boring: *The effect of the overuse of nouns in writing is the placement of strain on the verbs.* Instead, say this: *Overusing nouns places a strain on the verbs.*
- How many verbs are forms of *be* — *be, am, is, are, was, were, being, been*? If *be* verbs account for more than about a third of your total verbs, you are probably overusing them.
- Are verbs *active* wherever possible? Passive verbs are harder to read and remember than active ones. Although the passive voice has many uses, your writing will gain strength and energy if you use active verbs.
- Are your words *appropriate*? Check to be sure they are not too fancy — or too casual.

Proofreading the final draft

Take time for one last, careful proofreading, which means reading to correct any typographical errors or other inconsistencies in spelling and punctuation. To proofread most effectively, read through the copy aloud, making sure that you've used punctuation marks correctly and consistently, that all sentences are complete (unless you've used intentional fragments or run-ons for special effects)—and that no words are missing. Then go through the copy again, this time reading backward so that you can focus on each individual word and its spelling.

A student's revised draft

Following are the first three paragraphs from Emily Lesk's edited and proofread draft that she submitted to her instructor. Compare these paragraphs with those from her reviewed draft in 7b.

Student Writer

Emily Lesk

Emily Lesk

Professor Arraéz

Electric Rhetoric

November 15, 2013

Red, White, and Everywhere

America, I have a confession to make: I don't drink Coke. But don't call me a hypocrite just because I am still the proud owner of a bright red shirt that advertises it. Just call me an American.

Even before setting foot in Israel three years ago, I knew exactly where I could find the Coke T-shirt. The tiny shop in the central block of Jerusalem's Ben Yehuda Street did offer other designs, but the one with a bright white "Drink Coca-Cola Classic" written in Hebrew cursive across the chest was what drew in most of the dollar-carrying tourists. While waiting almost twenty minutes for my shirt (depicted in Fig. 1), I watched nearly every customer ahead of me ask for "the Coke shirt, *todah rabah* [thank you very much]."

At the time, I never thought it strange that I wanted one, too. After having absorbed sixteen years of Coca-Cola propaganda through everything from NBC's Saturday morning cartoon lineup to the concession stand at Camden Yards (the Baltimore Orioles' ballpark), I associated the shirt with singing along to the "Just for the Taste of It" jingle and with America's favorite pastime, not with a brown fizzy beverage I refused to consume. When I later realized the immensity of Coke's corporate power, I felt

Fig. 1. Hebrew Coca-Cola T-shirt. Personal photograph by author.

somewhat manipulated, but that didn't stop me from wearing the shirt. I still don it often, despite the growing hole in the right sleeve, because of its power as a conversation piece. Few Americans notice it without asking something like "Does that say Coke?" I usually smile and nod. Then they mumble a one-word compliment, and we go our separate ways. But rarely do they want to know what language the internationally recognized logo is written in. And why should they? They are interested in what they can relate to as Americans: a familiar red-and-white logo, not a foreign language. Through nearly a century of brilliant advertising strategies, the Coca-Cola Company has given Americans not only a thirst-quenching beverage but a cultural icon that we have come to claim as our own.

8 Reflecting

Research demonstrates a connection between careful reflection and learning: thinking back on what you've learned and assessing it help make that learning stick. As a result, first-year college writing courses are increasingly encouraging students to take time for such reflection. Whether or not your instructor asks you to write a formal reflection, whenever you finish a major piece of writing or a writing course, you should make time to think back over the experience and see what lessons you can learn from it.

8a   Reflect to present your work effectively.

You may find it useful (or you may be required) to reflect on the work you have done for a course as part of your preparation for submitting a portfolio of your best work.

Portfolio guidelines

In preparing a portfolio, use these tips:

- *Consider your purpose and audience.* Do you want to fulfill course requirements for an instructor, show work to a prospective employer, keep a record of what you've done for personal reasons, or something else? Answering these questions will help you decide what to include in the portfolio and whether it should be in print or electronic form.

- *Based on the portfolio's purpose, decide on the number of entries.* You may decide to include a wide range of materials—from essays, problem sets, and photos to web texts, multimedia presentations, a résumé, or anything else that is relevant—if readers can select only the pieces that interest them. For a portfolio that will be read from beginning to end, however, you should limit yourself to five to seven examples of your writing. You might include an academic essay that argues a claim, a personal essay, a brief report, writing based on research, significant correspondence, timed writing, or other work that you think shows your strengths as a writer.

- *Consider organization.* What arrangement—in chronological order, by genre, by topic—will make most sense to readers?

- *Think carefully about layout and design.* Will you include a menu, a table of contents, or appendices? How will you use color, font and type size, and other elements of design to enhance your portfolio (see Chapter 22)? Remember to label and date each piece of writing in the portfolio to help readers follow along easily. For print portfolios, number pages in consecutive order.

- *Edit and proofread* each piece in your portfolio and the reflective statement. Ask for responses from peers or an instructor.

Reflective statements

One of the most common writing assignments today is a reflective statement—often in the form of a letter, memo, or home page—that explains and analyzes a student's work in a writing course.

To create a reflective statement, think carefully about the impression it should give, and make sure your tone and style set the stage appropriately. Reflect on the strengths and weaknesses of your writing, using specific examples to provide evidence for each point you make. What are the most important things you have learned about writing—and about yourself as a writer—during the course?

If the reflective statement introduces your portfolio, follow your instructor's guidelines carefully. Unless asked to do otherwise, describe the portfolio's contents and explain why you have chosen each piece.

A STUDENT'S REFLECTIVE STATEMENT

Here is a shortened version of the cover letter that James Kung wrote to accompany his first-year writing portfolio.

Student Writer

James Kung

December 6, 2015

Dear Professor Ashdown:

"Writing is difficult and takes a long time." This simple yet powerful statement has been uttered so many times in our class that it has essentially become our motto. During this class, my persuasive writing skills have improved dramatically, thanks to many hours spent writing, revising, polishing, and thinking about my topic. The various drafts, revisions, and other materials in my portfolio show this improvement.

I entered this first-quarter Writing and Rhetoric class with both strengths and weaknesses. I have always written fairly well-organized essays. However, despite this strength, I struggled throughout the term to narrow and define the various aspects of my research-based argument.

The first aspect of my essay that I had trouble narrowing and defining was my major claim, or my thesis statement. In my "Proposal for Research-Based Argument," I proposed to argue about the case of Wen Ho Lee, the Los Alamos scientist accused of copying restricted government documents. I stated, "The Wen Ho Lee incident deals with the persecution of not only one man, but a whole ethnic group." You commented that the statement was a "sweeping claim" that would be "hard to support."

I spent weeks trying to rework that claim. Finally, as seen in my "Writer's Notebook 10/16/15," I realized that I had chosen the Lee case because of my belief that the political inactivity of Asian Americans contributed to the case against Lee. Therefore, I decided to focus on this issue in my thesis. Later I once again revised my claim, stating that the political inactivity did not cause but rather contributed to racial profiling in the Wen Ho Lee case.

I also had trouble defining my audience. I briefly alluded to the fact that my audience was a "typical American reader." However, I later decided to address my paper to an Asian American audience for two reasons. First, it would establish a greater ethos for myself as a Chinese American. Second, it would enable me to target the people the Wen Ho Lee case most directly affects: Asian Americans. As a result, in my final research-based argument, I was much more sensitive to the needs and concerns of my audience, and my audience trusted me more.

I hope to continue to improve my writing of research-based arguments.

Sincerely,

James Kung

James Kung

8b Reflect to learn.

Research shows that reflection is a key element in the move from writing for social reasons to writing for a wider public to accomplish bigger goals. When you reflect on your writing, you help ensure that what you have learned *transfers*—that is, that you will be able to use what you've learned in other disciplines and situations. Without time for reflection, you may feel that you are plunging from one assignment to the next, trying desperately to keep ahead of the syllabus, without being able to assimilate what you are learning. Try to make time to think about questions like these after every important piece of writing you do, either for school or for other purposes.

- What lessons have you learned from writing—from an individual piece of writing or an entire course?

Reflecting > Student Writing: Portfolio cover letter, James Kung

- From what you have learned, what can you apply to the work you will do for other classes and to the writing you do for personal reasons?
- What about your writing do you feel most confident about—and why do you feel this way?
- What about your writing do you think needs additional work, and what plans do you have for improving?
- What confusions did you have while writing, and what did you do to resolve them?
- What major questions do you still have?
- How has writing helped you clarify your thinking, extend your knowledge, or deepen your understanding?
- Identify a favorite passage in your writing, and then try to articulate what you like about it. Can you apply what you learn from this analysis to other pieces of writing?
- How would you describe your development as a writer?
- What goals do you have for yourself as a writer?

A STUDENT'S REFLECTIVE BLOG POST

Student Thanh Nguyen created a political poster for a course on immigration. On his personal blog, he posted the image that he created with a few reflective notes about what he had learned. Here is the image, along with a portion of his post:

It's not too obvious what I was trying to get at in the poster, which is my own fault in the design process. I replaced the cherubs/angels from Michelangelo's *Creation of Adam* with ICE agents and politicians to comment on their anti-immigrant practices. I guess I just wanted to address popular rhetoric dehumanizing undocumented folks in this country. They're people, too, you know? With families, lives, hopes, dreams, fears, and

Student Writing

beating hearts. Yet so many families are fractured because some children are forbidden to join their parents when deported, so many people are denied due process and proper trials because apparently you don't get them if you don't have a sheet of paper to legitimize your existence, and a lot of other messed-up stuff. As an artistic response to that, I just threw in a decapitated Statue of Liberty (lol stole/appropriated it from Cloverfield) and what I think she should say. . . .

Critical Reading **9**

I f you list all the reading you do in the course of a day, you will no doubt find that you are reading a lot—and that you are reading in many different ways for many different reasons, and using different tools and media. Reading critically means questioning, commenting, analyzing, and reflecting thoughtfully on a text—whether it's a white paper for a psychology class, a graphic novel, a Super Bowl ad, a business email, or a YouTube video. Any method you use to keep track of your questions and make yourself concentrate on a text can help you become a better critical reader.

9a Consider print and digital differences.

Onscreen reading is often social and collaborative, allowing you to connect with other readers, discuss what you've read, and thus turn reading into writing. Research suggests that onscreen readers tend to take shortcuts, scanning and skimming and jumping from link to link. Because screen reading can help you find content that relates to what you're looking for, it can be a powerful tool that you can use effectively in your college work.

But students today tell researchers that they still prefer to read print works when the reading needs to be absorbed and remembered. Psychologists find that students reading onscreen don't do nearly as much "metacognitive learning"—that is, learning that reflects on what has been learned and makes connections among the things learned—as readers of print texts do.

If you have a choice of media when you're asked to read a text, then, consider whether reading onscreen or in print will work better for your purposes. And if you must read a complex text onscreen rather than in print, be aware that you may need to try harder than usual to focus. Get in the habit of working through the steps described in this chapter—previewing (9b), annotating (9c), summarizing (9d), and analyzing (9e and f)—to ensure that you are reflecting and making appropriate connections, whether you're reading a printed page or a digital text.

9b   Preview the text.

Find out all you can about a text before beginning to look closely at it, considering its context, author, subject, genre, and design.

PREVIEWING THE CONTEXT

- Where have you encountered the work? Are you encountering the work in its original context? For example, an essay in a collection of readings may have been previously published in a magazine; a speech you watch on YouTube may have been delivered originally to a live or televised audience; a painting on a museum wall may have been created for a wealthy patron in a distant country centuries earlier.

CRITICAL READING: Preview

What do you expect to happen in this text?

WORLD PREMIERE

ASK:

What does the title tell you? Who created this work?

When, where, and how are you encountering the text?

How do genre, media, and design affect your expectations?

Prepare to engage the text.

- What can you infer from the original or current context of the work about its intended audience and purpose?

LEARNING ABOUT THE AUTHOR OR CREATOR

- What information can you find about the author or creator of the text?
- What purpose, expertise, and possible agenda might you expect this person to have? Where do you think the author or creator is coming from in this text?

PREVIEWING THE SUBJECT

- What do you know about the subject of the text?
- What opinions do you have about the subject, and on what are your opinions based?
- What would you like to learn about the subject?
- What do you expect the main point to be? Why?

CONSIDERING THE TITLE, MEDIUM, GENRE, AND DESIGN

- What does the title (or caption or other heading) indicate?
- What do you know about the medium (or media) in which the work appears? Is it a text on the web, a printed advertising brochure, a speech stored in iTunes, an animated cartoon on television, or some combination of media? What role does the medium play in achieving the purpose and connecting to the audience?
- What is the genre of the text—and what can it help illuminate about the intended audience or purpose? Why might the authors or creators have chosen this genre?
- How is the text presented? What do you notice about its formatting, use of color, visuals or illustrations, overall design, general appearance, and other design features?

Student preview of an assigned text

Fernando Sanchez and Sarah Lum, students in a first-year writing class, read and analyzed an academic article, "'Mistakes Are a Fact of Life': A National Comparative Study," by Andrea A. Lunsford and Karen J. Lunsford. Some of the preview notes they made before reading the article

Student Writer   Student Writer

Fernando Sanchez   Sarah Lum

appear below. (See 9c–e for additional steps in the critical reading from these students.)

This essay was published in *College Composition and Communication* in June 2008. According to the journal's website, "*College Composition and Communication* publishes research and scholarship in rhetoric and composition studies that supports college teachers in reflecting on and improving their practices in teaching writing and that reflects the most current scholarship and theory in the field." So the original audience was probably college writing teachers.

Information on context

The essay begins with these words from essayist Nikki Giovanni: "Mistakes are a fact of life. It is the response to the error that counts." The introduction explains that the article will talk about a study of first-year college writing and compare it to "a similar study conducted over twenty years ago."

Andrea A. Lunsford was an English professor and the director of the Program in Writing and Rhetoric at Stanford University when this article appeared in 2008. She is also the author of the book we are using in our writing class. Karen J. Lunsford is an associate professor of writing at the University of California, Santa Barbara.

About the authors

According to Google Scholar, both authors have published many articles and conducted a lot of research on writing, so they have experience that relates to this article.

Information on the authors' credibility

The authors will study writing from students across the country and see whether problems are increasing or whether mistakes are just "a fact of life." I am the subject of this study without even knowing it! My high school teachers used to tell me to be careful not to include any "Internet lingo" in my writing. . . . I wonder if students really are losing the ability to write because of technology?

Subject of article

I see that the authors are replicating a study done by Andrea Lunsford and Robert Connors in 1984, and they will give a detailed comparison between the two studies. This essay may say that making mistakes in writing may not be such a bad thing.

The title includes a quotation from the epigraph that opens the essay and that sets the theme for the whole article, indicating that the authors will focus on the mistakes that others point out in this generation of student writing.

Other preview information

The genre of this essay is a scholarly article published in a journal. This journal requires MLA documentation style for endnotes and for the list of works cited. The essay also uses headings to signal changes in topics within the essay. Eight tables provide data to back up what the authors are saying.

Information about genre and design

9c Read and annotate.

As you read a text for the first time, mark it up or take notes. Consider the text's content, author, intended audience, and genre and design.

READING FOR CONTENT

- What do you find confusing or unclear about the text? Where can you look for explanations or more information? Do you need background information in order to understand fully?
- What key terms and ideas—or key patterns—do you see? What key images stick in your mind?
- What sources or other works does this text cite, refer to, or allude to?

TALKING THE TALK

Critical Thinking

"Are criticizing and thinking critically the same thing?" *Criticize* can sometimes mean "find fault with," and you certainly don't have to be relentlessly negative to think critically. Instead, critical thinking means, first and foremost, asking good questions — and not simply accepting what you see at face value. By asking not only what words and images mean, but also how meaning gets across, critical thinkers consider why a text makes a particular claim, what writers may be leaving out or ignoring, and how to tell whether evidence is accurate and believable. If you're considering questions like these, then you're thinking critically.

CRITICAL READING: Read Carefully

• How does the content fit with what you already know?
• Which points do you agree with? Which do you disagree with? Why?

READING FOR AUTHOR/CREATOR AND AUDIENCE

• Do the authors or creators present themselves as you anticipated in your preview?
• For what audience was this text created? Are you part of its intended audience?
• What underlying assumptions can you identify in the text?
• Are the medium and genre appropriate for the topic, audience, and purpose?

READING FOR DESIGN, COMPOSITION, AND STYLE

• Is the design appropriate for the subject and genre?
• Does the composition serve a purpose — for instance, does the layout help you see what is more and less important in the text?
• Do words, images, sound, and other media work together well?
• How would you describe the style of the text? What contributes to this impression — word choice? references to research or popular culture? formatting? color? something else?

Student annotation of an assigned text

Following is an excerpt from Andrea A. Lunsford and Karen J. Luns-ford's essay "'Mistakes Are a Fact of Life': A National Comparative Study," with annotations made by Sarah Lum and Fernando San-chez. To read the full article with Sarah and Fernando's annotations, go to **macmillanhighered.com/everyday6e**.

"Mistakes Are a Fact of Life": A National Comparative Study

BY ANDREA A. LUNSFORD AND KAREN J. LUNSFORD

> Mistakes are a fact of life. It is the response to the error that counts.
> —NIKKI GIOVANNI, *Black Feeling, Black Talk, Black Judgment*

Perhaps it is the seemingly endless string of what have come to be called "Bushisms" ("We shouldn't fear a world that is more interacted") and the complex response to them from both right and left. Perhaps it is the hype over Instant Messaging lingo cropping up in formal writing and the debate among teachers over how to respond (Farmer 48). Perhaps it is the long series of attempts to loosen the grip of "standard" English on the public imagination, from the 1974 special issue of *College Composition and Communication* (*Students' Right to Their Own Language*) to a 2006 special issue of *College English* devoted to *Cross-Language Relations in Composition*. Or perhaps it is the number of recent reports, many of them commis-sioned by the government, that have be-moaned the state of student literacy and focused attention on what they deem signifi-cant failures at the college level (see especially the recent reports from the Spellings Commission and Derek Bok's *Our Underachieving Colleges*).

Fernando Sanchez: To an older audience, this is a good reference. To a much younger audience reading and researching this, "Bushisms" might not be a word in their vocabulary.

Sarah Lum: Perhaps text message lingo is not the main problem of student writing; rather it is the subjects students are currently interested in. They are reading less formal texts and are more engaged in social media. In the past, I read an essay in which a student had quoted the lyrics of a rapper rather than an author.

Whatever the reasons, and they are surely complex and multilayered, forms of language use have been much in the news, with charges of what student writers can and cannot (or should and should not) do all around us. The times seemed ripe, then, for taking a close look at a national sample of student writing to see what it might tell us about the current state of affairs. With that goal in mind, we drew up plans to conduct a national study of first-year college student writing and to compare our findings to those of a similar study conducted over twenty years ago.

"The Frequency of Formal Errors," or Remembering Ma and Pa Kettle

But we are getting a bit ahead of ourselves here. For now, flash back to the mid-1980s. Some readers may remember receiving a letter from Robert Connors and Andrea Lunsford asking them to participate in a national study of student writing by submitting a set of marked student papers from a first-year composition course. That call brought in well over 21,000 papers from 300 teachers around the country, and in fairly short order Andrea and Bob drew a random sample of 3,000 student papers stratified to be representative in terms of region of the country, size of institution, and type of institution. While they later analyzed patterns of teacher response to the essays as well as the particular spelling patterns that emerged (in that study, spelling was the most frequent student mistake by some 300 percent), they turned first to an analysis of which formal errors (other than spelling) were most common in this sample of student writing.

FS: This article will contain much content that older readers are already familiar with. It also includes phrases like "for now, flash back to the mid-1980s," implying the audience can easily remember those times.

SL: As frequent as misspelling is, I would expect that percentage to decrease in this age because we rely on computers to autocorrect our mistakes.

CRITICAL READING: Summarize

What was that all about?

ASK:

What is the overall *message* of the text?

Can you summarize it in your *own words*?

Would others get a **fair** and **accurate** impression from your summary?

Make sure that you understood the main points of the text.

9d Summarize the main ideas.

When you feel that you have read and thoroughly understood the text, try to summarize the contents in your own words. A summary *briefly* captures the main ideas of a text and omits information that is less important. Try to identify the key points in the text, find the essential evidence supporting those points, and explain the contents concisely and fairly, so that a reader unfamiliar with the original can make sense of it all. Deciding what to leave out can make summarizing a tricky task—but mastering this skill can serve you well in all the reading you do in your academic, professional, and civic life. To test your understanding—and to avoid unintentional plagiarism—it's wise to put the text aside while you write your summary. (For more information on writing a summary, see 14f.)

Student summary of an assigned text

Students Fernando Sanchez and Sarah Lum, whose critical reading notes appear in this chapter, summarized the "Mistakes" article. Here is Sarah's summary:

Student Writing

In "'Mistakes Are a Fact of Life': A National Comparative Study," Andrea and Karen Lunsford investigate the claim that students today can't write as well as students in the past. To determine how writing has changed over time, they replicated the 1984 Connors and Lunsford study of errors in student writing to find similarities and differences between the formal errors made by first-year writing students in 2006. Their findings reveal that the number of mistakes made two decades ago are consistent with the number of errors made today and that actually the rate of mistakes has stayed stable for a hundred years. The authors found that slang and shorthand commonly used by young adults do not interfere with college writing. The major difference between writing then and now is that students are writing more argument essays as opposed to personal narratives and that typical papers are two-and-a-half times longer now. We can't avoid making mistakes, but we can document them and figure out means of improvement.

Begins by identifying authors, title, and date of article, and by stating main goal of study

Summarizes major findings

Closes with comment that captures main point of article

9e   Analyze and reflect on the text.

When you feel that you understand the meaning of the text, move on to your analysis by asking additional questions about the text.

ANALYZING IDEAS AND EXAMPLES

- What are the main points in this text? Are they implied or explicitly stated?
- Which points do you agree with? Which do you disagree with? Why?
- Does anything in the text surprise you? Why, or why not?
- What kinds of examples does the text use? What other kinds of evidence does the text offer to back up the main points? Can you think of other examples or evidence that should have been included?
- Are viewpoints other than those of the author or creator included and treated fairly?
- How trustworthy are the sources the text cites or refers to?
- What assumptions does the text make? Are those assumptions valid? Why, or why not?

CRITICAL READING: Analyze

How does the text get its meaning across?

ASK:

How does the text accomplish its purposes?

Are the text and its creator *credible?* Are their assumptions valid?

How *effective* are the evidence, support, and design?

Assess your overall impression.

TALKING THE TALK

Visual Texts

"How can an image be a text?" In its traditional sense, a *text* involves words on paper. But now we spend at least as much time reading and analyzing images — including moving images — as we spend on printed words. So it makes sense to broaden the definition of "text" to include anything that sends a message. That's why images, ads, videos, films, and the like are often called *visual texts*.

ANALYZING FOR OVERALL IMPRESSION

- Do the authors or creators achieve their purpose? Why, or why not?
- What intrigues, puzzles, or irritates you about the text? Why?
- What else would you like to know?

Student analysis of an assigned text

After previewing, reading, annotating, and summarizing the article, students Sarah Lum and Fernando Sanchez analyzed the text. Here is Fernando's analysis:

Student Writing

Reading the first page gives the audience a good overview of what they are about to dive into. Andrea and Karen Lunsford clearly imply what side of the argument they will defend and expand on — that student errors have not increased over time. As I read, I noticed that the title quotation slowly and eloquently ties in with the argument. The authors' word choice (*positivity*, *optimism*, etc.) reminded me of this, and the phrase "mistakes are a fact of life" is also repeated several times to underline the main point.

States major finding of article

Shows how title quotation guides argument of entire essay

While a lot of people today think that students just can't write as well as we used to, this study proves the fear to be false. I am convinced by the results, which are based on careful analysis of a large number of student essays. One factor that did surprise me was an increase in student essay length. What happened between 1986 and 2006 that caused

Notes surprising aspect of essay and speculates on causes

such a huge change in length? The authors suggest that the change is related to use of technology, and this explanation makes sense to me.

> *Explains why he agrees with major point of essay*

The authors use clear and direct examples from other studies over a century, and the tables they use really help readers understand the differences between the studies. In fact, this was a major goal: the authors want readers to see for themselves the similarities and differences in student errors that studies have shown over the past hundred years. They have done a lot of research in order to find similar studies of error. In addition, one of the authors, Andrea Lunsford, was a researcher on a previous study. In my estimation, the authors achieved their purpose and have the evidence to support their conclusion. This article was well written, well explained, and well researched.

> *Notes effect of good examples and of tables representing findings*

> *Notes how authors establish credibility*

9f   Think critically about visual texts.

You can use the steps given in 9b–e to read any kind of text, from a scholarly article for a research project to an Instagram image. You may be at least as accustomed to reading visual texts as you are to reading words, whether or not you take time to make a formal analysis of what you see. But pausing to look closely and reflect on how a visual text works can make you more aware of how visuals convey information.

On p. 103, a Pulitzer Prize–winning photograph (by Craig F. Walker of the *Denver Post*) appears with its caption. This image appeared as part of a series documenting the experiences of a Colorado teenager, Ian Fisher, who joined the U.S. Army to fight in Iraq.

An analysis of this photograph made the following points:

> The couple are in the center of the photo — and at the center of our attention. But at this moment of choosing an engagement ring, they do not look "engaged" with each other. Kayla looks excited but uncertain, as if she knows that Ian feels doubts, but she hopes he will change his mind. She is looking right at him, with her body leaning toward him but her head leaning away: she looks very

> *Notes what is foregrounded in image and relates it to "main point" of visual*

© CRAIG F. WALKER/GETTY IMAGES

During a weekend home from his first assignment at Fort Carson, Colorado, Ian walked through a Denver-area mall with his new girlfriend, Kayla Spitzlberger, on December 15, 2007, and asked whether she wanted to go ring shopping. She was excited, but working out the financing made him nervous. They picked out the engagement ring in about five minutes, but Ian wouldn't officially propose until Christmas Day in front of her family. The couple had met in freshman math class but never really dated until now. The engagement would end before Valentine's Day.

tentative. Ian is looking away from Kayla, and the expression on his face suggests that he's already having second thoughts about the expense of the ring (we see his wallet on the counter by his elbow) and perhaps even about asking Kayla to marry him. The accompanying caption helps us interpret the image, telling us about the couple's brief history together and noting that the engagement will last less than two months after this moment. But the message comes through pretty clearly without words.

> Analyzes why they "do not look 'engaged' with each other"

> Shows how caption underscores image's main point

Ian and Kayla look as if they're trying on roles in this photograph. She looks ready to take the plunge, and he is resisting. These attitudes conform to stereotypical gender roles for a man and woman considering marriage (or going shopping, for that matter). The woman is expected to want the marriage and the ring; the man knows that he shouldn't show too much enthusiasm about weddings and shopping.

> Analysis suggests that people in the image conform to stereotypical gender roles

It's hard for the reader to tell whether Ian and Kayla really feel that they are making good or careful choices for their situation at this moment or whether they're just doing what they think they're supposed to do under the circumstances.

The reader also can't tell how the presence of the photographer, Craig F. Walker, affected the couple's actions. The photo is part of a series of images documenting Ian Fisher's life after joining the military, so Walker had probably spent a lot of time with Ian before this photo was taken. Did Ian want to give a particular impression of himself on this day? Were he and Kayla trying on "adult" roles in this situation? Were they feeling pressure to produce a memorable moment for the camera? And what was Walker thinking when he accompanied them to the mall and took this photograph? Did he foresee the end of their engagement when he captured this revealing moment? What was his agenda?

Notes that photographer's perspective may affect readers' understanding of image

Raises questions for further analysis

9g A student's critical reading of a text

Student Writer

Shuqiao Song

Following is an excerpt of a student essay written by Shuqiao Song, based on her critical reading of Alison Bechdel's graphic novel *Fun Home: A Family Tragicomic.* Shuqiao's critical reading involved looking closely at the words, at the images, and at how the words and images together create a very complex story. For Shuqiao Song's PowerPoint presentation of this essay, see 23f.

Shuqiao Song

Dr. Andrea Lunsford

English 87N

13 March 2014

Residents of a Dys*FUN*ctional *HOME*

In a 2008 online interview, comic artist Alison Bechdel
remarked, "I love words, and I love pictures. But especially, I
love them together — in a mystical way that I can't even explain"
("Stuck"). Indeed, in her graphic novel memoir, *Fun Home:
A Family Tragicomic,* text and image work together in a mystical
way: text *and* image. But using both image and text results not in a
simple summation but in a strange relationship — as strange as the
relationship between Alison Bechdel and her father. These strange
pairings have an alluring quality that makes Bechdel's *Fun Home*
compelling; for her, both text and image are necessary. As Bechdel
tells and shows us, alone, words can fail; alone, images deceive.
Yet her life story ties both concepts inextricably to her memories
and revelations such that only the interplay of text and image
offers the reader the rich complexity, honesty, and possibilities in
Bechdel's quest to understand and find closure for the past.

The idea that words are insufficient is not new — certainly
we have all felt moments when language simply fails us and we
are at a loss for words, moments like being "left . . . wordless" by
"the infinite gradations of color in a fine sunset" (Bechdel, *Fun*
150). In those wordless moments, we strain to express just what
we mean. Writers are especially aware of what is lost between word
and meaning; Bechdel's comment on the translation of Proust's *À la
Recherche du Temps Perdu* is a telling example of the troubling gap:

> After Dad died, an updated translation of Proust came out.
> *Remembrance of Things Past* was retitled *In Search of Lost
> Time*. The new title is a more literal translation

Margin note (right of opening paragraph): Introduces author of the work she is discussing, along with her major topic

First example in support of thesis

The Bechdels' elaborately restored house is the gilded, but tense, context of young Alison's familial relationships and a metaphor for her father's deceptions. "He used his skillful artifice not to make things, but to make things appear to be what they were not," Bechdel notes alongside an image of her father taking a photo of their family, shown in Fig. 2 (*Fun* 16). The scene represents the nature of her father's artifice; her father is *posing* a photo, an image of their family.

Fig. 2. Alison's father posing a family photo (Bechdel, *Fun* 16).

Second example in support of thesis

In that same scene, Bechdel also shows her own sleight of hand; she manipulates the scene and reverses her father's role and her own to show young Alison taking the photograph of the family and her father posing in Alison's place (Fig. 3). In the image, young Alison symbolizes Bechdel in the present—looking back through the camera

Fig. 3. Alison and her father trade places (Bechdel, *Fun* 17).

lens to create a portrait of her family. But unlike her father, she isn't using false images to deceive. Bechdel overcomes the treason of images by confessing herself as an "artificer" to her audience (*Fun* 16). Bechdel doesn't villainize the illusory nature of images; she repurposes their illusory power to . . .

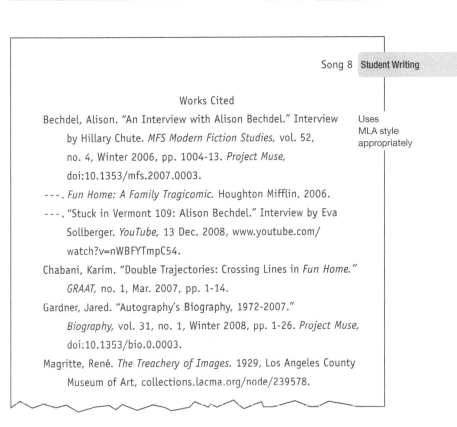

Song 8 | Student Writing

Works Cited

Bechdel, Alison. "An Interview with Alison Bechdel." Interview
by Hillary Chute. *MFS Modern Fiction Studies,* vol. 52,
no. 4, Winter 2006, pp. 1004-13. *Project Muse,*
doi:10.1353/mfs.2007.0003.

---. *Fun Home: A Family Tragicomic.* Houghton Mifflin, 2006.

---. "Stuck in Vermont 109: Alison Bechdel." Interview by Eva
Sollberger. *YouTube,* 13 Dec. 2008, www.youtube.com/
watch?v=nWBFYTmpC54.

Chabani, Karim. "Double Trajectories: Crossing Lines in *Fun Home.*"
GRAAT, no. 1, Mar. 2007, pp. 1-14.

Gardner, Jared. "Autography's Biography, 1972-2007."
Biography, vol. 31, no. 1, Winter 2008, pp. 1-26. *Project Muse,*
doi:10.1353/bio.0.0003.

Magritte, René. *The Treachery of Images.* 1929, Los Angeles County
Museum of Art, collections.lacma.org/node/239578.

Uses
MLA style
appropriately

Analyzing Arguments **10**

In one important sense, all language has an argumentative edge. When you greet friends, you wish to convince them that you're glad to see them. Even apparently objective news reporting has strong argumentative overtones: when a news outlet highlights a particular story, for example, the editors are arguing that this subject is more important than others. Since argument is so pervasive, you need to be able to recognize and use it effectively—and to question your own arguments as well as those put forth by others.

QUICK HELP

Analyzing an Argument

Here are some questions that can help you judge the effectiveness of an argument:

- What conclusions about the argument can you reach by playing both the believing and the doubting game? (10a)
- What cultural contexts inform the argument, and what do they tell you about where the writer is coming from? (10b)
- What emotional, ethical, and logical appeals is the writer making in support of the argument? (10c)
- How has the writer established credibility to write about the topic? (10c)
- What is the claim (or arguable statement)? Is the claim qualified in any way? (10d)
- What reasons and assumptions support and underlie the claim? (10d)
- What additional evidence backs up the assumption and claim? How current and reliable are the sources? (10d)
- How does the writer use visuals and media to support the argument?
- What fallacies can you identify, and what effect do they have on the argument's persuasiveness? (10e)
- What is the overall impression you get from analyzing the argument? Are you convinced?

10a Think critically about argument.

Critical thinking is a crucial component of argument, for it guides you in recognizing, formulating, and examining arguments. Here are some ways to think critically about argument:

- *Check understanding.* First, make sure you understand what is being argued and why. If you need to find out more about an unfamiliar subject to grasp the argument, do the research.
- *Play the believing—and the doubting—game.* Begin by playing the *believing game:* put yourself in the position of the person creating the argument to see the topic from that person's point of view as much as possible. Once you have given the argument sympathetic attention, play the *doubting game:* look skeptically at each claim, and examine each piece of evidence to see how well (or poorly) it supports the claim. Eventually, this process of believing and doubting will become natural.

- *Ask pertinent questions.* Whether you are thinking about others' ideas or your own, you should question unstated purposes and assumptions, the writer's qualifications, the context, the goal of the argument, and the evidence presented. What objections might be made to the argument?
- *Interpret and assess information.* All information that comes to you has a perspective — a spin. Your job is to identify the perspective and assess it, examining its sources and finding out what you can about its context.
- *Assess your own arguments.* The ultimate goal of all critical thinking is to reach your own conclusions. These, too, you must question and assess.

10b Recognize cultural contexts.

To understand as fully as possible the arguments of others, pay attention to clues to cultural context and to where the writer or creator is coming from. Put yourself in the position of the person creating the argument before looking skeptically at every claim and examining the evidence. Above all, watch out for your own assumptions as you analyze what you read or see. For example, just because you assume that the use of statistics as support for your argument holds more water than, say, precedent drawn from religious belief, you can't assume that all writers agree with you. Take a writer's cultural beliefs into account before you analyze an argument. (See Chapter 26.)

10c Identify an argument's basic appeals.

Aristotle categorized argumentative appeals into three types: emotional appeals that speak to readers' hearts and values (known to the ancient Greeks as *pathos*), ethical appeals that support the writer's character (*ethos*), and logical appeals that use facts and evidence (*logos*).

Emotional appeals

Emotional appeals stir your emotions and remind you of deeply held values. When politicians argue that the country needs more tax relief, they almost always use examples of one or more families they have met, stressing the concrete ways in which a tax cut would improve the quality of their lives. Doing so creates a strong emotional appeal. Some have criticized the use of emotional appeals in argument, claiming that they are a form of manipulation intended to mislead an audience. But emotional appeals are an important part of almost every argument. Critical readers are perfectly capable of "talking back" to such appeals by analyzing them, deciding which are acceptable and which are not.

Ethical appeals

Ethical appeals support the credibility, moral character, and goodwill of the argument's creator. These appeals are especially important for critical readers to recognize and evaluate. We may respect and admire an athlete, for example, but should we invest in the mutual funds the athlete promotes? To identify ethical appeals in arguments, ask yourself these questions: How does the creator of the argument show that he or she has really done the homework on the subject and is knowledgeable and credible about it? What sort of character does he or she build, and how? More important, is that character trustworthy? What does the creator of the argument do to show that he or she has the best interests of an audience in mind? Do those best interests match your own, and, if not, how does that alter the effectiveness of the argument?

Logical appeals

Logical appeals are viewed as especially trustworthy: "The facts don't lie," some say. Of course, facts are not the only type of logical appeals, which also include firsthand evidence drawn from observations, interviews, surveys and questionnaires, experiments, and personal experience; and secondhand evidence drawn from authorities, the testimony of others, statistics, and other print and online sources. Critical readers need to examine logical appeals just as carefully as emotional and ethical ones. What is the source of the logical appeal — and is that source trustworthy? Are all terms clearly defined? Has the logical evidence presented been taken out of context, and, if so, does that change its meaning?

Appeals in a visual argument

The poster on p. 111, from TurnAround, an organization devoted to helping victims of domestic violence, is "intended to strike a chord with abusers as well as their victims." The dramatic combination of words and image builds on an analogy between a child and a target and makes strong emotional and ethical appeals.

The bull's-eye that draws your attention to the center of the poster is probably the first thing you notice about the image. Then you may observe that the "target" is, in fact, a child's body; it also has arms, legs, and a head with wide, staring eyes. The heading "A child is not a target" reinforces the bull's-eye/child connection.

This poster's stark image and headline appeal to viewers' emotions, offering the uncomfortable reminder that children are often the victims of domestic violence. The design causes viewers to see a target first and only afterward recognize that the target is actually a child—an unsettling experience. But the poster also offers ethical appeals ("TurnAround can help") to show that the organization is

▶ Critical Reading > Tutorial: Reading visuals for audience
  Critical Reading > Tutorial: Reading visuals for purpose

credible and that it supports the worthwhile goal of ending "the cycle of domestic violence" by offering counseling and other support services. Finally, it uses the logical appeal of a statistic, noting that Turn-Around has served "more than 10,000 women, children and men each year" and giving specific information about where to get help.

10d Analyze the elements of argument.

According to philosopher Stephen Toulmin's framework for analyzing arguments, most arguments contain common features: a *claim* or *claims*; *reasons* for the claim; *assumptions*, whether stated or unstated, that underlie the argument (Toulmin calls these *warrants*); *evidence* or *backing*, such as facts, authoritative opinions, examples, and statistics; and *qualifiers* that limit the claim in some way.

ELEMENTS OF A TOULMIN ARGUMENT

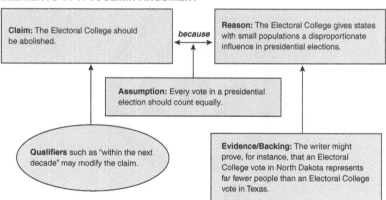

Claims

Claims (also referred to as arguable statements) are statements that the writer wants to prove. In longer essays, you may detect a series of linked claims or even several separate claims that you need to analyze before you agree to accept them. Claims worthy of arguing are those that are debatable: to say "Ten degrees Fahrenheit is cold" is a claim, but it is probably not debatable—unless you are describing northern Alaska, where ten degrees might seem balmy. In the example shown above, the claim that the Electoral College should be abolished is certainly arguable; a Google search will turn up numerous arguments for and against this claim.

Reasons

A claim is only as good as the reasons attached to it. If a student claims that course portfolios should be graded pass or fail because so many students in the class work full-time jobs, critical readers may question whether that reason is sufficient to support the claim. In the example on the preceding page, the writer gives a reason—that states with small populations have too much influence over the Electoral College—to support the claim of abolishing the institution. As you analyze claims, test each reason by asking how directly it supports the claim, how timely it is, and what counter-reasons you could offer to question it.

Assumptions

Putting a claim and reasons together often results in what Aristotle called an *enthymeme*, an argument that rests on an assumption the writer expects the audience to hold. These assumptions (which Toulmin calls *warrants*) that connect claim and reasons are often the hardest to detect in an argument, partly because they are often unstated, sometimes masking a weak link. As a result, it's especially important to identify the assumptions in arguments you are analyzing. Once the assumption is identified, you can test it against evidence and your own experience before accepting it. If a writer argues that the Electoral College should be abolished because states with small populations have undue influence on the outcome of presidential elections, what is the assumption underlying this claim and reason? It is that *presidential elections should give each voter the same amount of influence*. As a critical reader, remember that such assumptions are deeply affected by culture and belief; ask yourself, then, what cultural differences may be at work in your response to any argument.

Evidence or backing

Evidence, which Toulmin calls *backing*, also calls for careful analysis in arguments. In an argument about abolishing the Electoral College, the writer may offer as evidence a statistical analysis of the number of voters represented by an Electoral College vote in the least populous states and in the most populous states, a historical discussion of why the Founding Fathers developed the Electoral College system, or psychological studies showing that voters in states where one political party dominates feel disengaged from presidential elections. As a critical reader, you must evaluate each piece of evidence the writer offers, asking specifically how it relates to the claim, whether it is appropriate and timely, and whether it comes from a credible source.

Qualifiers

Qualifiers offer a way of limiting or narrowing a claim so that it is as precise as possible. Words or phrases that signal a qualification include *many, sometimes, in these circumstances,* and so on. Claims having no qualifiers can sometimes lead to overgeneralizations. For example, the statement *The Electoral College should be abolished* is less precise than *The Electoral College should be abolished by 2024.* Look carefully for qualifiers in the arguments you analyze, since they will affect the strength and reach of the claim.

Elements of a visual argument

Visual arguments can also be analyzed using these Toulmin methods. Look closely at the advertisement to the right. If you decide that this advertisement is claiming that people should adopt shelter pets, you might word a reason like this: *Dogs and cats need people, not just shelter.* You might note that the campaign assumes that people make pets happier (and that all pets deserve happiness)—and that the image backs up the overall message that this inquisitive, well-cared-for dog is happier living in a home with a human than in a

shelter. Considering unstated qualifiers (should *every* person consider adopting a shelter pet?) and thinking about potential evidence for the claim would help you complete an analysis of this visual argument.

10e   Think critically about fallacies.

Fallacies have traditionally been viewed as serious flaws that damage the effectiveness of an argument. But arguments are ordinarily fairly complex in that they always occur in some specific rhetorical situation and in some particular place and time; thus what looks like a fallacy in one situation may appear quite different in another. The best advice is to learn to identify fallacies but to be cautious in jumping to quick conclusions about them. Rather than thinking of them as errors you can use to discredit an arguer, you might think of them as barriers to common ground and understanding, since they often shut off rather than engender debate.

Verbal fallacies

AD HOMINEM

Ad hominem charges make a personal attack rather than focusing on the issue at hand.

▶ **Who cares what that fat loudmouth says about the health care system?**

GUILT BY ASSOCIATION

Guilt by association attacks someone's credibility by linking that person with a person or activity the audience considers bad, suspicious, or untrustworthy.

▶ **She does not deserve reelection; her husband had extramarital affairs.**

FALSE AUTHORITY

False authority is often used by advertisers who show famous actors or athletes testifying to the greatness of a product about which they may know very little.

▶ **He's today's greatest NASCAR driver—and he banks at National Mutual!**

BANDWAGON APPEAL

Bandwagon appeal suggests that a great movement is underway and the reader will be a fool or a traitor not to join it.

▶ **This new phone is everyone's must-have item. Where's yours?**

FLATTERY

Flattery tries to persuade readers by suggesting they are thoughtful, intelligent, or perceptive enough to agree with the writer.

▶ **You have the taste to recognize the superlative artistry of Bling diamond jewelry.**

IN-CROWD APPEAL

In-crowd appeal, a special kind of flattery, invites readers to identify with an admired and select group.

> ▶ **Want to know a secret that more and more of Middletown's successful young professionals are finding out about? It's Mountainbrook Manor condominiums.**

VEILED THREAT

Veiled threats try to frighten readers into agreement by hinting that they will suffer adverse consequences if they don't agree.

> ▶ **If Public Service Electric Company does not get an immediate 15 percent rate increase, its services to you may be seriously affected.**

FALSE ANALOGY

False analogies make comparisons between two situations that are not alike in important respects.

> ▶ **The volleyball team's sudden descent in the rankings resembled the sinking of the *Titanic*.**

BEGGING THE QUESTION

Begging the question is a kind of circular argument that treats a debatable statement as if it had been proved true.

> ▶ **Television news covered that story well; I learned all I know about it by watching TV.**

POST HOC FALLACY

The post hoc fallacy (from the Latin *post hoc, ergo propter hoc,* which means "after this, therefore caused by this") assumes that just because B happened *after* A, it must have been *caused* by A.

> ▶ **We should not rebuild the town docks because every time we do, a big hurricane comes along and damages them.**

NON SEQUITUR

A non sequitur (Latin for "it does not follow") attempts to tie together two or more logically unrelated ideas as if they were related.

> ▶ **If we can send a spaceship to Mars, then we can discover a cure for cancer.**

EITHER-OR FALLACY

The either-or fallacy insists that a complex situation can have only two possible outcomes.

> ▶ **If we do not build the new highway, businesses downtown will be forced to close.**

HASTY GENERALIZATION

A hasty generalization bases a conclusion on too little evidence or on bad or misunderstood evidence.

> ▶ **I couldn't understand the lecture today, so I'm sure this course will be impossible.**

OVERSIMPLIFICATION

Oversimplification claims an overly direct relationship between a cause and an effect.

> ▶ **If we prohibit the sale of alcohol, we will get rid of binge drinking.**

STRAW MAN

A straw-man argument misrepresents the opposition by pretending that opponents agree with something that few reasonable people would support.

> ▶ **My opponent believes that we should offer therapy to the terrorists. I disagree.**

Visual fallacies

Fallacies can also take the form of misleading images. The sheer power of images can make them especially difficult to analyze—people tend to believe what they see. Nevertheless, photographs and other visuals can be manipulated to present a false impression.

MISLEADING PHOTOGRAPHS

Faked or altered photos have existed since the invention of photography, and fakes continue to surface. On p. 118, for example, are an original photograph of an Iranian missile launch and the doctored image, showing a fourth launching missile, that Iran released to demonstrate its military might.

Today's technology makes such photo alterations easier than ever, if also easier to detect. But photographs need not be altered to try to fool viewers. Think of all the photos that make a politician look misleadingly bad or good. In these cases, you should closely examine the motives of those responsible for publishing the images.

MISLEADING CHARTS AND GRAPHS

Facts and statistics, too, can be presented in ways that mislead readers. For example, the following bar graph purports to deliver an argument about how differently Democrats, on the one hand, and Republicans and Independents, on the other, felt about a particular issue:

DATA PRESENTED MISLEADINGLY

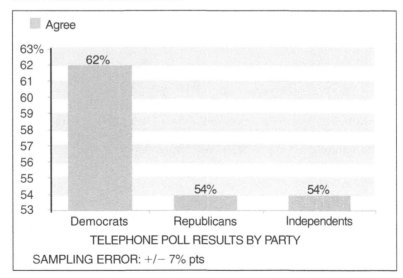

Look closely and you'll see a visual fallacy: the vertical axis starts not at zero but at 53 percent, so the visually large difference between the groups is misleading. In fact, a majority of all respondents agree about the issue, and only eight percentage points separate Democrats from Republicans and Independents (in a poll with a margin of error of +/− seven percentage points). Here's how the graph would look if the vertical axis began at zero:

DATA PRESENTED MORE ACCURATELY

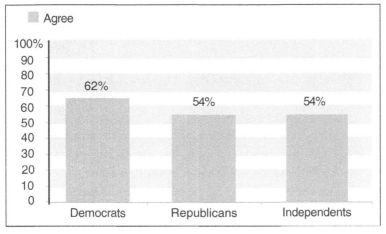

10f A student's rhetorical analysis

For a class assignment, Milena Ateyea was asked to analyze the emotional, ethical, and logical appeals in "Protecting Freedom of Expression at Harvard," an essay by Harvard president Derek Bok arguing that colleges should seek to persuade rather than to censor students who use speech or symbols that offend others.

Student Writer

Milena Ateyea

A Curse and a Blessing

Provocative
title suggests
mixed response
to Bok

Connects
article to her
own experi-
ence to build
credibility
(ethical appeal)

Brief overview
of Bok's
argument

Identifies Bok's
central claim

Links Bok's
claim to
strategies
he uses to
support it

Direct
quotations
show appeals
to emotion
through vivid
description

Bok establishes
common
ground
between two
positions

Emphasizes
Bok's credibility
(ethical appeal)

In 1991, when Derek Bok's essay "Protecting Freedom of
Expression at Harvard" was first published in the *Boston Globe*,
I had just come to America to escape the oppressive Communist
regime in Bulgaria. Perhaps my background explains why I
support Bok's argument that we should not put arbitrary limits
on freedom of expression. Bok wrote the essay in response to a
public display of Confederate flags and a swastika at Harvard, a
situation that created a heated controversy among the students.
As Bok notes, universities have struggled to achieve a balance
between maintaining students' right of free speech and avoiding
racist attacks. When choices must be made, however, Bok argues for
preserving freedom of expression.

In order to support his claim and bridge the controversy, Bok
uses a variety of rhetorical strategies. The author first immerses the
reader in the controversy by vividly describing the incident: two
Harvard students had hung Confederate flags in public view, thereby
"upsetting students who equate the Confederacy with slavery"
(51). Another student, protesting the flags, decided to display an
even more offensive symbol—the swastika. These actions provoked
heated discussions among students. Some students believed that
school officials should remove the offensive symbols, whereas others
suggested that the symbols "are a form of free speech and should
be protected" (51). Bok establishes common ground between the
factions: he regrets the actions of the offenders but does not believe
we should prohibit such actions just because we disagree with them.

The author earns the reader's respect because of his knowledge
and through his logical presentation of the issue. In partial support
of his position, Bok refers to U.S. Supreme Court rulings, which
remind us that "the display of swastikas or Confederate flags
clearly falls within the protection of the free-speech clause of the
First Amendment" (52). The author also emphasizes the danger of

the slippery slope of censorship when he warns the reader, "If we begin to forbid flags, it is only a short step to prohibiting offensive speakers" (52). Overall, however, Bok's work lacks the kinds of evidence that statistics, interviews with students, and other representative examples of controversial conduct could provide. Thus, his essay may not be strong enough to persuade all readers to make the leap from this specific situation to his general conclusion.

Throughout, Bok's personal feelings are implied but not stated directly. As a lawyer who was president of Harvard for twenty years, Bok knows how to present his opinions respectfully without offending the feelings of the students. However, qualifying phrases like "I suspect that" and "Under the Supreme Court's rulings, as I read them" could weaken the effectiveness of his position. Furthermore, Bok's attempt to be fair to all seems to dilute the strength of his proposed solution. He suggests that one should either ignore the insensitive deeds in the hope that students might change their behavior, or talk to the offending students to help them comprehend how their behavior is affecting other students.

Nevertheless, although Bok's proposed solution to the controversy does not appear at first reading to be very strong, it may ultimately be effective. There is enough flexibility in his approach to withstand various tests, and Bok's solution is general enough that it can change with the times and adapt to community standards.

In writing this essay, Bok faced a challenging task: to write a short response to a specific situation that represents a very broad and controversial issue. Some people may find that freedom of expression is both a curse and a blessing because of the difficulties it creates. As one who has lived under a regime that permitted very limited, censored expression, I am all too aware that I could not have written this response in 1991 in Bulgaria. As a result, I feel, like Derek Bok, that freedom of expression is a blessing, in spite of any temporary problems associated with it.

Marginal annotations:

Links Bok's credibility to use of logical appeals

Comments critically on kinds of evidence Bok's argument lacks

Reiterates Bok's credibility

Identifies qualifying phrases that may weaken claim

Analyzes weaknesses of Bok's proposed solution

Raises possibility that Bok's imperfect solution may work

Summarizes Bok's task

Ties conclusion back to title

Returns to own experience, which argues for accepting Bok's solution

Work Cited

Bok, Derek. "Protecting Freedom of Expression at Harvard." *Current Issues and Enduring Questions*, edited by Sylvan Barnet and Hugo Bedau, 6th ed., Bedford/St. Martin's, 2002, pp. 51–52. Originally published in *The Boston Globe*, 25 May 1991.

11 Constructing Arguments

Y ou respond to arguments all the time. When you see a stop sign and come to a halt, you've accepted the argument that stopping at such signs is a sensible thing to do. Unfortunately, constructing an effective argument of your own is not as easy as putting up a stop sign. Creating a thorough and convincing argument requires careful reasoning and attention to your audience and purpose.

11a Understand purposes for argument.

Although winning is an important purpose of argument, it is by no means the only purpose.

TO WIN The most traditional purpose of academic argument, arguing to win, is common in campus debating societies, in political debates, in trials, and often in business. The writer or speaker aims to present a position that will prevail over some other position.

TO CONVINCE Often, out-and-out defeat of another's position is not only unrealistic but undesirable. Instead, the goal might be to convince another person to change his or her mind. Doing so calls on a writer to provide *compelling reasons* for an audience to accept some or all of the writer's conclusions.

QUICK HELP

Reviewing Your Argument

- What is the purpose of your argument — to win? to convince others? to explore an issue? (11a)
- Is the point you want to make arguable? (11b)
- Have you formulated a strong working thesis that includes a clear claim and good reasons? (11c)
- Have you considered your audience sufficiently in shaping your appeals? (11e)
- How have you fully established your own credibility in the argument? (11f)
- How have you incorporated logical and emotional appeals into your argument? (11g and h)
- If you use sources, how effectively are they integrated into your argument? (11i)
- How is your argument organized? (11j)
- What design elements help you make your argument? (11k)

TO UNDERSTAND A writer often enters into a conversation with others to seek the best understanding of a problem, explore all approaches, and choose the best options. Argument to understand does not seek to control or conquer others or even to convince them. A writer's purpose in many situations — from trying to decide which job to pursue to exploring the best way to care for an elderly relative   will be to share information and perspectives in order to make informed political, professional, and personal choices.

TALKING THE TALK

Arguments

"Argument seems so negative — I don't want to attack anybody or contradict what someone else says." Sometimes — in law courts, for example — argument may call for attacking an opponent's credibility, and you may have used the word *argument* to describe a conversation in which the speakers said little more than "I did not!" and "You did, too!" But in college writing, argument usually means something much broader. Instead of attacking or contradicting, you will be expected to explore ideas and to work toward convincing yourself as well as others that these ideas are valuable.

11b Determine whether a statement can be argued.

At school, at home, or on the job, you will often need to convince someone or decide something. To do so, start with an arguable statement, which should meet three criteria:

1. It attempts to convince readers of something, change their minds about something, or urge them to do something—or it explores a topic in order to make a wise decision.
2. It addresses a problem for which no easily acceptable solution exists or asks a question to which no absolute answer exists.
3. It presents a position that readers might realistically have varying perspectives on.

ARGUABLE STATEMENT	Advertising in women's magazines contributes to the poor self-image that afflicts many young women.

This statement seeks to convince, addresses a problem—poor self-image among young women—that has no clear-cut solution, and takes a position many could disagree with.

UNARGUABLE STATEMENT	Women's magazines earn millions of dollars every year from advertising.

This statement does not present a position; it states a fact that can easily be verified and thus offers a poor basis for argument.

11c Make a claim and formulate a working thesis.

Once you have an arguable statement, you need to develop it into a working thesis (5b). One way to do so is to identify the elements of an argument (10d): the claim or arguable statement; one or more reasons for the claim; and assumptions—sometimes unstated—that underlie the claim and reasons.

To turn a claim into a working thesis for an argument, include at least one good reason to support the arguable statement.

REASON	Pesticides endanger the lives of farmworkers.
WORKING THESIS (CLAIM WITH REASON ATTACHED)	Because they endanger the lives of farmworkers, pesticides should be banned.

11d Examine your assumptions.

Once you have a working thesis, examine your assumptions to help test your reasoning and strengthen your argument. Begin by identifying underlying assumptions that support the working thesis.

WORKING THESIS	Because they endanger the lives of farmworkers, pesticides should be banned.
ASSUMPTION 1	Workers have a right to a safe working environment.
ASSUMPTION 2	Substances that endanger the lives of workers deserve to be banned.

Once you have a working thesis, you may want to use qualifiers to make it more precise and thus less susceptible to criticism. The preceding thesis might be qualified in this way:

▶ Because they *often* endanger the lives of farmworkers, *most* pesticides should be banned.

QUICK HELP

Showing Certainty in an Argument

How much certainty should you show when you're making an arguable claim? You may know that it's safer to say "*most* students believe" than "*all* students believe," but think carefully about when you should qualify or downplay a claim and when you can show greater confidence. Research conducted by Professor Laura Aull shows that expert academic writers in all disciplines tend to qualify their claims by using "hedges" — words such as *seems, might, may, generally, relatively, some,* or *likely* — and that expert writers are less likely to use intensifiers or "boosters" that show a high level of certainty — words such as *clearly, always, never,* and *must*. In contrast, student writers use many more "boosters" than "hedges." Learn from the experts: guard against overconfidence and aggressive critique of others' perspectives; overstating the truth of your claim can make you seem unfair or less credible to readers. Academic claims usually make room for alternative points of view, and they are more often qualified and cautious than absolutely certain.

11e   Shape your appeal to your audience.

Arguments and the claims they make are effective only if they appeal to the appropriate audience. For example, if you want to argue for increased lighting in parking garages on campus, you might appeal to students by citing examples drawn from their experiences of the safety problems in such dimly lit garages. If you are writing to university administrators, however, you might focus on the negative publicity associated with past attacks in campus garages and evoke the anger that such attacks cause in parents, alumni, and other influential groups.

11f   Establish credibility through ethical appeals.

To make your argument convincing, you must first gain the respect and trust of your readers, or establish credibility with them. In general, writers can establish credibility by making ethical appeals (10c) in four ways.

Knowledge

A writer can establish credibility first by establishing credentials. To decide whether you know enough to argue an issue credibly, consider the following questions:

- Can you provide information about your topic from sources other than your own knowledge?
- How reliable are your sources?
- If sources contradict one another, can you account for or resolve the contradictions?
- Would a personal experience relating to the issue help support your claim?

These questions may well show that you must do more research, check sources, resolve contradictions, refocus your working thesis, or even change your topic.

Common ground

Many arguments between people or groups are doomed to end without resolution because the two sides seem to occupy no starting

Building Ethos through Careful Restatement

Expert writers, says linguist Laura Aull, use "reformulation" or restatement to help build credibility and signal their own take on the evidence they're presenting. Phrases like *in other words*, *that is to say*, and *to be precise* show that a writer is interpreting information for the reader; *especially* or *in particular* emphasize what the writer finds particularly important; *in fact* or *indeed* or *as a matter of fact* show that a writer is contrasting an existing view. Expert writers use such phrases to restate and underscore their interpretation and introduce their own voices into their writing far more often than student writers do. Like transitions, these restatements help showcase the writer's reason for organizing the text in a particular way or emphasize the relation between ideas or parts of a text. How can you use restatement to build your ethos, or credibility? Look for — and ask peer reviewers to point out — opportunities to restate and clarify ideas.

point of agreement. The following questions can help you find common ground in presenting an argument. (See also Chapter 27.)

- What are the differing perspectives on this issue?
- What common ground can all sides agree on?
- How can you express such agreement clearly to all sides?
- How can you discover — and consider — opinions on this issue that differ from your own?
- How can you use language — occupational, regional, or ethnic varieties of English or languages other than English (28b–d) — to establish common ground with those you address?

FOR MULTILINGUAL WRITERS
Multilingual **Counting Your Own Experience**

You may have been told that your personal experience doesn't count in making academic arguments. If so, reconsider this advice, for showing an audience that you have relevant personal experience with a topic can carry strong persuasive appeal with many English-speaking readers.

Fairness

In arguing a position, writers must deal fairly with opposing arguments (also called counterarguments). Audiences are more inclined to listen to writers who seem to consider their opponents' views fairly than to those who ignore or distort such views. The following questions can help you discover ways of establishing yourself as open-minded and evenhanded:

- How can you show that you are taking into account all significant points of view?
- How can you demonstrate that you understand and sympathize with points of view other than your own?
- What can you do to show that you have considered evidence carefully, even when it does not support your position?

Some writers, instead of demonstrating fairness, may make unjustified attacks on an opponent's credibility. Avoid such attacks in your writing.

Visuals that make ethical appeals

SUSTAINABLE FOOD LABORATORY

In arguments and other kinds of writing, visuals can combine with text to help present a writer or an organization as trustworthy and credible. Like businesses, many institutions and individuals are using logos and other images to brand themselves as they wish the public to see them. The Sustainable Food Laboratory logo, seen here, suggests that the organization is concerned about both food production and the environment.

Visuals that make ethical appeals add to your credibility and fairness as a writer. Just as you probably consider the impression your Facebook profile photo makes on your audience, you should think about what kind of case you're making for yourself when you choose images and design elements for your argument.

11g   Use effective logical appeals.

Credibility alone cannot and should not carry the full burden of convincing readers. Indeed, many are inclined to think that the logic of the argument—the reasoning behind it—is as important as its ethos.

Examples, precedents, and narratives

Just as a picture can sometimes be worth a thousand words, so can a well-conceived example be extremely valuable in arguing a point. Examples are used most often to support generalizations or to bring abstractions to life. In making the general statement that popular media send the message that a woman must be thin to be attractive, you might include these examples:

> At the supermarket checkout, a tabloid publishes unflattering photographs of a young singer and comments on her apparent weight gain in shocked captions that ask "What happened?!?" Another praises a star for quickly shedding "ugly pounds" after the recent birth of a child. The cover of *Cosmopolitan* features a glamorously made-up and airbrushed actress in an outfit that reveals her remarkably tiny waist and flat stomach. Every woman in every advertisement in the magazine is thin—and the context makes it clear that readers are supposed to think that she is beautiful.

Precedents are examples taken from the past. If, as part of a proposal for increasing lighting in the library garage, you point out that the university has increased lighting in four other garages in the past year, you are arguing on the basis of precedent.

The following questions can help you check any use of example or precedent:

- How representative are the examples?
- Are the examples sufficient in strength or number to lead to a generalization?
- In what ways do they support your point?
- How closely does a precedent relate to the point you're trying to make? Are the situations really similar?
- How timely is the precedent? (What would have been applicable in 1920 is not necessarily applicable today.)

Because storytelling is universal, *narratives* can be very persuasive in helping readers understand and accept the logic of an argument. Narratives that use video and audio to capture the faces and voices of the people involved are often particularly compelling.

Stories drawn from your own experience can appeal particularly to readers, for they not only help make your point in true-to-life, human terms but also help readers know you better and therefore identify with you more closely.

When you include stories in an argument, ask yourself the following questions:

- Does the narrative support your thesis?

- Will the story's significance to the argument be clear to your readers?
- Is the story one of several good reasons or pieces of evidence—or does it have to carry the main burden of the argument?

In research writing, you must identify your sources for any examples, precedents, or narratives not based on your own knowledge.

Authority and testimony

Another way to support an argument logically is to cite an authority. The use of authority has figured prominently in the controversy over smoking. Since the U.S. surgeon general's 1964 announcement that smoking is hazardous to health, many Americans have quit smoking, largely persuaded by the authority of the scientists offering the evidence.

Ask the following questions to be sure you are using authorities effectively:

- Is the authority *timely*? (The argument that the United States should pursue a policy that was supported by Thomas Jefferson will probably fail since Jefferson's time was so radically different from ours.)
- Is the authority *qualified* to judge the topic at hand? (To cite a movie star in an academic essay on linguistics may not help your argument.)
- Is the authority likely to be *known and respected* by readers? (To cite an unfamiliar authority without identification will reduce the impact of the evidence.)
- Are the authority's *credentials* clearly stated and verifiable? (Especially with web-based sources, it is crucial to know whose authority guarantees the reliability of the information.)

Testimony—the evidence that an authority presents in support of a claim—is a feature of much contemporary argument. If testimony is timely, accurate, representative, and provided by a respected authority, then it, like authority itself, can add powerful support.

In research writing (see Chapters 12–16), you should cite your sources for authority and for testimony not based on your own knowledge.

Causes and effects

Showing that one event is the cause or the effect of another can help support an argument. Suppose you are trying to explain, in a petition to change your grade in a course, why you were unable to take the final examination. You would probably trace the causes of your failure to appear—your illness or the theft of your car, perhaps—so that the committee reading the petition would reconsider the effect—your not taking the examination.

Tracing causes often lays the groundwork for an argument, particularly if the effect of the causes is one we would like to change. In an environmental science class, for example, a student may argue that a national law regulating smokestack emissions from utility plants is needed because (1) acid rain on the East Coast originates from emissions at utility plants in the Midwest, (2) acid rain kills trees and other vegetation, (3) utility lobbyists have prevented Midwestern states from passing strict laws controlling emissions from such plants, and (4) if such laws are not passed, acid rain will soon destroy most eastern forests. In this case, the fourth point ties all of the previous points together to provide an overall argument from effect: if X, then Y.

Inductive and deductive reasoning

Traditionally, logical arguments are classified as using either inductive or deductive reasoning; in practice, the two almost always work together. Inductive reasoning is the process of making a generalization based on a number of specific instances. If you find you are ill on ten occasions after eating seafood, for example, you will likely draw the inductive generalization that seafood makes you ill. It may not be an absolute certainty that seafood is to blame, but the probability lies in that direction.

Deductive reasoning, on the other hand, reaches a conclusion by assuming a general principle (known as a major premise) and then applying that principle to a specific case (the minor premise). In practice, this general principle is usually derived from induction. The inductive generalization *Seafood makes me ill*, for instance, could serve as the major premise for the deductive argument *Since all seafood makes me ill, the shrimp on this buffet is certain to make me ill.*

Deductive arguments have traditionally been analyzed as syllogisms: reasoning that contains a major premise, a minor premise, and a conclusion.

MAJOR PREMISE   All people die.

MINOR PREMISE   I am a person.

CONCLUSION   I will die.

Syllogisms, however, are too rigid and absolute to serve in arguments about questions that have no absolute answers, and they often lack any appeal to an audience. Aristotle's more flexible alternative, the enthymeme, asks the audience to supply the implied major premise. Consider the following example:

> Because children who are bullied suffer psychological harm, schools should immediately discipline students who bully others.

You can analyze this enthymeme by restating it in the form of two premises and a conclusion.

MAJOR PREMISE   Schools should immediately discipline students who harm other children.

MINOR PREMISE   Being bullied causes psychological harm to children.

CONCLUSION   Schools should immediately discipline students who bully other children.

Note that the major premise is one the writer can count on an audience agreeing with or supplying: safety and common sense demand that schools should discipline children who harm other students. By implicitly asking the audience to supply this premise to the argument, the writer engages the audience's participation.

Toulmin's system (10d) looks for claims, reasons, and assumptions instead of major and minor premises.

CLAIM   Schools should immediately discipline students who bully other children.

REASON(S)   Being bullied causes psychological harm to children.

ASSUMPTION   Schools should discipline students who harm other children.

Note that in this system the assumption—which may be unstated—serves the same function as the assumed major premise in an enthymeme.

Whether it is expressed as a syllogism, an enthymeme, or a claim, a deductive conclusion is only as strong as the premise or reasons on which it is based.

Visuals that make logical appeals

Visuals that make logical appeals can be especially useful in arguments, since they present factual information that can be taken in at a glance. *Mother Jones* used this simple chart to carry a big message about income distribution in the United States. Consider how long it would take to explain all the information in this chart with words alone.

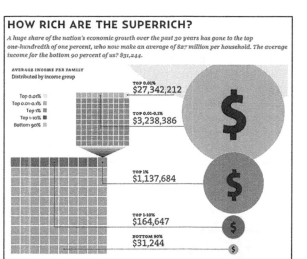

HOW RICH ARE THE SUPERRICH?

A huge share of the nation's economic growth over the past 30 years has gone to the top one-hundredth of one percent, who now make an average of $27 million per household. The average income for the bottom 90 percent of us? $31,244.

AVERAGE INCOME PER FAMILY
Distributed by income group

Top 0.01%
Top 0.01-0.1%
Top 1%
Top 1-10%
Bottom 90%

TOP 0.01%
$27,342,212

TOP 0.01-0.1%
$3,238,386

TOP 1%
$1,137,684

TOP 1-10%
$164,647

BOTTOM 90%
$31,244

2008 data. Includes capital gains. Source: Emmanuel Saez, University of California-Berkeley

11h Use appropriate emotional appeals.

Most successful arguments appeal to our hearts as well as to our minds — as is vividly demonstrated by the campaign to send aid to Nepal after a series of devastating earthquakes. Facts and figures (logical appeals) convince us that the problem is real and serious. What elicits an outpouring of support, however, is the arresting emotional power of stories and images of people affected by the disaster. But credible writers take particular care when they use emotional appeals; audiences can easily begin to feel manipulated when an argument tries too hard to appeal to their pity, anger, or fear.

Concrete descriptive details

Like photographs, vivid words can bring a moving immediacy to any argument. A student may amass facts and figures, including diagrams and maps, to illustrate the problem of wheelchair access to the library. But only when the student asks a friend who uses a wheelchair to accompany her to the library does the student writer discover the concrete details necessary to move readers. The student can then write, "Marie inched her heavy wheelchair up the steep entrance ramp, her arms straining, her face pinched with the sheer effort."

Figurative language

Figurative language, or figures of speech, can paint a detailed and vivid picture by making striking comparisons between something you are writing about and something else that helps a reader visualize, identify with, or understand it (29d).

Figures of speech include metaphors, similes, and analogies. Most simply, metaphors compare two things directly: *Richard the Lion-Hearted; old age is the evening of life.* Similes make comparisons using *like* or *as*: *Richard is as brave as a lion; old age is like the evening of life.* Analogies are extended metaphors or similes that compare an unfamiliar concept or process to a more familiar one.

Visuals that make emotional appeals

Visuals that make emotional appeals can also add substance to your argument. To make sure that such visual appeals will enhance your argument, test them out with several potential readers to see how they interpret the appeal. Consider, for example, this photograph depicting a Boston rally of gun-rights advocates. The image includes a group of protesters, one of whom is holding a sign saying "More gun laws will not stop mad men from killing," with a large yellow Gadsden flag in the foreground. Readers who generally oppose laws regulating gun ownership in the United States may feel very differently about this image than readers who tend to support restrictions on guns in private hands.

11i Consult sources.

In constructing an academic argument, it is often essential to use sources. The key to persuading people to accept your argument is providing good reasons; and even if your assignment doesn't specify that you must consult outside sources, they are often the most effective way of finding and establishing these reasons. Sources can help you to do the following:

- provide background information on your topic
- demonstrate your knowledge of the topic to readers

- cite authority and testimony in support of your thesis
- find opinions that differ from your own, which can help you sharpen your thinking, qualify your thesis if necessary, and demonstrate fairness to opposing arguments

For a more thorough discussion of finding, gathering, and evaluating sources, see Chapters 12–16.

11j Organize your argument.

Once you have assembled good reasons and evidence in support of an argumentative thesis, you must organize your material to present the argument convincingly. Although there is no universally favored, one-size-fits-all organizational framework, you may find it useful to try one of the following patterns.

The classical system

The system of argument often followed by ancient Greek and Roman orators is now referred to as *classical*. You can adapt the ancient format to written arguments as follows:

1. Introduction
   - Gain readers' attention and interest.
   - Establish your qualifications to write about your topic.
   - Establish common ground with readers.
   - Demonstrate fairness.
   - State or imply your thesis.

2. Background
   - Present any necessary background information, including relevant personal narrative.

3. Lines of argument
   - Present good reasons (including logical and emotional appeals) in support of your thesis.
   - Present reasons in order of importance, with the most important ones generally saved for last.
   - Demonstrate ways your argument may be in readers' best interest.

4. Alternative arguments
   - Examine alternative points of view.
   - Note advantages and disadvantages of alternative views.
   - Explain why one view is better than other(s).

5. Conclusion

- Summarize the argument if you choose.
- Elaborate on the implication of your thesis.
- Make clear what you want readers to think or do.
- Reinforce your credibility.

The Toulmin system

This simplified form of the Toulmin system (10d and 11g) can help you organize an argumentative essay:

1. Make your claim (arguable statement).

   ▶ **The federal government should ban smoking.**

2. Qualify your claim if necessary.

   ▶ **The ban would be limited to public places.**

3. Present good reasons to support your claim.

   ▶ **Smoking causes serious diseases in smokers.**

   ▶ **Nonsmokers are endangered by others' smoke.**

4. Explain the assumptions that underlie your claim and your reasons. Provide additional explanations for any controversial assumptions.

ASSUMPTION	The Constitution was established to "promote the general welfare."
ASSUMPTION	Citizens are entitled to protection from harmful actions by others.
ADDITIONAL EXPLANATION	The United States is based on a political system that is supposed to serve the basic needs of its people, including their health.

5. Provide additional evidence to support your claim (such as facts, statistics, testimony, and other logical, ethical, or emotional appeals).

STATISTICS	Cite the incidence of deaths attributed to secondhand smoke.
FACTS	Cite lawsuits won against large tobacco companies, including one that awarded billions of dollars to states in reparation for smoking-related health care costs.
FACTS	Cite bans on smoking already imposed on indoor public spaces in many cities.
AUTHORITY	Cite the surgeon general.

6. Acknowledge and respond to possible counterarguments.

COUNTER-   Smokers have rights, too.
ARGUMENT

RESPONSE   The suggested ban applies only to public places;
               smokers are free to smoke in private.

7. Finally, state your conclusion in the strongest way possible.

Rogerian or invitational argument

The psychologist Carl Rogers argued that people should not enter into disputes until they can thoroughly and fairly understand the other person's (or persons') perspectives. From Rogers's theory, rhetoricians Richard Young, Alton Becker, and Kenneth Pike adapted a four-part structure that is now known as "Rogerian argument":

- The introduction describes the issue, problem, or conflict in enough detail to demonstrate that the writer fully grasps and respects alternative points of view.
- The writer then fairly describes the contexts in which such alternative positions might be valid.
- The writer offers his or her position on the issue and explains in what circumstances and why that position would be valid.
- Finally, the writer explains how those who hold alternative positions can benefit from adopting the writer's position.

Like Rogerian argument, invitational rhetoric has as its goal getting people to work together effectively and to identify with each other; it aims for connection and collaboration. Such arguments call for structures that are closer to good two-way conversations or freewheeling dialogues than a linear march from thesis to conclusion. If you try developing such a conversational structure, you may find that it opens up a space in your argument for new perceptions and fresh ideas.

11k Consider design and delivery.

When someone asked the ancient orator Demosthenes to name the three most important parts of rhetoric, he said: *delivery, delivery, delivery.* In short, while what speakers said was important, the way they said it was of even greater importance. Today, we live in a time of information overload, when many powerful messages are vying for our attention. Getting and keeping an audience's attention is all about delivery. Figuring out the medium of delivery (print? digital? in-person?) and the appropriate genre is important, and so is designing the argument to appeal to your target audience.

- What medium will best get and hold your audience's attention? print? video? in-person or web presentation? social media site? Choosing just the right one is important to your success.
- What genre is most appropriate for your message? a report? a narrative? an essay? a brochure?
- What word choice, style, and tone will be most successful in delivering your message?
- Are any conventions expected in the kind of argument you are writing? Look for examples of similar arguments, or ask your instructor for information.
- What visual style will appeal to your intended readers, set a clear tone for your argument, and guide readers through your text? Spend time thinking about how the argument will look, and aim for a consistent visual design and for appealing fonts and colors.
- Are visual and media elements clearly integrated into your argument? Place images close to the text they illustrate, and label each one clearly. Make sure that audio and video files appear in appropriate places and are identified for users.

After you have a rough plan for delivering your argument, test it on friends and classmates, asking them what you need to change to make it more effective.

111   A student's argument essay

Student Writer

Benjy Mercer-Golden

In this argument essay, Benjy Mercer-Golden argues that socially conscious businesses and traditional for-profit businesses can learn from each other in ways that benefit businesses, consumers, and the environment. His essay has been annotated to point out the various parts of his argument as well as his use of good reasons, evidence, and appeals to logic and emotion.

Benjy Mercer-Golden

28 Nov. 2012

Lessons from Tree-Huggers and Corporate Mercenaries:

A New Model of Sustainable Capitalism

Televised images of environmental degradation—seagulls with
oil coating their feathers, smokestacks belching gray fumes—often
seem designed to shock, but these images also represent very real
issues: climate change, dwindling energy resources like coal and
oil, a scarcity of clean drinking water. In response, businesspeople
around the world are thinking about how they can make their
companies greener or more socially beneficial to ensure a brighter
future for humanity. But progress in the private sector has been
slow and inconsistent. To accelerate the move to sustainability,
for-profit businesses need to learn from the hybrid model of social
entrepreneurship to ensure that the company is efficient and
profitable while still working for social change, and more investors
need to support companies with long-term, revolutionary visions
for improving the world.

In fact, both for-profit corporations and "social good"
businesses could take steps to reshape their strategies. First, for-
profit corporations need to operate sustainably and be evaluated
for their performance with long-term measurements and incentives.
The conventional argument against for-profit companies deeply
embedding environmental and social goals into their corporate
strategies is that caring about the world does not go hand in hand
with lining pockets. This morally toxic case is also problematic
from a business standpoint. A 2012 study of 180 high-profile
companies by Harvard Business School professors Robert G. Eccles
and George Serafeim and London Business School professor Ioannis
Ioannou shows that "high sustainability companies," as defined by

Provocative
word choice
for title

Emotional
appeals
through use of
vivid imagery

Thesis
establishing
purpose

Claim related
to thesis

Opposing
viewpoint
to establish
writer's
credibility

Rebuttal

environmental and social variables, "significantly outperform their counterparts over the long term, both in terms of stock market and accounting performance." The study argues that the better financial returns of these companies are especially evident in sectors where "companies' products significantly depend upon extracting large amounts of natural resources" (Eccles et al.).

Transition referring to ideas in previous paragraph

Such empirical financial evidence to support a shift toward using energy from renewable sources to run manufacturing plants argues that executives should think more sustainably, but other underlying incentives need to evolve in order to bring about

Details of claim

tangible change. David Blood and Al Gore of Generation Investment Management, an investment firm focused on "sustainable investing for the long term" ("About Us"), wrote a groundbreaking white paper that outlined the perverse incentives company managers

Logical appeals using information and evidence in white paper

face. For public companies, the default practice is to issue earnings guidances—announcements of projected future earnings—every quarter. This practice encourages executives to manage for the short term instead of adding long-term value to their company and the earth (Gore and Blood). Only the most uncompromisingly green CEOs would still advocate for stricter carbon emissions standards at the company's factories if a few mediocre quarters left investors

Ethical appeal to companies

demanding that they be fired. Gore and Blood make a powerful case against requiring companies to be subjected to this "What have you done for me lately?" philosophy, arguing that quarterly earnings guidances should be abolished in favor of companies

Partial solution proposed

releasing information when they consider it appropriate. And to further persuade managers to think sustainably, companies need to change the way the managers get paid. Currently, the CEO of ExxonMobil is rewarded for a highly profitable year but is not held accountable for depleting nonrenewable oil reserves. A new model should incentivize thinking for the long run. Multiyear milestones for performance evaluation, as Gore and Blood suggest, are essential to pushing executives to manage sustainably.

But it's not just for-profit companies that need to rethink strategies. Social good–oriented leaders also stand to learn from the people often vilified in environmental circles: corporate CEOs. To survive in today's economy, companies building sustainable products must operate under the same strict business standards as profit-driven companies. Two social enterprises, Nika Water and Belu, provide perfect examples. Both sell bottled water in the developed world with the mission of providing clean water to impoverished communities through their profits. Both have visionary leaders who define the lesson that all environmental and social entrepreneurs need to understand: financial pragmatism will add far more value to the world than idealistic dreams. Nika Water founder Jeff Church explained this in a speech at Stanford University:

> Social entrepreneurs look at their businesses as nine parts cause, one part business. In the beginning, it needs to be nine parts business, one part cause, because if the business doesn't stay around long enough because it can't make it, you can't do anything about the cause.

When U.K.-based Belu lost £600,000 ($940,000) in 2007, it could only give around £30,000 ($47,000) to charity. Karen Lynch took over as CEO, cutting costs, outsourcing significant parts of the company's operations, and redesigning the entire business model; the company now donates four times as much to charity (Hurley). The conventional portrayal of do-gooders is that they tend to be terrible businesspeople, an argument often grounded in reality. It is easy to criticize the Walmarts of the world for caring little about

Margin notes:

Claim extended to socially responsible businesses

Logical appeals

Additional logical appeals

sustainability or social good, but the idealists with big visions who do not follow through on their promises because their businesses cannot survive are no more praiseworthy. Walmart should learn from nonprofits and social enterprises on advancing a positive environmental and social agenda, but idealist entrepreneurs should also learn from corporations about building successful businesses.

Return to thesis: businesses should learn from one another

The final piece of the sustainable business ecosystem is the investors who help get potentially world-changing companies off the ground. Industries that require a large amount of money to build complex products with expensive materials, such as solar power companies, rely heavily on investors—often venture capitalists based in California's Silicon Valley (Knight). The problem is that venture capitalists are not doing enough to fund truly groundbreaking companies. In an oft-cited blog post titled "Why Facebook Is Killing Silicon Valley," entrepreneur Steve Blank argues that the financial returns on social media companies have been so quick and so outsized that the companies with the *really* big ideas—like providing efficient, cheap, scalable solar power— are not being backed: "In the past, if you were a great [venture capitalist], you could make $100 million on an investment in 5–7 years. Today, social media startups can return hundreds of millions or even billions in less than 3 years." The point Blank makes is that what is earning investors lots of money right now is not what is best for the United States or the world.

Transition to second part of thesis signaled

Problem explained

Reasons in support of claim

There are, however, signs of hope. PayPal founder Peter Thiel runs his venture capital firm, the Founders Fund, on the philosophy that investors should support "flying cars" instead of new social media ventures (Packer). While the next company with the mission of making photo-sharing cooler or communicating with friends easier might be both profitable and valuable, Thiel and a select few

Transition signaling reason for optimism

Mercer-Golden 5

others fund technology that has the potential to solve the huge problems essential to human survival.

Reason presented

The world's need for sustainable companies that can build products from renewable energy or make nonpolluting cars will inevitably create opportunities for smart companies to make money. In fact, significant opportunities already exist for venture capitalists willing to step away from what is easy today and shift their investment strategies toward what will help us continue to live on this planet tomorrow—even if seeing strong returns may take a few more years. Visionaries like Blank and Thiel need more allies (and dollars) in their fight to help produce more pioneering, sustainable companies. And global warming won't abate before investors wise up. It is vital that this shift happen now.

Emotional appeal

When we think about organizations today, we think about nonprofits, which have long-term social missions, and corporations, which we judge by their immediate financial returns like quarterly earnings. That is a treacherous dichotomy. Instead, we need to see the three major players in the business ecosystem—corporations, social enterprises, and investors—moving toward a *single* model of long-term, sustainable capitalism. We need visionary companies that not only set out to solve humankind's biggest problems but also have the business intelligence to accomplish these goals, and we need investors willing to fund these companies. Gore and Blood argue that "the imperative for change has never been greater." We will see this change when the world realizes that sustainable capitalism shares the same goals as creating a sustainable environment. Let us hope that this realization comes soon.

Logical appeal

Thesis revisited

Quotation, restatement of thesis, and emotional appeal close argument

Mercer-Golden 6

Works Cited

"About Us." *Generation*, 2012, www.generationim.com/about/.

Blank, Steve. "Why Facebook Is Killing Silicon Valley." *Steveblank
.com*, 21 May 2012, steveblank.com/2012/05/21/why
-facebook-is-killing-silicon-valley/.

Church, Jeff. "The Wave of Social Entrepreneurship."
Entrepreneurial Thought Leaders Seminar, NVIDIA Auditorium,
Stanford, 11 Apr. 2012. Lecture.

Eccles, Robert G., et al. "The Impact of a Corporate Culture of
Sustainability on Organizational Process and Performance."
Working Knowledge, Harvard Business School, 14 Nov. 2011,
hbswk.hbs.edu/item/the-impact-of-corporate-sustainability
-on-organizational-process-and-performance.

Gore, Al, and David Blood. "Sustainable Capitalism." *Generation,*
15 Feb. 2012, www.generationim.com/media/pdf-generation
-sustainable-capitalism-v1.pdf.

Hurley, James. "Belu Boss Shows Bottle for a Turnaround."
Daily Telegraph, 28 Feb. 2012, www.telegraph.co.uk/finance/
businessclub/9109449/Belu-boss-shows-bottle-for
-a-turnaround.html.

Knight, Eric R. W. "The Economic Geography of Clean Tech
Venture Capital." Oxford University Working Paper Series in
Employment, Work, and Finance, 13 Apr. 2010. *Social Science
Research Network,* doi:10.2139/ssrn.1588806.

Packer, George. "No Death, No Taxes: The Libertarian Futurism of
a Silicon Valley Billionaire." *The New Yorker,* 28 Nov. 2011,
www.newyorker.com/magazine/2011/11/28/no-death-no
-taxes.

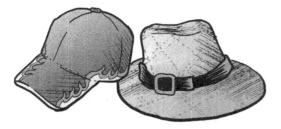

Coordination, Subordination, and Emphasis 30

Coordination and subordination are ways of joining ideas in sentences that show relationships between ideas and emphasize more important ideas. In speech, people tend to use *and* and *so* as all-purpose connectors.

> I've requested that information for you, and I will get back in touch shortly to let you know what's going on.

If you said this sentence aloud, you could provide clues about which parts of the sentence were most important by stressing certain words and phrases and by using facial expressions and gestures to provide hints about your meaning. But if you wrote the sentence rather than saying it, your reader might not be certain what you wanted to emphasize.

By choosing subordination, you convey that one part of the sentence or the other is more important. The emphasis here is on the promise to get back in touch, not on the request that has already happened:

> Having requested that information for you, I will get back in touch shortly to let you know what's going on.

You can also use other coordinating conjunctions to clarify the relationships between equally important ideas. Notice the different impression you would give by using *but* instead of *and*:

> I've requested that information for you, but I will get back in touch shortly to let you know what's going on.

All these sentences are grammatically correct, but all of them mean slightly different things. Choosing appropriate coordination and subordination allows your meaning to come through clearly.

QUICK HELP

Editing for Coordination, Subordination, and Emphasis

How do your ideas flow from one sentence to another? Do they connect smoothly and clearly? Are the more important ideas given more emphasis than less important ones?

- Look for strings of short sentences that might be combined to join related ideas. (30a)

  > The report was short*/,* ~~It~~ was persuasive*/;* ~~It~~ changed my mind.

  but it   *it*

- If you use *and* excessively, decide whether all the ideas are equally important. If they are not equal, edit to subordinate the less important ones. (30b)

- Make sure that the most important ideas appear in independent clauses that can stand alone as complete sentences. (30b)

  > *Even though the*
  > ~~The~~ report was short, ~~even though~~ it changed my mind.

- Identify the word or words you want to receive special emphasis. If those words are buried in the middle of a sentence, edit the sentence to change their position. The end and the beginning are generally the most emphatic. (30c)

- If a sentence includes a series of three or more words, phrases, or clauses, try to arrange the items in the series in climactic order, with the most important item last. (30c)

30a   Use coordination to relate equal ideas.

When used well, coordination relates separate but equal ideas. The element that links the ideas, usually a coordinating conjunction (*and, but, for, nor, or, so, yet*) or a semicolon, makes the precise relationship clear. The following sentences by N. Scott Momaday all use coordination, but the relationship between independent clauses differs in each sentence:

> They acquired horses, *and* their ancient nomadic spirit was suddenly free of the ground.

> There is perfect freedom in the mountains, *but* it belongs to the eagle and the elk, the badger and the bear.

▶ No longer were they slaves to the simple necessity of survival; they were a lordly and dangerous society of fighters and thieves, hunters and priests of the sun.
— N. SCOTT MOMADAY, *The Way to Rainy Mountain*

Momaday uses coordination in these sentences carefully in order to achieve very specific effects. In the first sentence, for example, the use of *and* gives a sense of adding on: "They acquired horses" *and*, of equal importance, "their ancient nomadic spirit was suddenly free." Momaday might have made other, equally correct choices, but they would have resulted in slightly different sentences. Compare these altered versions with Momaday's sentences. How do the changes affect your understanding?

▶ They acquired horses, *so* their ancient nomadic spirit was suddenly free of the ground.

▶ There is perfect freedom in the mountains; it belongs to the eagle and the elk, the badger and the bear.

In your own writing, think about exactly what information you want to convey with coordination. You, too, may have several correct options—so make the choice that works best for your situation and audience.

Coordination can help make explicit the relationship between two ideas.

▶ Generations have now grown up with *The Simpsons*/; Bart, Lisa, and Maggie never get older, but today's college students may have been watching the show since before they could talk.

Connecting these two sentences with a semicolon strengthens the connection between two closely related ideas.

When you connect ideas within a sentence, make sure the relationship between the ideas is clear.

▶ Surfing the Internet is a common way to spend leisure time, ~~and~~ *but* it should not replace human contact.

What does a common form of leisure have to do with replacing human contact? Changing *and* to *but* better relates the two ideas.

30b Use subordination to distinguish main ideas.

Subordination allows you to distinguish major points from minor points or to bring in supporting details. If, for instance, you put your main idea in an independent clause—words that could stand alone as a sentence (37e)—you might then put any less significant ideas in dependent clauses, phrases, or even single words. The following sentence italicizes the subordinated point:

▶ Mrs. Viola Cullinan was a plump woman *who lived in a three-bedroom house somewhere behind the post office.*
                                  – MAYA ANGELOU, "My Name Is Margaret"

The dependent clause adds important information about Mrs. Cullinan, but it is subordinate to the independent clause.

Choices about subordination

Notice that the choice of what to subordinate rests with the writer and depends on the intended meaning. Angelou might have given the same basic information differently.

▶ Mrs. Viola Cullinan, *a plump woman,* lived in a three-bedroom house somewhere behind the post office.

Subordinating the information about Mrs. Cullinan's size to that about her house would suggest a slightly different meaning, of course. When you write, think carefully about what you want to emphasize and subordinate information accordingly.

Subordination also establishes logical relationships among ideas. These relationships are often specified by relative pronouns—such as *which, who,* and *that*—and by subordinating conjunctions.

COMMON SUBORDINATING CONJUNCTIONS

after	if	though
although	in order that	unless
as	once	until
as if	since	when
because	so that	where
before	than	while
even though		

The following sentence italicizes the subordinate clause and underlines the subordinating word:

> She usually rested her smile until late afternoon _when_ her women friends dropped in and Miss Glory, the cook, served them cold drinks on the closed-in porch.
>> — MAYA ANGELOU, "My Name Is Margaret"

Using too many coordinate structures can be monotonous and can make it hard for readers to recognize the most important ideas. Subordinating lesser ideas can help highlight the main ideas.

> Many people check email in the evening, and so they turn on the
> *Though they*
> computer. ~~They~~ may intend to respond only to urgent messages, a
> *which*
> friend sends a link to a blog post, ~~and~~ they decide to read ~~it~~ for just a
> *Eventually,*
> short while~~.~~ ~~and~~ they get engrossed in Facebook, and they end up
>
> spending the whole evening in front of the screen.

> *Although our*
> ~~Our~~ new boss can be difficult, ~~although~~ she has revived and maybe
>
> even saved the division.

The editing puts the more important information—that she has saved part of the company—in an independent clause and subordinates the rest.

Excessive subordination

When too many subordinate clauses are strung together, readers may have trouble keeping track of the main idea.

TOO MUCH SUBORDINATION

> Philip II sent the Spanish Armada to conquer England, which was ruled by Elizabeth, who had executed Mary because she was plotting to overthrow Elizabeth, who was a Protestant, whereas Mary and Philip were Roman Catholics.

REVISED

> Philip II sent the Spanish Armada to conquer England, which was ruled by Elizabeth, a Protestant. She had executed Mary, a Roman Catholic like Philip, because Mary was plotting to overthrow her.

Putting the facts about Elizabeth executing Mary into an independent clause makes key information easier to recognize.

30c Use closing and opening positions for emphasis.

When you read a sentence, the part you are most likely to remember is the ending. This part of the sentence should move the writing forward by providing new information, as it does in the following example:

▶ **Employers today expect college graduates to have** *excellent writing skills.*

A less emphatic but still important position in a sentence is the opening, which often connects the new sentence with what has come before.

▶ **Today's employers want a college-educated workforce that can communicate well.** *Excellent writing skills* **are high on the list of qualifications.**

If you place relatively unimportant information in the memorable closing position of a sentence, you may undercut what you want to emphasize or give more emphasis to the closing words than you intend.

▶ *Last month, she*   *$500,000.*
 ~~She~~ gave ~~$500,000~~ to the school capital campaign ~~last month.~~
  ^   ^

Moving *$500,000* to the end of the sentence emphasizes the amount.

When you arrange ideas in order of increasing importance, power, or drama, your writing builds to a climax. By saving its most dramatic item for last, the following sentence makes its point forcefully and memorably:

▶ **After they've finished with the pantry, the medicine cabinet, and the attic, [neat people] will throw out the red geranium (too many leaves), sell the dog (too many fleas), and send the children off to boarding school (too many scuffmarks on the hardwood floors).**
         – SUSANNE BRITT, "Neat People vs. Sloppy People"

TALKING ABOUT STYLE

Anticlimax and Humor

Sometimes it's fun to turn the principle of climactic order upside down, opening with grand or exaggerated language only to end anticlimactically, with everyday words.

 He is a writer for the ages — the ages of four to eight.
         – DOROTHY PARKER

Parker builds up expectations at the beginning of the sentence — only to undercut them unexpectedly by shifting the meaning of *ages*. Having led readers to expect something dramatic, she makes us laugh, or at least smile, with words that are decidedly undramatic.

Consistency and Completeness **31**

I n conversation, you will hear inconsistent and incomplete structures all the time. For instance, during an interview with journalist
Bill Moyers, Jon Stewart discussed the supposed objectivity of news
reporting.

> But news has never been objective. It's always . . . what does every
> newscast start with? "Our top stories tonight." That's a list. That's a sub-
> jective . . . some editor made a decision: "Here's our top stories. Number
> one: There's a fire in the Bronx."

Because Stewart is talking casually, some of his sentences begin one
way but then move in another direction. The mixed structures pose
no problem for the viewer—they sound like conversations we hear
every day—but sentences such as these can be confusing in writing.

31a Revise faulty sentence structure.

One inconsistency that poses problems for
writers and readers alike is a mixed structure,
which results from beginning a sentence with
one grammatical pattern and then switching
to another one.

> MIXED   The fact that I get up at 5:00 AM,
>   a wake-up time that explains
>   why I'm always tired in the
>   evening.

The sentence starts out with a subject (*The fact*) followed by a dependent clause (*that I get up at 5:00 AM*). The sentence needs a predicate
to complete the independent clause, but instead it moves to another
phrase followed by a dependent clause (*a wake-up time that explains
why I'm always tired in the evening*), and what results is a fragment.

> REVISED   *The fact* that I get up at 5:00 AM *explains* why I'm always
>   tired in the evening.

> Deleting *a wake-up time that* changes the rest of the sentence into a
> predicate.

REVISED   *I get up* at 5:00 AM, a wake-up time that explains why I'm always tired in the evening.

Deleting *The fact that* turns the beginning of the sentence into an independent clause.

(For information about subjects and predicates, see 37b and c; for information about independent and dependent clauses, see 37e.)

31b Match up subjects and predicates.

Another kind of mixed structure, called faulty predication, occurs when a subject and predicate do not fit together grammatically or simply do not make sense together. Many cases of faulty predication result from using forms of *be* when another verb would be stronger.

▶ A characteristic that I admire is a̶ ̶p̶e̶r̶s̶o̶n̶ ̶w̶h̶o̶ ̶i̶s̶ ̶g̶e̶n̶e̶r̶o̶u̶s̶. *generosity.*

A person is not a characteristic.

▶ The rules of the corporation e̶x̶p̶e̶c̶t̶ *require* employees to be on time.

Rules cannot expect anything.

Constructions using *is when, is where,* and *the reason . . . is because* are used frequently in informal contexts, but they may be inappropriate in academic writing because they describe a noun using an adverb clause (37e).

▶ A stereotype is w̶h̶e̶n̶ ̶s̶o̶m̶e̶o̶n̶e̶ ̶c̶h̶a̶r̶a̶c̶t̶e̶r̶i̶z̶e̶s̶ *an unfair characterization of* a group. u̶n̶f̶a̶i̶r̶l̶y̶.

▶ A confluence is w̶h̶e̶r̶e̶ *a place* two rivers join to form one.

▶ T̶h̶e̶ ̶r̶e̶a̶s̶o̶n̶ I like to play soccer i̶s̶ ̶b̶e̶c̶a̶u̶s̶e̶ it provides aerobic exercise.

31c Use elliptical structures carefully.

Sometimes writers omit a word in a compound structure. This type of structure, known as an elliptical structure, is appropriate when the word omitted later in the compound is exactly the same as the word earlier in the compound.

▶ **That bell belonged to the figure of Miss Duling as though it grew directly out of her right arm, as wings grew out of an angel or a tail [grew] out of the devil.** — EUDORA WELTY, *One Writer's Beginnings*

If the omitted word does not match a word in the other part of the compound, readers might be confused, so the omission is inappropriate in formal writing.

▶ **His skills are weak, and his performance** **only average.**

The verb *is* does not match the verb in the other part of the compound (*are*), so the writer needs to include it.

31d Check for missing words.

The best way to catch inadvertent omissions is to proofread carefully.

▶ **The new website makes it easier to look** *at* **and choose from the**

company's inventory.

QUICK HELP

Editing for Consistency and Completeness

- If you find an especially confusing sentence, check to see whether it has a subject and a predicate. If not, revise as necessary. (31a) If you find both a subject and a predicate, and you are still confused, see whether the subject and verb make sense together. (31b)

- Revise any *is when*, *is where*, and *reason . . . is because* constructions. (31b)

▶ Spamming is ~~where companies send~~ *the practice of sending* electronic junk mail.

- Check all comparisons for completeness. (31e)

▶ We like Lisa better than *we like* Margaret.

31e Make comparisons complete, consistent, and clear.

When you compare two or more things, the comparison must be complete, logically consistent, and clear.

▶ I was embarrassed because my parents were so different. *from my friends' parents.*

Different from what? Adding *from my friends' parents* tells readers what the comparison is being made with.

UNCLEAR   Aneil always felt more affection for his brother than his sister.

CLEAR   Aneil always felt more affection for his brother than his sister did.

CLEAR   Aneil always felt more affection for his brother than he did for his sister.

32 Parallelism

Parallel grammatical structures show up in many familiar phrases: *sink or swim, rise and shine, shape up or ship out.* If you look and listen for these structures, you will see parallelism in everyday use. Bumper stickers often use parallel grammatical structures to make their messages memorable (*Minds are like parachutes; both work best when open*), but the pleasing effects of parallel structures can benefit any kind of writing.

32a Make items in a series parallel.

Parallelism makes a series both graceful and easy to follow.

▶ In the eighteenth century, armed forces could fight *in open fields* and *on the high seas.* Today, they can clash *on the ground anywhere, on the sea, under the sea,* and *in the air.*
    – DONALD SNOW AND EUGENE BROWN, *The Contours of Power*

QUICK HELP

Editing for Parallelism

- Look for any series of three or more items, and make all of the items parallel in structure. (32a)
- Be sure items in lists and in related headings are parallel. (32a)
- Check for places where two ideas are paired in the same sentence. Often these ideas will appear on either side of *and, but, or, nor, for, so,* or *yet,* or after each part of *both . . . and, either . . . or, neither . . . nor, not only . . . but also, whether . . . or,* or *just as . . . so.* Edit to make the two ideas parallel in structure. (32b)
- Check any parallel structures to make sure that you have included all necessary words — prepositions, the *to* of the infinitive, and so on. (32c)

The parallel phrases, as well as the parallel structure of the sentences themselves, highlight the contrast between warfare in the eighteenth century and warfare today.

In the following sentences, note how the revisions make all items in the series parallel:

▶ The quarter horse skipped, pranced, and ~~was sashaying.~~ *sashayed.*

▶ The children ran down the hill, skipped over the lawn, and *jumped* into the swimming pool.

▶ The duties of the job include babysitting, housecleaning, and *preparing* ~~preparation of~~ meals.

Items in a list, in a formal outline, and in headings in a writing project should be parallel.

▶ Kitchen rules: (1) Coffee to be made only by library staff. (2) Coffee service to be closed at 4:00 PM. (3) Doughnuts to be kept in cabinet.
  Coffee materials not to be handled by faculty.
  (4) ~~No faculty members should handle coffee materials.~~

32b Make paired ideas parallel.

Parallel structures can help you pair two ideas effectively. The more nearly parallel the two structures are, the stronger the connection between the ideas will be.

▶ *History became* popular, and *historians became* alarmed.

> – WILL DURANT

▶ **I *type* in one place, but I *write* all over the house.**

> – TONI MORRISON

▶ **Writers are often more interesting on the page than they are in**

the flesh.
~~person.~~
^

In these examples, the parallel structures help readers see an important contrast between two ideas or acts.

Coordinating conjunctions

When you link ideas with a coordinating conjunction—*and*, *but*, *or*, *nor*, *for*, *so*, or *yet*—try to make the ideas parallel in structure.

                                      who is
▶ **Consult a friend in your class or who is good at math.**
                                  ^

                                                         accepts
▶ **The wise politician promises the possible and ~~should accept~~ the**
                                                     ^

inevitable.

In both sentences, the editing links the two ideas by making them parallel.

Correlative conjunctions

Use the same structure after both parts of a correlative conjunction: *either . . . or*, *both . . . and*, *neither . . . nor*, *not . . . but*, *not only . . . but also*, *just as . . . so*, and *whether . . . or*.

                                                            live in
▶ **I wanted not only to go away to school but also to New England.**
                                                        ^

Balancing *to go* with *to live* links the two ideas and makes the sentence easier to read.

32c Include all necessary words.

In addition to making parallel elements grammatically similar, be sure to include any words—prepositions, articles, verb forms, and so on—that are necessary for clarity, grammar, or idiom.

▶ We'll move to a town in the Southwest or *in* Mexico.

> To a town in Mexico or to Mexico in general? The editing makes the meaning clear.

Shifts  **33**

A shift in writing is an abrupt change that results in inconsistency. Sometimes a writer or speaker will shift deliberately, as linguist Geneva Smitherman does in this passage from *Word from the Mother*: "There are days when I optimistically predict that Hip Hop will survive—and thrive. . . . In the larger realm of Hip Hop culture, there is cause for optimism as we witness Hip Hop younguns tryna git they political activist game togetha."

Smitherman's shift from formal academic language to vernacular speech calls out for and holds our attention. Although writers make shifts for good rhetorical reasons, unintentional shifts in verb tenses, pronouns, and tone can be confusing to readers.

33a Revise unnecessary shifts in verb tense.

If the verbs in a passage refer to actions occurring at different times, they may require different tenses. Be careful, however, not to change tenses for no reason.

▶ A few countries produce almost all of the world's illegal drugs, but
  addiction *affects* ~~affected~~ many countries.

33b Revise unnecessary shifts in mood.

Be careful not to shift from one mood to another without good reason. The mood of a verb can be indicative (he *closes* the door), imperative (*close* the door), or subjunctive (if the door *were closed*) (38h).

> Keep your eye on the ball, and ~~you should~~ bend your knees.

33c Revise unnecessary shifts in voice.

Do not shift without reason between the active voice (she *sold* it) and the passive voice (it *was sold*). Sometimes a shift in voice is justified, but often it only confuses readers (38g).

>   *me*
> Two youths approached me/ and ~~I was~~ asked for my wallet.

The original sentence shifts from the active (*youths approached*) to the passive (*I was asked*), so it is unclear who asked for the wallet. Making both verbs active clears up the confusion.

33d Revise unnecessary shifts in person and number.

Unnecessary shifts in point of view among first person (*I, we*), second person (*you*), and third person (*he, she, it, they*), or between singular and plural subjects, can be very confusing to readers.

>   *You*
> ~~Someone~~ can do well on this job if you budget your time.

Is the writer making a general statement or giving advice? Eliminating the shift eliminates this confusion.

33e Revise shifts between direct and indirect discourse.

Multilingual

When you quote someone's exact words, you are using direct discourse: *She said, "I'm an editor."* When you report what someone says without repeating the exact words, you are using indirect discourse: *She says she is an editor.* Shifting between direct and indirect discourse in the same sentence can cause problems, especially with questions.

> **QUICK HELP**
> ### Confusing Shifts
>
> - Make sure you have a reason for shifting from one verb tense to another. (33a)
> - Revise any shifts in mood — perhaps from an indicative statement to an imperative — that are not necessary. (33b)
> - Check for shifts from active (*She asks questions*) to passive voice (*Questions are asked*). Are they intentional? (33c)
> - Make sure you have good reasons for any shifts in person or number — from *we* to *you*, for example. (33d)
> - Check your writing for consistency in tone and word choice. (33f)

               he
▶ **Viet asked what could he do to help?.**

The editing eliminates an awkward shift by reporting Viet's question indirectly. It could also be edited to quote Viet directly: *Viet asked, "What can I do to help?"*

33f Revise shifts in tone and word choice.

Tone, a writer's attitude toward a topic or audience, is related to word choice and to overall formality or informality. Watch out for tone or diction shifts that can confuse readers and leave them wondering what your real attitude is (3f).

INCONSISTENT TONE

The question of child care forces a society to make profound decisions about its economic values. Can most families with young children actually live adequately on only one salary? If some conservatives had their way, June Cleaver would still be stuck in the kitchen baking cookies for Wally and the Beaver and waiting for Ward to bring home the bacon, except that, with only one income, the Cleavers would be lucky to afford hot dogs.

In this version, the first two sentences set a serious, formal tone by discussing child care in fairly general, abstract terms. But in the third sentence, the writer shifts suddenly to sarcasm, to references to television characters of an earlier era, and to informal language like *stuck* and *bring home the bacon*. Readers cannot tell whether the writer is presenting a serious analysis or preparing for a humorous satire. The revision makes the tone consistently formal.

The question of child care forces a society to make profound decisions about its economic values. Can most families with young children actually live adequately on only one salary? Some conservatives believe that women with young children should not work outside the home, but many mothers are forced to do so for financial reasons.

34 Conciseness

I f you have a Twitter account, you know a lot about being concise—that is, about getting messages across without wasting words (Twitter limits writers to 140 characters). Recently, *New York Times* editor Bill Keller decided to start a discussion by tweeting, "Twitter makes you stupid. Discuss." That little comment drew a large number of responses, including one from his wife that read, "I don't know if Twitter makes you stupid, but it's making you late for dinner. Come home."

No matter how you feel about the effects of Twitter on the brain (or stomach!), you can make any writing more effective by using clear structures and choosing words that convey exactly what you mean to say.

34a Eliminate unnecessary words.

Sometimes writers say that something is large *in size* or red *in color* or that two ingredients should be combined *together*. The italicized words are unnecessarily repetitive; delete such redundant words.

▶ ~~Compulsory attendance~~ *Attendance* at assemblies is required.

▶ Many different forms of hazing occur, such as physical ~~abuse~~ and mental abuse.

Meaningless modifiers

Many modifiers are so overused that they have little meaning.

MEANINGLESS MODIFIERS

absolutely, awfully, definitely, fine, great, interesting, quite, really, very

QUICK HELP

Editing for Conciseness

- Look for redundant words. If you are unsure about a certain word, read the sentence without it; if meaning is not affected, leave the word out. (34a)
- Take out empty words — words like *aspect* or *factor*, *definitely* or *very*. (34a)
- Replace wordy phrases with a single word. Instead of *because of the fact that*, try *because*. (34a)
- Reconsider any sentences that begin with *it is* or *there is/are*. Unless they create special emphasis, try recasting the sentences without these words. (34b)

Wordy phrases

Wordy phrases can be reduced to a word or two with no loss in meaning.

WORDY	CONCISE
at all times	always
at that point in time	then
at the present time	now / today
due to the fact that	because
for the purpose of	for
in order to	to
in spite of the fact that	although
in the event that	if

34b Simplify sentence structure.

Using simple grammatical structures can strengthen your sentences considerably.

▶ Hurricane Katrina, ~~which was certainly~~ one of the most powerful

storms ever to hit the Gulf Coast, caused damage. *widespread* ~~to a very wide area.~~

Deleting unnecessary words and replacing five words with one tightens the sentence and makes it easier to read.

▶ When ~~she was~~ questioned about her previous job, she seemed

        and
nervous. ~~She also~~ tried to change the subject.
      ^

Combining two sentences produces one concise sentence.

There is, there are, *and* it is

Sometimes expletive constructions—*there is, there are,* and *it is*—can introduce a topic effectively; often, however, your writing will be better without them.

     Many
▶ ~~There are many~~ people ~~who~~ fear success because they believe they do
     ^

not deserve it.

       Presidential   *need*
▶ ~~It is necessary for presidential~~ candidates to perform well on television.
     ^   ^

Active voice

Some writing situations call for the passive voice (38g), but it is always wordier than the active—and often makes for dull or even difficult reading.

    Gower
▶ ~~In Gower's research, it was~~ found that pythons often dwell in
   ^

trees.

Wordy noun forms

Forming nouns from verbs, a process sometimes called *nominalization,* can help make prose more concise—for example, using *abolition* instead of *the process of abolishing*—but it can also make a sentence wordy and hard to read.

          assessing
▶ The firm is now ~~engaged in an assessment of~~ its procedures for
           ^

   developing
~~the development of~~ new products.
 ^

The original sentence sounds pretentious, and the noun phrases cloud the message. In contrast, the edited version is clear and forceful.

Sentence Variety **35**

Row upon row of trees identical in size and shape may appeal to our sense of orderliness, but in spite of that appeal, the rows soon become boring. Constant uniformity in anything, in fact, soon gets tiresome. Variety is important in sentence structures because too much uniformity results in dull, listless prose. This chapter examines ways to revise sentences by creating variety in length and in openings.

35a Vary sentence length.

Is there a "just right" length for a particular sentence or idea? The answer depends partly on your purpose, intended audience, and topic. But note that after one or more long sentences with complex ideas or images, the punch of a short sentence can be refreshing.

▶ To become a doctor, you spend so much time in the tunnels of preparation—head down, trying not to screw up, just going from one day to the next—that it is a shock to find yourself at the other end, with someone offering you a job. *But the day comes.*
— ATUL GAWANDE, *Better*

QUICK HELP

Editing for Sentence Variety

- Count the number of words in each of your sentences. If the difference between the longest and shortest sentences is small — say, five words or fewer — try revising your sentences to create greater variety. (35a)

- If many sentences have fewer than ten words, consider whether any of them require additional detail or should be combined with other sentences.

- How do your sentences open? If all or most of them open with a subject, try recasting some sentences to begin with a transition, a phrase, or a dependent clause. (35b)

35b Vary sentence openings.

If sentence after sentence begins with a subject, a passage may become monotonous or hard to read.

▶ The way football and basketball are played is as interesting as the
Because football   *each*
players. ~~Football~~ is a game of precision./, ~~Each~~ play is diagrammed to
                                        however,
accomplish a certain goal. Basketball , is a game of endurance.
In fact, a
~~A~~ basketball game looks like a track meet; the team that drops of

exhaustion first, loses. Basketball players are often compared to
          their
artists/, ~~The players'~~ graceful moves and slam dunks are their

masterpieces.

The editing adds variety by using a subordinating word (*Because*) and a prepositional phrase (*In fact*) and by linking sentences. Varying sentence openings prevents the passage from seeming to jerk or lurch along.

You can add variety to your sentence openings by using transitions, various kinds of phrases, and dependent clauses.

TRANSITIONAL EXPRESSIONS

▶ *In contrast,* our approach will save time and money.

▶ *Nevertheless,* the show must go on.

▶ *However,* the report is accurate.

▶ *Additionally,* my client insists on immunity from prosecution.

PHRASES

▶ *Before dawn,* tired commuters drink their first cups of coffee.

▶ *Frustrated by the delays,* the drivers started honking their horns.

▶ *To qualify for flight training,* one must be in excellent physical condition.

▶ *Our hopes for victory dashed,* we started home.

DEPENDENT CLAUSES

▶ *What they want* is a place to call home.

▶ *Because the hills were dry,* the fire spread rapidly.

▶ *When the police appeared wearing riot gear,* the protesters stopped chanting, stared for a moment, and then scattered.

▶ *Although you may not consider a cell phone a necessity,* a homeless veteran will not be able to find a job without one.

TALKING ABOUT STYLE

Technical Writing

For some types of writing, varying sentence structure and length is not always appropriate. Many technical writers, particularly those who write manuals that will be translated into other languages, must follow stringent rules for sentence structure and length. One computer company, for example, requires writers to adhere to a strict subject-verb-object order and limit all of their sentences to no more than fifteen words. Learn the style conventions of your field as fully as possible, and then bring them to bear on your own sentence revisions.

Parts of Speech 36

G rammatical correctness alone is not enough to ensure that a sentence is effective and artful — or that it serves an appropriate purpose in your writing. Understanding grammatical structures can, however, help you produce sentences that are appropriate and effective as well as grammatically correct. The English language includes eight different categories of words called the *parts of speech* — verbs, nouns, pronouns, adjectives, adverbs, prepositions, conjunctions, and interjections. Many English words can function as more than one part of speech. When you *book an airplane flight*, the word *book* is a verb; when you *take a good book to the beach*, it is a noun; and when you have *book knowledge*, it is an adjective.

36a Verbs

Verbs move the meaning of sentences along by showing action (*glance, speculate*), occurrence (*become, happen*), or being (*be, seem*). Verbs change form to show *time, person, number, voice,* and *mood* (Chapter 38).

TIME	we *work*, we *worked*
PERSON	I *work*, she *works*
NUMBER	one person *works*, two people *work*
VOICE	she *asks*, she *is asked*
MOOD	we *see*, if I *were to see*

Helping verbs (also called *auxiliary verbs*) combine with main verbs to create verb phrases. Auxiliaries include the forms of *be, do,* and *have*, which are also used as main verbs, and *can, could, may, might, must, shall, should, will,* and *would* (38b).

▶ I *could have danced* all night.

▶ She *would prefer* to learn Italian rather than Spanish.

▶ When *do* you *need* the spreadsheet?

36b Nouns

Nouns name persons (*aviator, child*), places (*lake, library*), things (*truck, suitcase*), or concepts (*happiness, balance*). Proper nouns, which are capitalized, name specific persons, places, things, or concepts: *Bill, Iowa, Supreme Court, Buddhism.* Collective nouns (40d) name groups: *flock, jury.*

Most nouns change from singular (one) to plural (more than one) when you add *-s* or *-es: horse, horses; kiss, kisses.* Some nouns, however, have irregular plural forms: *woman, women; mouse, mice; deer, deer.* Noncount nouns (39a) cannot be made plural because they name things that cannot easily be counted: *dust, peace, prosperity.*

The possessive form of a noun shows ownership. Possessive forms add an apostrophe plus *-s* to most singular nouns or just an apostrophe to most plural nouns: *the horse's owner, the boys' department.*

Nouns are often preceded by the article (or determiner) *a, an,* or *the: a rocket, an astronaut, the launch* (39b).

FOR MULTILINGUAL WRITERS

Multilingual　**Count and Noncount Nouns**

Do people conduct *research* or *researches*? See 39a for a discussion of count and noncount nouns.

36c Pronouns

Pronouns often take the place of nouns or other words functioning as nouns so that you do not have to repeat words that have already been mentioned. A word or word group that a pronoun replaces or refers to is called the antecedent of the pronoun (41f).

ANTECEDENT　　　　　　　　　　　　　　　　PRONOUN
▶ Caitlin refused the invitation even though *she* wanted to go.

Pronouns fall into several categories.

PERSONAL PRONOUNS

Personal pronouns refer to specific persons or things. Each can take several forms (*I, me, my, mine*) depending on its function in the sentence (41a).

▶ **When Keisha saw the dogs again,** *she* **called** *them,* **and** *they* **ran to** *her.*

POSSESSIVE PRONOUNS

Possessive pronouns (*my, mine, your, yours, her, hers, his, its, our, ours, their, theirs*) are personal pronouns that indicate ownership (41a and 50a).

▶ *My* **roommate lost** *her* **keys.**

REFLEXIVE PRONOUNS

Reflexive pronouns refer to the subject of the sentence or clause in which they appear. They end in *-self* or *-selves*: *myself, yourself, himself, herself, itself, oneself, ourselves, yourselves, themselves.*

▶ **The seals sunned** *themselves* **on the warm rocks.**

INTENSIVE PRONOUNS

Intensive pronouns have the same form as reflexive pronouns. They emphasize a noun or another pronoun.

▶ **He decided to paint the apartment** *himself.*

INDEFINITE PRONOUNS

Indefinite pronouns do not refer to specific nouns, although they may refer to identifiable persons or things. The following is a partial list:

all, another, anybody, both, each, either, everything, few, many, most, neither, none, no one, nothing, one, some, something

▶ *Everybody* **screamed, and** *someone* **fainted, when the lights went out.**

DEMONSTRATIVE PRONOUNS

Demonstrative pronouns (*this, that, these, those*) identify or point to specific nouns.

▶ *These* **are Peter's books.**

INTERROGATIVE PRONOUNS

Interrogative pronouns (*who, which, what*) are used to ask questions.

▶ *Who* **can help set up the chairs for the meeting?**

RELATIVE PRONOUNS

Relative pronouns (*who, which, that, what, whoever, whichever, whatever*) introduce dependent clauses and relate the dependent clause to the rest of the sentence (37e). The interrogative pronoun *who* and the relative pronouns *who* and *whoever* have different forms depending on how they are used in a sentence (41b).

 ▶ Maya, *who* hires interns, is the manager *whom* you should contact.

RECIPROCAL PRONOUNS

Reciprocal pronouns (*each other, one another*) refer to individual parts of a plural antecedent.

 ▶ The business failed because the partners distrusted *each other*.

36d Adjectives

Adjectives modify (limit the meaning of) nouns and pronouns, usually by describing, identifying, or quantifying those words (see Chapter 42). Adjectives that identify or quantify are sometimes called *determiners* (39b).

 ▶ The *red* Corvette ran off the road. [describes]
 ▶ *That* Corvette needs to be repaired. [identifies]
 ▶ We saw *several other* Corvettes race by. [quantifies]

In addition to their basic forms, most descriptive adjectives have other forms that allow you to make comparisons: *small, smaller, smallest; foolish, more foolish, most foolish, less foolish, least foolish*.

 ▶ This year's attendance was *smaller* than last year's.

Adjectives usually precede the words they modify, though they may follow linking verbs: *The car was defective*. Many pronouns (36c) can function as identifying adjectives when they are followed by a noun.

 ▶ *That* is a dangerous intersection. [pronoun]
 ▶ *That* intersection is dangerous. [identifying adjective]

Other kinds of adjectives that identify or quantify are the articles *a, an*, and *the* (39b) and numbers (*three, sixty-fifth, five hundred*).

Proper adjectives, which are capitalized (53b), are formed from or relate to proper nouns (*Egyptian, Emersonian*).

☑ Parts of Speech > LearningCurve: Verbs, adjectives, and adverbs

36e Adverbs

Adverbs modify verbs, adjectives, other adverbs, or entire clauses (see Chapter 42). Many adverbs end in -*ly*, though some do not (*always*, *never*, *very*, *well*), and some words that end in -*ly* are not adverbs but adjectives (*friendly*, *lovely*). One of the most common adverbs is *not*.

▶ **Business writers** *frequently* **communicate with strangers.** [modifies the verb *communicate*]

▶ **How can they attract customers in an** *increasingly* **difficult economy?** [modifies the adjective *difficult*]

▶ **They must work** *especially* **hard to avoid offending readers.** [modifies the adverb *hard*]

▶ *Obviously,* **they need to weigh their words with care.** [modifies the independent clause that makes up the rest of the sentence]

Adverbs often answer the questions *when? where? why? how? to what extent?*

Many adverbs, like many adjectives, take different forms when making comparisons: *forcefully, more forcefully, most forcefully, less forcefully, least forcefully.*

Conjunctive adverbs modify an entire clause, and they express the connection in meaning between that clause and the preceding clause (or sentence). Common conjunctive adverbs include *however, furthermore, therefore,* and *likewise.* (See 36g.)

36f Prepositions

Prepositions express relationships — in space, time, or other senses — between nouns or pronouns and other words in a sentence.

▶ **We did not want to leave** *during* **the game.**

▶ **The contestants waited nervously** *for* **the announcement.**

A prepositional phrase (see Chapter 44) begins with a preposition and ends with the noun or pronoun it connects to the rest of the sentence.

▶ **Drive** *across* **the bridge and go** *down* **the avenue** *past* **three stoplights.**

SOME COMMON PREPOSITIONS

about	at	down	near	since
above	before	during	of	through
across	behind	except	off	toward
after	below	for	on	under
against	beneath	from	onto	until
along	beside	in	out	up
among	between	inside	over	upon
around	beyond	into	past	with
as	by	like	regarding	without

SOME COMPOUND PREPOSITIONS

according to	except for	instead of
as well as	in addition to	next to
because of	in front of	out of
by way of	in place of	with regard to
due to	in spite of	

Research for this book shows that many writers—including native speakers of English—have trouble choosing appropriate prepositions. If you are not sure which preposition to use, consult your dictionary, or use search engines or online databases to choose one (see 29e).

36g Conjunctions

Conjunctions connect words or groups of words to each other and tell something about the relationship between these words.

Coordinating conjunctions

Coordinating conjunctions (30a) join equivalent structures, such as two or more nouns, pronouns, verbs, adjectives, adverbs, prepositions, conjunctions, phrases, or clauses.

▶ A strong *but* warm breeze blew across the desert.
▶ Please print *or* type the information on the application form.
▶ Taiwo worked two shifts today, *so* she is tired tonight.

COORDINATING CONJUNCTIONS

and	but	for	nor	or	so	yet

Correlative conjunctions

Correlative conjunctions join equal elements, and they come in pairs.

▶ *Both* Bechtel *and* Kaiser submitted bids on the project.

▶ Maisha *not only* sent a card *but also* visited me in the hospital.

CORRELATIVE CONJUNCTIONS

both . . . and	just as . . . so	not only . . . but also
either . . . or	neither . . . nor	whether . . . or

Subordinating conjunctions

Subordinating conjunctions (30b) introduce adverb clauses and signal the relationship between the adverb clause and another clause, usually an independent clause. For instance, in the following sentence, the subordinating conjunction *while* signals a time relationship, letting us know that the two events in the sentence happened simultaneously:

▶ Sweat ran down my face *while* I frantically searched for my child.

SOME COMMON SUBORDINATING CONJUNCTIONS

after	if	unless
although	in order that	until
as	once	when
as if	since	where
because	so that	whether
before	than	while
even though	that	who
how	though	why

Conjunctive adverbs

Conjunctive adverbs connect independent clauses and often act as transitional expressions (47e) that show how the second clause relates to the first clause. As their name suggests, conjunctive adverbs can act as both adverbs and conjunctions because they modify the second clause in addition to connecting it to the preceding clause.

▶ The cider tasted bitter; *however,* each of us drank a tall glass of it.

▶ The cider tasted bitter; each of us, *however,* drank a tall glass of it.

SOME CONJUNCTIVE ADVERBS

also	however	moreover	similarly
anyway	incidentally	namely	still
besides	indeed	nevertheless	then
certainly	instead	next	therefore
finally	likewise	now	thus
furthermore	meanwhile	otherwise	undoubtedly

36h Interjections

Interjections express surprise or emotion: *oh, ouch, hey*. Interjections often stand alone. Even when they are included in a sentence, they do not relate grammatically to the rest of the sentence.

▶ *Hey*, **no one suggested that we would find an easy solution to this problem.**

37 Parts of Sentences

The grammar of your first language comes to you almost automatically. Listen in on a conversation between two four-year-olds:

AUDREY: My new bike that Aunt A got me has a red basket and a loud horn, and I love it.

LILA: Can I ride it?

AUDREY: Yes, as soon as I take a turn.

This simple conversation features sophisticated grammar—the subordination of one clause to another, a compound object, and a number of adjectives—used effortlessly. If you are like many English speakers, you may never really have reflected on the details of how the language works. Paying close attention to how you put sentences together can help you understand the choices available to you whenever you write.

37a The basic grammar of sentences

A sentence is a grammatically complete group of words that expresses a thought. Words in a sentence can be identified by parts of speech (see Chapter 36), but you should also understand how words and phrases function in sentences.

Subjects and predicates

To be grammatically complete, a sentence must contain both a subject, which identifies what the sentence is about, and a predicate, which says or asks something about the subject or tells the subject to do something.

SUBJECT	PREDICATE
I	have a dream.
The rain in Spain	stays mainly in the plain.
Her skill as an archer	makes her a formidable opponent.

TALKING THE TALK

Understanding Grammatical Terms

"I never learned any grammar." You may lack *conscious* knowledge of grammar and grammatical terms (and if so, you are not alone — American students today rarely study English grammar). But you probably understand the ideas that grammatical terms such as *auxiliary verb* and *direct object* represent, even if the terms themselves are unfamiliar. Brushing up on the terms commonly used to talk about grammar will make it easier for you and your instructor — as well as other readers and reviewers — to share a common language when you discuss the best ways to get your ideas across clearly and with few distractions.

Some sentences contain only a one-word predicate with an implied subject; for example, *Stop!* is a complete sentence, with the unspoken subject *you*. Most sentences, however, contain some words that expand upon the basic subject and predicate.

The central elements of subjects and predicates are nouns (36b) and verbs (36a).

```
┌── SUBJECT ──┐ ┌─── PREDICATE ───┐
        NOUN     VERB
```
▶ A solitary **figure waited** on the platform.

```
┌───── SUBJECT ─────┐ ┌───── PREDICATE ──────┐
  NOUN                    VERB
```
▶ Her **skill** as an archer **makes** her a formidable opponent.

Conventional English word order

Multilingual

In general, subjects, verbs, and objects must all be placed in specific positions within a sentence.

SUBJECT VERB OBJECT ADVERB
▶ **Mario left Venice reluctantly.**

The only word in this sentence that you can move is the adverb *reluctantly* (*Mario reluctantly left Venice* or *Reluctantly, Mario left Venice*). The three key elements of subject, verb, and object rarely move out of their normal order.

QUICK HELP

Basic Sentence Patterns

1. Subject / verb
   ```
   ┌ S ┐┌ V ┐
   ```
   ▶ **Babies drool.**

2. Subject / verb / subject complement
   ```
   ┌ S ┐┌ V ┐┌ SC ┐
   ```
   ▶ **Babies smell sweet.**

3. Subject / verb / direct object
   ```
   ┌ S ┐┌ V ┐┌ DO ┐
   ```
   ▶ **Babies drink milk.**

4. Subject / verb / indirect object / direct object
   ```
   ┌ S ┐┌ V ┐┌── IO ──┐┌ DO ┐
   ```
   ▶ **Babies give grandparents pleasure.**

5. Subject / verb / direct object / object complement
   ```
   ┌ S ┐┌ V ┐┌ DO ┐┌ OC ┐
   ```
   ▶ **Babies keep parents awake.**

Sentence patterns

Knowing a word's part of speech (see Chapter 36) helps you understand how to use it, but you also have to look at the part it plays in a particular sentence. In the following sentences, the noun *description* plays different roles:

> SUBJECT
> ▶ This *description* conveys the ecology of the Everglades.

> DIRECT OBJECT
> ▶ I read a *description* of the ecology of the Everglades.

In the first sentence, *description* serves as the subject of the verb *conveys*, while in the second it serves as the direct object of the verb *read*.

37b Subjects

The subject of a sentence identifies what the sentence is about. The simple subject consists of one or more nouns (36b) or pronouns (36c); the complete subject consists of the simple subject with all its modifiers.

> ▶ **Baseball** is a summer game.

> ┌────── COMPLETE SUBJECT ──────┐
> ▶ **Sailing over the fence, the ball** crashed through Mr. Wilson's window.

> ┌────── COMPLETE SUBJECT ──────┐
> ▶ **Those who sit in the bleachers** have the most fun.

A compound subject contains two or more simple subjects joined with a coordinating conjunction (*and, but, or*) or a correlative conjunction (*both . . . and, either . . . or, neither . . . nor, not only . . . but also*). (See 36g.)

> ▶ **Baseball** *and* **softball** developed from cricket.

> ▶ **Both baseball** *and* **softball** developed from cricket.

Subject positions

The subject usually comes before the predicate (37a), but sometimes writers reverse this order to achieve a particular effect.

> ▶ Up to the plate stepped *Casey.*

In questions, the subject appears between the helping verb and the main verb.

▶ Can *statistics* lie?

▶ How did the *manager* turn these players into a winning team?

In sentences beginning with *there* or *here* followed by a form of the verb *be*, the subject always follows the verb. *There* and *here* are never the subject.

▶ There was no *joy* in Mudville.

Explicit subjects

Multilingual

While many languages can omit a sentence subject, English very rarely allows this. You might write *Responsible for analyzing data* on a résumé, but in most varieties of spoken and written English, you must state the subject explicitly. In fact, with only a few exceptions, all clauses in English must have an explicit subject.

>   *it*

▶ They took the Acela Express to Boston because was fast.
                                                         ^

English even requires a kind of "dummy" subject to fill the subject position in certain kinds of sentences.

▶ *It* is raining.

▶ *There* is a strong wind.

Imperative sentences (37f), which express requests or commands, are an exception to the rule of explicit subjects; the subject *you* is usually implied rather than stated.

▶ *(You)* Keep your eye on the ball.

37c Predicates

In addition to a subject, every sentence has a predicate, which asserts or asks something about the subject or tells the subject to do something. The key word of most predicates is a verb. The simple predicate of a sentence consists of the main verb and any auxiliaries; the complete predicate includes the simple predicate and any modifiers of the verb and any objects or complements (37a) and their modifiers.

> ┌─────── COMPLETE PREDICATE ───────┐

▶ Both of us are planning to major in history.

A compound predicate contains two or more verbs that have the same subject, usually joined by a coordinating or a correlative conjunction (36g).

▶ Omar shut the book, put it back on the shelf, *and* sighed.

On the basis of how they function in predicates, verbs can be divided into three categories: linking, transitive, and intransitive.

Linking verbs

A linking verb connects a subject with a subject complement (sc), a word or word group that identifies or describes the subject.

```
       S    V    ┌──── SC ─────┐
```
▶ Christine *is* an excellent teacher.

```
     S   V   SC
```
▶ She *is* patient.

A subject complement can be either a noun or pronoun (*teacher*) or an adjective (*patient*).

The forms of *be*, when used as main verbs, are common linking verbs. Other verbs, such as *appear, become, feel, grow, look, make, seem, smell*, and *sound*, can also function as linking verbs, depending on the sense of the sentence.

```
   ┌──── S ─────┐   V       SC
```
▶ The neighborhood *looked* prosperous.

Transitive verbs

Multilingual

A transitive verb expresses action that is directed toward a noun or pronoun called the *direct object* (DO).

```
     S    V    ┌──── DO ─────┐
```
▶ He *peeled* all the rutabagas.

Here, the subject and verb do not express a complete thought. The direct object completes the thought by saying *what* he peeled.

A direct object may be followed by an object complement (oc), a word or word group that describes or identifies the direct object. Object complements may be adjectives, as in the first example below, or nouns, as in the second example.

```
   S V  ┌──────────── DO ─────────────┐ ┌──── OC ────┐
```
▶ I *find* cell-phone conversations in restaurants very annoying.

```
    S       V       DO     ┌──── OC ────┐
```
▶ Alana *considers* Keyshawn her best friend.

Some transitive verbs may also be followed by an indirect object (IO), which is the recipient of the direct object. The indirect object tells to whom or what, or for whom or what, the verb does its action.

┌────── S ──────┐ V   IO ┌──── DO ────┐
▶ **The sound of the traffic** *gave* **me a splitting headache.**

Transitive verbs typically require you to state the object explicitly. For example, you can't just say *Give!* even if it is clear that you mean *Give me the phone.*

Intransitive verbs

Multilingual

An intransitive verb does not have a direct object.

┌────── S ──────┐   V
▶ **The Red Sox** *persevered.*

┌──── S ────┐   V
▶ **Their fans** *watched* **anxiously.**

The verb *persevered* has no object (it makes no sense to ask, *persevered what?*), and the verb *watched* is directed toward an object that is implied but not expressed.

Some verbs that express action can be only transitive or only intransitive, but most can be used either way, with or without a direct object.

┌──── S ────┐   V   ┌── DO ──┐
▶ **The butler** *opened* **the door.** [transitive]

┌──── S ────┐   V
▶ **The door** *opened* **silently.** [intransitive]

37d Phrases

A phrase is a group of words that lacks a subject or a predicate or both.

Noun phrases

Made up of a noun and all its modifiers, a noun phrase can function in a sentence as a subject, object, or complement.

┌──────── SUBJECT ────────┐
▶ *Delicious, gooey peanut butter* **is surprisingly healthful.**

┌──────────── OBJECT ────────────┐
▶ **I craved** *a green salad with plenty of fresh vegetables.*

┌─ COMPLEMENT ─┐
▶ **Soup is** *a popular lunch.*

Verb phrases

A main verb and its auxiliary verbs make up a verb phrase, which can function in a sentence only as a verb.

▶ Frank *can swim* for a long time.

▶ His headaches *might have been caused* by tension.

Prepositional phrases

A prepositional phrase begins with a preposition and includes a noun or pronoun (the object of the preposition) and any modifiers of the object. Prepositional phrases usually function as adjectives or adverbs.

ADJECTIVE
▶ Our house *in Maine* was a cabin.

ADVERB
▶ *From Cadillac Mountain,* you can see the northern lights.

Verbal phrases

Verbals look like verbs, but they function as nouns, adjectives, or adverbs. There are three kinds of verbals: participles, gerunds, and infinitives.

PARTICIPLES AND PARTICIPIAL PHRASES

The present participle is the *-ing* form of a verb (*spinning*). The past participle of most verbs ends in *-ed* (*accepted*), but some verbs have an irregular past participle (*worn, frozen*). Participles function as adjectives (42a).

▶ A kiss awakened the *dreaming* princess.

▶ The cryptographers deciphered the *hidden* meaning in the

message.

Participial phrases, which also act as adjectives, consist of a present or past participle and any modifiers, objects, or complements.

▶ *Irritated by the delay,* Luisa complained.

▶ A dog *howling at the moon* kept me awake.

GERUNDS AND GERUND PHRASES

The gerund has the same *-ing* form as the present participle but functions as a noun.

SUBJECT
▶ *Writing* takes practice.

DIRECT OBJECT
▶ The organization promotes *recycling.*

Gerund phrases, which function as nouns, consist of a gerund and any modifiers, objects, or complements.

┌────────── SUBJECT ──────────┐
▶ *Opening their eyes to the problem* was not easy.

┌────── DIRECT OBJECT ──────┐
▶ They suddenly heard *a loud wailing from the sandbox.*

INFINITIVES AND INFINITIVE PHRASES

The infinitive is the *to* form of a verb (*to dream, to be*). An infinitive can function as a noun, an adjective, or an adverb.

┌ NOUN ┐
▶ She wanted *to write.*

ADJECTIVE
▶ They had no more time *to waste.*

┌ ADVERB ┐
▶ The corporation was ready *to expand.*

Infinitive phrases consist of an infinitive and any modifiers, objects, or complements. Like infinitives, they function as nouns, adjectives, or adverbs.

┌────── NOUN ──────┐
▶ My goal is *to be a biology teacher.*

┌── ADJECTIVE ──┐
▶ A party *to end the semester* would be a good idea.

┌── ADVERB ──┐
▶ *To perfect a draft,* always proofread carefully.

INFINITIVE-GERUND CONFUSION

Multilingual

In general, infinitives tend to indicate intentions, desires, or expectations, and gerunds tend to indicate facts. Knowing whether to use an infinitive or a gerund in a sentence can be a challenge for many students.

INFINITIVES TO STATE INTENTIONS

▶ Kumar *expected to get* a good job after graduation.

▶ Last year, Fatima *decided to change* her major.

▶ The strikers have *refused to go* back to work.

Verbs such as *expect*, *decide*, and *refuse*, which indicate intentions, must always be followed by an infinitive.

GERUNDS TO STATE FACTS

▶ Jerzy *enjoys going* to the theater.

▶ We *resumed working* after our coffee break.

▶ Kim *appreciated getting* a card from Sean.

Verbs like *enjoy*, *resume*, and *appreciate*, which indicate that something has actually happened, can be followed only by gerunds, not by infinitives.

OTHER RULES AND GUIDELINES

A few verbs can be followed by either an infinitive or a gerund. With some, such as *begin* and *continue*, the choice doesn't affect the meaning. With others, however, the difference is important.

▶ Carlos was working as a medical technician, but he *stopped to study* English.

The infinitive shows that Carlos quit because he intended to study English.

▶ When Carlos left the United States, he *stopped studying* English.

The gerund indicates that Carlos gave up his English studies when he left.

You can use only a gerund—never an infinitive—right after a preposition.

▶ This fruit is safe for ~~to eat.~~ *eating.*

▶ This fruit is safe ~~for~~ to eat.

▶ This fruit is safe for *us* to eat.

Consult a learner's dictionary for more information on whether to follow a verb with an infinitive or a gerund.

Absolute phrases

An absolute phrase usually includes a noun or pronoun and a participle. It modifies an entire sentence rather than a particular word and is usually set off from the rest of the sentence with commas (47c).

▶ I stood on the deck, *the wind whipping my hair.*

▶ *My fears laid to rest,* I set off on my first solo flight.

Appositive phrases

An appositive phrase is a noun phrase that renames the noun or pronoun that immediately precedes it (47c).

▶ The report, *a hefty three-volume work,* included more than ninety recommendations.

▶ We had a single desire, *to change the administration's policies.*

37e   Clauses

A clause is a group of words containing a subject and a predicate. There are two kinds of clauses: independent and dependent. Independent clauses (also known as main clauses) can stand alone as complete sentences.

▶ The window is open.

Pairs of independent clauses may be joined with a comma and a coordinating conjunction (*and, but, for, nor, or, so, yet*).

▶ The window is open, so the room feels cool.

Like independent clauses, dependent clauses (also referred to as subordinate clauses) contain a subject and a predicate. They cannot stand alone as complete sentences, however, for they begin with a subordinating word—a subordinating conjunction (36g) or a relative pronoun (36c)—that connects them to an independent clause.

▶ Because the window is open, the room feels cool.

The subordinating conjunction *because* transforms the independent clause *the window is open* into a dependent clause. In doing so, it indicates a causal relationship between the two clauses.

Dependent clauses function as nouns, adjectives, or adverbs.

Noun clauses

Multilingual

Noun clauses are always contained within another clause. They usually begin with a relative pronoun (*that, which, what, who, whom, whose, whatever, whoever, whomever, whichever*) or with *when, where, whether, why,* or *how.*

▶ *What the archeologists found* **was startling.**
SUBJECT

▶ **She explained** *that the research was necessary.*
DIRECT OBJECT

▶ **The mystery was** *why the ancient city had been abandoned.*
SUBJECT COMPLEMENT

▶ **They were looking for** *whatever information was available.*
OBJECT OF PREPOSITION

Like a noun, a noun clause is an integral part of the sentence; for example, in the second sentence the independent clause is not just *She explained* but *She explained that the research was necessary.* This complex sentence is built out of two sentences; one of them (*The research was necessary*) is embedded in the other (*She explained [something]*). The relative pronoun *that* introduces the noun clause that is the object of *explained.*

A *that* clause can serve as the subject of a sentence, but the effect is very formal.

▶ *That the city had been abandoned* **was surprising.**
SUBJECT

In less formal contexts, and in spoken English, a long noun clause is usually moved to the end of the sentence and replaced with the "dummy subject" *it.*

▶ *It* **was surprising** *that the city had been abandoned.*

Adjective clauses

Multilingual

Adjective clauses modify nouns and pronouns in another clause. Usually, they immediately follow the words they modify.

▶ **The surgery,** *which took three hours,* **was a complete success.**

▶ **It was performed by the surgeon** *who had developed the procedure.*

▶ **The hospital was the one** *where I was born.*

Sometimes the relative pronoun introducing an adjective clause may be omitted, as in the following examples:

▶ That is one book [*that*] *I intend to read.*

▶ The company [*that*] *the family had invested in* grew rapidly.

To see how the adjective clause fits into this sentence, rewrite it as two sentences: *The company grew rapidly. The family had invested in it.* To make *The family had invested in it* a relative clause, change it to a relative pronoun and move it to the beginning of the clause: *The family had invested in it* becomes *that the family had invested in.* Then position the new clause after the word it describes (in this case, *company*): *The company that the family had invested in grew rapidly.*

In very formal writing, when the pronoun you are changing is the object of a preposition, select *which* (or *whom* for people) and move the whole prepositional phrase to the beginning of the clause: *The company in which the family had invested grew rapidly.* In many American English contexts, however, such constructions may sound too formal, so consider your audience carefully.

Adverb clauses

Adverb clauses modify verbs, adjectives, or other adverbs. They begin with a subordinating conjunction (36g). Like adverbs, they usually tell when, where, why, how, or to what extent.

▶ We hiked *where few other hikers went.*

▶ My backpack felt heavier *than it ever had.*

▶ Climbers ascend Mount Everest *because it is there.*

37f Types of sentences

Like words, sentences can be categorized both grammatically and functionally.

Grammatical sentence structure

Grammatically, sentences may be simple, compound, complex, or compound-complex.

SIMPLE SENTENCES

A simple sentence consists of one independent clause and no dependent clause. The subject or the verb, or both, may be compound.

┌─────────── INDEPENDENT CLAUSE ───────────┐
▶ **The trailer is surrounded by a wooden deck.**

┌─────────────── INDEPENDENT CLAUSE ───────────────┐
▶ **Pompeii and Herculaneum disappeared under tons of lava and ash.**

COMPOUND SENTENCES

A compound sentence consists of two or more independent clauses and no dependent clause. The clauses may be joined by a comma and a coordinating conjunction (36g) or by a semicolon.

┌────── INDEPENDENT CLAUSE ──────┐ ┌ INDEPENDENT CLAUSE ┐
▶ **Occasionally a car goes up the dirt trail, and dust flies everywhere.**

┌────── INDEPENDENT CLAUSE ──────┐ ┌────── INDEPENDENT CLAUSE ──────┐
▶ **Alberto is obsessed with soccer; he eats, breathes, and lives the game.**

COMPLEX SENTENCES

A complex sentence consists of one independent clause and at least one dependent clause.

┌ INDEPENDENT CLAUSE ┐┌────── DEPENDENT CLAUSE ──────┐
▶ **Many people believe that anyone can earn a living.**

┌──── DEPENDENT CLAUSE ────┐ ┌───── INDEPENDENT CLAUSE ─────┐
▶ **As I awaited my interview, I sat with another candidate**

┌─ DEPENDENT CLAUSE ─┐
who smiled nervously.

COMPOUND-COMPLEX SENTENCES

A compound-complex sentence consists of two or more independent clauses and at least one dependent clause.

INDEPENDENT CLAUSE ┌── DEPENDENT CLAUSE ──┐ INDEPENDENT CLAUSE
▶ **I complimented Luis when he finished the job, and he seemed pleased.**

┌── INDEPENDENT CLAUSE ──┐ ┌── INDEPENDENT CLAUSE ──┐
▶ **The actors performed well, but the audience hated the play,**

┌────── DEPENDENT CLAUSE ──────┐
which was confusing and far too long.

Sentence function

In terms of function, sentences can be declarative (making a statement), interrogative (asking a question), imperative (giving a command), or exclamatory (expressing strong feeling).

DECLARATIVE	He sings with the Grace Church Boys' Choir.
INTERROGATIVE	How long has he sung with them?
IMPERATIVE	Comb his hair before the performance starts.
EXCLAMATORY	What voices those boys have!

38   Verbs and Verb Phrases

Restaurant menus often spotlight verbs in action. One famous place in Boston, for instance, offers to bake, broil, pan-fry, deep-fry,

poach, sauté, fricassée, blacken, or scallop any of the fish entrées on its menu. To someone ordering—or cooking—at this restaurant, the important distinctions lie entirely in the verbs.

When used skillfully, verbs can be the heartbeat of prose, moving it along, enlivening it, carrying its action. (See Chapter 40 for advice on subject-verb agreement.)

38a   Understand the five forms of verbs.

Except for *be*, all English verbs have five forms.

BASE FORM	PAST TENSE	PAST PARTICIPLE	PRESENT PARTICIPLE	-S FORM
talk	talked	talked	talking	talks
adore	adored	adored	adoring	adores

BASE FORM	We often *go* to Legal Sea Foods.
PAST TENSE	Grandpa always *ordered* bluefish.
PAST PARTICIPLE	Grandma *has tried* the oyster stew.
PRESENT PARTICIPLE	Juanita *is getting* the shrimp platter.
-S FORM	The chowder *needs* salt and pepper.

QUICK HELP

Editing the Verbs in Your Own Writing

- Check verb endings that cause you trouble. (38a and c)
- Double-check forms of *lie* and *lay*, *sit* and *set*, *rise* and *raise*. See that the words you use are appropriate for your meaning. (38d)
- If you are writing about a literary work, remember to refer to the action in the work in the present tense. (38e)
- If you have problems with verb tenses, use the guidelines in 38e to check your verbs.
- Check all uses of the passive voice for appropriateness. (38g)
- Check all verbs used to introduce quotations, paraphrases, and summaries. (15b) If you rely on *say*, *write*, and other very general verbs, try substituting more vivid, specific verbs (*claim*, *insist*, and *wonder*, for instance).

-s and -es endings

Except with *be* and *have*, the *-s* form consists of the base form plus *-s* or *-es*. In standard English, this form indicates action in the present for third-person singular subjects. All singular nouns; the personal pronouns *he*, *she*, and *it*; and many other pronouns (such as *this*, *anyone*, *everything*, and *someone*) are third-person singular.

	SINGULAR	PLURAL
FIRST PERSON	I wish	we wish
SECOND PERSON	you wish	you wish
THIRD PERSON	he/she/it *wishes*	they wish
	Joe *wishes*	children wish
	someone *wishes*	many wish

Forms of be

Be has three forms in the present tense and two in the past tense.

BASE FORM	be
PAST PARTICIPLE	been
PRESENT PARTICIPLE	being
PRESENT TENSE	I *am*, he/she/it *is*, we/you/they *are*
PAST TENSE	I/he/she/it *was*, we/you/they *were*

TALKING ABOUT STYLE

Everyday Use of *Be*

Spoken varieties of English may follow rules for the use of *be* that differ from the rules of most academic English. For instance, you may have heard speakers say "She ain't here now" (instead of *She isn't here now*) or "He be at work every Saturday" (instead of *He is at work every Saturday*). You may sometimes want to quote dialogue featuring such spoken usages when you write or to use what linguists refer to as "habitual *be*" in writing to particular audiences. In most academic and professional writing, however, you will want to follow the conventions of academic English. (For help on using varieties of English appropriately, see Chapter 28.)

38b   Form verb phrases appropriately.

English sentences must have at least one verb or verb phrase that is not simply an infinitive (*to write*), a gerund (*writing*), or a participle (*written*) without any helping verbs. Use helping (also called *auxiliary*) verbs with a main verb—a base form, present participle, or past participle—to create verb phrases.

The most common auxiliaries are forms of *be*, *have*, and *do*. *Have* is used to form perfect tenses that indicate completed action (38e); *be* is used with progressive forms that show continuing action (38e) and to form the passive voice (38g).

▶ The engineers *have considered* possible problems. [completed action]

▶ The college *is building* a new dormitory. [continuing action]

▶ The activists *were warned* to stay away. [passive voice]

As an auxiliary, *do* is used to show emphasis, to form questions, and to make negative statements.

▶ I *do respect* my opponent's viewpoint. [emphasis]

▶ *Do* you *know* the answer? [question]

▶ He *does* not *like* wearing a tie. [negative statement]

Helping (auxiliary) verb order

Multilingual

Verb phrases can be built up out of a main verb and one or more auxiliaries.

▶ Immigration figures *have been rising* every year.

Verb phrases have strict rules of order. The only permissible change to word order is to form a question, moving the first auxiliary to the beginning of the sentence: *Have immigration figures been rising every year?*

When two or more auxiliaries appear in a verb phrase, they must follow a particular order based on the type of auxiliary:

1. A modal (*can, could, may, might, must, shall, should, will, would,* or *ought to*)
2. A form of *have* used to indicate a perfect tense (38e)
3. A form of *be* used to indicate a progressive tense (38e)
4. A form of *be* used to indicate the passive voice, followed by a past participle (38g)

Very few sentences include all four kinds of auxiliaries.

	Modal	Perfect *Have*	Progressive *Be*	Passive *Be*	Main Verb	
Sonia	—	has	—	been	invited	to visit Prague.
Her arrange-ments	will	—	—	be	made	by the relatives.
The invitation	must	have	—	been	sent	in the spring.
She	—	has	been	—	studying	Czech.
She	may	—	be	—	feeling	nervous.
She	might	have	been	—	expecting	to travel elsewhere.
The trip	will	have	been	being	planned	for months by the time she leaves.

Modals

The modal auxiliaries—*can, could, may, might, shall, should, will, would, must,* and *ought to*—indicate future action, possibility, necessity, or obligation.

▶ They *will explain* the procedure. [future action]
▶ You *can see* three states from the top of the mountain. [possibility]

▶ Students *must manage* their time wisely. [necessity]

▶ They *should examine* the results of the study. [obligation]

No verb phrase can include more than one modal.

       be able to
▶ She will ~~can~~ speak Czech much better soon.

USING MODALS FOR REQUESTS OR INSTRUCTIONS

Modals are often used in requests and instructions. If you use a modal such as *could* or *would*, you are politely acknowledging that the person you are talking to may be unable or unwilling to do what you ask.

▶ *Could* you bring me a pillow?

Modals appearing in instructions usually indicate whether an action is suggested or required:

1. You *can* / You *may* post your work online. [Posting online is allowed.]
2. You *should* submit your report electronically. [Posting online is recommended or required.]
3. You *must* / You *will* submit your report electronically. [Posting online is required.]

USING MODALS TO SHOW DOUBT OR CERTAINTY

Modals can also indicate how confident the writer is about his or her claims. Using *may* or *might* results in a tentative suggestion, while *will* indicates complete confidence:

▶ The study *might help explain* the findings of previous research.

▶ The study *will help explain* the findings of previous research.

Phrases with modals

Multilingual

Use the base form of a verb after a modal.

▶ Alice *can read* Latin.

▶ Sanjay *should have studied* for the test.

In many other languages, modals such as *can* and *must* are followed by an infinitive (*to* + base form). In English, only the base form follows a modal.

▶ Alice can ~~to~~ read Latin.

Notice that a modal auxiliary never changes form to agree with the subject.

For the most part, modals refer to present or future time. When you want to use a modal to refer to the past, you follow the modal with a perfect form of the main verb (see 38e).

► If you have a fever, you *should see* a doctor.

► If you had a fever, you *should have seen* a doctor.

The modal *must* is a special case. The past tense of *must* is *had to* or *needed to*.

► You *must renew* your visa by the end of this week.

► You *had to renew* / You *needed to renew* your visa by last Friday.

Note, too, the different meanings of the negative forms *must not* and *don't have to*.

► You *must not go* to the party. [You are forbidden to go.]

► You *don't have to go* to the party. [You are not required to go, but you may.]

38c Use appropriate forms of irregular verbs.

A verb is regular when its past tense and past participle are formed by adding -*ed* or -*d* to the base form.

BASE FORM	PAST TENSE	PAST PARTICIPLE
love	loved	loved
honor	honored	honored
obey	obeyed	obeyed

A verb is irregular when it does not follow the -*ed* or -*d* pattern. If you are not sure whether a verb form is regular or irregular, or what the correct form is, consult the following list or a dictionary. Dictionaries list any irregular forms under the entry for the base form.

Some common irregular verbs

BASE FORM	PAST TENSE	PAST PARTICIPLE
arise	arose	arisen
be	was/were	been
beat	beat	beaten
become	became	become
begin	began	begun

BASE FORM	PAST TENSE	PAST PARTICIPLE
bite	bit	bitten, bit
blow	blew	blown
break	broke	broken
bring	brought	brought
broadcast	broadcast	broadcast
build	built	built
burn	burned, burnt	burned, burnt
burst	burst	burst
buy	bought	bought
catch	caught	caught
choose	chose	chosen
come	came	come
cost	cost	cost
dig	dug	dug
dive	dived, dove	dived
do	did	done
draw	drew	drawn
dream	dreamed, dreamt	dreamed, dreamt
drink	drank	drunk
drive	drove	driven
eat	ate	eaten
fall	fell	fallen
feel	felt	felt
fight	fought	fought
find	found	found
fly	flew	flown
forget	forgot	forgotten, forgot
freeze	froze	frozen
get	got	gotten, got
give	gave	given
go	went	gone
grow	grew	grown
hang (suspend)[1]	hung	hung
have	had	had

---

[1]*Hang* meaning "execute by hanging" is regular: *hang, hanged, hanged.*

BASE FORM	PAST TENSE	PAST PARTICIPLE
hear	heard	heard
hide	hid	hidden
hit	hit	hit
keep	kept	kept
know	knew	known
lay	laid	laid
lead	led	led
leave	left	left
lend	lent	lent
let	let	let
lie (recline)[2]	lay	lain
lose	lost	lost
make	made	made
mean	meant	meant
meet	met	met
prove	proved	proved, proven
put	put	put
read	read	read
ride	rode	ridden
ring	rang	rung
rise	rose	risen
run	ran	run
say	said	said
see	saw	seen
send	sent	sent
set	set	set
shake	shook	shaken
shoot	shot	shot
show	showed	showed, shown
shrink	shrank	shrunk
sing	sang	sung
sink	sank	sunk
sit	sat	sat
sleep	slept	slept

---

[2]*Lie* meaning "tell a falsehood" is regular: *lie, lied, lied.*

BASE FORM	PAST TENSE	PAST PARTICIPLE
speak	spoke	spoken
spend	spent	spent
spring	sprang, sprung	sprung
stand	stood	stood
steal	stole	stolen
strike	struck	struck, stricken
swim	swam	swum
swing	swung	swung
take	took	taken
tear	tore	torn
throw	threw	thrown
wake	woke, waked	waked, woken
wear	wore	worn
write	wrote	written

38d   Choose between *lie* and *lay, sit* and *set, rise* and *raise.*

These pairs of verbs cause confusion because both verbs in each pair have similar-sounding forms and related meanings. In each pair, one of the verbs is transitive, meaning that it is followed by a direct object (*I laid the cloth on the table*). The other is intransitive, meaning that it does not have an object (*He lay on the floor when his back ached*). The best way to avoid confusing these verbs is to memorize their forms and meanings.

BASE FORM	PAST TENSE	PAST PARTICIPLE	PRESENT PARTICIPLE	-S FORM
lie (recline)	lay	lain	lying	lies
lay (put)	laid	laid	laying	lays
sit (be seated)	sat	sat	sitting	sits
set (put)	set	set	setting	sets
rise (get up)	rose	risen	rising	rises
raise (lift)	raised	raised	raising	raises

✓ Grammar > LearningCurve: Verbs
  Grammar > LearningCurve: Verbs for multilingual writers

> *lie*
> ▶ The doctor asked the patient to l̶a̶y̶ on his side.
> ⌄

> *set*
> ▶ She s̶a̶t̶ the vase on the table.
> ⌄

> *rose*
> ▶ He r̶a̶i̶s̶e̶d̶ up in bed and glared at us.
> ⌄

38e Use verb tenses appropriately.

Multilingual

Verb tenses show when the action takes place. The three simple tenses are the present tense, the past tense, and the future tense.

PRESENT TENSE	I *ask*, I *write*
PAST TENSE	I *asked*, I *wrote*
FUTURE TENSE	I *will ask*, I *will write*

More complex aspects of time are expressed through progressive, perfect, and perfect progressive forms of the simple tenses.

PRESENT PROGRESSIVE	she *is asking*, she *is writing*
PAST PROGRESSIVE	she *was asking*, she *was writing*
FUTURE PROGRESSIVE	she *will be asking*, she *will be writing*
PRESENT PERFECT	she *has asked*, she *has written*
PAST PERFECT	she *had asked*, she *had written*
FUTURE PERFECT	she *will have asked*, she *will have written*
PRESENT PERFECT PROGRESSIVE	she *has been asking*, she *has been writing*
PAST PERFECT PROGRESSIVE	she *had been asking*, she *had been writing*
FUTURE PERFECT PROGRESSIVE	she *will have been asking*, she *will have been writing*

The simple tenses locate an action only within the three basic time frames of present, past, and future. Progressive forms express continuing actions; perfect forms express actions completed before another action or time in the present, past, or future; perfect progressive forms express actions that continue up to some point in the present, past, or future.

Present tense

SIMPLE PRESENT

Use the simple present to indicate actions occurring now and those occurring habitually.

▶ I *eat* breakfast every day at 8:00 AM.

▶ Love *conquers* all.

Use the simple present when writing about action in literary works.

> *realizes*   *is*
▶ Ishmael slowly ~~realized~~ all that ~~was~~ at stake in the search for the
                    ^   ^

    white whale.

General truths or scientific facts should be in the simple present, even when the predicate of the sentence is in the past tense.

>   *makes*
▶ Pasteur demonstrated that his boiling process ~~made~~ milk safe.
                                                ^

When you are quoting, summarizing, or paraphrasing a work, in general use the present tense.

>   *writes*
▶ Keith Walters ~~wrote~~ that the "reputed consequences and promised
                ^

    blessings of literacy are legion."

But in an essay using APA (American Psychological Association) style, report your experiments or another researcher's work in the past tense (*wrote, noted*) or the present perfect (*has reported*). (See Chapter 61.)

>   *noted*
▶ Comer (1995) ~~notes~~ that protesters who deprive themselves of food
            ^

    are seen as "caring, sacrificing, even heroic" (p. 5).

PRESENT PROGRESSIVE

Use the present progressive form when an action is in progress now. The present progressive uses a present form of *be* (*am, is, are*) and the *-ing* form of the main verb.

▶ He *is directing* a new film.

In contrast, use the simple present tense for actions that frequently occur in the present, but that are not necessarily happening now.

SIMPLE PRESENT   PRESENT PROGRESSIVE
▶ My sister *drives* a bus. She *is taking* a vacation now.

With an appropriate expression of time, you can use the present progressive to indicate a scheduled event in the future.

▶ We *are having* friends over for dinner tomorrow night.

Some verbs are rarely used in progressive forms in formal writing. These verbs are said to express unchanging conditions or mental states: *believe, belong, hate, know, like, love, need, own, resemble, understand.* However, in spoken and informal written English, progressive forms like *I'm loving this* and *You're not understanding me correctly* are becoming increasingly common.

PRESENT PERFECT

The present perfect tense indicates actions begun in the past and either completed at some unspecified time in the past or continuing into the present. To form the present perfect, use a present form of *have* (*has, have*) and a perfect participle such as *talked*.

▶ Uncontrolled logging *has destroyed* many tropical forests.

PRESENT PERFECT PROGRESSIVE

Use the present perfect progressive form to indicate continuous actions begun in the past and continuing into the present. To form the present perfect progressive, use the present perfect form of *be* (*have been, has been*) and the *-ing* form of the main verb.

▶ Since September, he *has been writing* a novel in his spare time.

Past tense

In the past tense, you can use simple past, past progressive, past perfect, and past perfect progressive forms.

SIMPLE PAST

Use the simple past to indicate actions or conditions that occurred at a specific time and do not extend into the present.

▶ Germany *invaded* Poland on September 1, 1939.

PAST PROGRESSIVE

Use the past progressive when an action was in progress in the past. It is used relatively infrequently in English, and it focuses on duration or calls attention to a past action that went on at the same time as something else. The present progressive uses a past form of *be* (*was*, *were*) and the *-ing* form of the main verb.

▶ Lenin *was living* in exile in Zurich when the tsar was overthrown.

PAST PERFECT

Use the past perfect to indicate actions or conditions completed by a specific time in the past or before some other past action occurred. To form the past perfect, use *had* and a perfect participle such as *talked*.

▶ By the fourth century, Christianity *had become* the state religion.

PAST PERFECT PROGRESSIVE

Use the past perfect progressive form to indicate a continuing action or condition in the past that had already been happening when some other past action happened. (You will probably need the simple past tense for the other past action.) To form the past perfect progressive, use the past perfect form of *be* (*had been*) and the *-ing* form of the main verb.

▶ Carter *had been planning* a naval career until his father died.

Future tense

The future tense includes simple, progressive, perfect, and perfect progressive forms.

SIMPLE FUTURE

Use the simple future (*will* plus the base form of the verb) to indicate actions or conditions that have not yet begun.

▶ The exhibition *will come* to Washington in September.

FUTURE PROGRESSIVE

Use the future progressive to indicate continuing actions or conditions in the future. The future progressive uses the future form of *be* (*will be*) and the *-ing* form of the main verb.

▶ The loans *will be coming* due over the next two years.

FUTURE PERFECT

Use the future perfect to indicate actions or conditions that will be completed by or before some specified time in the future. To form the future perfect, use *will have* and a perfect participle such as *talked*.

▶ **By next summer, she *will have published* the results of the research study.**

FUTURE PERFECT PROGRESSIVE

Use the future perfect progressive to indicate continuing actions or conditions that will be completed by some specified time in the future. To form the future perfect progressive, use the future perfect form of *be* (*will have been*) and the *-ing* form of the main verb.

▶ **As of May 1, I *will have been living* in Tucson for five years.**

QUICK HELP

Editing Verb Tenses

If you have trouble with verb tense in standard English, make a point of checking for these common trouble spots as you proofread.

- Problems with verb form: writing *seen* for *saw*, for example, which confuses the past-participle and past-tense forms. (38c)
- Problems with tense: using the simple past (*Uncle Charlie arrived*) when meaning requires the present perfect (*Uncle Charlie has arrived*). (38e)
- Think carefully before using a regional or ethnic variety of English in situations calling for standard academic English. (See Chapter 28.)

38f Sequence verb tenses effectively.

Careful and accurate use of tenses is important for clear writing. Even the simplest narrative describes actions that take place at different times; when you use the appropriate tense for each action, readers can follow such time changes easily.

▶ **By the time he *lent* her the money, she *had declared* bankruptcy.**

Use an infinitive (*to* plus a base form: *to go*) to indicate actions occurring at the same time as or later than the action of the predicate verb.

▶ **Each couple *hopes to win* the dance contest.**

The hoping is in the present; the winning is in the future.

Use a present participle (base form plus *-ing*) to indicate actions occurring at the same time as that of the predicate verb.

> ▶ *Seeking to relieve unemployment,* **Roosevelt established several public works programs.**

A past participle or a present-perfect participle (*having* plus a past participle) indicates actions occurring before that of the predicate verb.

> ▶ *Flown*
>   ~~Flying~~ **to the front, the troops joined their hard-pressed comrades.**
>   ^
>
> The past participle *flown* shows that the flying occurred before the joining.

> ▶ *Having crushed*
>   ~~Crushing~~ **all opposition at home, he launched a war of conquest.**
>   ^
>
> He launched the war after he crushed the opposition.

One common error is to use *would* in both clauses of a sentence with an *if* clause. Use *would* only in one clause.

> ▶ *had*
>   **If I** ~~would have~~ **played harder, I would have won.**
>   ^

38g   Use active and passive voice effectively.

Voice tells whether the subject is acting (*he questions us*) or being acted upon (*he is questioned*). When the subject is acting, the verb is in the active voice; when the subject is being acted upon, the verb is in the passive voice.

ACTIVE VOICE   The storm *uprooted* huge pine trees.

PASSIVE VOICE   Huge pine trees *were uprooted* by the storm.

The passive voice uses the appropriate form of the auxiliary verb *be* followed by the past participle of the main verb: *he is being questioned, he was questioned, he will be questioned, he has been questioned.*

Most contemporary writers use the active voice as much as possible because it livens up their prose. Passive-voice verbs often make a passage hard to understand and remember. In addition, writers sometimes use the passive voice to avoid taking responsibility for what they have written. A government official who admits that "mistakes were made" skirts the question: who made them?

To shift a sentence from the passive to the active voice, make the performer of the action the subject of the sentence, and make the recipient of the action an object.

► *My sister took the*
The prizewinning photograph. ~~was taken by my sister.~~

The passive voice can work to good advantage in some situations. Journalists often use the passive voice when the performer of an action is unknown or less important than the recipient.

► **Colonel Muammar el-Qaddafi** *was killed* **during an uprising.**

Much technical and scientific writing uses the passive voice to highlight what is being studied.

► **The volunteers' food intake** *was* **closely** *monitored.*

38h Understand mood and conditional sentences.

The mood of a verb indicates the attitude of the writer. The indicative mood states facts and opinions or asks questions. The imperative mood gives commands and instructions. The subjunctive mood (used mainly in clauses beginning with *that* or *if*) expresses wishes or conditions that are contrary to fact.

INDICATIVE	I *did* the right thing.
IMPERATIVE	*Do* the right thing.
SUBJUNCTIVE	If I *had done* the right thing, I would not be in trouble now.

Subjunctives

The present subjunctive uses the base form, no matter what the subject of the verb is.

► **It is important that children** *be* **psychologically ready for a new sibling.**

The past subjunctive is the same as the simple past except for the verb *be*, which uses *were* for all subjects.

► **He spent money as if he** *had* **infinite credit.**
► **If the store** *were* **better located, it would attract more customers.**

Subjunctive mood

Because the subjunctive can create a rather formal tone, many people today tend to substitute the indicative mood in informal conversation.

▶ If I *was* a better swimmer, I would try out for the team. [informal]

For academic and professional writing, use the subjunctive in the following contexts:

CLAUSES EXPRESSING A WISH

▶ He wished that his mother *were* still living nearby.

AS IF AND *AS THOUGH* CLAUSES

▶ He started down the trail as if he *were* walking on ice.

THAT CLAUSES EXPRESSING A REQUEST OR DEMAND

▶ The job requires that the employee *be* in good physical condition.

IF CLAUSES EXPRESSING A CONDITION THAT DOES NOT EXIST

▶ If the sale of tobacco *were* banned, tobacco companies would suffer a great loss.

One common error is to use *would* in both clauses. Use the subjunctive in the *if* clause and *would* in the main clause.

       had
▶ If I ~~would have~~ played harder, I would have won.

Conditional sentences

Multilingual

Sentences that use an *if* clause don't always require subjunctive forms. Each of the following conditional sentences makes different assumptions about whether or not the *if* clause is true.

▶ If you *practice* writing frequently, you *know* what your chief problems are.

This sentence assumes that what is stated in the *if* clause is probably true. Any tense that is appropriate may be used in both the *if* clause and the main clause.

▶ If you *practice* writing for the rest of this term, you *will understand* the process better.

This sentence makes a prediction. The main clause uses the future tense (*will understand*) or a modal that can indicate future time (*may understand*). The *if* clause uses the present tense.

▶ If you *practiced* writing every single day, it *would* eventually *seem* much easier to you.

This sentence indicates doubt. In the *if* clause, the verb is past subjunctive, even though it refers to future time. The main clause contains *would* + the base form of the main verb.

▶ **If you *practiced* writing on Mars, you *would find* no one to read your work.**

This sentence imagines an impossible situation. The past subjunctive is used in the *if* clause, although past time is not being referred to, and *would* + the base form is used in the main clause.

▶ **If you *had practiced* writing in ancient Egypt, you *would have used* hieroglyphics.**

This sentence shifts the impossibility to the past; obviously, you aren't going to find yourself in ancient Egypt. But a past impossibility demands a form that is "more past": the past perfect in the *if* clause and *would* + the perfect form of the verb in the main clause.

Nouns and Noun Phrases

Although all languages have nouns, English nouns differ from those in some other languages in various ways, such as their division into count and noncount nouns and the use of plural forms, articles, and other modifiers.

39a Use count and noncount nouns appropriately.

Multilingual

Nouns in English can be either count nouns or noncount nouns. Count nouns refer to distinct individuals or things that can be directly counted: *a doctor, an egg, a child; doctors, eggs, children.* Noncount nouns refer to masses, collections, or ideas without distinct parts: *milk, rice, courage.* You cannot count noncount nouns except with a preceding phrase: *a glass of milk, three grains of rice, a little courage.*

Count nouns usually have singular and plural forms: *tree, trees.* Noncount nouns usually have only a singular form: *grass.*

COUNT	NONCOUNT
people (plural of person)	humanity
tables, chairs, beds	furniture
letters	mail
pebbles	gravel
suggestions	advice

Some nouns can be either count or noncount, depending on their meaning.

COUNT   Before video games, children played with *marbles.*

NONCOUNT   The palace floor was made of *marble.*

When you learn a new noun in English, you need to determine whether it is count, noncount, or both. Many dictionaries provide this information.

39b Use determiners appropriately.
Multilingual

Determiners are words that identify or quantify a noun, such as <u>*this*</u> *study,* <u>*all*</u> *people,* <u>*his*</u> *suggestions.*

COMMON DETERMINERS

- the articles *a, an, the*
- *this, these, that, those*
- *my, our, your, his, her, its, their*
- possessive nouns and noun phrases (<u>*Sheila's*</u> *paper,* <u>*my friend's*</u> *book*)
- *whose, which, what*
- *all, both, each, every, some, any, either, no, neither, many, much, (a) few, (a) little, several, enough*
- the numerals *one, two,* etc.

These determiners . . .	. . . can precede these noun types	Examples
a, an, each, every	singular count nouns	*a* book *an* American *each* word *every* Buddhist
this, that	singular count nouns noncount nouns	*this* book *that* milk
(a) little, much	noncount nouns	*a little* milk *much* affection
some, any, enough	noncount nouns plural count nouns	*some* milk *any* fruit *enough* trouble *some* books *any* questions *enough* problems
the	singular count nouns plural count nouns noncount nouns	*the* doctor *the* doctors *the* information
these, those, (a) few, *many, both, several*	plural count nouns	*these* books *those* plans *a few* ideas *many* students *both* hands *several* trees

Determiners with singular count nouns

Every singular count noun must be preceded by a determiner. Place any adjectives between the determiner and the noun.

► *my*
sister
^

► *the*
growing population
^

► *that*
old neighborhood
^

Determiners with plural or noncount nouns

Noncount and plural nouns sometimes have determiners and sometimes do not. For example, *This research is important* and *Research is important* are both acceptable but have different meanings.

39c Use articles conventionally.

Multilingual

Articles (*a, an,* and *the*) are a type of determiner. In English, choosing which article to use—or whether to use an article at all—can be challenging. Although there are exceptions, the following general guidelines can help.

The articles a *or* an

Use the indefinite articles *a* and *an* with singular count nouns. Use *a* before a consonant sound (*a car*) and *an* before a vowel sound (*an uncle*). Consider sound rather than spelling: *a house, an hour.*

A or *an* tells readers they do not have enough information to identify specifically what the noun refers to. Compare these sentences:

▶ I need *a* new coat for the winter.

▶ I saw *a* coat that I liked at Dayton's, but it wasn't heavy enough.

The coat in the first sentence is hypothetical. Since it is indefinite to the writer and the reader, it is used with *a,* not *the.* The second sentence refers to an actual coat, but since the writer cannot expect the reader to know which one, it is used with *a* rather than *the.*

If you want to speak of an indefinite quantity rather than just one indefinite thing, use *some* or *any* with a noncount noun or a plural count noun. Use *any* in negative sentences and questions.

▶ This stew needs *some* more salt.

▶ I saw *some* plates that I liked at Gump's.

▶ This stew doesn't need *any* more salt.

▶ Do you have *any* sandwiches left?

The article the

Use the definite article *the* with both count and noncount nouns whose identity is known or is about to be made known to readers. The necessary information for identification can come from the noun phrase itself, from elsewhere in the text, from context, from general knowledge, or from a superlative.

> *the*
> ► Let's meet at ̬fountain in front of Dwinelle Hall.

The phrase *in front of Dwinelle Hall* identifies the specific fountain.

> ► Last Saturday, a fire that started in a restaurant spread to a nearby
> *The store*
> clothing store. ~~Store~~ was saved, although it suffered water damage.

The word *store* is preceded by *the*, which directs our attention to the information in the previous sentence, where the store is first identified.

> *the*
> ► She asked him to shut ̬door when he left her office.

The context shows that she is referring to her office door.

> *The pope*
> ► ~~Pope~~ is expected to visit Africa in October.

There is only one living pope.

> *the*
> ► Bill is now ̬best singer in the choir.

The superlative *best* identifies the noun *singer*.

No article (the zero article)

Noncount and plural count nouns can be used without an article or any other determiner when making generalizations:

> ► In this world nothing is certain but death and taxes.
> — BENJAMIN FRANKLIN

Franklin refers not to a particular death or specific taxes but to death and taxes in general, so no article is used with *death* or with *taxes*.

English differs from many other languages that use the definite article to make generalizations. In English, a sentence like *The ants live in colonies* can refer only to particular, identifiable ants, not to ants in general.

It is sometimes possible to make general statements with *the* or *a/an* and singular count nouns.

> ► *First-year college students* are confronted with many new experiences.
> ► *A first-year student* is confronted with many new experiences.
> ► *The first-year student* is confronted with many new experiences.

These sentences all make the same general statement, but the emphasis of each sentence is different. The first sentence refers to first-year college students as a group, the second focuses on a hypothetical student taken at random, and the third sentence, which is characteristic of formal written style, projects the image of a typical student as representative of the whole class.

40   Subject-Verb Agreement

In everyday terms, the word *agreement* refers to an accord of some sort: friends agree to go to a movie; the United States and Russia negotiate an agreement about reducing nuclear arms. In most sentences, making subjects and verbs agree is fairly simple; only a few subject-verb constructions cause confusion.

40a Understand subject-verb agreement.

In academic varieties of English, verbs must agree with their subjects in number (singular or plural) and in person (first, second, or third).

To make a verb in the present tense agree with a third-person singular subject, add -s or -es to the base form.

▶ A vegetarian diet lowers the risk of heart disease.

To make a verb in the present tense agree with any other subject, use the base form of the verb.

▶ I *miss* my family.
▶ They *live* in another state.

The verbs *have* and *be* do not follow the -s or -es pattern with third-person singular subjects. *Have* changes to *has*; *be* has irregular forms in both the present and past tenses and in the first person as well as the third person. (See Chapter 38.)

▶ War *is* hell.
▶ The soldier *was* brave beyond the call of duty.

In some varieties of proper African American or regional English, third-person singular verb forms do not end with -s or -es: *She go to*

QUICK HELP

Editing for Subject-Verb Agreement

- Identify the subject that goes with each verb. Cover up any words between the subject and the verb to identify agreement problems more easily. (40b)
- Check compound subjects. Those joined by *and* usually take a plural verb form. With those subjects joined by *or* or *nor*, however, the verb agrees with the part of the subject closest to the verb. (40c)
- Check collective-noun subjects. These nouns take a singular verb form when they refer to a group as a single unit but a plural form when they refer to the multiple members of a group. (40d)
- Check indefinite-pronoun subjects. Most take a singular verb form. *Both*, *few*, *many*, *others*, and *several* take a plural form; and *all*, *any*, *enough*, *more*, *most*, *none*, and *some* can be either singular or plural, depending on the noun they refer to. (40e)

---

work every day. In most academic writing, however, your audience will expect third-person singular verb forms to end in *-s* or *-es* (38a).

40b Make separated subjects and verbs agree.

Make sure the verb agrees with the subject and not with another noun that falls in between.

▶ A vase of flowers makes a room attractive.

▶ Many books on the best-seller list ~~has~~ *have* little literary value.

The simple subject is *books*, not *list*.

Be careful when you use phrases beginning with *as well as*, *along with*, *in addition to*, *together with*, or similar prepositions. They do not make a singular subject plural.

▶ A passenger, as well as the driver, ~~were~~ *was* injured in the accident.

Though this sentence has a grammatically singular subject, it suggests the idea of a plural subject. The sentence makes better sense with a compound subject: *The driver and a passenger were injured in the accident.*

40c   Make verbs agree with compound subjects.

Two or more subjects joined by *and* generally require a plural verb form.

▶ Tony and his friend commute from Louisville.

▶ A backpack, a canteen, and a rifle ~~was~~ issued to each recruit.
       were

When subjects joined by *and* are considered a single unit or refer to the same person or thing, they take a singular verb form.

▶ George W. Bush's older brother and political ally was the governor of

Florida.

▶ Drinking and driving ~~remain~~ a major cause of highway fatalities.
                      remains

> In this sentence, *drinking and driving* is considered a single activity, and a singular verb is used.

If the word *each* or *every* precedes subjects joined by *and,* the verb form is singular.

▶ Each boy and girl chooses one gift to take home.

With subjects joined by *or* or *nor,* the verb agrees with the part closest to the verb.

▶ Neither my roommate nor my neighbors *like* my loud music.

▶ Either the witnesses or the defendant ~~are~~ lying.
                                        is

If you find this sentence awkward, put the plural noun closest to the verb: *Either the defendant or the witnesses are lying.*

40d   Make verbs agree with collective nouns.

Collective nouns—such as *family, team, audience, group, jury, crowd, band, class,* and *committee*—refer to a group. Collective nouns can take either singular or plural verb forms, depending on whether they refer to the group as a single unit or to the multiple members of the group. The meaning of a sentence as a whole is your guide to whether a collective noun refers to a unit or to the multiple parts of a unit.

▶ **After deliberating, the jury** *reports* **its verdict.**

The jury acts as a single unit.

▶ **The jury still** *disagree* **on a number of counts.**

The members of the jury act as multiple individuals.

scatter
▶ **The duck family** ~~scatters~~ **when the cat approaches.**

Family here refers to the many ducks; they cannot scatter as one.

Treat fractions that refer to singular nouns as singular and those that refer to plural nouns as plural.

SINGULAR   Two-thirds of the park *has* burned.

PLURAL   Two-thirds of the students *were* commuters.

Even though *eyeglasses*, *scissors*, *pants*, and other such words refer to single items, they take plural verbs because they are made up of pairs.

▶ **Where** *are* **my reading glasses?**

Treat phrases starting with *the number of* as singular and with *a number of* as plural.

SINGULAR   The number of applicants for the internship *was* amazing.

PLURAL   A number of applicants *were* put on the waiting list.

40e Make verbs agree with indefinite pronouns.

Indefinite pronouns do not refer to specific persons or things. Most take singular verb forms.

SOME COMMON INDEFINITE PRONOUNS

another	each	much	one
any	either	neither	other
anybody	everybody	nobody	somebody
anyone	everyone	no one	someone
anything	everything	nothing	something

▶ Of the two jobs, neither *holds* much appeal.

▶ Each of the plays ~~depict~~ a hero undone by a tragic flaw. *(depicts)*

Both, few, many, others, and *several* are plural.

▶ Though many *apply,* few *are* chosen.

All, any, enough, more, most, none, and *some* can be singular or plural, depending on the noun they refer to.

▶ All of the cake *was* eaten.

▶ All of the candidates *promise* to improve the schools.

40f   Make verbs agree with *who, which,* and *that.*

When the relative pronouns *who, which,* and *that* are used as a subject, the verb agrees with the antecedent of the pronoun.

▶ Fear is an ingredient that *goes* into creating stereotypes.

▶ Guilt and fear are ingredients that *go* into creating stereotypes.

Problems often occur with the words *one of the.* In general, *one of the* takes a plural verb, while *only one of the* takes a singular verb.

▶ Carla is one of the employees who always ~~works~~ overtime. *(work)*

Some employees always work overtime. Carla is among them. Thus *who* refers to *employees,* and the verb is plural.

▶ Ming is the only one of the employees who always ~~work~~ overtime. *(works)*

Only one employee always works overtime, and that employee is Ming. Thus *one,* and not *employees,* is the antecedent of *who,* and the verb form is singular.

40g Make linking verbs agree with subjects.

A linking verb should agree with its subject, which usually precedes the verb, not with the subject complement, which follows it (37a).

> ▶ Three key treaties *are* is the topic of my talk.

The subject is *treaties*, not *topic*.

> ▶ Nero Wolfe's passion *was* were orchids.

The subject is *passion*, not *orchids*.

40h Make verbs agree with subjects ending in -s.

Some words that end in -s appear plural but are singular and thus take singular verb forms.

> ▶ Measles still *strikes* strike many Americans.

Some nouns of this kind (such as *statistics* and *politics*) may be either singular or plural, depending on context.

SINGULAR Statistics *is* a course I really dread.

PLURAL The statistics in that study *are* highly questionable.

40i Make verbs agree with subjects that follow.

In English, verbs usually follow subjects. When this order is reversed, make the verb agree with the subject, not with a noun that happens to precede it.

> ▶ Beside the barn *stand* stands silos filled with grain.

The subject is *silos*; it is plural, so the verb must be *stand*.

In sentences beginning with *there is, there are, there was,* or *there were,* the word *there* serves only as a placeholder; the subject follows the verb.

▶ There are five basic positions in classical ballet.

The subject, *positions,* is plural, so the verb must also be plural.

40j   **Make verbs agree with titles and words used as words.**

▶ *One Writer's Beginnings* ~~describe~~ describes Eudora Welty's childhood.

▶ *Steroids* ~~are~~ is a little word that packs a big punch in the world of sports.

41   Pronouns

As words that stand in for nouns, pronouns carry a lot of weight in everyday language. These directions show one of the reasons why it's important to use pronouns clearly:

> When you see a dirt road turning left off Winston Lane, follow it for two more miles.

The listener may not know whether *it* means the dirt road or Winston Lane. Pronouns can improve understanding, but only when they're used carefully and accurately.

41a   **Consider a pronoun's role in the sentence.**

Most speakers of English know intuitively when to use *I, me,* and *my.* Our choices reflect differences in case, the form a pronoun takes to indicate how it acts in a sentence. Pronouns acting as subjects are in the subjective case (*I*); those acting as objects are in the objective case (*me*); those acting as possessives are in the possessive case (*my*).

SUBJECTIVE PRONOUNS	OBJECTIVE PRONOUNS	POSSESSIVE PRONOUNS
I	me	my/mine
we	us	our/ours
you	you	your/yours
he/she/it	him/her/it	his/her/hers/its
they	them	their/theirs
who/whoever	whom/whomever	whose

QUICK HELP

Editing Pronouns

- Are all pronouns after forms of the verb *be* in the subjective case? *It's me* is common in spoken English, but in formal writing use *It is I.* (41a)

- To check for use of *who* and *whom* (and *whoever* and *whomever*), try substituting *he* or *him*. If *he* is correct, use *who* (or *whoever*); if *him*, use *whom* or *whomever*. (41b)

- In compound structures, make sure any pronouns are in the same case they would be in if used alone (*She and Jake were living in Spain*). (41c)

- When a pronoun follows *than* or *as*, complete the sentence mentally. If the pronoun is the subject of an unstated verb, it should be subjective (*I like her better than he [likes her]*). If it is the object of an unstated verb, make it objective (*I like her better than [I like] him*). (41d)

- If you have used *he*, *his*, or *him* to refer to *everyone* or another singular indefinite pronoun that includes both males and females, revise the sentence. (41f)

- For each pronoun, identify the specific word that it refers to in the sentence (its antecedent). If you cannot find one specific word, supply one. If the pronoun refers to more than one word, revise the sentence. (41g)

- Check each use of *it*, *this*, *that*, and *which* to be sure the pronoun refers to a specific word. (41g)

- Be sure that any use of *you* refers to your specific reader or readers. (41g)

Subjective case

A pronoun should be in the subjective case (*I, we, you, he/she/it, they, who, whoever*) when it is a subject, a subject complement, or an appositive renaming a subject or subject complement.

SUBJECT

She was passionate about recycling.

SUBJECT COMPLEMENT

The main supporter of the recycling program was *she*.

APPOSITIVE RENAMING A SUBJECT OR SUBJECT COMPLEMENT

Three colleagues — Peter, John, and *she* — worked on the program.

Americans routinely use the objective case for subject complements, especially in conversation: *Who's there? It's me.* If the subjective case for a subject complement sounds stilted or awkward (*It's I*), try rewriting the sentence using the pronoun as the subject (*I'm here*).

> *She was the*
> ▶ ~~The~~ first person to see Kishore after the awards. ~~was she.~~

Objective case

Use the objective case (*me, us, you, him/her/it, them*) when a pronoun functions as a direct or indirect object, an object of a preposition, an appositive renaming an object, or a subject of an infinitive.

DIRECT OBJECT

The boss surprised *her* with a big raise.

INDIRECT OBJECT

The owner gave *him* a reward.

OBJECT OF A PREPOSITION

Several friends went with *me*.

APPOSITIVE RENAMING AN OBJECT

The students elected two representatives, Joan and *me*.

SUBJECT OF AN INFINITIVE

The students convinced *him* to vote for the school bond.

Possessive case

Use the possessive case when a pronoun shows possession or ownership. The adjective forms of possessive pronouns (*my, our, your, his/her/its, their, whose*) are used before nouns or gerunds, and noun forms (*mine, ours, yours, his/hers/its, theirs, whose*) take the place of a possessive noun. Possessive pronouns do not include apostrophes (50a).

BEFORE A NOUN

The sound of *her* voice came right through the walls.

IN PLACE OF A POSSESSIVE NOUN

The responsibility is *hers*.

Pronouns before a gerund should be in the possessive case.

▶ I remember ~~him~~ singing.
        his

His modifies the gerund *singing*.

41b Use *who, whoever, whom,* and *whomever* appropriately.

A common problem with pronoun case is deciding whether to use *who* or *whom*. Even when traditional grammar requires *whom*, many Americans use *who* instead, especially in informal writing and speech. Nevertheless, you should understand the difference between *who* and *whom* so that you can make informed choices in situations such as formal college writing. The most common confusion with *who* and *whom* occurs when they begin a question and when they introduce a dependent clause.

TALKING THE TALK

Correctness or Stuffiness?

"I think *Everyone has their opinion* sounds better than *Everyone has his or her opinion*. And nobody says *whom*. Why should I write that way?" Over time, the conventions governing certain usages — such as *who* versus *whom*, or *their* versus *his or her* when it refers to an indefinite pronoun like *everyone* — have become much more relaxed. To many Americans, *Whom did you talk to?* and *No one finished his or her test* — both of which are technically "correct" — sound unpleasantly fussy. However, other people object to less formal constructions such as *Who did you talk to?* and *No one finished their test*. Unfortunately, you can't please everyone. Use whatever you are most comfortable with in speaking, but be more careful in formal writing. If you don't know whether your audience will prefer more or less formality, try recasting your sentence.

Questions

You can determine whether to use *who* or *whom* at the beginning of a question by answering the question using a personal pronoun. If the answer is *he*, *she*, or *they*, use *who*; if it is *him*, *her*, or *them*, use *whom*.

> *Whom*
> ▶ ~~Who~~ did you visit?
>   ^

> I visited *them*. *Them* is objective; thus *whom* is correct.

> *Who*
> ▶ ~~Whom~~ do you think wrote the story?
>   ^

> I think *she* wrote the story. *She* is subjective; thus *who* is correct.

Dependent clauses

The case of a pronoun in a dependent clause is determined by its purpose in the clause, no matter how that clause functions in the sentence. If the pronoun acts as a subject or subject complement in the clause, use *who* or *whoever*. If the pronoun acts as an object in the clause, use *whom* or *whomever*.

> *whoever*
> ▶ The center is open to ~~whomever~~ wants to use it.
>   ^

> *Whoever* is the subject of the clause *whoever wants to use it*. (The clause is the object of the preposition *to*, but the clause's function in the sentence does not affect the case of the pronoun.)

> *whom*
> ▶ The new president was not ~~who~~ she had expected.
>   ^

> Here, *whom* is the object of the verb *had expected* in the clause *whom she had expected*.

If you are not sure which case to use, try separating the dependent clause from the rest of the sentence. Rewrite the clause as a new sentence, and substitute a personal pronoun for *who(ever)* or *whom(ever)*. If the pronoun is in the subjective case, use *who* or *whoever*; if it is in the objective case, use *whom* or *whomever*.

> ▶ The minister glared at (*whoever/whomever*) made any noise.

> Isolate the clause *whoever/whomever made any noise*. Substituting a personal pronoun gives you *they made any noise*. *They* is in the subjective case; therefore, *The minister grimaced at <u>whoever</u> made any noise.*

▶ The minister glared at whoever ~~she thought~~ made any noise.

Ignore such expressions as *he thinks* and *she says* when you isolate the clause.

41c Consider case in compound structures.

When a pronoun is part of a compound subject, complement, object, or appositive, put it in the same case you would use if the pronoun were alone.

▶ When ~~him~~ and Zelda were first married, they lived in New York.
    he

▶ The boss invited ~~she~~ and her family to dinner.
    her

▶ This morning saw yet another conflict between my sister and ~~I.~~
    me.

▶ Both panelists—Javonne and ~~me~~—were stumped.
    I

To decide whether to use the subjective or objective case in a compound structure, mentally delete the rest of the compound and try the pronoun alone.

▶ Come to the park with Anh and ~~I.~~
    me.

Mentally deleting *Anh and* results in *Come to the park with I.* Rewrite as *Come to the park with Anh and me.*

41d Consider case in elliptical constructions.

In elliptical constructions, some words are understood but left out. When an elliptical construction ends in a pronoun, put the pronoun in the case it would be in if the construction were complete.

▶ His sister has always been more athletic than *he* [is].

In some elliptical constructions, the case of the pronoun depends on the meaning intended.

▶ Willie likes Lily more than *she* [likes Lily].

She is the subject of the omitted verb *likes*.

▶ **Willie likes Lily more than [he likes]** *her*.

Her is the object of the omitted verb *likes*.

41e   Use *we* and *us* appropriately before a noun.

If you are unsure about whether to use *we* or *us* before a noun, recast the sentence without the noun. Use whichever pronoun would be correct if the noun were omitted.

▶ **Us fans never give up hope.**
   We

Without *fans*, *we* would be the subject.

▶ **The Rangers depend on we fans.**
   us

Without *fans*, *us* would be the object of a preposition.

41f   Make pronouns agree with antecedents.

The antecedent of a pronoun is the word the pronoun refers to. The antecedent usually appears before the pronoun—earlier in the sentence or in the prior sentence. Pronouns and antecedents are said to agree when they match up in person, number, and gender.

SINGULAR   The choirmaster raised *his* baton.

PLURAL   The boys picked up *their* music.

Compound antecedents

Compound antecedents joined by *and* require plural pronouns.

▶ *My parents and I* **tried to resolve** *our* **disagreement.**

When *each* or *every* precedes a compound antecedent, however, it takes a singular pronoun.

▶ *Every plant* **and** *animal* **has** *its* **own ecological niche.**

With a compound antecedent joined by *or* or *nor*, the pronoun agrees with the nearer or nearest antecedent. If the parts of the antecedent are of different genders, however, this kind of sentence can be awkward or ambiguous and may need to be revised.

AWKWARD   Neither Annie nor Barry got *his* work done.

REVISED   Annie didn't get *her* work done, and neither did Barry.

When a compound antecedent contains both singular and plural parts, the sentence may sound awkward unless the plural part comes last.

▶ **Neither the newspaper nor the radio stations would reveal *their* sources.**

Collective-noun antecedents

A collective noun that refers to a single unit (*herd, team, audience*) requires a singular pronoun.

▶ **The audience fixed *its* attention on center stage.**

When such an antecedent refers to the multiple parts of a unit, however, it requires a plural pronoun.

▶ **The director chose this cast because *they* had experience in the roles.**

Indefinite-pronoun antecedents

Indefinite pronouns are those that do not refer to specific persons or things. Most indefinite pronouns are always singular; a few are always plural. Some can be singular or plural depending on the context.

▶ *One* **of the ballerinas lost *her* balance.**

▶ *Many* **in the audience jumped to *their* feet.**

SINGULAR   Some of the furniture was showing *its* age.

PLURAL   Some of the farmers abandoned *their* land.

Sexist pronouns

Indefinite pronouns often serve as antecedents that may be either male or female. Writers used to use a masculine pronoun, known as the generic *he*, to refer to such indefinite pronouns. However, such wording ignores or even excludes females.

QUICK HELP

Editing Out Generic *He, His, Him*

Everyone should know his *legal rights.*

Here are three ways to express the same idea without *his*:

1. Revise to make the antecedent a plural noun.
   All citizens should know their *legal rights.*
2. Revise the sentence altogether.
   Everyone should have some knowledge of basic legal rights.
3. Use both masculine and feminine pronouns.
   Everyone should know his or her *legal rights.*

   This third option, using both masculine and feminine pronouns, can be awkward, especially when repeated several times in a passage.

   A fourth option replaces *his* with the plural *their*. Although this gender-neutral solution is increasingly common, some audiences will consider it unacceptably informal.

When the antecedent is *anybody, each, everybody,* or *everyone,* some people avoid the generic *he* by using a plural pronoun.

▶ **Everyone should know** *their* **legal rights.**

You will hear such sentences in conversation and see them in writing. However, if you are writing for situations in which formal choices are expected, be aware that many people believe that it's a mistake to use the plural *their* with singular antecedents such as *anybody, each,* and *everyone.*

41g Make pronouns refer to clear antecedents.

The antecedent of a pronoun is the word the pronoun substitutes for. If a pronoun is too far from its antecedent, readers will have trouble making the connection between the two.

Ambiguous antecedents

Readers have trouble when a pronoun can refer to more than one antecedent.

▶ **The car went over the bridge just before** ~~it~~ the bridge **fell into the water.**

What fell into the water — the car or the bridge? The revision makes the meaning clear.

▶ Kerry told Ellen, *"I* she should be ready soon."

Reporting Kerry's words directly, in quotation marks, eliminates the ambiguity.

Vague use of *it, this, that, and* which

The words *it, this, that,* and *which* often function as a shortcut for referring to something mentioned earlier. But such shortcuts can cause confusion for readers. Like other pronouns, each must refer to a specific antecedent.

▶ When the senators realized the bill would be defeated, they tried to
The entire effort
postpone the vote but failed. It was a fiasco.

▶ Nancy just found out that she won the lottery, *and that news* which explains her

sudden resignation from her job.

Indefinite use of *you, it, and* they

In conversation, we frequently use *you, it,* and *they* in an indefinite sense in such expressions as *you never know; in the paper, it said;* and *they say.* In academic and professional writing, however, use *you* only to mean "you, the reader," and *they* or *it* only to refer to a clear antecedent.

▶ Commercials try to make *people* you buy without thinking.

▶ *The* On the Weather Channel/ it reported that an earthquake devastated

parts of Pakistan.

▶ *Many restaurants in France* In France, they allow dogs. in many restaurants.

Possessive antecedents

A possessive may *suggest* a noun antecedent but does not serve as a clear antecedent.

▶ In *her* Alexa's formal complaint, *Alexa* she showed why the test question was

wrong.

42 Adjectives and Adverbs

As words that describe other words, adjectives and adverbs can add liveliness and color to writing, helping writers show rather than just tell. In addition, adjectives and adverbs often provide indispensable meanings to the words they modify. In basketball, for example, there is an important difference between a *flagrant* foul and a *technical* foul, or an *angry* coach and an *abusively angry* coach. In each instance, the modifiers are crucial to accurate communication.

42a Understand adjectives and adverbs.

Adjectives modify nouns and pronouns, answering the question *which? how many?* or *what kind?* Adverbs modify verbs, adjectives, other adverbs, or entire clauses; they answer the question *how? when? where?* or *to what extent?* Many adverbs are formed by adding *-ly* to adjectives (*slight, slightly*), but many are not (*outdoors, very*). And some words that end in *-ly* are adjectives (*lovely, homely*). To tell adjectives and adverbs apart, identify the word's function in the sentence.

QUICK HELP

Editing Adjectives and Adverbs

- Scrutinize each adjective and adverb. Consider synonyms for each one to see whether you have chosen the best word possible.

- See if a more specific noun would eliminate the need for an adjective (*mansion* rather than *enormous house*, for instance); do the same with verbs and adverbs.

- Consider adding an adjective or adverb that might make your writing more vivid or specific.

- Make sure all adjectives modify nouns or pronouns and all adverbs modify verbs, adjectives, or other adverbs. Check especially for proper use of *good* and *well*, *bad* and *badly*, *real* and *really*. (42c)

- Make sure all comparisons are complete. (42d)

- If English is not your first language, check that adjectives are in the right order. (42g)

- Avoid using too many adverbs and adjectives in your writing. (42h)

42b Use adjectives after linking verbs.

When adjectives come after linking verbs, they usually describe the subject: *I am patient*. Note that in specific sentences, some verbs may or may not act as linking verbs—*look, appear, sound, feel, smell, taste, grow,* and *prove,* for instance. When a word following one of these verbs modifies the subject, use an adjective; when the word modifies the verb, use an adverb.

ADJECTIVE **Fluffy looked angry.**

ADVERB **Fluffy looked angrily at the poodle.**

Linking verbs suggest a state of being, not an action. In the preceding examples, *looked angry* suggests the state of being angry; *looked angrily* suggests an angry action.

42c Use adverbs to modify verbs, adjectives, and adverbs.

In everyday conversation, you will often hear (and perhaps use) adjectives in place of adverbs. When you write in formal academic English, however, use adverbs to modify verbs, adjectives, and other adverbs.

► You can feel the song's meter if you listen ~~careful~~ *carefully.*

► The audience was ~~real~~ *really* disappointed by the show.

Good *and* well, bad *and* badly

The modifiers *good, well, bad,* and *badly* cause problems for many writers because the distinctions between *good* and *well* and between *bad* and *badly* are often not observed in conversation. *Good* and *bad* are always adjectives, and both can be used after a linking verb. In formal writing, do not use them to modify a verb, an adjective, or an adverb; use *well* or *badly* instead.

► The weather looks *good* today.

► He plays the trumpet ~~good~~ *well* and the trombone ~~bad~~ *badly.*

Badly is an adverb and can modify a verb, an adjective, or another adverb. Do not use it after a linking verb in formal writing; use *bad* instead.

▶ I feel b̶a̶d̶l̶y̶ for the Cubs' fans.
_(bad above badly)

Problems also arise because *well* can function as either an adjective or an adverb. As an adjective, *well* means "in good health"; as an adverb, it means "in a good manner" or "thoroughly."

ADJECTIVE   After a week of rest, Julio felt *well* again.

ADVERB   She plays *well* enough to make the team.

Regional modifiers (right *smart*, wicked *fun*)

Most regions have certain characteristic adjectives and adverbs. Some of the most colorful are intensifiers, adverbs meaning *very* or *absolutely*. In parts of the South, for example, and particularly in Appalachia, you are likely to hear the following: *He paid a right smart price for that car* or *She was plumb tuckered out.* In New England, you might hear *That party was wicked fun.* In each of these cases, the adverb (*right, plumb, wicked*) acts to intensify the meaning of the adjective (*smart, tuckered out, fun*).

As with all language, use regional adjectives and adverbs when they are appropriate (28c). In writing about a family member in Minnesota, for example, you might well quote her, bringing midwestern expressions into your writing. For most academic writing, however, you should use academic English.

FOR MULTILINGUAL WRITERS

Multilingual **Adjectives with Plural Nouns**

In Spanish, Russian, and many other languages, adjectives agree in number with the nouns that they modify. In English, however, adjectives do not change their number this way: *her kittens are cute* (not *cutes*).

42d Choose appropriate comparative and superlative forms.

Most adjectives and adverbs have three forms: positive, comparative, and superlative.

POSITIVE	COMPARATIVE	SUPERLATIVE
large	larger	largest
early	earlier	earliest
careful	more careful	most careful
delicious	more delicious	most delicious
happily	more happily	most happily

▶ Canada is *larger* than the United States.

▶ My son needs to be *more careful* with his money.

▶ This is the *most delicious* coffee we have tried.

▶ They are the *most happily* married couple I know.

The comparative and superlative of most short (one-syllable and some two-syllable) adjectives are formed by adding -*er* and -*est*. With some two-syllable adjectives, longer adjectives, and most adverbs, use *more* and *most*: *scientific, more scientific, most scientific; elegantly, more elegantly, most elegantly*. If you are not sure whether a word has -*er* and -*est* forms, consult the dictionary entry for the simple form.

Irregular forms

A number of adjectives and adverbs have irregular comparative and superlative forms.

POSITIVE	COMPARATIVE	SUPERLATIVE
good	better	best
well	better	best
bad	worse	worst
badly	worse	worst
little (quantity)	less	least
many, some, much	more	most

Comparatives or superlatives

In academic writing, use the comparative to compare two things; use the superlative to compare three or more.

▶ Rome is a much *older* city than New York.

▶ Damascus is one of the ~~older~~ cities in the world.
   oldest

▶ Which of the two candidates is the ~~strongest~~ for the job?
   stronger

Double comparatives and superlatives

Double comparatives and superlatives, used in some informal contexts, use both *more* or *most* and the *-er* or *-est* ending. Occasionally they can act to build a special emphasis, as in the title of Spike Lee's movie *Mo' Better Blues*. In college writing, however, double comparatives and superlatives may count against you. Make sure not to use *more* or *most* before adjectives or adverbs ending in *-er* or *-est* in formal situations.

▶ Paris is the ~~most~~ loveliest city in the world.

Incomplete comparisons

Even if you think your audience will understand an implied comparison, you will be safer if you make sure that comparisons in formal writing are complete and clear (31e).

▶ The patients taking the drug appeared healthier.
   than those receiving a placebo.

Absolute concepts

Some readers consider modifiers such as *perfect* and *unique* to be absolute concepts; according to this view, a construction such as *more unique* is illogical because a thing is either unique or it isn't, so modified forms of the concept don't make sense. However, many seemingly absolute words have multiple meanings, all of which are widely accepted as correct. For example, *unique* may mean *one of a kind* or *unequaled*, but it can also simply mean *distinctive* or *unusual*.

If you think your readers will object to a construction such as *more perfect* (which appears in the U.S. Constitution) or *somewhat unique*, then avoid such uses.

Multiple negatives

Multiple negatives such as *I can't hardly see you* have a long history in English (and in other languages) and can be found in the works of Chaucer and Shakespeare. In the eighteenth century, however, in an effort to make English more logical, double negatives came to be labeled as incorrect. In college writing, you may well have reason to quote passages that include them (whether from Shakespeare, Toni Morrison, or your grandmother), but it is safer to avoid other uses of double negatives in academic writing.

42e Consider nouns as modifiers.

Sometimes a noun can function as an adjective by modifying another noun, as in *chicken soup* or *money supply*. If noun modifiers pile up, however, they can make your writing harder to understand.

> AWKWARD   The cold war–era Rosenberg espionage trial and
>   execution continues to arouse controversy.

> REVISED   The Rosenbergs' trial and execution for espionage
>   during the cold war continues to arouse controversy.

42f Understand adjectives ending in -*ed* and -*ing*.

Multilingual

Many verbs refer to feelings—for example, *bore, confuse, excite, frighten, interest*. The present participles of such verbs, which end in -*ing*, and the past participles, which end in -*ed*, can be used as adjectives (36d).

Use the -*ed* (past participle) form to describe a person having the feeling.

▶ The *frightened* boy started to cry.

Use the -*ing* (present participle) form to describe the thing or person causing the feeling.

▶ The *frightening* movie gave him nightmares.

Be careful not to confuse the two types of adjectives.

     interested
▶ I am ~~interesting~~ in African literature.

                    interesting.
▶ African literature seems ~~interested.~~

42g Put adjectives in order.

Multilingual

Modifiers are words that give more information about a noun; that is, they *modify* the meaning of the noun in some way. Some modifiers precede the noun, and others follow it, as indicated in the chart below.

If there are two or more adjectives, their order is variable, but English has strong preferences, described below.

- Subjective adjectives (those that show the writer's opinion) go before objective adjectives (those that merely describe): *these old-fashioned kitchen tiles.*

- Adjectives of size generally come early: *these large old-fashioned kitchen tiles.*

- Adjectives of color generally come late: *these beautiful blue kitchen tiles.*

- Adjectives derived from proper nouns or from nouns that refer to materials generally come after color terms and right before noun modifiers: *these beautiful blue Portuguese ceramic kitchen tiles.*

- All other objective adjectives go in the middle, separated by commas (see 47d): *these decorative, heat-resistant, old-fashioned blue Portuguese ceramic kitchen tiles.*

Very long noun phrases are usually out of place in most kinds of writing. Academic and professional types of writing tend to avoid long strings of adjectives.

Modifier Type	Arrangement	Examples
determiners	at the beginning of the noun phrase	*these* old-fashioned tiles
all or *both*	before any other determiners	*all* these tiles
numbers	after any other determiners	these *six* tiles
noun modifiers	directly before the noun	these *kitchen* tiles
adjectives	between determiners and noun modifiers	these *old-fashioned* kitchen tiles
phrases or clauses	after the noun	the tiles *on the wall* the tiles *that we bought*

42h Avoid overuse of adverbs and adjectives.

In formal academic writing, expert writers tend to use adverbs and adjectives sparingly. So take a tip from the experts: using fewer modifiers can ensure that each adjective or adverb has a greater impact on your writing.

Adverbs

In his memoir *On Writing*, novelist Stephen King says, "I believe the road to hell is paved in adverbs, and I will shout it from the rooftops." Note that he doesn't say he will shout it *loudly*, since readers already know that shouting is loud. Many adverbs are simply redundant:

▶ Tourists meandered ~~aimlessly~~ in the garden.

> The verb *meandered* means "wandered aimlessly," so *aimlessly* is unnecessary.

In academic writing, avoid redundant adverbs, and omit adverbs that are so overused that they have little meaning anymore, such as *definitely, absolutely,* and *extremely.*

Adjectives

Adjectives can also lead to redundancy. Ask yourself whether you need to say "the *large* mountain" or whether your readers will know that a mountain is large. When you overuse adjectives, you can simply bog down readers.

▶ The author responded to the ~~wonderful cheery~~ smiles lighting up all of the ~~happy, delighted~~ faces in the ~~listening~~ audience.

Adjectives and adverbs in informal writing

As always, consider the context when deciding whether you are overusing adjectives and adverbs. Repetition that would be inappropriate in formal contexts can add effective emphasis in informal writing, as in the hashtag *#sosososcared* or a status update saying "I'm massively, insanely psyched for the show tonight."

43 Modifier Placement

Consider the following notice in a guidebook:

> Visit the old Dutch cemetery where early settlers are buried from noon to five daily.

Does the old cemetery really bury early settlers for five hours every day? Repositioning the modifier *from noon to five daily* eliminates the confusion and makes it clear when the cemetery is open: *From noon to five daily, visit the old Dutch cemetery where early settlers are buried.* To be effective, modifiers should refer clearly to the words they modify and be placed close to those words.

43a Revise misplaced modifiers.

Modifiers can cause confusion or ambiguity if they are not close enough to the words they modify or if they seem to modify more than one word in the sentence.

QUICK HELP

Editing for Misplaced or Dangling Modifiers

1. Identify all the modifiers in each sentence, and draw an arrow from each modifier to the word it modifies.
2. If a modifier is far from the word it modifies, try to move the two closer together. (43a)
3. Does any modifier seem to refer to a word other than the one it is intended to modify? If so, move the modifier so that it refers clearly to only the intended word. (43a and b)
4. If you cannot find the word to which a modifier refers, revise the sentence: supply such a word, or revise the modifier itself so that it clearly refers to a word already in the sentence. (43c)

---

on voodoo
▶ She teaches a seminar this term ~~on voodoo~~ at Skyline College.
⌃

The voodoo was not at the college; the seminar is.

He   *billowing from every window.*
▶ ~~Billowing from every window,~~ he saw clouds of smoke.
⌃   ⌃

People cannot billow from windows.

After he lost the 1962 gubernatorial race,
▶ Nixon told reporters that he planned to get out of politics. ~~after he~~
⌃   ⌃

~~lost the 1962 gubernatorial race.~~

The unedited sentence implies that Nixon planned to lose the race.

Limiting modifiers

Be especially careful with the placement of limiting modifiers such as *almost, even, just, merely,* and *only.* In general, these modifiers should be placed right before or after the words they modify. Putting them in other positions may produce not just ambiguity but a completely different meaning.

AMBIGUOUS	The court *only* hears civil cases on Tuesdays.
CLEAR	The court hears *only* civil cases on Tuesdays.
CLEAR	The court hears civil cases on Tuesdays *only*.

In the first sentence, placing *only* before *hears* makes the meaning ambiguous. Does the writer mean that civil cases are the only cases heard on Tuesdays or that those are the only days when civil cases are heard?

almost
▶ The city ~~almost~~ spent $20 million on the new stadium.
⌃

The original sentence suggests the money was almost spent; moving *almost* makes clear that the amount spent was almost $20 million.

Squinting modifiers

If a modifier can refer to either the word before it or the word after it, it is a squinting modifier. Put the modifier where it clearly relates to only a single word.

SQUINTING	Students who practice writing *often* will benefit.
REVISED	Students who *often* practice writing will benefit.
REVISED	Students who practice writing will *often* benefit.

43b   Revise disruptive modifiers.

Disruptive modifiers interrupt the connections between parts of a grammatical structure or a sentence, making it hard for readers to follow the progress of the thought.

> *If they are cooked too long, vegetables will*
> ▶ ~~Vegetables will, if they are cooked too long,~~ lose most of their
> ^
> nutritional value.

A modifier placed between the *to* and verb of an infinitive (*to boldly go*) is known as a split infinitive. Once considered a serious writing error, split infinitives are no longer taboo. Few readers will object to a split infinitive in a clear and understandable sentence.

> ▶ Students need to *really* know the material to pass the exam.

Sometimes, however, split infinitives can be distracting to readers—especially when more than one word comes between the parts of the infinitive. In such cases, move the modifier before or after the infinitive, or reword the sentence, to remove the distracting interruption.

> *surrender*
> ▶ Hitler expected the British to fairly quickly. ~~surrender.~~
> ^   ^

43c   Revise dangling modifiers.

Dangling modifiers modify nothing in particular in the rest of a sentence. They often *seem* to modify something that is implied but not actually present in the sentence. Dangling modifiers frequently appear at the beginnings or ends of sentences.

> DANGLING   Driving nonstop, Salishan Lodge is located two hours
>   from Portland.
>
> REVISED   Driving nonstop from Portland, you can reach Salishan
>   Lodge in two hours.

To revise a dangling modifier, often you need to add a subject that the modifier clearly refers to. In some cases, however, you have to revise the modifier itself, turning it into a phrase or a clause.

> *our family gave away*
> ▶ Reluctantly, the hound ~~was given away~~ to a neighbor.
> ^
> In the original sentence, was the dog reluctant, or was someone else who is not mentioned reluctant?

> *When he was*
> ~~As~~ a young boy, his grandmother told stories of her years as a country
> ^
>
> schoolteacher.

His grandmother was never a young boy.

> *My*
> ~~Thumbing through the magazine, my~~ eyes automatically noticed the
> ^
> *as I was thumbing through the magazine.*
> perfume ads/
> ^

Eyes cannot thumb through a magazine.

Prepositions and Prepositional Phrases   **44**

W ords such as *to, from, over,* and *under* show the relations between
other words; these words are prepositions, and they are one of
the more challenging elements of English writing. You will need to
decide which preposition to use for your intended meaning and
understand how to use verbs that include prepositions, such as *take
off, pick up,* and *put up with.*

44a Use prepositions idiomatically.
Multilingual

Even if you know where to use a preposition, it can be difficult to determine which preposition to use. Each of the most common prepositions
has a wide range of applications, and this range never coincides exactly
from one language to another. See, for example, how *in* and *on* are used
in English.

> The peaches are *in* the refrigerator.
> The peaches are *on* the table.
> Is that a diamond ring *on* your finger?

The Spanish translations of these sentences all use the same preposition (*en*), a fact that might lead you astray in English.

> *on*
> Is that a ruby ring ~~in~~ your finger?
> ^

QUICK HELP

Using Prepositions Idiomatically

1. **Keep in mind typical examples of each preposition.**

   IN The peaches are *in* the refrigerator.

      There are still some pickles *in* the jar.

      The book you are looking for is *in* the bookcase.

   Here the object of the preposition *in* is a container that encloses something.

   ON The peaches are *on* the table.

      There are still some pickles *on* the plate.

      The book you are looking for is *on* the top shelf.

   Here the object of the preposition *on* is a horizontal surface with which something is in direct contact.

2. **Learn other examples that show some similarities and some differences in meaning.**

   IN You shouldn't drive *in* a snowstorm.

   Here there is no container, but like a container, the falling snow surrounds the driver. The preposition *in* is used for other weather-related expressions as well: *in a tornado, in the sun, in the rain*.

   ON Is that a diamond ring *on* your finger?

   The preposition *on* is used to describe things we wear: *the hat on his head*, *the shoes on her feet*, *the tattoo on his back*.

3. **Use your imagination to create mental images that can help you remember figurative uses of prepositions.**

   IN Michael is *in* love.

   The preposition *in* is often used to describe a state of being: *in love*, *in pain*, *in a panic*. As a way to remember this, you might imagine the person immersed *in* this state of being.

4. **Try to learn prepositions not in isolation but as part of a system.** For example, in identifying the location of a place or an event, you can use the three prepositions *at, in,* and *on.*
     At specifies the exact point in space or time.

   AT There will be a meeting tomorrow *at* 9:30 AM *at* 160 Main Street.

   Expanses of space or time within which a place is located or an event takes place might be seen as containers and so require *in.*

   IN I arrived *in* the United States *in* January.

   On must be used in two cases: with the names of streets (but not the exact address) and with days of the week or month.

   ON The airline's office is *on* Fifth Avenue.

      I'll be moving to my new apartment *on* September 30.

There is no easy solution to the challenge of using English prepositions idiomatically. Digital tools, such as search engines and online
databases of English usage (29e), can help you see how other writers
have expressed a particular idiom. You can also try the strategies in
the box on p. 402.

44b Use two-word verbs idiomatically.

Multilingual

Some words that look like prepositions do not always function as prepositions. Consider the following two sentences:

▶ The balloon rose *off* the ground.

▶ The plane took *off* without difficulty.

In the first sentence, *off* is a preposition that introduces the prepositional phrase *off the ground*. In the second, *off* does not function as a
preposition. Instead, it combines with *took* to form a two-word verb
with its own meaning. Such a verb is called a phrasal verb, and the
word *off*, when used this way, is called an adverbial particle. Many
prepositions can function as particles to form phrasal verbs.

Phrasal verbs

The verb + particle combination that makes up a phrasal verb is a
single entity that often cannot be torn apart.

> *off*
▶ The plane took without difficulty. ~~off.~~

However, when a phrasal verb takes a direct object (37a), the particle
may sometimes be separated from the verb by the object.

▶ I *picked up my baggage* at the terminal.

▶ I *picked my baggage up* at the terminal.

If a personal pronoun (such as *it*, *her*, or *him*) is used as the direct
object, that pronoun must separate the verb from its particle.

▶ I *picked it up* at the terminal.

Prepositional verbs

Some idiomatic two-word verbs are not phrasal verbs.

▶ We *ran into* our neighbor on the train.

Here, *into* is a preposition, and *our neighbor* is its object. You can't separate the verb from the preposition (*We ran our neighbor into on the train* does not make sense in English). Verbs like *run into* are called prepositional verbs.

Notice that *run into our neighbor* is different from a normal verb and prepositional phrase, such as *run into a room*. The combination *run + into* has a special meaning, "meet by chance," that you could not guess from the meanings of *run* and *into*.

English has many idiomatic prepositional verbs. Here is a small sample.

PREPOSITIONAL VERB	MEANING
take after	resemble (usually a parent or older relative)
get over	recover from
count on	trust

Other prepositional verbs have predictable meanings but require you to use a particular preposition that you should learn along with the verb: *depend on, look at, listen to, approve of.*

Finally, look out for phrasal-prepositional verbs such as the following, which include a verb, a particle, and a preposition in a set order.

PHRASAL-PREPOSITIONAL VERB	MEANING
put up with	tolerate
look forward to	anticipate with pleasure
get away with	avoid punishment for

45 Comma Splices and Fused Sentences

Writers sometimes use comma splices for special effects. In advertising and other slogans, comma splices can provide a catchy rhythm.

> Dogs have owners, cats have staff. — BUMPER STICKER

45a Identify comma splices and fused sentences.

A comma splice results from placing only a comma between two independent clauses, as in this tweet:

▶ **One thing is certain, girls everywhere need education.**

A related construction is a fused, or run-on, sentence, which results from joining two independent clauses with no punctuation or connecting word between them. As a fused sentence, the tweet above would read *One thing is certain girls everywhere need education.*

Using comma splices is increasingly common in writing that aims for a casual, informal feel, but comma splices and fused sentences in academic writing are likely to draw an instructor's criticism. If you use comma splices and fused sentences in formal writing, be sure your audience can tell that you are doing so for a special effect.

45b Separate the clauses into two sentences.

The simplest way to revise comma splices or fused sentences is to separate them into two sentences.

COMMA SPLICE	**My mother spends long hours every spring tilling the soil and moving manure, *This* this part of gardening is nauseating.**
FUSED SENTENCE	**My mother spends long hours every spring tilling the soil and moving manure. *This* this part of gardening is nauseating.**

If the two clauses are very short, making them two sentences may sound abrupt and terse, so some other method of revision is probably preferable.

QUICK HELP

Editing for Comma Splices and Fused Sentences

If you find no punctuation between two of your independent clauses — groups of words that can stand alone as sentences — you have identified a fused sentence. If you find two such clauses joined only by a comma, you have identified a comma splice. Revise comma splices and fused sentences with one of these methods.

1. Separate the clauses into two sentences. (45b)

   ▶   Education is an elusive idea,/. ^*It*^ it means different things to different people.

2. Link the clauses with a comma and a coordinating conjunction (*and, but, or, nor, for, so,* or *yet*). (45c)

   ▶   Education is an elusive idea, ^*for*^ it means different things to different people.

3. Link the clauses with a semicolon. (45d)

   ▶   Education is an elusive idea,/; it means different things to different people.

   If the clauses are linked with only a comma and a conjunctive adverb — a word like *however, then, therefore* — add a semicolon.

   ▶   Education is an elusive idea,/; ^*indeed,*^ it means different things to different people.

4. Recast the two clauses as one independent clause. (45e)

   ▶   ^*An elusive idea, education*^ ~~Education is an elusive idea,~~ it means different things to different people.

5. Recast one independent clause as a dependent clause. (45f)

   ▶   Education is an elusive idea,/ ^*because*^ it means different things to different people.

6. In informal writing, link the clauses with a dash. (45g)

   ▶   Education is an elusive idea,/— it means different things to different people.

45c Link the clauses with a comma and a coordinating conjunction.

If the two clauses are closely related and equally important, join them with a comma and a coordinating conjunction (*and, but, or, nor, for, so,* or *yet*). (See 30a.)

COMMA
SPLICE

and
I got up feeling bad, I feel even worse now.
       ∧

FUSED
SENTENCE

but
I should pay my tuition, I need a new car.
       ∧

45d Link the clauses with a semicolon.

If the ideas in the two clauses are closely related and you want to give them equal emphasis, link them with a semicolon.

COMMA
SPLICE

This photograph is not at all realistic/; it even uses
       ∧
dreamlike images to convey its message.

FUSED
SENTENCE

The practice of journalism is changing dramatically;
       ∧
advances in technology have sped up news cycles.

Be careful when you link clauses with a conjunctive adverb or a transitional phrase. You must precede such words and phrases with a semicolon (see Chapter 48), with a period, or with a comma combined with a coordinating conjunction (30a).

COMMA
SPLICE

Many developing countries have very high birthrates/;
       ∧
therefore, most of their citizens are young.
        ∧

FUSED
SENTENCE

Many developing countries have very high birthrates.
       T   ∧
therefore, most of their citizens are young.
        ∧

FUSED
SENTENCE

and
Many developing countries have very high birthrates,
       ∧
therefore, most of their citizens are young.
        ∧

SOME CONJUNCTIVE ADVERBS AND TRANSITIONAL PHRASES

also	in contrast	next
anyway	indeed	now
besides	in fact	otherwise
certainly	instead	similarly
finally	likewise	still
furthermore	meanwhile	then
however	moreover	therefore
in addition	namely	thus
incidentally	nevertheless	undoubtedly

FOR MULTILINGUAL WRITERS

Multilingual **Judging Sentence Length**

In U.S. academic contexts, readers sometimes find a series of short sentences "choppy" and undesirable. If you want to connect two independent clauses into one sentence, be sure to join them using one of the methods discussed in this chapter so that you avoid creating a comma splice or fused sentence. Another useful tip for writing in American English is to avoid writing several very long sentences in a row. If you find this pattern in your writing, try breaking it up by including a shorter sentence occasionally.

TALKING ABOUT STYLE

Comma Splices in Context

Spliced and fused sentences appear frequently in literary and journalistic writing, where they can create momentum with a breathless rush of details:

> Bald eagles are common, ospreys abound, we have herons and mergansers and kingfishers, we have logging with Percherons and Belgians, we have park land and nature trails, we have enough oddballs, weirdos, and loons to satisfy anybody.
> — ANNE CAMERON

Context is critical. Depending on audience, purpose, and situation, structures commonly considered errors can actually be appropriate and effective.

45e Rewrite the clauses as one independent clause.

Sometimes you can reduce two spliced or fused independent clauses to a single independent clause.

COMMA
SPLICE

Most
A large part of my mail is advertisements/ most of the
                                         ^   *and*
rest is bills.

45f Rewrite one independent clause as a dependent clause.

When one independent clause is more important than the other, try converting the less important one to a dependent clause (30b).

COMMA
SPLICE

which reacted against mass production,
The arts and crafts movement, called for handmade
                             ^
objects/. it reacted against mass production.
       ^

In the revision, the writer chooses to emphasize the first clause, the one describing what the movement advocated, and to make the second clause, the one describing what it reacted against, into a dependent clause.

FUSED
SENTENCE

Although
Zora Neale Hurston is regarded as one of America's
^
major novelists, she died in obscurity.
               ^

In the revision, the writer chooses to emphasize the second clause and to make the first one into a dependent clause by adding the subordinating conjunction *although*.

45g Link the two clauses with a dash.

In informal writing, you can use a dash to join the two clauses, especially when the second clause elaborates on the first clause.

COMMA
SPLICE

Exercise trends come and go/ this year yoga is hot.
                          ^

46 Sentence Fragments

S entence fragments are often used to make writing sound conversational, as in this Facebook status update:

> Realizing that there are no edible bagels in this part of Oregon. Sigh.

 Fragments—groups of words that are punctuated as sentences but are not sentences—are often seen in intentionally informal writing and in public writing, such as advertising, that aims to attract attention or give a phrase special emphasis. But you should think carefully before using fragments in academic or professional writing, where some readers might regard them as errors.

46a Identify sentence fragments.

A group of words must meet three criteria to form a complete sentence. If it does not meet all three, it is a fragment. Revise a fragment by combining it with a nearby sentence or by rewriting it as a complete sentence.

1. A sentence must have a subject (37b).
2. A sentence must have a verb, not just a verbal. A verbal cannot function as a sentence's verb without an auxiliary verb (37d).

   VERB   The terrier is *barking.*

   VERBAL   The terrier *barking.*

3. Unless it is a question, a sentence must have at least one clause that does not begin with a subordinating word (36g). Following are some common subordinating words:

although	if	when
as	since	where
because	that	whether
before	though	which
how	unless	who

46b Revise phrase fragments.

Phrases are groups of words that lack a subject, a verb, or both (37d). When verbal phrases, prepositional phrases, noun phrases, and appositive phrases are punctuated like sentences, they become fragments. To revise these fragments, attach them to an independent clause, or make them a separate sentence.

▶ NBC is broadcasting the debates. ~~With~~ *with* discussions afterward.

With discussions afterward is a prepositional phrase, not a sentence. The editing combines the phrase with an independent clause.

▶ The town's growth is controlled by zoning laws. ~~A~~ *a* strict set of regulations for builders and corporations.

A strict set of regulations for builders and corporations is an appositive phrase renaming the noun *zoning laws*. The editing attaches the fragment to the sentence containing that noun.

▶ Kamika stayed out of school for three months after Linda was born.
She did so to
~~To~~ recuperate and to take care of the baby.

To recuperate and to take care of the baby includes verbals, not verbs. The revision—adding a subject (*she*) and a verb (*did*)—turns the fragment into a separate sentence.

Fragments beginning with transitions

If you introduce an example or explanation with one of the following transitions, be certain you write a sentence, not a fragment.

also	for example	like
as a result	for instance	such as
besides	instead	that is

▶ Joan Didion has written on many subjects. ~~Such~~ *such* as the Hoover Dam and migraine headaches.

The second word group is a phrase, not a sentence. The editing combines it with an independent clause.

46c   Revise compound-predicate fragments.

A compound predicate consists of two or more verbs, along with their modifiers and objects, that have the same subject. Fragments occur when one part of a compound predicate lacks a subject but is punctuated as a separate sentence. These fragments usually begin with *and, but,* or *or.* You can revise them by attaching them to the independent clause that contains the rest of the predicate.

> ▶ They sold their house. ~~And~~ moved into an apartment.

    and

46d   Revise dependent-clause fragments.

Dependent clauses contain both a subject and a verb, but they cannot stand alone as sentences; they depend on an independent clause to complete their meaning. Dependent clauses usually begin with words such as *after, because, before, if, since, though, unless, until, when, where, while, who, which,* and *that.* You can usually combine dependent-clause fragments with a nearby independent clause.

> ▶ When I decided to work part-time. I gave up a lot of my earning
>
>   potential.

If you cannot smoothly attach a clause to a nearby independent clause, try deleting the opening subordinating word and turning the dependent clause into a sentence.

> ▶ The majority of injuries in automobile accidents occur in two ways.
>
>   *An*
>   ~~When an~~ occupant either is hurt by something inside the car or is
>
>   thrown from the car.

47 Commas

Commas often play a crucial role in meaning. See how important the comma is in the following directions for making hot cereal:

> Add Cream of Wheat slowly, stirring constantly.

That sentence tells the cook to *add the cereal slowly*. If the comma came before the word *slowly*, however, the cook might add all of the cereal at once and *stir slowly*. Using commas correctly can help you communicate more effectively.

 **Use commas to set off introductory words, phrases, and clauses.**

▶ However, health care costs keep rising.

▶ In the end, only you can decide.

▶ Wearing new running shoes, Logan prepared for the race.

▶ To win the contest, Connor needed skill and luck.

▶ Pencil poised in anticipation, Audrey waited for the drawing contest to begin.

▶ While her friends watched, Lila practiced her gymnastics routine.

QUICK HELP

Editing for Commas

Research for this book shows that five of the twenty most common errors in college writing involve commas. Check your writing for the following errors:

1. Check every sentence that doesn't begin with the subject to see whether it opens with an introductory element (a word, phrase, or clause that describes the subject or tells when, where, how, or why the main action of the sentence occurs). In these cases, use a comma to separate the introductory material from the main part of the sentence. (47a)

2. Look at every sentence that contains one of the conjunctions *and*, *but*, *or*, *nor*, *for*, *so*, or *yet*. If the groups of words both before and after the conjunction function as complete sentences, you have a compound sentence. Make sure to use a comma before the conjunction. (47b)

3. Look at each adjective clause beginning with *which*, *who*, *whom*, *whose*, *when*, or *where*, and at each phrase and appositive. (37e) Is the element essential to the meaning of the sentence? If the sentence would be unclear without it, do not set off the element with commas. (47c)

4. Make sure that adjective clauses beginning with *that* are not set off with commas. Do not use commas between subjects and verbs, verbs and objects or complements, or prepositions and objects; to separate parts of compound constructions other than compound sentences; to set off restrictive clauses; or before the first or after the last item in a series. (47c and d)

5. Do not use a comma alone to separate sentences; this would create a comma splice (see Chapter 45).

▶ If candidates expect to be taken seriously, they should suggest solutions for the problems of ordinary Americans.

Some writers omit the comma if the introductory element is short and does not seem to require a pause after it.

▶ *At the racetrack* Henry lost his entire paycheck.

However, you will seldom be wrong if you use a comma after an introductory element.

47b   Use commas with conjunctions that join clauses in compound sentences.

A comma usually precedes a coordinating conjunction (*and, but, or, nor, for, so,* or *yet*) that joins two independent clauses in a compound sentence (37e).

▶ The title sounds impressive, but *administrative clerk* is just another word for *photocopier.*

▶ The show started at last, and the crowd grew quiet.

With very short clauses, you can sometimes omit the comma.

▶ She saw her chance and she took it.

Always use the comma if there is any chance the sentence will be misread without it.

▶ I opened the junk drawer, and the cabinet door jammed.

Use a semicolon rather than a comma when the clauses are long and complex or contain their own commas.

▶ When these early migrations took place, the ice was still confined to the lands in the far north; but eight hundred thousand years ago, when man was already established in the temperate latitudes, the ice moved southward until it covered large parts of Europe and Asia.
— ROBERT JASTROW, *Until the Sun Dies*

47c   Use commas to set off nonrestrictive elements.

Nonrestrictive elements are word groups that do not limit, or restrict, the meaning of the noun or pronoun they modify. Setting nonrestrictive elements off with commas shows your readers that the information is not essential to the meaning of the sentence. Restrictive elements, on the other hand, *are* essential to meaning and should *not* be set off with commas. The same sentence may mean different things with and without the commas:

▶ The bus drivers rejecting the management offer remained on strike.
▶ The bus drivers, rejecting the management offer, remained on strike.

The first sentence says that only *some* bus drivers, the ones rejecting the offer, remained on strike. The second says that *all* the drivers did.

Since the decision to include or omit commas affects how readers interpret your sentence, you should think especially carefully about what you mean and use commas (or omit them) accordingly.

RESTRICTIVE   Drivers *who have been convicted of drunken driving* should lose their licenses.

In the preceding sentence, the clause *who have been convicted of drunken driving* is essential because it explains that only drivers who have been convicted of drunken driving should lose their licenses. Therefore, it is *not* set off with commas.

NONRESTRICTIVE   The two drivers involved in the accident, *who have been convicted of drunken driving,* should lose their licenses.

In the second sentence, however, the clause *who have been convicted of drunken driving* is not essential to the meaning because it merely provides more information about what it modifies, *The two drivers involved in the accident.* Therefore, the clause is set off with commas.

To decide whether an element is restrictive or nonrestrictive, read the sentence without the element, and see if the deletion changes the meaning of the rest of the sentence.

- If the deletion does change the meaning, the element is probably restrictive, and you should not set it off with commas.
- If it does not change the meaning, the element is probably nonrestrictive and requires commas.

Adjective and adverb clauses

An adjective clause that begins with *that* is always restrictive; do not set it off with commas. An adjective clause beginning with *which* may be either restrictive or nonrestrictive; however, some writers prefer to use *which* only for nonrestrictive clauses, which they set off with commas.

RESTRICTIVE CLAUSES

▶ The claim *that men like seriously to battle one another to some sort of finish* is a myth.
    – JOHN MCMURTRY, "Kill 'Em! Crush 'Em! Eat 'Em Raw!"

The *that* clause is necessary to the meaning because it explains which claim is a myth; therefore, the clause is not set off with commas.

▶ The man / who rescued Jana's puppy / won her eternal gratitude.

The *who* clause is necessary to the meaning because only the man who rescued the puppy won the gratitude; therefore, the clause takes no commas.

NONRESTRICTIVE CLAUSES

▶ I borrowed books from the rental library of Shakespeare and Company, *which was the library and bookstore of Sylvia Beach at 12 rue de l'Odeon.*   — ERNEST HEMINGWAY, *A Moveable Feast*

The clause describing Shakespeare and Company is not necessary to the meaning of the sentence and therefore is set off with a comma.

In general, set off an adverb clause that follows a main clause only if it begins with *although, even though, while,* or another subordinating conjunction expressing contrast.

▶ He uses semicolons frequently, while she prefers periods and short

   sentences.

The clause *while she prefers periods and short sentences* expresses contrast; therefore, it is set off with a comma.

Do *not* set off any other adverb clause that follows a main clause.

▶ Remember to check your calculations / before you submit the form.

Phrases

Participial phrases may be restrictive or nonrestrictive. Prepositional phrases are usually restrictive, but sometimes they are not essential to the meaning of a sentence and are set off with commas (37d).

NONRESTRICTIVE PHRASES

▶ Frédéric Chopin, in poor health, still composed prolifically.

The phrase *in poor health* does not limit the meaning of *Frédéric Chopin* and so is set off with commas.

Appositives

An appositive renames a nearby noun (37d). When an appositive is not essential to identify what it renames, it is set off with commas.

NONRESTRICTIVE APPOSITIVES

▶ Jon Stewart‸ an actor and comic‸ became a respected political commentator.

Jon Stewart's name identifies him; the appositive *an actor and comic* provides extra information.

RESTRICTIVE APPOSITIVES

▶ Mozart's opera/*The Marriage of Figaro*/was considered revolutionary.

The appositive is restrictive because Mozart wrote more than one opera.

47d Use commas with items in a series.

▶ **He has plundered our seas, ravaged our coasts, burnt our towns, and destroyed the lives of our people.** – Declaration of Independence

You may see a series with no comma after the next-to-last item, particularly in newspaper writing. Occasionally, however, omitting the comma can cause confusion.

▶ **All the cafeteria's vegetables—broccoli, green beans, peas‸ and carrots—were cooked to a gray mush.**

Without the comma after *peas,* you wouldn't know if there were three choices (the third being a *mixture* of peas and carrots) or four.

When the items in a series contain commas of their own or other punctuation, separate them with semicolons rather than commas (48b).

Coordinate adjectives, those that relate equally to the noun they modify, should be separated by commas.

▶ **The long‸ twisting‸ muddy road led to a shack in the woods.**

In a sentence like *The cracked bathroom mirror reflected his face,* however, *cracked* and *bathroom* are not coordinate because *bathroom mirror* is the equivalent of a single word, which is modified by *cracked.* Hence, they are *not* separated by commas.

You can usually determine whether adjectives are coordinate by inserting *and* between them. If the sentence makes sense with the *and,* the adjectives are coordinate and should be separated by commas.

▶ They are sincere *and* talented *and* inquisitive researchers.

The sentence makes sense with the *and*s, so the adjectives should be separated by commas: *They are sincere, talented, inquisitive researchers.*

▶ Byron carried an elegant *and* pocket watch.

The sentence does not make sense with *and*, so the adjectives *elegant* and *pocket* should not be separated by commas: *Byron carried an elegant pocket watch.*

47e Use commas to set off parenthetical and transitional expressions.

Parenthetical expressions add comments or information. Because they often interrupt the flow of a sentence or digress, they are usually set off with commas.

▶ Some studies have shown that chocolate, of all things, helps to prevent tooth decay.

▶ Roald Dahl's stories, it turns out, were often inspired by his own childhood.

Transitional expressions, conjunctive adverbs (words such as *however* and *furthermore*), and other words and phrases used to connect parts of sentences are usually set off with commas (6e).

▶ Ozone is a by-product of dry cleaning, for example.

▶ Ceiling fans are, moreover, less expensive than air conditioners.

47f Use commas to set off contrasting elements, interjections, direct address, and tag questions.

CONTRASTING ELEMENTS

▶ On official business it was she, *not my father*, one would usually hear on the phone or in stores.
　　　　– RICHARD RODRIGUEZ, "Aria: A Memoir of a Bilingual Childhood"

INTERJECTIONS

▶ *My God*, who wouldn't want a wife?
　　　　　　　　　　　　– JUDY BRADY, "I Want a Wife"

DIRECT ADDRESS

▶ Remember, *sir,* that you are under oath.

TAG QUESTIONS

▶ The governor did not veto the unemployment bill, *did she*?

 47g Use commas with dates, addresses, titles, and numbers.

Dates

Use a comma between the day of the week and the month, between the day of the month and the year, and between the year and the rest of the sentence, if any.

▶ The attacks on the morning of Tuesday, September 11, 2001, took the United States by surprise.

Do not use commas with dates in inverted order or with dates consisting of only the month and the year.

▶ She dated the letter *26 August 2015*.
▶ Thousands of Germans swarmed over the wall in *November 1989*.

Addresses and place-names

Use a comma after each part of an address or place-name, including the state if there is no ZIP code. Do not precede a ZIP code with a comma.

▶ Forward my mail to the Department of English, The Ohio State University, Columbus, Ohio 43210.

▶ Portland, Oregon, is much larger than Portland, Maine.

Titles

Use commas to set off a title such as *MD* or *PhD* from the name preceding it and from the rest of the sentence. The titles *Jr.* and *Sr.*, however, often appear without commas.

▶ Oliver Sacks, MD, has written about the way the mind works.

▶ Martin Luther King Jr. was one of the twentieth century's greatest orators.

Numbers

In numerals of five digits or more, use a comma between each group of three, starting from the right.

▶ **The city's population rose to *158,000* in the 2000 census.**

The comma is optional within numerals of four digits but never occurs in four-digit dates, street addresses, or page numbers.

▶ **The college had an enrollment of *1,789* [or *1789*] in the fall of 2008.**

▶ **My grandparents live at *2428* Loring Place.**

▶ **Turn to page *1566*.**

47h Use commas to set off most quotations.

Commas set off a quotation from words used to introduce or identify the source of the quotation. A comma following a quotation goes inside the closing quotation mark. (See 52d for advice about using colons instead of commas to introduce quotations.)

▶ **A German proverb warns, "Go to law for a sheep, and lose your cow."**

▶ **"All I know about grammar, " said Joan Didion, "is its infinite power."**

Do not use a comma after a question mark or exclamation point.

▶ **"What's a thousand dollars?/" asks Groucho Marx in Cocoanuts. "Mere chicken feed. A poultry matter."**

▶ **"Out, damned spot!/" cries Lady Macbeth.**

Do not use a comma when you introduce a quotation with *that*.

▶ **The writer of Ecclesiastes concludes that/ "all is vanity."**

Do not use a comma before an indirect quotation—one that does not use the speaker's exact words.

▶ **Patrick Henry declared/ that he wanted either liberty or death.**

47i Use commas to prevent confusion.

Sometimes commas are necessary to make sentences easier to read or understand.

▶ The members of the dance troupe strutted in͵ in matching costumes.

▶ Before͵ I had planned to major in biology.

 47j **Eliminate unnecessary commas.**

Excessive use of commas can spoil an otherwise fine sentence.

Around restrictive elements

Do not use commas to set off restrictive elements—elements that limit, or define, the meaning of the words they modify or refer to (47c).

▶ I don't let my children watch films/that are violent.

▶ A law/reforming campaign financing/was passed in 2002.

▶ My only defense/against my allergies/is to stay indoors.

▶ The actor/Chiwetel Ejiofor/might win this award.

Between subjects and verbs, verbs and objects or complements, and prepositions and objects

Do not use a comma between a subject and its verb, a verb and its object or complement, or a preposition and its object. This rule holds true even if the subject, object, or complement is a long phrase or clause.

▶ Watching movies late at night/is a way for me to relax.

▶ Parents must decide/how much television their children may watch.

▶ The winner of/the community-service award stepped forward.

In compound constructions

In compound constructions (other than compound sentences—see 47b), do not use a comma before or after a coordinating conjunction that joins the two parts.

▶ Improved health care/and more free trade were two of the administration's goals.

The *and* here joins parts of a compound subject, which should not be separated by a comma.

▶ **Donald Trump was born rich/and used his money to make more money.**

The *and* here joins parts of a compound predicate, which should not be separated by a comma.

Before the first or after the last item in a series

▶ **The auction included/furniture, paintings, and china.**

▶ **The swimmer took slow, elegant, powerful/strokes.**

48 Semicolons

The following public-service announcement, posted in New York City subway cars, reminded commuters what to do with a used newspaper at the end of the ride:

> Please put it in a trash can; that's good news for everyone.

The semicolon in the subway announcement separates two clauses that could have been written as separate sentences. Semicolons, which create a pause stronger than that of a comma but not as strong as the full pause of a period, show close connections between related ideas.

48a Use semicolons to link independent clauses.

Though a comma and a coordinating conjunction often join independent clauses, semicolons provide writers with subtler ways of signaling closely related clauses. The clause following a semicolon often restates an idea expressed in the first clause; it sometimes expands on or presents a contrast to the first.

▶ **Immigration acts were passed; newcomers had to prove, besides moral correctness and financial solvency, their ability to read.**
— MARY GORDON, "More Than Just a Shrine"

Gordon uses a semicolon to join the two clauses, giving the sentence an abrupt rhythm that suits the topic: laws that imposed strict requirements.

A semicolon should link independent clauses joined by conjunctive adverbs such as *therefore, however,* and *indeed* or transitional expressions such as *in fact, in addition,* and *for example* (36g).

▶ **The circus comes as close to being the world in microcosm as anything I know; in a way, it puts all the rest of show business in the shade.**
— E. B. WHITE, "The Ring of Time"

If two independent clauses joined by a coordinating conjunction contain commas, you may use a semicolon instead of a comma before the conjunction to make the sentence easier to read.

▶ **Every year, whether the Republican or the Democratic party is in office, more and more power drains away from the individual to feed vast reservoirs in far-off places; and we have less and less say about the shape of events which shape our future.**
— WILLIAM F. BUCKLEY JR., "Why Don't We Complain?"

48b Use semicolons to separate items in a series containing other punctuation.

Ordinarily, commas separate items in a series (47d). But when the items themselves contain commas or other marks of punctuation, using semicolons to separate the items will make the sentence clearer and easier to read.

▶ **Anthropology encompasses archeology, the study of ancient civilizations through artifacts; linguistics, the study of the structure and development of language; and cultural anthropology, the study of language, customs, and behavior.**

QUICK HELP

Editing for Semicolons

- If you use semicolons, be sure they appear only between independent clauses — groups of words that can stand alone as sentences (48a) — or between items in a series. (48b)
- If you find few or no semicolons in your writing, ask yourself whether you should add some. Would any closely related ideas in two sentences be better expressed in one sentence with a semicolon? (48a)

48c Revise misused semicolons.

A comma, not a semicolon, should separate an independent clause from a dependent clause or phrase.

- **The police found fingerprints;, which they used to identify the thief.**
- **The new system would encourage students to register for courses online;, thus streamlining registration.**

A colon, not a semicolon, should introduce a series or list.

- **The reunion tour includes the following bands;: Urban Waste, Murphy's Law, Rapid Deployment, and Ism.**

49 End Punctuation

Periods, question marks, and exclamation points often appear in advertising to create special effects or draw readers along from line to line.

You have a choice to make.
Where can you turn for advice?
Ask our experts today!

QUICK HELP

Editing for End Punctuation

- If all or almost all of your sentences end with periods, see if some of them might be phrased more effectively as questions or exclamations. (49a–c)
- Check to be sure you use question marks appropriately. (49b)
- If you use exclamation points, consider whether each is justified. Does the sentence call for extra emphasis? If in doubt, use a period instead. (49c)

End punctuation tells us how to read each sentence—as a matter-of-fact statement, a query, or an emphatic request. Making appropriate choices with end punctuation allows readers to understand exactly what you mean.

49a Use periods appropriately.

Use a period to close sentences that make statements or give mild commands.

▶ **All books are either dreams or swords.** – AMY LOWELL

▶ **Don't use a fancy word if a simpler word will do.**
         – GEORGE ORWELL, "Politics and the English Language"

A period also closes indirect questions, which report rather than ask questions.

▶ **I asked how old the child was.**

▶ **We all wonder who will win the election.**

Until recently, periods have been used with most abbreviations in American English (see Chapter 54). However, more and more abbreviations are appearing without periods.

Mr.	MD	BC *or* B.C.
Ms.	PhD	BCE *or* B.C.E.
Mrs.	MBA	AD *or* A.D.
Jr.	RN	AM *or* a.m.
Dr	Sen	PM *or* p.m.

Some abbreviations rarely if ever appear with periods. These include the postal abbreviations of state names, such as *FL* and *TN* (though the traditional abbreviations, such as *Fla.* and *Tenn.,* do call for periods), and most groups of initials (*GE, CIA, AIDS, UNICEF*). If you are not sure whether a particular abbreviation should include periods, check a dictionary, or follow the style guidelines (such as those of the Modern Language Association) you are using in a research paper.

49b Use question marks appropriately.

Use a question mark to close sentences that ask direct questions.

▶ **Have you finished the essay, or do you need more time?**

Question marks do not close *indirect* questions, which report rather than ask questions.

> ► She asked whether I opposed his nomination?.

Do not use a comma or a period immediately after a question mark that ends a direct quotation (51f).

> ► "Am I my brother's keeper?/" Cain asked.

> ► Cain asked, "Am I my brother's keeper?"/

Questions in a series may have question marks even when they are not separate sentences.

> ► I often confront a difficult choice: should I go to practice? finish my homework? spend time with my friends?

A question mark in parentheses can be used to indicate that a writer is unsure of a date, a figure, or a word.

> ► Quintilian died in 96 CE (?).

49c Use exclamation points appropriately.

Use an exclamation point to show surprise or strong emotion.

> ► In those few moments of geologic time will be the story of all that has happened since we became a nation. And what a story it will be!
> — JAMES RETTIE, "But a Watch in the Night"

Today, we live in a world of many exclamations. But use exclamation points sparingly in academic work because they can distract your readers or suggest that you are exaggerating. In general, try to create emphasis through diction and sentence structure rather than with exclamation points.

> ► This university is so large, so varied, that attempting to tell someone everything about it would take three years!.

Do not use a comma or a period after an exclamation point that ends a direct quotation.

> ► On my last visit, I looked out the sliding glass doors and ran breathlessly to Connor in the kitchen: "There's a *huge* black pig in the backyard!"/   — ELLEN ASHDOWN, "Living by the Dead"

49d Consider end punctuation in informal writing.

In informal writing, especially texts and tweets with character limits, writers today are increasingly likely to omit end punctuation entirely. In informal writing that does use end punctuation, research shows that ellipses (. . .), or "dots," are on the rise; they can signal a trailing off of a thought or leave open the possibility of further communication. Exclamation marks can convey an excited or a chatty tone, so they are used more frequently in social media and other informal writing situations than in academic writing. And some writers have argued that ending informal writing with a period rather than no punctuation at all can suggest that the writer is irritated. The meaning of end punctuation is changing in informal contexts, so pay attention to how others communicate, and use what you learn in your own social writing.

Apostrophes 50

The little apostrophe can make a big difference in meaning. The following sign at a neighborhood swimming pool, for instance, says something different from what the writer probably intended:

> Please deposit your garbage (and your guests) in the trash receptacles before leaving the pool area.

The sign indicates that guests should be put in the trash. Adding a single apostrophe would offer a more neighborly statement: *Please deposit your garbage (and your guests') in the trash receptacles before leaving the pool area* asks that the guests' garbage, not the guests themselves, be thrown away.

50a Use apostrophes appropriately to show possession.

The possessive case denotes ownership or possession of one thing by another.

QUICK HELP

Editing for Apostrophes

- Check each noun that ends in *-s* and shows possession. Is the apostrophe in the right place, either before or after the *-s*? (50a)
- Check the possessive form of each indefinite pronoun, such as *someone's*. Be sure the apostrophe comes before the *-s*. (50a)
- Check each personal pronoun that ends with *-s* (*yours, his, hers, its, ours, theirs*) to make sure it does not include an apostrophe. (50a)
- Does each *it's* mean *it is* or *it has*? If not, remove the apostrophe. (50b)
- Make sure other contractions use apostrophes correctly. (50b)

Singular nouns and indefinite pronouns

Add an apostrophe and *-s* to form the possessive of most singular nouns, including those that end in *-s*, and of indefinite pronouns (36c). Do not use apostrophes with the possessive forms of personal pronouns: *yours, his, hers, its, ours, theirs*.

▶ The *bus's* fumes overpowered her.

▶ *Star Wars* made George *Lucas's* fortune.

▶ *Anyone's* guess is as good as mine.

Plural nouns

To form the possessive case of plural nouns not ending in *-s*, add an apostrophe and *-s*.

▶ The *men's* department sells business attire.

For plural nouns ending in *-s*, add only the apostrophe.

▶ The three *clowns'* costumes were bright green and orange.

Compound nouns

For compound nouns, make the last word in the group possessive.

▶ The *secretary of state's* speech was televised.

▶ My *in-laws'* disapproval dampened our enthusiasm for the new house.

Two or more nouns

To signal individual possession by two or more owners, make each noun possessive.

▶ **Great differences exist between** *Jerry Bruckheimer's* **and** *Ridley Scott's* **films.**

Bruckheimer and Scott have produced different films.

To signal joint possession, make only the last noun possessive.

▶ *Wallace and Gromit's* **creator is Nick Park.**

Wallace and Gromit have the same creator.

50b   Use apostrophes in contractions.

Contractions are two-word combinations formed by leaving out certain letters, which are indicated by an apostrophe.

it is, it has/it's	I would, I had/I'd	will not/won't
was not/wasn't	he would, he had/he'd	let us/let's
I am/I'm	would not/wouldn't	cannot/can't
he is, he has/he's	do not/don't	who is, who
you will/you'll	does not/doesn't	has/who's

Contractions are common in conversation and informal writing. Academic and professional work, however, often calls for greater formality.

Use of it's *and* its

Its is the possessive form of *it*. *It's* is a contraction for *it is* or *it has*.

▶ **This disease is unusual;** *its* **symptoms vary from person to person.**

▶ *It's* **a difficult disease to diagnose.**

50c   Avoid apostrophes in most plural forms.

Many style guides now advise against using apostrophes for any plurals.

▶ **The gymnasts need marks of** *8s* **and** *9s* **to qualify for the finals.**

Others use an apostrophe and *-s* to form the plural of numbers, letters, and words referred to as terms.

▶ **The five** *Shakespeare's* **in the essay were spelled five different ways.**

Check your instructor's preference.

51 Quotation Marks

As a way of bringing other people's words into your own, quotations can be a powerful writing tool.

Mrs. Macken encourages parents to get books for their children, to read to them when they are "li'l," and when they start school to make certain they attend regularly. She holds herself up as an example of "a millhand's daughter who wanted to be a schoolteacher and did it through sheer hard work."
— SHIRLEY BRICE HEATH, *Ways with Words*

The writer lets her subject speak for herself—and lets readers hear Mrs. Macken's voice.

51a Use quotation marks to identify direct quotations.

▶ The president asked Congress to "try common sense."

▶ She smiled and said, "Son, this is one incident that I will never forget."

Use quotation marks to enclose the words of each speaker within running dialogue. Mark each shift between speakers with a new paragraph.

"I want no proof of their affection," said Elinor; "but of their engagement I do."
"I am perfectly satisfied of both."
"Yet not a syllable has been said to you on the subject, by either of them." — JANE AUSTEN, *Sense and Sensibility*

Use single quotation marks for a quotation within a quotation. Open and close the quoted passage with double quotation marks, and change any quotation marks that appear *within* the quotation to single quotation marks.

▶ Baldwin says, "The title 'The Uses of the Blues' does not refer to music; I don't know anything about music."

> **QUICK HELP**
>
> **Editing for Quotation Marks**
>
> - Use quotation marks around direct quotations and titles of short works. (51a and c)
> - Do not use quotation marks around set-off quotations of more than four lines of prose or more than three lines of poetry, or around titles of long works. Consult a style guide, such as that of the Modern Language Association (MLA), for guidelines. (51b and c)
> - Use quotation marks to signal irony and invented words, but do so sparingly. (51e)
> - Check other punctuation used with closing quotation marks. (51f)
>
>   Periods and commas should be *inside* the quotation marks.
>
>   Colons, semicolons, and footnote numbers should be *outside*.
>
>   Question marks, exclamation points, and dashes should be *inside* if they are part of the quoted material, *outside* if they are not.
> - Never use quotation marks around indirect quotations. (51g)
> - Do not use quotation marks just to add emphasis to words. (51g)

51b Punctuate block quotations and poetry appropriately.

If the prose passage you wish to quote is more than four typed lines, set the quotation off by starting it on a new line and indenting it one inch from the left margin. This format, known as block quotation, does not require quotation marks.

> In "Suspended," Joy Harjo tells of her first awareness of jazz as a child:
>
> > My rite of passage into the world of humanity occurred then, via jazz. The music made a startling bridge between the familiar and strange lands, an appropriate vehicle, for . . . we were there when jazz was born. I recognized it, that humid afternoon in my formative years, as a way to speak beyond the confines of ordinary language. I still hear it. (84)

This block quotation, including the ellipsis dots and the page number in parentheses at the end, follows the style of the Modern Language Association (MLA). The American Psychological Association (APA) has different guidelines for setting off block quotations. (See Chapters 57 and 61.)

When quoting poetry, if the quotation is brief (fewer than four lines), include it within your text. Separate the lines of the poem with slashes, each preceded and followed by a space, in order to tell the reader where one line of the poem ends and the next begins.

> In one of his best-known poems, Robert Frost remarks, "Two roads diverged in a yellow wood, and I — / I took the one less traveled by / And that has made all the difference" (lines 18–20).

To quote more than three lines of poetry, indent the block one inch from the left margin. Do not use quotation marks. Take care to follow the spacing, capitalization, punctuation, and other features of the original poem.

> The duke in Robert Browning's poem "My Last Duchess" is clearly a jealous, vain person, whose arrogance is illustrated through this statement:
>
> > She thanked men — good! but thanked
> > Somehow — I know not how — as if she ranked
> > My gift of a nine-hundred-years-old name
> > With anybody's gift. (lines 31–34)

51c   Use quotation marks for titles of short works.

Quotation marks are used to enclose the titles of short poems, short stories, articles, essays, songs, sections of books, and episodes of television and radio programs.

▶ **"Dover Beach" moves from calmness to sadness.** [poem]
▶ **Alice Walker's "Everyday Use" is about more than just quilts.** [short story]
▶ **The *Atlantic* published an article entitled "Illiberal Education."** [article]
▶ **In "Photography," Susan Sontag considers the role of photography in our society.** [essay]
▶ **The *Nature* episode "Echo of the Elephants" portrays ivory hunters unfavorably.** [television series episode]

Use italics rather than quotation marks for the titles of television series, magazines, movies, and other long works (see 55a).

51d Use quotation marks appropriately for definitions.

▶ In social science, the term *sample size* means "the number of individuals being studied in a research project."
— Kathleen Stassen Berger and Ross A. Thompson,
The Developing Person through Childhood and Adolescence

Use italics for words used as a term, like *sample size* above (see 55b).

51e Use quotation marks to identify irony and invented terms.

To show readers that you are using a word or phrase ironically or that you made it up, enclose it in quotation marks.

▶ The "banquet" consisted of dried-out chicken and canned vegetables.

The quotation marks suggest that the meal was anything but a banquet.

▶ Your whole first paragraph or first page may have to be guillotined in any case after your piece is finished: it is a kind of "forebirth."
— Jacques Barzun, "A Writer's Discipline"

The writer made up the term *forebirth.*

51f Follow conventions for other punctuation with quotation marks.

Periods and commas go *inside* closing quotation marks.

▶ "Don't compromise yourself," said Janis Joplin. "You are all you've got."

When you follow MLA style for documenting a short quotation, place the period *after* the parentheses with source information (see Chapter 58).

▶ In places, de Beauvoir "sees Marxists as believing in subjectivity" (Whitmarsh 63).

For more information on using a comma with a quotation, see 47h.

Colons, semicolons, and footnote numbers go *outside* closing quotation marks.

▶ I felt one emotion after finishing "Eveline": sorrow.

▶ Everything is dark, and "a visionary light settles in her eyes"; this vision, this light, is her salvation.

▶ Tragedy is defined by Aristotle as "an imitation of an action that is serious and of a certain magnitude."[1]

Question marks, exclamation points, and dashes go *inside* if they are part of the quoted material, *outside* if they are not.

PART OF THE QUOTATION

▶ The cashier asked, "Would you like to super-size that?"

▶ "Jump!" one of the firefighters shouted.

NOT PART OF THE QUOTATION

▶ What is the theme of "The Birth-Mark"?

▶ "Break a leg"—that phrase is supposed to bring good luck.

51g Revise misused quotation marks.

Do not use quotation marks for indirect quotations—those that do not use someone's exact words.

▶ Our mother told us that ⸤she was sure she would never forget the incident.⸥

Do not use quotation marks just to add emphasis to particular words or phrases.

▶ Michael said that his views might not be ⸤politically correct⸥ but that he wasn't going to change them for anything.

▶ Much time was spent speculating about their ⸤relationship.⸥

Do not use quotation marks around slang or colloquial language; they create the impression that you are apologizing for using those words. If you have a good reason to use slang or a colloquial term, use it without quotation marks.

▶ After our twenty-mile hike, we were ready to ⸤turn in.⸥

> **FOR MULTILINGUAL WRITERS**
>
> **Multilingual** **Quoting in American English**
>
> Remember that the way you mark quotations in American English (" ") may not be the same as in other languages. In French, for example, quotations are marked with *guillemets* or angle quotes (« »), while in German, quotations take split-level marks („ "). Writers of British English use single quotation marks first and, when necessary, double quotation marks for quotations within quotations. If you are writing for an American audience, be careful to follow the U.S. conventions governing quotation marks.

Other Punctuation Marks 52

P arentheses, brackets, dashes, colons, slashes, and ellipses are everywhere. Every URL includes colons and slashes, and dashes and ellipses are increasingly common in writing that expresses conversational informality.

You can also use these punctuation marks for more formal purposes: to signal relationships among parts of sentences, to create particular rhythms, and to help readers follow your thoughts.

52a Use parentheses appropriately.

Use parentheses to enclose material that is of minor or secondary importance in a sentence—material that supplements, clarifies, comments on, or illustrates what precedes or follows it.

> ▶ Inventors and men of genius have almost always been regarded as fools at the beginning (and very often at the end) of their careers.
> — FYODOR DOSTOYEVSKY

> ▶ During my research, I found problems with the flat-rate income tax (a single-rate tax with no deductions).

Textual citations

> ▶ Freud and his followers have had a most significant impact on the ways abnormal functioning is understood and treated (Joseph, 1991).
> — RONALD J. COMER, *Abnormal Psychology*

> ▶ Zamora notes that Kahlo referred to her first self-portrait, given to a close friend, as "your Botticelli" (110).

The first in-text citation shows the style of the American Psychological Association (APA); the second, the style of the Modern Language Association (MLA).

Numbers or letters in a list

> ▶ Five distinct styles can be distinguished: (1) Old New England, (2) Deep South, (3) Middle American, (4) Wild West, and (5) Far West or Californian. — ALISON LURIE, *The Language of Clothes*

Other punctuation marks with parentheses

A period may be placed either inside or outside a closing parenthesis, depending on whether the parenthetical text is part of a larger sentence. A comma, if needed, is always placed *outside* a closing parenthesis (and never before an opening one).

> ▶ Gene Tunney's single defeat in an eleven-year career was to a flamboyant and dangerous fighter named Harry Greb ("The Human Windmill"), who seems to have been, judging from boxing literature, the dirtiest fighter in history. — JOYCE CAROL OATES, "On Boxing"

Parentheses, commas, and dashes

In general, use commas when the material to be set off is least interruptive (47c, e, and f), parentheses when it is more interruptive, and dashes when it is the most interruptive (52c).

52b Use brackets appropriately.

Use brackets to enclose parenthetical elements in material that is itself within parentheses and to enclose explanatory words or comments that you are inserting into a quotation.

Material within parentheses

> ▶ Eventually the investigation had to examine the major agencies (including the previously sacrosanct National Security Agency [NSA]) that were conducting covert operations.

Material within quotations

> ▶ Massing notes that "on average, it [Fox News] attracts more than eight million people daily—more than double the number who watch CNN."

The bracketed words *Fox News* clarify what *it* refers to in the original quotation.

In the quotation in the following sentence, the artist Gauguin's name is misspelled. The bracketed word *sic,* which means "so," tells readers that the person being quoted—not the writer who has picked up the quotation—made the mistake.

▶ **One admirer wrote, "She was the most striking woman I'd ever seen—a sort of wonderful combination of Mia Farrow and one of Gaugin's [*sic*] Polynesian nymphs."**

52c Use dashes appropriately.

Dashes give more emphasis than parentheses to the material they enclose. Many word-processing programs automatically convert two typed hyphens into a solid dash.

▶ **The pleasures of reading itself—who doesn't remember?—were like those of Christmas cake, a sweet devouring.**
—EUDORA WELTY, "A Sweet Devouring"

Explanatory material

▶ **Indeed, several of modern India's greatest scholars—such as the Mughal historian Muzaffar Alam of the University of Chicago—are madrasa graduates.** —WILLIAM DALRYMPLE

Material at the end of a sentence

▶ **In the twentieth century it has become almost impossible to moralize about epidemics—except those which are transmitted sexually.**
—SUSAN SONTAG, *AIDS and Its Metaphors*

A sudden change in tone

▶ **New York is a catastrophe—but a magnificent catastrophe.**
—LE CORBUSIER

Summary or explanation

▶ **In walking, the average adult person employs a motor mechanism that weighs about eighty pounds—sixty pounds of muscle and twenty pounds of bone.** —EDWIN WAY TEALE

Hesitation in speech

▶ As the officer approached his car, the driver stammered, "What — what have I done?"

52d Use colons appropriately.

Use a colon to introduce explanations or examples and to separate some elements from one another.

Explanation, example, or appositive

▶ The men may also wear the getup known as Sun Belt Cool: a pale beige suit, open-collared shirt (often in a darker shade than the suit), cream-colored loafers and aviator sunglasses.
– ALISON LURIE, *The Language of Clothes*

Series, list, or quotation

▶ At the baby's one-month birthday party, Ah Po gave him the Four Valuable Things: ink, inkslab, paper, and brush.
– MAXINE HONG KINGSTON, *China Men*

▶ The teachers wondered: "Do boys and girls really learn differently?"

The preceding example could have taken a comma instead of a colon (see 47h). Use a colon rather than a comma to introduce a quotation when the lead-in is a complete sentence on its own.

▶ The State of the Union address contained one surprising statement: "America is addicted to oil."

Colons with other elements

SALUTATIONS IN FORMAL LETTERS

▶ Dear Dr. Chapman:

BIBLICAL CHAPTERS AND VERSES

▶ I Corinthians 3:3–5

HOURS, MINUTES, AND SECONDS

▶ 4:59 PM
▶ 2:15:06

TITLES AND SUBTITLES

▶ *The Joy of Insight:*
Passions of a Physicist

RATIOS

▶ a ratio of 5:1

CITIES AND PUBLISHERS IN
BIBLIOGRAPHIC ENTRIES

▶ Boston: Bedford, 2015

Unnecessary colons

Do not put a colon between a verb and its object or complement—
unless the object is a quotation.

▶ Some natural fibers are: cotton, wool, silk, and linen.

Do not put a colon between a preposition and its object or after such
expressions as *such as, especially,* and *including.*

▶ In poetry, additional power may come from devices such as: simile,
metaphor, and alliteration.

52e Use slashes appropriately.

Use a slash to separate alternatives.

▶ Then there was Daryl, the cabdriver/bartender.
> — JOHN L'HEUREUX, *The Handmaid of Desire*

Use slashes to mark line divisions between two or three lines of
poetry quoted within running text. When using a slash to separate
lines of poetry, precede and follow it with a space (51b).

▶ In Sonnet 29, the persona states, "For thy sweet love rememb'red
such wealth brings / That then I scorn to change my state with kings."

Slashes also separate parts of fractions and Internet addresses.

52f Use ellipses appropriately.

Ellipses, or ellipsis points, are three equally spaced dots. Ellipses
usually indicate that something has been omitted from a quoted passage, but they can also signal a pause or hesitation in speech in the
same way that a dash can.

Omissions

Just as you should carefully use quotation marks around any material that you quote directly from a source, so you should carefully
use ellipses to indicate that you have left out part of a quotation that
otherwise appears to be a complete sentence.

The ellipses in the following example indicate two omissions—one in the middle of the sentence and one at the end. When you omit the last part of a quoted sentence, add a period after the ellipses, for a total of four dots. Be sure a complete sentence comes before and after the four points. If you are adding your own ellipses to a quotation that already has other ellipses, enclose yours in brackets.

ORIGINAL TEXT

▶ The quasi-official division of the population into three economic classes called high-, middle-, and low-income groups rather misses the point, because as a class indicator the amount of money is not as important as the source.   – PAUL FUSSELL, "Notes on Class"

WITH ELLIPSES

▶ As Paul Fussell argues, "The quasi-official division of the population into three economic classes . . . rather misses the point. . . ."

If your shortened quotation ends with a source (such as a page number, a name, or a title), follow these steps:

1. Use three ellipsis points but no period after the quotation.
2. Add the closing quotation mark, closed up to the third ellipsis point.
3. Add the source documentation in parentheses.
4. Use a period to indicate the end of the sentence.

▶ Packer argues, "The Administration is right to reconsider its strategy . . ." (34).

Hesitation

▶ Then the voice, husky and familiar, came to wash over us—"The winnah, and still heavyweight champeen of the world . . . Joe Louis."
          – MAYA ANGELOU, *I Know Why the Caged Bird Sings*

53   Capital Letters

Capital letters are a key signal in everyday life. Look around any store to see their importance: you can shop for Levi's or *any* blue jeans, for Coca-Cola or *any* cola, for Kleenex or *any* tissue. As these examples show, one of the most common reasons for capitalizing a word is to indicate that it is part of a name or title—of a brand, person, article, or something else.

QUICK HELP

Editing for Capitalization

- Capitalize the first word of each sentence. If you quote a poem, follow its original capitalization. (53a)
- Check to make sure you have appropriately capitalized proper nouns and proper adjectives. (53b)
- Review where you have used titles of people or of works to be sure you have capitalized them correctly. (53b and c)
- Double-check the capitalization of geographical directions (*north* or *North*?), family relationships (*dad* or *Dad*?), and seasons of the year (*winter*, not *Winter*). (53d)

53a Capitalize the first word of a sentence or line of poetry.

Capitalize the first word of a sentence. If you are quoting a full sentence, capitalize the first word of the quotation.

 Kennedy said, "Let us never negotiate out of fear."

Capitalization of a sentence following a colon is optional.

 Gould cites the work of Darwin: The [*or the*] theory of natural selection incorporates the principle of evolutionary ties among all animals.

Capitalize a sentence within parentheses unless the parenthetical sentence is inserted into another sentence.

 Gould cites the work of Darwin. (Other researchers cite more recent evolutionary theorists.)

 Gould cites the work of Darwin (see page 150).

When citing poetry, follow the capitalization of the original poem. Though most poets capitalize the first word of each line in a poem, some poets do not.

 Morning sun heats up the young beech tree
leaves and almost lights them into fireflies

– JUNE JORDAN, "Aftermath"

53b Capitalize proper nouns and proper adjectives.

Capitalize proper nouns (those naming specific persons, places, and things) and most proper adjectives (those formed from proper nouns). All other nouns are common nouns and are not capitalized unless they begin a sentence or are used as part of a proper noun: *a street* or *the street where you live,* but *Elm Street.* The following list shows proper nouns and adjectives on the left and related common nouns and adjectives on the right.

PEOPLE

Ang Lee	the film's director
Nixonian	political

NATIONS, NATIONALITIES, ETHNIC GROUPS, AND LANGUAGES

Brazil, Brazilian	their native country, his citizenship
Italian American	an ethnic group

PLACES

Pacific Ocean	an ocean
Hawaiian Islands	tropical islands

STRUCTURES AND MONUMENTS

the Lincoln Memorial	a monument
the Eiffel Tower	a landmark

SHIPS, TRAINS, AIRCRAFT, AND SPACECRAFT

the *Queen Mary*	a cruise ship
the *City of New Orleans*	the 6:00 train

ORGANIZATIONS, BUSINESSES, AND GOVERNMENT INSTITUTIONS

United Auto Workers	a trade union
Library of Congress	certain federal agencies

ACADEMIC INSTITUTIONS AND COURSES

University of Maryland	a state university
Political Science 102	my political science course

HISTORICAL EVENTS AND ERAS

the Easter Uprising	a rebellion
the Renaissance	the fifteenth century

RELIGIONS AND RELIGIOUS TERMS

God   a deity

the Qur'an   a holy book

Catholicism, Catholic   a religion, their religious affiliation

TRADE NAMES

Nike   running shoes

Cheerios   cereal

Product names

Some contemporary companies use capitals called *InterCaps* in the middle of their own or their product's names. Follow the style you see in company advertising or on the product itself—*eBay, FedEx, iTunes.*

Titles of individuals

Capitalize titles used before a proper name. When used alone or following a proper name, most titles are not capitalized. One common exception is the word *president,* which many writers capitalize whenever it refers to the president of the United States.

Chief Justice Roberts   John Roberts, the chief justice

Professor Lisa Ede   my English professor

Dr. Edward A. Davies   Edward A. Davies, our doctor

FOR MULTILINGUAL WRITERS

Multilingual **Learning English Capitalization**

Capitalization systems vary considerably among languages, and some languages (Arabic, Chinese, Hindi, and Hebrew, for example) do not use capital letters at all. English may be the only language to capitalize the first-person singular pronoun (*I*), but Dutch and German capitalize some forms of the second-person pronoun (*you*). German capitalizes all nouns; English used to capitalize more nouns than it does now (see, for instance, the Declaration of Independence).

53c   Capitalize titles of works.

Capitalize most words in titles of books, articles, stories, speeches, essays, plays, poems, documents, films, paintings, and musical compositions. Do not capitalize an article (*a, an, the*), a preposition, a conjunction, or the *to* in an infinitive unless it is the first or last word in a title or subtitle.

Walt Whitman: A Life	Declaration of Independence
"As Time Goes By"	*Charlie and the Chocolate Factory*
"Shooting an Elephant"	*Rebel without a Cause*

53d   Revise unnecessary capitalization.

Do not capitalize a compass direction unless the word designates a specific geographic region.

▶ Voters in the South and much of the West tend to favor socially conservative candidates.

▶ John Muir headed ~~West,~~ *west,* motivated by the need to explore.

Do not capitalize a word indicating a family relationship unless the word is used as part of the name or as a substitute for the name.

▶ I could always tell when Mother was annoyed with Aunt Rose.

▶ When she was a child, my ~~Mother~~ *mother* shared a room with my ~~Aunt.~~ *aunt.*

Do not capitalize seasons of the year and parts of the academic or financial year.

spring	fall semester
winter	winter term
autumn	third-quarter earnings

Capitalizing entire words and phrases in online writing gives them emphasis. On social media, writers may capitalize a few words or phrases for comic effect ("*I am shocked, SHOCKED to hear you say that!*"). But note that using all capital letters makes writing in digital environments feel like shouting. In email and professional writing, use italics, boldface, or underlining for emphasis.

Abbreviations and Numbers

A ny time you look up an address, you see an abundance of abbreviations and numbers, as in the following movie theater listing from a Google map of Berkeley, California:

Oaks Theater   1875 Solano Av   Brk

Abbreviations and numbers allow writers to present detailed information in a small amount of space.

 54a **Abbreviate some titles before and all titles after proper names.**

Ms. Susanna Moller   Henry Louis Gates Jr.
Mr. Aaron Oforlea   Karen Lancry, MD
Dr. Cheryl Gold   Samuel Cohen, PhD

Other titles — including religious, academic, and government titles — should be spelled out in academic writing. In other writing, they can be abbreviated before a full name but should be written out when used with only a last name.

Rev. Fleming Rutledge   Reverend Rutledge
Prof. Vershawn Young   Professor Young
Gen. Colin Powell   General Powell

Do not use both a title and an academic degree with a person's name. Use one or the other. Instead of *Dr. Beverly Moss, PhD,* write *Dr. Beverly Moss* or *Beverly Moss, PhD.* (Note that academic degrees such as *RN* and *PhD* often appear without periods; see 49a.)

54b Abbreviate years and hours appropriately.

You can use the following abbreviations with numerals. Notice that AD precedes the numeral; all other abbreviations follow the numeral. Today, BCE and CE are generally preferred over BC and AD, and periods in all four of these abbreviations are optional.

> 399 BCE ("before the common era") *or* 399 BC ("before Christ")

> 49 CE ("common era") *or* AD 49 (*anno Domini,* Latin for "year of our Lord")

> 11:15 AM (*or* a.m.)

> 9:00 PM (*or* p.m.)

For these abbreviations, you may use full-size capital letters or small caps, a typographical option in word-processing programs.

54c Abbreviate some business, government, and science terms.

As long as you can be sure your readers will understand them, use common abbreviations such as *PBS, NASA, DNA,* and *CIA.* If an abbreviation may be unfamiliar, however, spell out the full term the first time you use it, and give the abbreviation in parentheses. After that, you can use the abbreviation by itself.

> ▶ The Comprehensive Test Ban (CTB) Treaty was first proposed in the 1950s. For those nations signing it, the CTB would bring to a halt all nuclear weapons testing.

54d Use abbreviations in official company names.

Use such abbreviations as *Co., Inc., Corp.,* and *&* if they are part of a company's official name. Do not, however, use these abbreviations in most other contexts.

corporation
▶ Sears, Roebuck & Co. was the only large ~~corp.~~ in town.

Bros.
▶ Paola has a part-time job at the Warner ~~Brothers~~ store in the mall.

54e Use Latin abbreviations appropriately.

In general, avoid these Latin abbreviations except when citing sources:

cf.	compare (*confer*)
e.g.	for example (*exempli gratia*)
et al.	and others (*et alia*)
etc.	and so forth (*et cetera*)
i.e.	that is (*id est*)
N.B.	note well (*nota bene*)
P.S.	postscript (*postscriptum*)

for example,
▶ Many firms have policies to help working parents—~~e.g.,~~ flexible

hours, parental leave, and day care.

▶ Before the conference began, Haivan unpacked the name tags,
and so forth.
programs, pens, ~~etc.~~

54f Use symbols and unit abbreviations appropriately.

Symbols such as %, +, $, and = are acceptable in charts and graphs. Dollar signs are acceptable with figures: *$11* (but not with words: *eleven dollars*). Units of measurement can be abbreviated in charts and graphs (*4 in.*) but not in the body of a paper (*four inches*).

54g Use other abbreviations according to convention.

Some abbreviations required in notes and in source citations are not appropriate in the body of a paper.

TALKING ABOUT STYLE

Abbreviations and Numbers in Different Fields

Use of abbreviations and numbers varies in different fields. See a typical example from a biochemistry textbook:

> The energy of a green photon . . . is 57 kilocalories per mole (kcal/mol). An alternative unit of energy is the joule (J), which is equal to 0.239 calorie; 1 kcal/mol is equal to 4.184 kJ/mol.
> – LUBERT STRYER, *Biochemistry*

These two sentences demonstrate how useful figures and abbreviations can be; reading the same sentences would be very difficult if the numbers and units of measurement were all written out.

Become familiar with the conventions governing abbreviations and numbers in your field. The following reference books provide guidelines:

MLA Handbook for Writers of Research Papers for literature and the humanities

Publication Manual of the American Psychological Association for the social sciences

Scientific Style and Format: The CSE Manual for Authors, Editors, and Publishers for the natural sciences

The Chicago Manual of Style for the humanities

AIP Style Manual for physics and the applied sciences

CHAPTER AND PAGES	chapter, page, pages (*not* ch., p., pp.)
MONTHS	January, February (*not* Jan., Feb.)
STATES AND NATIONS	California, Mexico (*not* Calif., Mex.)
	Two exceptions are Washington, D.C., and U.S.

54h Spell out numbers expressed in one or two words.

If you can write out a number in one or two words, do so. Use figures for longer numbers.

thirty-eight

▶ Her screams were heard by ~~38~~ *thirty-eight* people, none of whom called the police.

▶ A baseball is held together by ~~two hundred sixteen~~ *216* red stitches.

If one of several numbers *of the same kind* in the same sentence requires a figure, you should use figures for all the numbers in that sentence.

▶ An audio system can range in cost from ~~one hundred dollars~~ to $2,599.

$100

54i Spell out numbers that begin sentences.

When a sentence begins with a number, either spell out the number or rewrite the sentence.

▶ ~~119~~ years of CIA labor cost taxpayers sixteen million dollars.

One hundred nineteen

Most readers find it easier to read figures than three-word numbers; thus the best solution may be to rewrite this sentence: *Taxpayers spent sixteen million dollars for 119 years of CIA labor.*

54j Use figures according to convention.

ADDRESSES	23 Main Street; 175 Fifth Avenue
DATES	September 17, 1951; 6 June 1983; 4 BCE; the 1860s
DECIMALS AND FRACTIONS	65.34; 8½
PERCENTAGES	77 percent (*or* 77%)
EXACT AMOUNTS OF MONEY	$7,348; $1.46 trillion; $2.50; thirty-five (*or* 35) cents
SCORES AND STATISTICS	an 8–3 Red Sox victory; a verbal score of 600; an average age of 22; a mean of 53
TIME OF DAY	6:00 AM (*or* a.m.)

FOR MULTILINGUAL WRITERS

Multilingual **Using the Term *Hundred***

The term *hundred* is used idiomatically in English. When it is linked with numbers like two, eight, and so on, the word *hundred* remains singular: *Eight hundred years have passed and still old animosities run deep.* Add the plural -s to *hundred* only when no number precedes the term: *Hundreds of priceless books were lost in the fire.*

55   Italics

The slanted type known as *italics* is more than just a pretty type-face. Indeed, italics give words special meaning or emphasis. In the sentence "Many people read *People* on the subway every day," the italics (and the capital letter) tell readers that *People* is a publication.

QUICK HELP

Editing for Italics

- Check that all titles of long works are italicized. (55a)
- If you use any words, letters, or numbers as terms, make sure they are in italics. (55b)
- Italicize any non-English words or phrases that are not in an English dictionary. (55c)

55a   Italicize titles of long works.

In general, use italics for titles of long works; use quotation marks for shorter works (51c).

BOOKS	*Fun Home: A Family Tragicomic*
CHOREOGRAPHIC WORKS	Agnes de Mille's *Rodeo*
FILMS AND VIDEOS	*Selma*
LONG MUSICAL WORKS	*Brandenburg Concertos*
LONG POEMS	*Bhagavad Gita*
MAGAZINES AND JOURNALS	*Ebony,* the *New England Journal of Medicine*
NEWSPAPERS	the *Cleveland Plain Dealer*
PAINTINGS AND SCULPTURE	Georgia O'Keeffe's *Black Iris*
PAMPHLETS	Thomas Paine's *Common Sense*
PLAYS	*The Book of Mormon*
RADIO SERIES	*All Things Considered*

RECORDINGS   *Nevermind*

TELEVISION SERIES   *House of Cards*

55b Italicize words, letters, and numbers used as terms.

▶ On the back of his jersey was the famous 24.

▶ One characteristic of some New York speech is the absence of postvocalic *r*—for example, pronouncing the word *four* as "fouh."

55c Italicize non-English words and phrases.

Italicize words from other languages unless they have become part of English—like the French "bourgeois" or the Italian "pasta," for example. If a word is in an English dictionary, it does not need italics.

▶ At last one of the phantom sleighs gliding along the street would come to a stop, and with gawky haste Mr. Burness in his fox-furred *shapka* would make for our door.   —VLADIMIR NABOKOV, *Speak, Memory*

Hyphens 56

H yphens are undoubtedly confusing to many people—hyphen problems are now one of the twenty most common surface errors in student writing. The confusion is understandable. Over time, the conventions for hyphen use in a given word can change (*tomorrow* was once spelled *to-morrow*). New words, even compounds such as *firewall*, generally don't use hyphens, but controversy continues to rage over whether to hyphenate *email* (or is it *e-mail*?). And some words are hyphenated when they serve one kind of purpose in a sentence and not when they serve another.

QUICK HELP

Editing for Hyphens

- Double-check compound words to be sure they are properly closed up, separated, or hyphenated. If in doubt, consult a dictionary. (56a)
- Check all terms that have prefixes or suffixes to see whether you need hyphens. (56b)
- Do not hyphenate two-word verbs or word groups that serve as subject complements. (56c)

56a   Use hyphens with compound words.

Some compounds are one word (*rowboat, pickup*), some are separate words (*hard drive*), and some require hyphens (*sister-in-law*). You should consult a dictionary to be sure. However, the following conventions can help you decide when to use hyphens with compound words.

Compound adjectives

Hyphenate most compound adjectives that precede a noun but not those that follow a noun.

a *well-liked* boss	My boss is *well liked.*
a *six-foot* plank	The plank is *six feet long.*

In general, the reason for hyphenating compound adjectives is to facilitate reading.

▶ Designers often use potted plants as living-room dividers.

Without the hyphen, *living* may seem to modify *room dividers.*

Never hyphenate an *-ly* adverb and an adjective.

▶ They used a widely-distributed mailing list.

Fractions and compound numbers

Use a hyphen to write out fractions and to spell out compound numbers from twenty-one to ninety-nine.

one-seventh	thirty-seven
two and seven-sixteenths	three hundred fifty-four thousand

56b Use hyphens with prefixes and suffixes.

Most words containing prefixes or suffixes are written without hyphens: *antiwar, gorillalike.* Here are some exceptions:

BEFORE CAPITALIZED BASE WORDS	un-American, non-Catholic
WITH FIGURES	pre-1960, post-1945
WITH CERTAIN PREFIXES AND SUFFIXES	all-state, ex-partner, self-possessed, quasi-legislative, mayor-elect, fifty-odd
WITH COMPOUND BASE WORDS	pre-high school, post-cold war
FOR CLARITY OR EASE OF READING	re-cover, anti-inflation, troll-like

Re-cover means "cover again"; the hyphen distinguishes it from the word *recover,* meaning "get well." In *anti-inflation* and *troll-like*, the hyphens separate confusing clusters of vowels and consonants.

56c Avoid unnecessary hyphens.

Unnecessary hyphens are at least as common a problem as omitted ones. Do not hyphenate the parts of a two-word verb such as *depend on, turn off,* or *tune out* (44b).

▶ Every player must pick⁄up a medical form before football tryouts.

The words *pick up* act as a verb and should not be hyphenated.

However, be careful to check that two words do indeed function as a verb in the sentence (36a); if they function as an adjective, a hyphen may be needed.

▶ Let's sign up for the early class.

The verb *sign up* should not have a hyphen.

▶ Where is the sign-up sheet?

The compound adjective *sign-up,* which modifies the noun *sheet,* needs a hyphen.

Do not hyphenate a subject complement—a word group that follows a linking verb (such as a form of *be* or *seem*) and describes the subject (37b).

▶ Audrey is almost eleven⁄years⁄old.

The Basics of MLA Style  57

Different rhetorical situations call for different approaches to citing sources—that is, for different ways of answering the question "Says who?" If you're reading a popular magazine, you probably won't expect the writer to provide careful source citations or a list of references at the end of an article. If you're posting material on a blog, you might follow conventions for citation by simply linking to the material you're talking about. But in other situations, including most academic writing, you will be expected to follow a more rigorous system for citing the information you use. Many courses in English ask writers to follow MLA style, the system developed by the Modern Language Association. For further reference, consult Chapters 58–60 or the *MLA Handbook,* Eighth Edition (2016).

57a Think about what readers need from you.

Why does academic work call for very careful citation practices when writing for the general public may not? The answer to that question is pretty easy: readers of your academic work (your instructor, other students, perhaps even researchers and professionals in your field) expect to get certain information from source citations:

- Source citations demonstrate that while you may not yet be a recognized expert on the topic, you've nevertheless done your homework, and you are a part of the conversation surrounding it. You include sources that you find credible and that provide evidence and good reasons to back up your claims, as well as sources that you need to respond to or refute (see 14a). Careful citation shows your readers what you know, where you stand, and what you think is important.

- Source citations show that you understand the need to give credit when you make use of someone else's intellectual property. Especially in academic writing, when it's better to be safe than sorry, include a citation for any source you think you might need to cite. (See Chapter 15 for details.)
- Source citations give explicit directions to guide readers who want to look for themselves at the works you're using.

The guidelines for MLA style (or APA or *Chicago*—if you are asked to use these systems, see Chapters 61–67) help you with this last purpose, giving you instructions on exactly what information to include in your citation and how to format that information.

57b Consider the context of your sources.

New kinds of sources crop up regularly, and each new medium once required new guidelines from MLA. But the *MLA Handbook*, 8th Edition, provides advice writers can use to cite any kind of source. There are often several "correct" ways to cite a source, so you will need to think carefully about *your own context* for using the source so you can identify the pieces of information that you should emphasize or include and any other information that might be helpful to your readers.

Elements of MLA citations

The first step is to identify elements that are commonly found in most works writers cite.

AUTHOR AND TITLE

The first two elements, both of which are needed for many sources, are the author's name and the title of the work. Each of these elements is followed by a period.

| **Author.** |
| **Title.** |

Even in these elements, your context is important. The author of a novel may be obvious, but who is the "author" of a television episode? The director? The writer? The show's creator? The star? The answer may depend on the focus of your own work. If an actor's performance is central to your discussion, then MLA guidelines ask you to identify the actor as the author. If the plot is your focus, you might name the writer of the episode as the author.

CONTAINER

The next step is to identify elements of what the MLA calls the "container" for the work. The context in which you are discussing the source and the context in which you find the source will help you determine what counts as a container — and whether you need a container other than the title — in each case. A standalone source, such as a print novel, won't require you to name a separate container. If you watch a movie in a theater, you won't identify a container. But if you watch the same movie as part of a DVD box set of the director's work, the container title is the name of the box set. If you read an article in a print journal, the first container is the journal the article appears in. If you read it online, the journal may also be part of a second, larger container, such as a database. Thinking about a source as nested in larger containers may help you to visualize how a citation works.

The elements you may include in the "container" part of your citation include the title of the larger container; the names of contributors such as editors or translators; the version or edition; the volume and issue numbers; the publisher or sponsor; the date of publication; and a location such as the page numbers, URL, or DOI. These elements are separated by commas, and the end of the container is marked with a period.

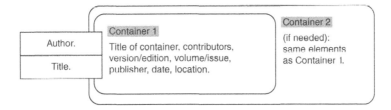

Most sources won't include *all* these pieces of information, so include only the elements that are available and relevant to create an acceptable citation. If you need a second container, you simply add it after the first one. You will find many examples of how elements and containers are combined to create citations in Chapters 58–59.

Examples from student work

ARTICLE IN A DATABASE

David Craig, whose research writing appears in Chapter 60, found a potentially useful article in Academic Search Premier, a database he accessed through his library website. Many databases are digital collections of articles that originally appeared in print periodicals, and the articles usually have the same written-word content as they did in print form, without changes or updates. Database sources have usually been carefully reviewed before publication, either by an editor, an editorial board, or peer reviewers. While finding information in an article from a database is not a surefire guarantee of credibility, such information is often more authoritative than much of what you find for free on the web. (See 13b.)

From the page shown below, David Craig was able to click through to read the full text of the article. He printed this computer screen in case he needed to cite the article: the image has all the information that he would need to create a complete MLA citation, including the original print publication information for the article, the name of the database, and the location (here, a "digital object identifier" or DOI, which provides the source's permanent location).

A SOURCE FROM A DATABASE

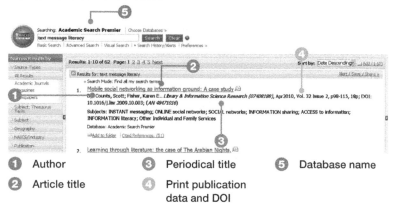

1 Author   **3** Periodical title   **5** Database name
2 Article title   **4** Print publication
                            data and DOI

A complete citation for this article would look like this:

Counts, Scott, and Karen E. Fisher. "Mobile Social Networking as Information
    Ground: A Case Study." *Library and Information Science Research*, vol. 32,
    no. 2, Apr. 2010, pp. 98-115. *Academic Search Premier*, doi:10.1016/j
    .lisr.2009.10.003.

Note that the periodical, *Library and Information Science Research*, is the first "container" of the article, and the database, *Academic Search Premier*, is the second "container." Notice, too, that the first container includes just four relevant elements—the journal title, number (here, that means the volume and issue numbers), date, and page numbers; and the second container includes just two—the database title and location. Publisher information is not required for journals and databases.

OTHER KINDS OF SOURCES

While researching her presentation on Alison Bechdel's graphic memoir *Fun Home* (see Chapter 23), Shuqiao Song came across a brief video interview with Bechdel on YouTube that she wanted to play for her audience. However, the YouTube post noted that the interview had originally appeared on a web series called *Stuck in Vermont*. At first Shuqiao was puzzled: should she be citing a video, an interview, a work from a website, or something else? She used the information available on YouTube and followed the "container" template, naming Bechdel (who is speaking in the video clip) as the author, with the interviewer identified after the title of the piece.

Bechdel, Alison. "Stuck in Vermont 109: Alison Bechdel." Interview by

Eva Sollberger. *YouTube*, 13 Dec. 2008, www.youtube.com/

watch?v=nWBFYTmpC54.

57c   Plan and connect your citations.

MLA citations appear in two connected parts—the brief in-text citation, usually in parentheses in the body of your written text, and the full citation in the list of works cited, to which the in-text citation directs your readers. The most straightforward in-text citations include the author's name and the page number, but many variations on this basic format are discussed in Chapter 58.

In the text of his research essay (see Chapter 60), David Craig paraphrases material from the print book *Language Play* by linguist David Crystal. As shown here, he cites the book page on which the original information appears in a parenthetical reference that points readers to the entry for "Crystal, David" in his list of works cited. He also cites statistics from a report that he found on a website sponsored by the nonprofit Pew Internet and American Life Project. The report, like many online texts, does not include page numbers. These examples show just two of the many ways to cite sources using in-text citations and a list of works cited. You'll need to make case-by-case decisions based on the types of sources you include.

for good reason. According to David Crystal, an internationally recognized scholar of linguistics at the University of Wales, as young children develop and learn how words string together to express ideas, they go through many phases of language play. The singsong rhymes and nonsensical chants of preschoolers are vital to learning language, and a healthy appetite for wordplay leads to a better command of language later in life (182).

Craig 10

end in SAT

h Is Yielding

Concern. College

Board, 2002.

Crystal, David. *Language Play.* U of Chicago P, 1998.

Ferguson, Niall. "Texting Makes U Stupid." *Newsweek,* vol. 158, no. 12, 19 Sept. 2011, p. 11. *EBSCOHost,* connection.ebscohost.com/c/articles/65454341/texting-makes-u-stupid.

Leibowitz, Wendy R. "Technology Transforms Writing and the Teaching of Writing." *Chronicle of Higher Education,* 26 Nov. 1999, pp. A67-A68.

Lenhart, Amanda. *Teens, Smartphones, & Texting.* Pew Research Center, 19 Mar. 2012, www.pewinternet.org/files/old-media//Files/Reports/2012/PIP_Teens_Smartphones_and_Texting.pdf.

Lenhart, Amanda, et al. *Writing, Technology & Teens.* Pew Research Center, 24 Apr. 2008, www.pewinternet.org/2008/04/24/writing-technology-and-teens/.

Lenhart, Amanda, and Oliver Lewis. *Teenage Life Online: The Rise of the Instant-Message Generation and the Internet's Impact on Friendships and Family Relationships.* Pew Research Center, 21 June 2001, www.pewinternet.org/2001/06/20/the-rise-of-the-instant-message-generation/.

is rising among the young. According to the Pew Internet & American Life Project, 85 percent of those aged twelve to seventeen at least occasionally write text messages, instant messages, or comments on social networking sites (Lenhart et al.) In 2001, the most conservative estimate based on

n'?" Bedford Bits, 9 Apr. 2015, /the-english-community/bedford ma-queen.

Text-Messaging Skills Can Score 11 Mar. 2005, www ssc.html.

"SAT Trends 2011." *Collegeboard.org,* 14 Sept. 2011, research.collegeboard.org/programs/sat/data/archived/cb-seniors-2011/tables.

57d   Include notes as needed.

MLA citation style asks you to include explanatory notes for information or comments that don't readily fit into your text but are needed for clarification or further explanation. In addition, MLA permits bibliographic notes for offering information about or evaluation of a source, or to list multiple sources that relate to a single point. Use superscript numbers in the text to refer readers to the notes, which may appear as endnotes (under the heading *Notes* on a separate page immediately before the list of works cited) or as footnotes at the bottom of each page where a superscript number appears.

EXAMPLE OF SUPERSCRIPT NUMBER IN TEXT

Although such communication relies on the written word, many messagers disregard standard writing conventions. For example, here is a snippet from an IM conversation between two teenage girls:[1]

EXAMPLE OF EXPLANATORY NOTE

1. This transcript of an IM conversation was collected on 20 Nov. 2014. The teenagers' names are concealed to protect privacy.

57e Format MLA manuscripts appropriately.

The MLA recommends the following format for the manuscript of a research-based print project. If you are creating a nonprint project or have formatting questions, it's always a good idea to check with your instructor before preparing your final draft.

For detailed guidelines on formatting a list of works cited, see Chapter 59. For a sample student essay in MLA style, see Chapter 60.

- *First page and title page.* The MLA does not require a title page. Type each of the following items on a separate line on the first page, beginning one inch from the top and flush with the left margin: your name, the instructor's name, the course name and number, and the date. Double-space between each item; then double-space again and center the title. Double-space between the title and the beginning of the text.

- *Margins and spacing.* Leave one-inch margins at the top and bottom and on both sides of each page. Double-space the entire text, including set-off quotations, notes, and the list of works cited. Indent the first line of a paragraph one-half inch.

- *Page numbers.* Include your last name and the page number on each page, one-half inch below the top and flush with the right margin.

- *Long quotations.* Set off a long quotation (one with more than four typed lines) in block format by starting it on a new line and indenting each line one-half inch from the left margin. Do not enclose the passage in quotation marks (15b).

- *Headings.* MLA style allows, but does not require, headings. Many students and instructors find them helpful.

- *Visuals.* Place tables, photographs, drawings, charts, graphs, and other figures as near as possible to the relevant text. (See 15c for guidelines on incorporating visuals into your text.) Tables should have a label and number (*Table 1*) and a clear caption.

The label and caption should be aligned on the left, on separate lines. Give the source information below the table. All other visuals should be labeled *Figure* (abbreviated *Fig.*), numbered, and captioned. The label and caption should appear on the same line, followed by the source information. Remember to refer to each visual in your text, indicating how it contributes to the point you are making.

58 MLA Style for In-Text Citations

I n MLA style, a citation in the text of an essay is required for every quotation, paraphrase, summary, or other material requiring documentation (see 15f). In-text citations document material from other sources with both signal phrases and parenthetical references. Parenthetical references should include the information your readers need to locate the full reference in the list of works cited at the end of the text (Chapter 59). An in-text citation in MLA style aims to give the reader two kinds of information: (1) it indicates *which source* on the works-cited page the writer is referring to, and (2) it explains *where in the source* the material quoted, paraphrased, or summarized can be found, if the source has page numbers or other numbered sections.

The basic MLA in-text citation includes the author's last name either in a signal phrase introducing the source material (15b) or in parentheses at the end of the sentence. For sources with stable page numbers, it also includes the page number in parentheses at the end of the sentence.

SAMPLE CITATION USING A SIGNAL PHRASE

In his discussion of Monty Python routines, Crystal notes that the group relished "breaking the normal rules" of language (107).

SAMPLE PARENTHETICAL CITATION

A noted linguist explains that Monty Python humor often relied on "bizarre linguistic interactions" (Crystal 108).

(For digital sources without print page numbers, see model 3.)

DIRECTORY TO MLA STYLE

In-text citations

1. Author named in a signal phrase, *469*
2. Author named in a parenthetical reference, *469*
3. Digital or nonprint source, *470*
4. Two authors, *470*
5. Three or more authors, *470*
6. Organization as author, *470*
7. Unknown author, *471*
8. Author of two or more works cited in the same project, *471*
9. Two or more authors with the same last name, *471*
10. Indirect source (author quoting someone else), *471*
11. Multivolume work, *471*
12. Work in an anthology or collection, *472*
13. Government source, *472*
14. Entire work, *472*
15. Two or more sources in one citation, *472*
16. Personal communication or social media source, *472*
17. Literary work, *472*
18. Sacred text, *473*
19. Encyclopedia or dictionary entry, *473*
20. Visual, *474*

Note in the following examples where punctuation is placed in relation to the parentheses.

1. AUTHOR NAMED IN A SIGNAL PHRASE

The MLA recommends using the author's name in a signal phrase to introduce the material and citing the page number(s), if any, in parentheses.

> Lee claims that his comic-book creation, Thor, was actually "the first regularly published superhero to speak in a consistently archaic manner" (199).

2. AUTHOR NAMED IN A PARENTHETICAL REFERENCE

When you do not mention the author in a signal phrase, include the author's last name before the page number(s), if any, in parentheses. Do not use punctuation between the author's name and the page number(s).

> The word *Bollywood* is sometimes considered an insult because it implies that Indian movies are merely "a derivative of the American film industry" (Chopra 9).

3. DIGITAL OR NONPRINT SOURCE

Give enough information in a signal phrase or in parentheses for readers to locate the source in your list of works cited. Many works found online or in electronic databases lack stable page numbers; you can omit the page number in such cases. However, if you are citing a work with stable pagination, such as an article in PDF format, include the page number in parentheses.

DIGITAL SOURCE WITHOUT STABLE PAGE NUMBERS

As a *Slate* analysis has noted, "Prominent sports psychologists get praised for their successes and don't get grief for their failures" (Engber).

DIGITAL SOURCE WITH STABLE PAGE NUMBERS

According to Whitmarsh, the British military had experimented with using balloons for observation as far back as 1879 (328).

If the source includes numbered sections, paragraphs, or screens, include the abbreviation *sec.*, *par.*, or *scr.* and the number in parentheses.

Sherman notes that the "immediate, interactive, and on-the-spot" nature of Internet information can make nondigital media seem outdated (sec. 32).

4. TWO AUTHORS

Use both the authors' last names in a signal phrase or in parentheses.

Gilbert and Gubar point out that in the Grimm version of "Snow White," the king "never actually appears in this story at all" (37).

5. THREE OR MORE AUTHORS

Use the first author's last name and *et al.* ("and others").

Similarly, as Belenky et al. assert, examining the lives of women expands our understanding of human development (7).

6. ORGANIZATION AS AUTHOR

Give the group's full name or a shortened form of it in a signal phrase or in parentheses.

Any study of social welfare involves a close analysis of "the impacts, the benefits, and the costs" of its policies (Social Research Corporation iii).

7. UNKNOWN AUTHOR

Use the full title, if it is brief, in your text—or a shortened version of the title in parentheses.

> One analysis defines *hype* as "an artificially engendered atmosphere of
> hysteria" (*Today's Marketplace* 51).

8. AUTHOR OF TWO OR MORE WORKS CITED IN THE SAME PROJECT

If your list of works cited has more than one work by the same author, include a shortened version of the title of the work that you are citing in a signal phrase or in parentheses to prevent reader confusion.

> Gardner shows readers their own silliness in his description of a "pointless,
> ridiculous monster, crouched in the shadows, stinking of dead men, murdered
> children, and martyred cows" (*Grendel* 2).

9. TWO OR MORE AUTHORS WITH THE SAME LAST NAME

Include the author's first *and* last names in a signal phrase or first initial and last name in a parenthetical reference.

> Children will learn to write if they are allowed to choose their own
> subjects, James Britton asserts, citing the Schools Council study of the
> 1960s (37-42).

10. INDIRECT SOURCE (AUTHOR QUOTING SOMEONE ELSE)

Use the abbreviation *qtd. in* to indicate that you are quoting from someone else's report of a source.

> As Arthur Miller says, "When somebody is destroyed everybody finally
> contributes to it, but in Willy's case, the end product would be virtually the
> same" (qtd. in Martin and Meyer 375).

11. MULTIVOLUME WORK

In a parenthetical reference, note the volume number first and then the page number(s), with a colon and one space between them.

> Modernist writers prized experimentation and gradually even sought to blur
> the line between poetry and prose, according to Forster (3: 150).

If you name only one volume of the work in your list of works cited, include only the page number in the parentheses.

12. WORK IN AN ANTHOLOGY OR COLLECTION

For an essay, short story, or other piece of prose reprinted in an anthology, use the name of the author of the work, not the editor of the anthology, but use the page number(s) from the anthology.

> Narratives of captivity play a major role in early writing by women in the United States, as demonstrated by Silko (219).

13. GOVERNMENT SOURCE

Because entries for sources authored by government agencies will appear on your list of works cited under the name of the country (see Chapter 59, item 79), your in-text citation for such a source should include the name of the country as well as the name of the agency responsible for the source.

> To reduce the agricultural runoff into the Chesapeake Bay, the United States Environmental Protection Agency has argued that "[h]igh nutrient loading crops, such as corn and soybean, should be replaced with alternatives in environmentally sensitive areas" (26).

14. ENTIRE WORK

Include the reference in the text, without any page numbers.

> In *Into the Wild*, Krakauer both criticizes and admires the solitary impulses of its young hero, which end up killing him.

15. TWO OR MORE SOURCES IN ONE CITATION

Separate the information with semicolons.

> Economists recommend that *employment* be redefined to include unpaid domestic labor (Clark 148; Nevins 39).

16. PERSONAL COMMUNICATION OR SOCIAL MEDIA SOURCE

Provide information that will allow readers to locate the source in your list of works cited, such as a name (if you know it) or username.

> George Hahn posted a self-portrait with a Citibike on Instagram with the caption, "Citibike is fabulous. Don't let anyone tell you differently."

17. LITERARY WORK

Because literary works are often available in many different editions, cite the page number(s) from the edition you used followed by a semicolon; then give other identifying information that will lead readers to the passage in any edition. Indicate the act and/or scene in a play (*37; sc. 1*). For a novel, indicate the part or chapter (*175; ch. 4*).

> In utter despair, Dostoyevsky's character Mitya wonders aloud about the
>
> "terrible tragedies realism inflicts on people" (376; bk. 8, ch. 2).

For a poem, cite the part (if there is one) and line(s), separated by a period.

> Whitman speculates, "All goes onward and outward, nothing collapses, / And
>
> to die is different from what anyone supposed, and luckier" (6.129-30).

If you are citing only line numbers, use the word *line(s)* in the first reference (*lines 21–22*) and the line numbers alone in subsequent references.

> The duke criticizes his late wife for having a "heart . . . too soon made glad"
>
> (line 22).

For a verse play, give only the act, scene, and line numbers, separated by periods.

> The witches greet Banquo as "Lesser than Macbeth, and greater" (1.3.65).

18. SACRED TEXT

To cite a sacred text such as the Qur'an or the Bible, give the title of the edition you used, then the book, chapter, and verse (or their equivalent), separated by a period. In your text, spell out the names of books. In parenthetical references, use abbreviations for books with names of five or more letters (*Gen.* for *Genesis*).

> He ignored the admonition "Pride goes before destruction, and a haughty
>
> spirit before a fall" (*New Oxford Annotated Bible,* Prov. 16.18).

19. ENCYCLOPEDIA OR DICTIONARY ENTRY

An entry for a reference work that does not list an author's name—for example, an encyclopedia or dictionary—will appear on the works-cited list under the entry's title. Enclose the title in quotation marks and place it in parentheses. Omit the page number if the reference work arranges entries alphabetically.

> The term *prion* was coined by Stanley B. Prusiner from the words
>
> *proteinaceous* and *infectious* and a suffix meaning *particle* ("Prion").

20. VISUAL

When you include an image in your text, number it and include a parenthetical reference that precedes the image in your text (*see Fig. 2*). Number figures (photos, drawings, cartoons, maps, graphs, and charts) and tables separately. Each visual should include a caption with the figure or table number and information about the source (see the box on p. 506).

> This trend is illustrated in a chart distributed by the College Board as part of its 2011 analysis of aggregate SAT data (see Fig. 1).

Soon after the preceding sentence, readers find the following figure and caption (see Chapter 60):

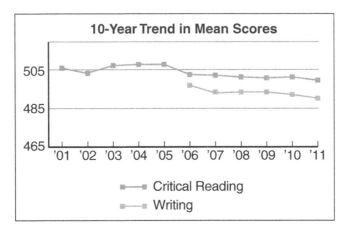

Fig. 1. Ten-year trend in mean SAT reading and writing scores (2001-2011). Data source: "SAT Trends 2011."

An image that you create might appear with a caption like this:

> Fig. 4. Young woman reading a magazine. Personal photograph by author.

MLA Style for a List of Works Cited **59**

A list of works cited is an alphabetical list of the sources you have referred to in your essay. (If your instructor asks you to list everything you have read as background, call the list *Works Consulted*.) Begin the works-cited list on a separate page or slide after the text of your project and any notes, under the centered heading *Works Cited* (not italicized or in quotation marks).

- Do not indent the first line of each entry, but indent subsequent lines for the entry one-half inch. (This makes the author names easy to scan.) Double-space the entire list.

- List sources alphabetically by authors' last names or by title for works without authors. For titles beginning with the article *A, An,* or *The,* don't count the article when alphabetizing.

QUICK HELP

Citing Sources That Don't Match Any Model Exactly

What should you do if your source doesn't match the model exactly? Suppose, for instance, that your source is a translated essay that appears in the fifth edition of an anthology.

- Identify a basic model to follow. If you decide that your source looks most like an essay in an anthology, you would start with a citation that looks like model 10. Include the author (if given) and title.

- Enter as many of the elements of the "container" (see 57b) as you can find: title of the larger container, if any; other contributors, such as editor or translator; version or edition number; publisher; date; page numbers or other location information such as a URL or DOI. End the container with a period. If the container is nested in a larger container, collect the information from the second container as well.

- If you aren't sure how to arrange the pieces to create a combination model, ask your instructor.

To cite a source for which you cannot find a model, collect as much information as you can find with the goal of helping your readers find the source for themselves, if possible. Then look at the models in this section to see which one most closely matches the type of source you are using. If possible, seek your instructor's advice to find the best model.

- List the author's last name first, followed by a comma and the first name. If a source has more than one author, subsequent authors' names appear first name first (see model 2).
- Italicize titles of books and long works. Put titles of articles and other short works in quotation marks.

DIRECTORY TO MLA STYLE

Works-cited entries

Guidelines for author listings

1. One author, *478*
2. Multiple authors, *478*
3. Organization or group author, *478*
4. Unknown author, *479*
5. Author using a pseudonym (pen name) or screen name, *479*
6. Two or more works by the same author, *479*

Print books

7. Basic format for a book, *479*
   SOURCE MAP, *482–83*
8. Author and editor both named, *480*
9. Editor, no author named, *480*
10. Anthology, *480*
11. Work in an anthology or chapter in a book with an editor, *480*
12. Two or more items from the same anthology, *481*
13. Translation, *481*
14. Book with both translator and editor, *481*
15. Translation of a section of a book, *481*
16. Translation of a book by an unknown author, *481*
17. Book in a language other than English, *481*
18. Graphic narrative, *484*
19. Edition other than the first, *484*
20. One volume of a multivolume work, *484*
21. More than one volume of a multivolume work, *484*
22. Preface, foreword, introduction, or afterword, *484*
23. Entry in a reference book, *485*
24. Book that is part of a series, *485*
25. Republication (modern edition of an older book), *485*
26. More than one publisher's name, *485*
27. A title within the title, *485*
28. Sacred text, *485*

Articles and short works in print periodicals

29. Article in a print journal, *486*
30. Article in a print magazine, *486*
    SOURCE MAP, *488–89*
31. Article in a print newspaper, *486*
32. Editorial in a print periodical, *486*
33. Letter to the editor of a print periodical, *486*
34. Review in a print periodical, *487*
35. Interview in a print periodical, *487*
36. Unsigned article in a print periodical, *487*

Works-cited entries, continued

Digital written-word sources

37. Work from an online database, *487*
    SOURCE MAP, *492–93*
38. Article from a journal on the web, *490*
39. Article from a magazine on the web, *490*
40. Article from a newspaper on the web, *490*
41. Digital book, *491*
42. Part of a digital book, *491*
43. Online poem, *491*
44. Online editorial or letter to the editor, *494*
45. Online review, *494*
46. Short work from a website, *494*
    SOURCE MAP, *496–97*
47. Entire website, *494*
48. Entry in an online reference work or wiki, *495*
49. Academic course or department website, *498*
50. Blog, *498*
51. Post or comment on a blog or discussion group, *499*
52. Tweet, *499*
53. Posting on a social networking site, *499*
54. Email or message, *500*

Visual, audio, multimedia, and live sources

55. Film (theatrical, DVD, or other format), *500*
56. Online video clip, *500*
57. Television broadcast, *500*
58. Television on the web, *501*
59. Radio broadcast, *501*
60. Radio on the web, *501*
61. Television or radio interview, *502*
62. Online interview, *502*
63. Personal interview, *502*
64. Sound recording, *502*
65. Musical composition, *503*
66. Published score, *503*
67. Video game, *503*
68. Computer software or app, *503*
69. Lecture or speech (live), *503*
70. Lecture or speech on the web, *504*
71. Live performance, *504*
72. Podcast (streaming), *504*
73. Downloaded digital file, *504*
74. Work of art or photograph, *504*
75. Map or chart, *505*
76. Cartoon or comic strip, *505*
77. Advertisement, *505*

Other sources (including digital versions)

78. Report or pamphlet, *506*
79. Government publication, *506*
80. Published proceedings of a conference, *507*
81. Dissertation, *507*
82. Dissertation abstract, *507*
83. Unpublished letter, *507*
84. Manuscript or other unpublished work, *508*
85. Legal source, *508*

Guidelines for author listings

The list of works cited is arranged alphabetically. The in-text citations in your writing point readers toward particular sources on the list (see Chapter 58).

NAME CITED IN SIGNAL PHRASE IN TEXT

Crystal explains . . .

. . . (Crystal 107).

Crystal, David.

Models 1–6 explain how to arrange author names. The information that follows the name depends on the type of work you are citing—a print book (models 7–28); a print periodical (models 29–36); a written text from a digital source, such as an article from a website or database (models 37–54); sources from art, film, comics, or other media, including live performances (models 55–77); or academic, government, and legal sources (models 78–85). Consult the model that most closely resembles the source you are using.

1. ONE AUTHOR

Put the last name first, followed by a comma, the first name (and initial, if any), and a period.

Crystal, David.

2. MULTIPLE AUTHORS

For two authors, list the first author's last name first (see model 1). Follow this with a comma, the word *and*, and the name of the second author with the first name first.

Stiglitz, Joseph E., and Bruce C. Greenwald.

For three or more authors, list the first author followed by a comma and *et al.* ("and others").

Lupton, Ellen, et al.

3. ORGANIZATION OR GROUP AUTHOR

Give the name of the group, government agency, corporation, or other organization listed as the author.

Getty Trust.

United States, Government Accountability Office.

4. UNKNOWN AUTHOR

When the author is not identified, begin the entry with the title, and alphabetize by the first important word. Italicize titles of books and long works, but put titles of articles and other short works in quotation marks.

"California Sues EPA over Emissions."

New Concise World Atlas.

5. AUTHOR USING A PSEUDONYM (PEN NAME) OR SCREEN NAME

Give the author's name as it appears in the source, followed by the real name in parentheses. If you don't know the author's real name, use only the pseudonym or screen name.

Atrios (Duncan Black).

JennOfArk.

6. TWO OR MORE WORKS BY THE SAME AUTHOR

Arrange the entries alphabetically by title. Include the author's name in the first entry, but in subsequent entries, use three hyphens followed by a period. (For the basic format for citing a book, see model 7. For the basic format for citing an article from an online newspaper, see model 40.)

Chopra, Anupama. "Bollywood Princess, Hollywood Hopeful." *The New York Times,* 10 Feb. 2008, nyti.ms/1QEtNpF.

---. *King of Bollywood: Shah Rukh Khan and the Seductive World of Indian Cinema.* Warner Books, 2007.

Note: Use three hyphens only when the work is by *exactly* the same author(s) as the previous entry.

Print books

7. BASIC FORMAT FOR A BOOK

Begin with the author name(s). (See models 1–6.) Then include the title and subtitle, the publisher, and the publication year. The source map on pp. 482–83 shows where to find this information in a typical book.

Crystal, David. *Language Play.* U of Chicago P, 1998.

Note: Place a period and a space after the name, title, and date. Place a comma after the publisher, and in the publisher's name, omit *Co.* or *Inc.*, and abbreviate *University* and *Press* to *U* and *P.*

8. AUTHOR AND EDITOR BOTH NAMED

> Bangs, Lester. *Psychotic Reactions and Carburetor Dung.* Edited by Greil
>
> Marcus, Alfred A. Knopf, 1988.

To cite the editor's contribution instead, begin the entry with the editor's name.

> Marcus, Greil, editor. *Psychotic Reactions and Carburetor Dung.* By Lester
>
> Bangs, Alfred A. Knopf, 1988.

9. EDITOR, NO AUTHOR NAMED

> Wall, Cheryl A., editor. *Changing Our Own Words: Essays on Criticism, Theory,*
>
> *and Writing by Black Women.* Rutgers UP, 1989.

10. ANTHOLOGY

Cite an entire anthology the same way you would cite a book with an editor and no named author (see model 9).

> Walker, Dale L., editor. *Westward: A Fictional History of the American West.*
>
> Forge Books, 2003.

11. WORK IN AN ANTHOLOGY OR CHAPTER IN A BOOK WITH AN EDITOR

List the author(s) of the selection; the selection title, in quotation marks; the title of the book, italicized; the words *edited by* and the name(s) of the editor(s); publication information; and the abbreviation *pp.* with the selection's page numbers.

> Komunyakaa, Yusef. "Facing It." *The Seagull Reader,* edited by Joseph Kelly,
>
> W. W. Norton, 2000, pp. 126-27.

Note: To provide original publication information for a reprinted selection, use the original publication information as a second "container" (see 57b):

> Byatt, A. S. "The Thing in the Forest." *The O. Henry Prize Stories 2003,* edited
>
> by Laura Furman, Anchor Books, 2003, pp. 3-22. Originally published in
>
> *The New Yorker,* 3 June 2002, pp. 80-89.

12. TWO OR MORE ITEMS FROM THE SAME ANTHOLOGY

List the anthology as one entry (see model 10). Also list each of the selections separately with a cross-reference to the anthology.

Estleman, Loren D. "Big Tim Magoon and the Wild West." Walker, pp. 391-404.

Salzer, Susan K. "Miss Libbie Tells All." Walker, pp. 199-212.

13. TRANSLATION

Bolaño, Roberto. *2666*. Translated by Natasha Wimmer, Farrar, Straus and

Giroux, 2008.

14. BOOK WITH BOTH TRANSLATOR AND EDITOR

List the editor's and translator's names after the title, in the order they appear on the title page.

Kant, Immanuel. *"Toward Perpetual Peace" and Other Writings on Politics,*

Peace, and History. Edited by Pauline Kleingeld, translated by David L.

Colclasure, Yale UP, 2006.

15. TRANSLATION OF A SECTION OF A BOOK

If different translators have worked on various parts of the book, identify the translator of the part you are citing.

García Lorca, Federico. *"The Little Mad Boy."* Translated by W. S. Merwin. *The*

Selected Poems of Federico García Lorca, edited by Francisco García Lorca

and Donald M. Allen, Penguin, 1955, pp. 51-53.

16. TRANSLATION OF A BOOK BY AN UNKNOWN AUTHOR

Place the title first unless you wish to emphasize the translator's work.

Grettir's Saga. Translated by Denton Fox and Hermann Palsson. U of Toronto P,

1974.

17. BOOK IN A LANGUAGE OTHER THAN ENGLISH

Include a translation of the title in brackets, if necessary.

Benedetti, Mario. *La borra del café* [*The Coffee Grind*]. Editorial Sudamericana,

2000.

MLA SOURCE MAP: Books

Take information from the book's title page and copyright page (on the reverse side of the title page), not from the book's cover or a library catalog.

1 **Author.** List the last name first. End with a period. For variations, see models 2–6.

2 **Title.** Italicize the title and any subtitle; capitalize all major words. End with a period.

3 **Publisher.** Identify the publisher's name as given on the book's title page. If more than one publisher appears on the title page, separate the names with a slash, leaving a space before and after the slash. If no publisher is listed on the title page, check the copyright page. Abbreviate *University* and *Press* as *U* and *P* (*Oxford UP*). Omit terms such as *Company* and *Incorporated.* Follow the publisher's name with a comma.

4 **Year of publication.** If more than one copyright date is given, use the most recent one. End with a period.

A citation for the book on p. 483 would look like this:

Patel, Raj. *The Value of Nothing: How to Reshape Market Society and Redefine Democracy.* Picador, 2009.

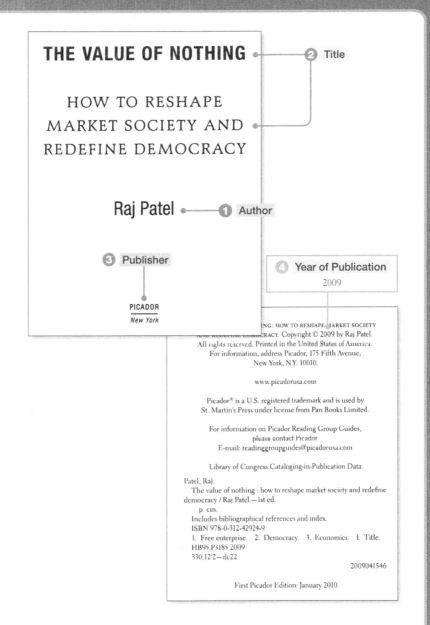

THE VALUE OF NOTHING

2 Title

HOW TO RESHAPE MARKET SOCIETY AND REDEFINE DEMOCRACY

Raj Patel

1 Author

3 Publisher

4 Year of Publication

2009

PICADOR
New York

...ING: HOW TO RESHAPE MARKET SOCIETY AND REDEFINE DEMOCRACY. Copyright © 2009 by Raj Patel. All rights reserved. Printed in the United States of America. For information, address Picador, 175 Fifth Avenue, New York, N.Y. 10010.

www.picadorusa.com

Picador® is a U.S. registered trademark and is used by St. Martin's Press under license from Pan Books Limited.

For information on Picador Reading Group Guides, please contact Picador
E-mail: readinggroupguides@picadorusa.com

Library of Congress Cataloging-in-Publication Data

Patel, Raj.
The value of nothing : how to reshape market society and redefine democracy / Raj Patel.—1st ed.
p. cm.
Includes bibliographical references and index.
ISBN 978-0-312-42924-9
1. Free enterprise. 2. Democracy. 3. Economics. I. Title.
HB95.P3185 2009
330.12'2—dc22

2009041546

First Picador Edition: January 2010

18. GRAPHIC NARRATIVE

If the words and images are created by the same person, cite a graphic narrative just as you would a book (model 7).

Bechdel, Alison. *Are You My Mother? A Comic Drama.* Houghton Mifflin

Harcourt, 2012.

If the work is a collaboration, indicate the author or illustrator who is most important to your research before the title of the work. List other contributors after the title, in the order of their appearance on the title page. Label each person's contribution to the work.

Stavans, Ilan, writer. *Latino USA: A Cartoon History.* Illustrated by Lalo

Arcaraz, Basic Books, 2000.

19. EDITION OTHER THAN THE FIRST

Walker, John A. *Art in the Age of Mass Media.* 3rd ed., Pluto P, 2001.

20. ONE VOLUME OF A MULTIVOLUME WORK

Give the number of the volume cited after the title. Including the total number of volumes after the publication date is optional.

Ch'oe, Yong-Ho, et al., editors. *Sources of Korean Tradition.* Vol. 2, Columbia

UP, 2000. 2 vols.

21. MORE THAN ONE VOLUME OF A MULTIVOLUME WORK

Ch'oe, Yong-Ho, et al., editors. *Sources of Korean Tradition.* Columbia UP,

2000. 2 vols.

22. PREFACE, FOREWORD, INTRODUCTION, OR AFTERWORD

Following the writer's name, describe the contribution. After the title, indicate the book's author (with *by*) or editor (with *edited by*).

Atwan, Robert. Foreword. *The Best American Essays 2002,* edited by Stephen

Jay Gould, Houghton Mifflin, 2002, pp. viii-xii.

Moore, Thurston. Introduction. *Confusion Is Next: The Sonic Youth Story,* by

Alec Foege, St. Martin's P, 1994, p. xi.

23. ENTRY IN A REFERENCE BOOK

For a well-known encyclopedia, note the edition (if identified) and year of publication. If the entries are alphabetized, omit publication information and page number.

Kettering, Alison McNeil. "Art Nouveau." *World Book Encyclopedia,* 2002 ed.

24. BOOK THAT IS PART OF A SERIES

After the date, cite the series name (and number, if any) from the title page.

Nichanian, Marc, and Vartan Matiossian, editors. *Yeghishe Charents: Poet of the Revolution.* Mazda, 2003. Armenian Studies Series 5.

25. REPUBLICATION (MODERN EDITION OF AN OLDER BOOK)

Indicate the original publication date after the title.

Austen, Jane. *Sense and Sensibility.* 1813. Dover Publications, 1996.

26. MORE THAN ONE PUBLISHER'S NAME

If the title page gives two publishers' names, separate them with a slash. Include spaces on both sides of the slash.

Hornby, Nick. *About a Boy.* Riverhead / Penguin Putnam, 1998.

27. A TITLE WITHIN THE TITLE

Do not italicize the title of a book or other standalone work when it appears within the title. If a title within the title identifies an article or other short work, italicize as usual and place the article title in quotation marks.

Mullaney, Julie. *Arundhati Roy's* The God of Small Things: *A Reader's Guide.* Continuum, 2002.

Rhynes, Martha. *"I, Too, Sing America": The Story of Langston Hughes.* Morgan Reynolds Publishing, 2002.

28. SACRED TEXT

To cite any individual published editions of sacred books, begin the entry with the title.

Qur'an: The Final Testament (Authorized English Version) with Arabic Text. Translated by Rashad Khalifa, Universal Unity, 2000.

Articles and short works in print periodicals

Begin with the author name(s). (See models 1–6.) Then include the article title, the title of the periodical, the date and volume information, and the page numbers. If an article skips page numbers, put the first page number and a plus sign (*28+*). The source map on pp. 488–89 shows where to find all of this information in a sample periodical.

29. ARTICLE IN A PRINT JOURNAL

Follow the journal title with a comma; the abbreviation *vol.* and volume number; a comma; the abbreviation *no.;* the issue number; a comma; the day (if given), month (abbreviated except for May, June, or July), and year (or season and year) of publication; a comma; the abbreviation *p.* or *pp.;* and the page numbers.

> Gigante, Denise. "The Monster in the Rainbow: Keats and the Science of Life."
>
> *PMLA*, vol. 117, no. 3, May 2002, pp. 433-48.

30. ARTICLE IN A PRINT MAGAZINE

Provide the date from the magazine cover.

> Sanneh, Kelefa. "Skin in the Game." *The New Yorker*, 24 Mar. 2014, pp. 48-55.

> Taubin, Amy. "All Talk?" *Film Comment*, Nov.-Dec. 2007, pp. 45-47.

31. ARTICLE IN A PRINT NEWSPAPER

Include the edition (if listed) and the section number or letter (if listed).

> Fackler, Martin. "Japan's Foreign Minister Says Apologies to Wartime Victims
>
> Will Be Upheld." *The New York Times*, 9 Apr. 2014, late ed., p. A6.

Note: For locally published newspapers, add the city in brackets after the name if it is not part of the name: *Globe and Mail [Toronto].*

32. EDITORIAL IN A PRINT PERIODICAL

Include the writer's name, if given, and the title, if any. End with the label *Editorial.*

> "California Dreaming." *The Nation*, 25 Feb. 2008, p. 4. Editorial.

33. LETTER TO THE EDITOR OF A PRINT PERIODICAL

Include the writer's name, if given, and the title, if any. Provide relevant information for the type of source, and end with the label *Letter.*

> MacEwan, Valerie. *The Believer*, vol. 12, no. 1, Jan. 2014, p. 4. Letter.

34. REVIEW IN A PRINT PERIODICAL

Include the writer's name and the title of the review. If no title is given, write *Review of* and the title of the work under review, without italics or quotation marks.

> Nussbaum, Emily. "Change Agents: Review of *The Americans* and *Silicon*
>
> *Valley.*" *The New Yorker*, 31 Mar. 2014, p. 68.

> Schwarz, Benjamin. Review of *The Second World War: A Short History*, by
>
> R. A. C. Parker. *The Atlantic Monthly*, May 2002, pp. 110-11.

35. INTERVIEW IN A PRINT PERIODICAL

List the person interviewed as the author, the title of the interview (if any), and the label *Interview*, along with the interviewer's name, if relevant and not already stated.

> Blume, Judy. "Judy Blume in Conversation with Lena Dunham." Interview.
>
> *The Believer*, vol. 12, no. 1, Jan. 2014, pp. 39+.

36. UNSIGNED ARTICLE IN A PRINT PERIODICAL

> "Performance of the Week." *Time*, 6 Oct. 2003, p. 18.

Digital written-word sources

Digital sources such as websites differ from print sources in the ease with which they can be changed, updated, or eliminated. The most commonly cited digital sources are documents from websites and databases.

37. WORK FROM AN ONLINE DATABASE

The basic format for citing a work from a database appears in the source map on pp. 492–93.

For a periodical article that you access in an online database through a library subscription service, begin with the author's name (if given); the title of the work, in quotation marks; the title of the periodical, italicized; and the volume/issue and date of the print version of the work (see models 29–36). Next, include the page numbers from the print version. Then give the name of the online database, italicized, and a DOI or permalink for the article; if neither is available, give the URL of the database home page, omitting the protocol (*http://*).

> Collins, Ross F. "Cattle Barons and Ink Slingers: How Cow Country Journalists
>
> Created a Great American Myth." *American Journalism*, vol. 24, no. 3,
>
> Summer 2007, pp. 7-29. *Communication and Mass Media Complete*,
>
> www.ebscohost.com/academic/communication-mass-media-complete.

MLA SOURCE MAP: Articles in Print Periodicals

① **Author.** List the last name first. End with a period. For variations, see models 2–6.

② **Article title.** Put the title and any subtitle in quotation marks; capitalize all major words. Place a period inside the closing quotation mark.

③ **Periodical title.** Italicize the title; capitalize all major words. End with a comma.

④ **Volume and issue / Date of publication.** Give the volume number, abbreviated *vol.,* and the issue number, abbreviated *no.,* if the periodical provides them. List the day (if given), month (abbreviated except for May, June, and July), and year (or season and year) of publication. Put commas after the volume, issue, and date.

⑤ **Page numbers.** Give the abbreviation *p.* (for "page") or *pp.* (for "pages") and the inclusive page numbers. If the article skips pages, put the first page number and a plus sign. End with a period.

A citation for the article on p. 489 would look like this:

Quart, Alissa. "Lost Media, Found Media: Snapshots from the Future of Writing." *Columbia Journalism Review,* May/June 2008, pp. 30-34.

③ Periodical Title

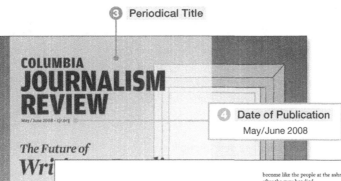

COLUMBIA
**JOURNALISM
REVIEW**
May/June 2008 · cjr.org

④ Date of Publication
May/June 2008

The Future of

Wri...

Nonfiction's...
ALISSA QUAR...

Kindle isn't i...
EZRA KLEIN...

UNDER TH...
A reporter r...
that got him...
CAMERON MC...

LOVE THY...
The religion...
TIM TOWNSE...

---

② Article Title

Lost Media,
Found Media

Snapshots from the future of writing

BY ALISSA QUART

① Author

ALISSA QUART

If there were an ashram for people who worship contemplative long-form journalism, it would be the Nieman Conference on Narrative Journalism. This March, at the Sheraton Boston Hotel, hundreds of journalists, authors, students, and aspirants came for the weekend event. Seated on metal chairs in large conference rooms, we learned about muscular storytelling (the Q-shaped narrative structure—who knew?). We sipped cups of coffee and ate bagels and heard about reporting history through letters and public documents and how to evoke empathy for our subjects, particularly our most marginal ones. As we listened to reporters discussing great feats—exposing Walter Reed's fetid living quarters for wounded soldiers, for instance—we also renewed our pride in our profession. In short, the conference exemplified the best of the older media models, the ones that have so recently fallen into economic turmoil.

Yet even at the weekend's strongest lectures on interview techniques or the long-form profile, we couldn't ignore the digital elephant in the room. We all knew as writers that the kinds of pieces we were discussing require months of work to be both deep and refined, and that we were all hard-pressed for the time and the money to do that. It was always hard for nonfiction writers, but something seems to have changed. For those of us who believed in the value of the journalism and literary nonfiction of the past, we had become like the people at the ashram after the guru has died.

Right now, journalism is more or less divided into two camps, which I will call Lost Media and Found Media. I went to the Nieman conference partially because I wanted to see how the forces creating this new division are affecting and afflicting the Lost Media world that I love best, not on the institutional level, but for reporters and writers themselves. This world includes people who write for all the newspapers and magazines that are currently struggling with layoffs, speedups, hiring freezes, buyouts, the death or shrinkage of film- and book-review sections, limits on expensive investigative work, the erasure of foreign bureaus, and the general narrowing of institutional ambition. It includes freelance writers competing with hordes of ever younger competitors willing to write and publish online for free, the fade-out of established journalistic career paths, and, perhaps most crucially, a muddled sense of the meritorious, as blogs level and scramble the value and status of print publications, and of professional writers. The glamour and influence once associated with a magazine elite seem to have faded, becoming a sort of pastiche of winsome articles about yearning and boxers and dinners at Elaine's.

Found Media-ites, meanwhile, are the bloggers, the contributors to Huffington Post-type sites that aggregate blogs, as well as other work that somebody else paid for, and the new nonprofits and pay-per-article schemes that aim to save journalism from 20 percent profit-margin demands. Although these elements are often disparate, together they compose the new media landscape. In economic terms, I mean all the outlets for nonfiction writing that seem to be thriving in the new era or striving to fill niches that Lost Media is giving up in a new order. Stylistically, Found Media tends to feel spontaneous, almost accidental. It's a domain dominated by the young, where writers get points not for following traditions or burnishing them but for amateur and hybrid vigor, for creating their own venues and their own genres. It is about public expression and community—not quite John Dewey's Great Community, which the critic Eric Alterman alluded to in a recent *New Yorker* article on newspapers, but rather a fractured form of Dewey's ideal: call it Great Communities.

To be a Found Media journalist or pundit, one need not be elite, expert, or trained; one must simply produce punchy intellectual property that is in conversation with groups of

Illustration by Tomer Hanuka

⑤ Page Numbers
30–34

QUICK HELP

Citing Articles From Databases

1. Provide the author of the work. End with a period.
2. Give the title of the article you are citing, in quotation marks. Put a period inside the closing quotation mark.
3. Give the title of the periodical, italicized, and a comma.
4. Give the volume (abbreviated *vol.*), a comma, the issue number (abbreviated *no.*), and a comma.
5. Give the most complete date of publication you can find (day, month, and year; month and year; or season and year). Abbreviate months except May, June, and July. End with a comma.
6. Give the abbreviation *p.* or *pp.* and the print page numbers. End with a period.
7. Give the name of the database, italicized, followed by a comma.
8. Provide a permalink or DOI, if you can find one. If not, give the URL of the database home page. End with a period.

38. ARTICLE FROM A JOURNAL ON THE WEB

Begin an entry for an online journal article as you would one for a print journal article (see model 29). End with the online location (permalink, DOI, or URL) and a period.

> Clark, Msia Kibona. "Hip Hop as Social Commentary in Accra and Dar es
> Salaam." *African Studies Quarterly,* vol. 13, no. 3, Summer 2012,
> pp. 23–46, asq.africa.ufl.edu/files/Clark-V13Is3.pdf.

39. ARTICLE FROM A MAGAZINE ON THE WEB

List the author, article title, and name of the magazine. Then identify the date of publication, and provide a permalink or DOI, if one is available, or a URL.

> Landhuis, Esther. "Is Dementia Risk Falling?" *Scientific American,* 25 Jan.
> 2016, www.scientificamerican.com/article/is-dementia-risk-falling/.

40. ARTICLE FROM A NEWSPAPER ON THE WEB

After the name of the newspaper, give the publication date and the permalink (if you can find one) or URL.

Shyong, Frank. "Sriracha Showdown Intensifies as Irwindale Declares
Public Nuisance." *Los Angeles Times,* 10 Apr. 2014, articles.latimes
.com/2014/apr/10/local/la-me-ln-sriracha-irwindale-public
-nuisance-20140410.

41. DIGITAL BOOK

Provide information as for a print book (see models 7–28); then give the
digital container title and any other relevant information, including the
location.

Euripides. *The Trojan Women.* Translated by Gilbert Murray, Oxford UP, 1915.
Internet Sacred Text Archive, 2011, www.sacred-texts.com/cla/eurip/
troj_w.htm.

If you read the book on an e-reader such as a Kindle or Nook, specify
the type of reader file you used.

Schaap, Rosie. *Drinking with Men: A Memoir.* Riverhead / Penguin, 2013.
Kindle.

42. PART OF A DIGITAL BOOK

Cite as you would a part of a print book (see models 11 and 22) for
the first container (see 57b). For the second container, give the title,
the date, and the DOI, permalink, or URL.

Riis, Jacob. "The Genesis of the Gang." *The Battle with the Slum,* Macmillan,
1902. *Bartleby.com: Great Books Online,* 2015, www.bartleby.com/175/
9.html.

43. ONLINE POEM

Include the poet's name, the title of the poem, and the print publication information (if any) for the first container (see 57b). For the
second container, give the title, the date, and the DOI, permalink,
or URL.

Geisel, Theodor. "Too Many Daves." *The Sneetches and Other Stories,* Random
House, 1961. *Poetry Foundation,* 2015, www.poetryfoundation.org/
poem/171612.

MLA SOURCE MAP: Articles from Databases

Library subscriptions—such as EBSCOhost and Academic Search Premier—provide access to huge databases of articles.

1 **Author.** List the last name first. End with a period. For variations, see models 2–6.

2 **Article title.** Enclose the title and any subtitle in quotation marks. End with a period.

3 **Periodical title.** Italicize it. Follow it with a comma.

4 **Volume and issue / Date of publication.** List the volume and issue number, separated by commas. Use the abbreviations *vol.* and *no.* Then, add the date of publication, including the day (if given), month, and year, in that order. Follow it with a comma.

5 **Page numbers.** Give the inclusive page numbers, using the abbreviations *p.* or *pp.* End with a period.

6 **Database name.** Italicize the name of the database. End with a comma.

7 **Location.** Give the DOI or other permalink, if available. If not, give the URL for the home page of the database.

A citation for the article on p. 493 would look like this:

Arnett, Robert P. "*Casino Royale* and Franchise Remix: James Bond as Superhero." *Film Criticism,* vol. 33, no. 3, Spring 2009, pp. 1-16. *Academic Search Premier,* www.ebscohost.com/academic/academic -search-premier.

Title:	**Casino Royale and Franchise Remix: James Bond as Superhero.**
Authors:	Arnett, Robert P.1
Source:	Film Criticism; Spring2009, Vol. 33 Issue 3, p1-16, 16p
Document Type:	Article
Subject Terms:	*JAMES Bond films *FILM genres *BOND, James (Fictitious character) *SUPERHERO films
Reviews & Products:	CASINO Royale (Film)
People:	CRAIG, Daniel
Abstract:	The article discusses the role of the film "Casino Royale" in remixing the James Bond franchise. The author believes that the remixed Bond franchise has shifted its genre to a superhero franchise. When Sony acquired MGM in 2004, part of its plans is to transform the 007 franchise at par with "Spiderman." The remixed franchise re-aligns its franchise criteria with those established by superhero films. The author cites "Casino Royale's" narrative structure as an example of the success of the film as franchise remixed for the future. The portrayal of Bond as a superhero by actor Daniel Craig is discussed.
Author Affiliations:	1Associate professor, Department of Communication and Theatre Arts, Old Dominion University
ISSN:	01635069
Accession Number:	47966995
Database:	Academic Search Premier

493

44. ONLINE EDITORIAL OR LETTER TO THE EDITOR

Include the author's name (if given) and the title (if any). Follow the appropriate model for the type of source you are using. (Check the directory on pp. 476–77.) End with the label *Editorial* or *Letter*.

> "Migrant Children Deserve a Voice in Court." *The New York Times*, 8 Mar. 2016, nyti.ms/1LO8bKK. Editorial.

> Starr, Evva. "Local Reporting Thrives in High Schools." *The Washington Post*, 4 Apr. 2014, wpo.st/7hmJ1. Letter.

45. ONLINE REVIEW

Cite an online review as you would a print review (see model 34). End with the name of the website, the date of publication, and the URL or permalink.

> O'Hehir, Andrew. "Aronofsky's Deranged Biblical Action Flick." *Salon*, 27 May 2014, www.salon.com/2014/03/27/noah_aronofskys_deranged_biblical _action_flick/.

46. SHORT WORK FROM A WEBSITE

For basic information for citing a work on a website that is not part of a regularly published journal, magazine, or newspaper, see the source map on pp. 496–97. Include all of the following elements that are available: the author; the title of the document, in quotation marks; the name of the website, italicized; the name of the publisher or sponsor (if the name is different from the name of the site); the date of publication; and the location. If the site gives no date, end with *Accessed* and your date of access.

> Bali, Karan. "Kishore Kumar." *Upperstall.com*, upperstall.com/profile/ kishore-kumar/. Accessed 2 Mar. 2016.

> "Our Mission." *Trees for Life International*, 2011, www.treesforlife.org/ our-work/our-mission.

47. ENTIRE WEBSITE

Follow the guidelines for a work from the web, beginning with the name of the author or editor (if any), followed by the title of the website, italicized; the name of the sponsor or publisher (if different

QUICK HELP

Citing Works From Websites

1. Provide the author of the work, if you can find one. End with a period.
2. Give the title of the work you are citing, ending with a period. If the work is part of a larger container (such as a video on YouTube), put the title in quotation marks.
3. If the title you identified is not the name of the website, list the website title, in italics, followed by a comma.
4. If the site's publisher or sponsor is different from the title of the site, identify the publisher or sponsor, followed by a comma. If the names are very similar, omit the publisher.
5. Give the date of publication or latest update, followed by a comma.
6. Give a permalink (if you can find one) or URL. End with a period.
7. If the work does not include any date, add "Accessed" and the day, month (abbreviated, except for May, June, or July), and year you accessed the source. End with a period. If you provided a date before the URL, omit the access date.

from the name of the site; otherwise, omit the sponsor or publisher); the date of publication or last update; and the location.

> Glazier, Loss Pequeño, director. *Electronic Poetry Center.* State U of New York
>
> Buffalo, 1996-2016, epc.buffalo.edu/.

> *Weather.com.* Weather Channel Interactive, 1995-2016, weather.com/.

For a personal website, include the name of the person who created the site; the title, in quotation marks if it is part of a larger work or italicized if it is not, or (if there is no title) a description such as *Home page*, not italicized; the name of the larger site, if different from the personal site's title; the publisher or sponsor of the site (if different from the site title); the date; and the URL. If the site is undated, end with your date of access.

> Enright, Mike. *Menright.com.* www.menright.com. Accessed 30 Mar. 2016.

48. ENTRY IN AN ONLINE REFERENCE WORK OR WIKI

Begin with the title unless the author is named. (A wiki, which is collectively edited, will not include an author.) Treat an online reference entry as you would a short work from a website (see model 46).

MLA SOURCE MAP: Works from Websites

You may need to browse other parts of a site to find some of the following elements, and some sites may omit elements. Uncover as much information as you can.

1 **Author.** List the last name first. End with a period. If no author is given, begin with the title. For variations, see models 2–6.

2 **Title of work.** Enclose the title and any subtitle of the work in quotation marks.

3 **Title of website.** Give the title of the entire website, italicized. Follow it with a comma.

4 **Publisher or sponsor.** Look for the sponsor's name at the bottom of the home page. If the sponsor's name is approximately the same as the site title, omit the sponsor. Follow it with a comma.

5 **Date of publication or latest update.** Give the most recent date, followed by a period.

6 **Location.** Give a permalink, if you can find one, or the site's URL, followed by a period.

7 **Date of access.** If the site is undated, end with *Accessed* and the date.

A citation for the work on p. 497 would look like this:

Tønnesson, Øyvind. "Mahatma Gandhi, the Missing Laureate." *Nobelprize.org*, 2015, www.nobelprize.org/nobel_prizes/themes/peace/gandhi/.

6 Location　　　**3 Title of Website**　　**2 Title of Work**

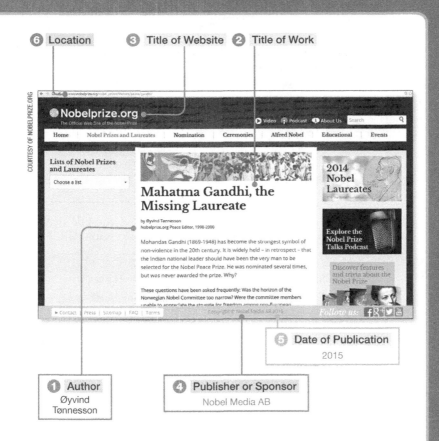

5 Date of Publication
2015

1 Author
Øyvind
Tønnesson

4 Publisher or Sponsor
Nobel Media AB

Include the title of the entry; the name of the work, italicized; the sponsor or publisher; the date of the latest update; and the location (permalink or URL). Before using a wiki as a source, check with your instructor.

> Cartwright, Mark. "Apollo." *Ancient History Encyclopedia*, 18 May 2012, www
> .ancient.eu/apollo/.

> "Gunpowder Plot." *Wikipedia*, 4 Mar. 2016, en.wikipedia.org/wiki/Gunpowder
> _Plot.

49. ACADEMIC COURSE OR DEPARTMENT WEBSITE

For a course site, include the name of the instructor, the title of the course, the title of the site in italics, the date, and the location (URL).

> Creekmur, Corey K., and Philip Lutgendorf. Topics in Asian Cinema:
> Popular Hindi Cinema. *U of Iowa*, Spring 2007, www.uiowa.edu/
> indiancinema/article/syllabus-introductory-university-course
> -popular-hindi-cinema.

For a department website, give the department name, the description *Department home page*, the institution (in italics), the date, and the URL. If the site is undated, end with your access date.

> English Department home page. *Amherst College*, www.amherst.edu/
> academiclife/departments/english. Accessed 5 Apr. 2016.

50. BLOG

For an entire blog, give the author's name, if any; the title of the blog, italicized; the sponsor or publisher of the blog (if any); the date; and the URL. If the site is undated, end with your access date.

> Levy, Carla Miriam. *Filmi Geek*. 2006-2015, www.filmigeek.com/.

> *Little Green Footballs*. littlegreenfootballs.com. Accessed 4 Mar. 2016.

Note: To cite a blogger who writes under a pseudonym, begin with the pseudonym and then put the writer's real name (if you know it) in parentheses. (See model 5, p. 479.)

> Atrios (Duncan Black). *Eschaton*. www.eschatonblog.com/. Accessed 8 Mar.
> 2016.

51. POST OR COMMENT ON A BLOG OR DISCUSSION GROUP

Give the author's name; the title of the post, in quotation marks; the title of the site, italicized; the date of the post; and the URL.

> Edroso, Roy. "Going Down with the Flagship." *Alicublog,* 24 Feb. 2016,
>
> alicublog.blogspot.com/2016/02/going-down-with-flagship.html.

For a comment on an online post, give the writer's name or screen name (see model 5); a label such as *Comment on,* not italicized; the title of the article commented on, in quotation marks; and the label *by* and the article author's name. End with the citation information for the original article and the URL for the comment.

> JennOfArk. Comment on "Going Down with the Flagship," by Roy Edroso.
>
> *Alicublog,* 24 Feb. 2016, alicublog.blogspot.com/2016/02/going-down
>
> -with-flagship.html#disqus_thread.

52. TWEET

Begin with the writer's Twitter handle, and put the real name, if known, in parentheses. Include the entire tweet, in quotation marks. Give the site name in italics (*Twitter*), the date and time of the message, and the URL for the tweet.

> @Lunsfordhandbks (Andrea A. Lunsford). "Technology & social media have
>
> changed the way we write. That doesn't mean literacy has declined
>
> https://community.macmillan.com/groups/macmillan-news
>
> /blog/2016/02/24/the-literacy-revolution... @MacmillanLearn."
>
> *Twitter,* 24 Feb. 2016, 10:17 a.m., twitter.com/LunsfordHandbks/
>
> status/702512638937460736.

53. POSTING ON A SOCIAL NETWORKING SITE

To cite a posting on Facebook, Instagram, or another social networking site, include the writer's name; up to 140 characters of the posting, in quotation marks (or a description such as *Photograph,* not italicized and not in quotation marks, if no text appears); the name of the site, italicized; the date of the post; and the location of the post (URL).

> Cannon, Kevin. "Portrait of Norris Hall in #Savannah, GA — home (for a few
>
> more months, anyway) of #SCAD's sequential art department." *Instagram,*
>
> Mar. 2014, www.instagram.com/p/lgmqk4i6DC/.

54. EMAIL OR MESSAGE

Include the writer's name; the subject line, in quotation marks, if one is provided, or a descriptive label such as *Text message*; *Received by* (not italicized or in quotation marks) followed by the recipient's name; and the date of the message.

> Carbone, Nick. "Screen vs. Print Reading." Received by Karita dos Santos,
>
> 17 Apr. 2013.

Visual, audio, multimedia, and live sources

55. FILM (THEATRICAL, DVD, OR OTHER FORMAT)

If you cite a particular person's work, start with that name. If not, start with the title of the film; then name the director, distributor, and year of release. Other contributors, such as writers or performers, may follow the director. If you cite a feature found only on a disc, treat the film as the first "container" and the disc as the second "container" (see 57b).

> Bale, Christian, performer. *The Big Short*. Directed by Adam McKay, Paramount
>
> Pictures, 2015.

> Lasseter, John. Introduction. *Spirited Away*, directed by Hayao Miyazaki, 2001.
>
> Walt Disney Video, 2003, disc 1.

> *Shree 420*. Directed by Raj Kapoor, performances by Kapoor and Nargis,
>
> R. K. Films, 1955.

56. ONLINE VIDEO CLIP

Cite an online video as you would a short work from a website (see model 46).

> Weber, Jan. "As We Sow, Part 1: Where Are the Farmers?" *YouTube*,
>
> 15 Mar. 2008, www.youtube.com/watch?v=_cdcDpMf6qE.

57. TELEVISION BROADCAST

Begin with the title of the program, italicized (for an entire series), or the title of the episode, in quotation marks. Then list important contributors (narrator, writer, director, actors); season and episode number (for a specific episode); the network; the local station and city, if the show appeared on a local channel; and the broadcast date(s). To cite a particular person's work, begin with that name (see model 55). When citing an entire series, give inclusive dates.

> *Breaking Bad.* Created by Vince Gilligan, performances by Bryan Cranston,
> Aaron Paul, Anna Gunn, AMC, 2008-2013.

> "Time Zones." *Mad Men,* written by Matthew Weiner, directed by Scott
> Hornbacher, season 7, episode 1, AMC, 13 Apr. 2014.

58. TELEVISION ON THE WEB

For a show accessed on a network website, begin as for a television broadcast (model 57). After the network, include the date of posting and the URL.

> "Time Zones." *Mad Men,* written by Matthew Weiner, directed by Scott
> Hornbacher, season 7, episode 1, AMC, 13 Apr. 2014, www.amc.com/
> shows/mad-men/season-7/episode-01-time-zones.

59. RADIO BROADCAST

If you are citing a particular episode or segment, begin with the title, in quotation marks. Then give the program title in italics. List important contributors (narrator, writer, director, actors); the network; the local station and city, if the show appeared locally; and the broadcast date(s). To cite a particular person's work, begin with that name.

> "Tarred and Feathered." *This American Life,* narrated by Ira Glass, WNYC,
> New York, 11 Apr. 2013.

60. RADIO ON THE WEB

For a show or segment accessed on the web, begin as for a radio broadcast (model 59). After the network, include the date of posting, the website title, and the URL.

> "Obama's Failures Have Made Millennials Give Up Hope." *The Rush
> Limbaugh Show,* narrated by Rush Limbaugh, Premiere Radio
> Networks, 14 Apr. 2014, *RushLimbaugh.com,* www.rushlimbaugh.com/
> daily/2014/04/14/obama_s_failures_have_made_millennials_give
> _up_hope.

61. TELEVISION OR RADIO INTERVIEW

List the person interviewed and then the title, if any. If the interview has no title, use the label *Interview* and name the interviewer, if relevant. Then identify the source. End with information about the program and the date(s) the interview took place.

> Russell, David O. Interview by Terry Gross. *Fresh Air,* WNYC, New York,
>
> 20 Feb. 2014.

Note: If you found an archived version of a television or radio interview online, provide the date of the interview, the name of the website, and the location (URL or permalink).

> Revkin, Andrew. Interview by Terry Gross. *Fresh Air,* NPR, 14 June 2006, www
>
> .npr.org/templates/story/story.php?storyId=5484338.

62. ONLINE INTERVIEW

Start with the name of the person interviewed. Give the title, if there is one. If not, give a descriptive label such as *Interview*, neither italicized nor in quotation marks, and the interviewer's name, if relevant. In the second "container" (57b), include the title of the site, sponsor or publisher (if there is one), the date of publication, and the URL.

> Ladd, Andrew. "What Ends: An Interview with Andrew Ladd." Interview by Jill.
>
> *Looks & Books,* 25 Feb. 2014, www.looksandbooks.com/2014/02/25/
>
> what-ends-an-interview-with-andrew-ladd/.

63. PERSONAL INTERVIEW

List the person interviewed; the label *Telephone interview, Personal interview,* or *E-mail interview;* and the date the interview took place.

> Freedman, Sasha. Personal interview, 10 Nov. 2014.

64. SOUND RECORDING

List the name of the person or group you wish to emphasize (such as the composer, conductor, or band); the title of the recording or composition; the artist, if appropriate; the manufacturer; and the year of issue. If you are citing a particular song or selection, include its title, in quotation marks.

> Bach, Johann Sebastian. *Bach: Violin Concertos.* Performances by Itzhak
>
> Perlman and Pinchas Zukerman, English Chamber Orchestra, EMI, 2002.
>
> Sonic Youth. "Incinerate." *Rather Ripped,* Geffen, 2006.

Note: If you are citing instrumental music that is identified only by form, number, and key, do not underline, italicize, or enclose it in quotation marks.

> Grieg, Edvard. Concerto in A minor, op. 16. Conducted by Eugene Ormandy,
>
> Philadelphia Orchestra, RCA, 1989.

65. MUSICAL COMPOSITION

When you are not citing a specific published version, first give the composer's name, followed by the title.

> Mozart, Wolfgang Amadeus. *Don Giovanni,* K527.

> Mozart, Wolfgang Amadeus. Symphony no. 41 in C major, K551.

66. PUBLISHED SCORE

Cite a published score as you would a book. If you include the date the composition was written, do so immediately after the title.

> Schoenberg, Arnold. *Chamber Symphony No. 1 for 15 Solo Instruments, Op. 9.*
>
> 1906. Dover, 2002.

67. VIDEO GAME

Start with the developer or author (if any). After the title, give the distributor and the date of publication.

> Harmonix. *Rock Band Blitz.* MTV Games, 2012.

Note: If you play the game on the web, give the URL after the date.

68. COMPUTER SOFTWARE OR APP

Cite as a video game (see model 67), giving the available information about the version, distributor, and date.

> *Angry Birds.* Version 4.1.0. Rovio, 2014.

69. LECTURE OR SPEECH (LIVE)

List the speaker; the title (if any), in quotation marks; the sponsoring institution or group; the place; and the date. Add the label "Lecture" or "Speech" after the date if readers will not otherwise be able to identify the work.

> Eugenides, Jeffrey. Portland Arts and Lectures. Arlene Schnitzer Concert Hall,
>
> Portland, OR, 30 Sept. 2003.

70. LECTURE OR SPEECH ON THE WEB

Cite as you would a short work from a website (model 46).

> Burden, Amanda. "How Public Spaces Make Cities Work." *TED.com,* Mar. 2014,
>
> www.ted.com/talks/amanda_burden_how_public_spaces_make_cities
>
> _work.

71. LIVE PERFORMANCE

List the title, the appropriate names (such as the writer or performer), the place, and the date. To cite a particular person's work, begin the entry with that name.

> *The Sea Ranch Songs.* By Aleksandra Vrebalov, performed by The Kronos
>
> Quartet, White Barn, The Sea Ranch, CA, 23 May 2015.

72. PODCAST (STREAMING)

Cite a podcast that you view or listen to online as you would a short work from a website (model 46).

> Fogarty, Mignon. "Begs the Question: Update." *QuickandDirtyTips.com,*
>
> Macmillan, 6 Mar. 2014, www.quickanddirtytips.com/education/
>
> grammar/begs-the-question-update.

73. DOWNLOADED DIGITAL FILE

A citation for a file that you can download — one that exists independently, not only on a website — begins with citation information required for the type of source (a photograph or sound recording, for example).

> *Officers' Winter Quarters, Army of Potomac, Brandy Station.* Mar. 1864, Prints
>
> and Photographs Division, Library of Congress, www.loc.gov/item/
>
> 90708676/.

> "Return to the Giant Pool of Money." *This American Life,* narrated by Ira
>
> Glass, NPR, 25 Sept. 2009, www.thisamericanlife.org/radio-archives/
>
> episode/390/Return-To-The-Giant-Pool-of-Money.

74. WORK OF ART OR PHOTOGRAPH

List the artist's or photographer's name; the work's title, italicized; and the date of composition. Then cite the name of the museum or other location and the city. To cite a reproduction in a book, add the publication information (see the second model below). To cite artwork found online, after the location, add the title of the database or website, italicized, and the URL or permalink.

Bronzino, Agnolo. *Lodovico Capponi*. 1550-55, Frick Collection, New York.

General William Palmer in Old Age. 1810, National Army Museum, London.

> *White Mughals: Love and Betrayal in Eighteenth-Century India,* by William Dalrymple, Penguin, 2002, p. 270.

Hassam, Childe. *Isles of Shoals*. 1899, Minneapolis Institute of Arts,

> collections.artsmia.org/art/45/isles-of-shoals-childe-hassam.

75. MAP OR CHART

Cite a map or chart as you would a book or a short work within a longer work. For an online source, include the location. End with the label *Map* or *Chart* if needed for clarity.

"Australia." *Perry-Castañeda Library Map Collection,* U of Texas, 1999, www.lib

> .utexas.edu/maps/australia/australia_pol99.jpg.

California. Rand McNally, 2002. Map.

76. CARTOON OR COMIC STRIP

List the artist's name; the title (if any) of the cartoon or comic strip, in quotation marks; and the usual publication information for a print periodical (see models 29–36) or a short work from a website (model 46). You may end the entry with a label (*Cartoon* or *Comic strip*) for clarity.

Flake, Emily. *The New Yorker,* 13 Apr. 2015, p. 66. Cartoon.

Munroe, Randall. "Heartbleed Explanation." *xkcd.com,* xkcd.com/1354/. Comic strip.

77. ADVERTISEMENT

Include the label *Advertisement*.

Ameritrade. *Wired,* Jan. 2014, p. 47. Advertisement.

Lufthansa. *The New York Times,* 16 Apr. 2014, www.nytimes.com. Advertisement.

QUICK HELP

Citing Visuals That Appear in Your Text

If you choose to include images in your text, you need to cite and caption them correctly (see p. 474).

- For a work that you have created, the works-cited entry should begin with a descriptive phrase from the image's caption ("L.A. Bus Stop"), a label ("Photograph by author"), and the date.

- For a visual reproduced from another source, you can include the complete citation information in the caption, or you can indicate the source to allow readers to find it on the list of works cited. If you give the complete citation in the caption and do not cite the visual elsewhere in your text, you can omit the visual from your works-cited page.

Other sources (including digital versions)

If an online version is not shown in this section, use the appropriate model for the source and then end with a DOI, permalink, or URL.

78. REPORT OR PAMPHLET

Follow the guidelines for a print book (models 7–28) or a digital book (model 41).

> Rainie, Lee, and Maeve Duggan. *Privacy and Information Sharing.* Pew
>
>   Research Center, 14 Jan. 2016, www.pewinternet.org/files/2016/01/
>
>   PI_2016.01.14_Privacy-and-Info-Sharing_FINAL.pdf.

79. GOVERNMENT PUBLICATION

Begin with the author, if identified. Otherwise, start with the name of the government, followed by the agency. For congressional documents, cite the number, session, and house of Congress; the type (*Report, Resolution, Document*); and the number. End with the publication information. The print publisher is often the Government Printing Office. For online versions, follow the models for a short work from a website (model 46), an entire website (model 47), or a downloadable file (model 73).

> Gregg, Judd. *Report to Accompany the Genetic Information Act of 2003.* US
>
>   108th Congress, 1st session, Senate Report 108-22, Government Printing
>
>   Office, 2003.

United States, Department of Health and Human Services, National
Institutes of Health. *Keep the Beat Recipes: Deliciously Healthy
Dinners.* Oct. 2009, healthyeating.nhlbi.nih.gov/pdfs/Dinners
_Cookbook_508-compliant.pdf.

80. PUBLISHED PROCEEDINGS OF A CONFERENCE

Cite the proceedings as you would a book.

Cleary, John, and Gary Gurtler, editors. *Proceedings of the Boston Area
Colloquium in Ancient Philosophy 2002.* Brill Academic Publishers, 2003.

81. DISSERTATION

Enclose the title in quotation marks. Add the label *Dissertation,* the
school, and the year the work was accepted.

Thompson, Brian. "I'm Better Than You and I Can Prove It: Games, Expertise,
and the Culture of Competition." Dissertation, Stanford U, 2015.

Note: Cite a published dissertation as a book, adding the identification
Dissertation and the university after the title.

82. DISSERTATION ABSTRACT

Cite the abstract as you would an unpublished dissertation (see model
81). For the abstract of a dissertation that uses *Dissertation Abstracts
International*, include the volume, year, and page number.

Huang-Tiller, Gillian C. "The Power of the Meta-Genre: Cultural, Sexual, and
Racial Politics of the American Modernist Sonnet." Dissertation, U of
Notre Dame, 2000. Abstract. *Dissertation Abstracts International,* vol. 61,
2000, p. 1401.

Moore, Courtney L. "Stress and Oppression: Identifying Possible Protective
Factors for African American Men." Dissertation, Chicago School of
Professional Psychology, 2016. Abstract. *ProQuest Dissertations and
Theses,* search.proquest.com/docview/1707351557.

83. UNPUBLISHED LETTER

Cite a published letter as a work in an anthology (see model 11). If
the letter is unpublished, follow this form:

Anzaldúa, Gloria. Letter to the author, 10 Sept. 2002.

84. MANUSCRIPT OR OTHER UNPUBLISHED WORK

List the author's name; the title (if any) or a description of the material; any identifying numbers; and the name and location of the library or research institution housing the material, if applicable.

> Woolf, Virginia. "The Searchlight." Series III, Box 4, Item 184. Papers of
>
> Virginia Woolf, 1902-1956, Smith College, Northampton.

85. LEGAL SOURCE

To cite a court case, give the names of the first plaintiff and defendant, the case number, the name of the court, and the date of the decision. To cite an act, give the name of the act followed by its Public Law (*Pub. L.*) number, the date the act was enacted, and its Statutes at Large (*Stat.*) cataloging number.

> Citizens United vs. FEC. 558 US 310. Supreme Court of the US. 2010. *Legal*
>
> *Information Institute,* Cornell U Law School, www.law.cornell.edu/supct/
>
> pdf/08-205P.ZS.

> Museum and Library Services Act of 2003. Pub. L. 108-81. Stat. 117.991.
>
> 25 Sept. 2003.

Note: You do not need an entry in the list of works cited when you cite articles of the U.S. Constitution and laws in the U.S. Code.

60 A Student Research Essay, MLA Style

Student Writer

David Craig

David Craig's research project appears on the following pages. In preparing this essay, he followed the MLA guidelines described in this chapter. His complete project appears with an activity at **macmillanhighered.com/everyday6e**.

David Craig

Professor Turkman

English 219

18 December 2014

Name, instructor, course, and date aligned at left

Messaging: The Language of Youth Literacy

Title centered

The English language is under attack. At least, that is what many people seem to believe. From concerned parents to local librarians, everyone seems to have a negative comment on the state of youth literacy today. They fear that the current generation of grade school students will graduate with an extremely low level of literacy, and they point out that although language education hasn't changed, kids are having more trouble reading and writing than in the past. When asked about the cause of this situation, many adults pin the blame on technologies such as texting and instant messaging, arguing that electronic shortcuts create and compound undesirable reading and writing habits and discourage students from learning conventionally correct ways to use language. But although the arguments against messaging are passionate, evidence suggests that they may not hold up.

Opens with attention-getting statement

Background on the problem of youth literacy

Explicit thesis statement concludes introductory paragraph

The disagreements about messaging shortcuts are profound, even among academics. John Briggs, an English professor at the University of California, Riverside, says, "Americans have always been informal, but now the informality of precollege culture is so ubiquitous that many students have no practice in using language in any formal setting at all" (qtd. in McCarroll). Such objections are not new; Sven Birkerts of Mount Holyoke College argued in 1999 that "[students] read more casually. They strip-mine what they read" online and consequently produce "quickly generated, casual prose" (qtd. in Leibowitz A67). However, academics are also among the defenders of texting and instant messaging (IM), with

Indirect quotation uses "qtd. in" and name of web source on list of works cited

Marginal annotations indicate effective choices or MLA-style formatting.

Writer's last name and page number at upper right corner of every page

some suggesting that messaging may be a beneficial force in the development of youth literacy because it promotes regular contact with words and the use of a written medium for communication.

Definition and example of messaging

Texting and instant messaging allow two individuals who are separated by any distance to engage in real-time, written communication. Although such communication relies on the written word, many messagers disregard standard writing conventions. For example, here is a snippet from an IM conversation between two teenage girls:[1]

> Teen One: sorry im talkinto like 10 ppl at a time
>
> Teen Two: u izzyful person
>
> Teen Two: kwel
>
> Teen One: hey i g2g

As this brief conversation shows, participants must use words to communicate via texting and messaging, but their words do not

Writer considers argument that youth literacy is in decline

have to be in standard English.

The issue of youth literacy does demand attention because standardized test scores for language assessments, such as the verbal and writing sections of the College Board's SAT, have

Figure explained in text and cited in parenthetical reference

declined in recent years. This trend is illustrated in a chart distributed by the College Board as part of its 2011 analysis of aggregate SAT data (see Fig. 1).

Discussion of Figure 1

The trend lines illustrate a significant pattern that may lead to the conclusion that youth literacy is on the decline. These lines display the ten-year paths (from 2001 to 2011) of reading and writing scores, respectively. Within this period, the average verbal score dropped a few points—and appears to be headed toward a

Explanatory note adds information not found on list of works cited

further decline in the future.

1. This transcript of an IM conversation was collected on 20 Nov. 2014. The teenagers' names are concealed to protect privacy.

Craig 3   Student Writing
MLA

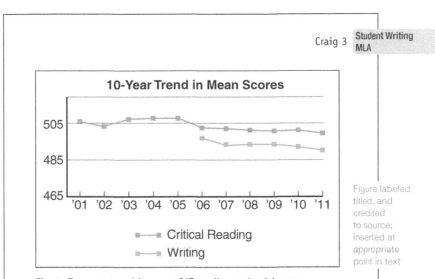

10-Year Trend in Mean Scores

■——■ Critical Reading
■——■ Writing

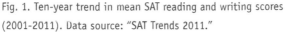

Figure labeled, titled, and credited to source; inserted at appropriate point in text

Fig. 1. Ten-year trend in mean SAT reading and writing scores (2001-2011). Data source: "SAT Trends 2011."

Based on the preceding statistics, parents and educators appear to be right about the decline in youth literacy. And this trend coincides with another phenomenon: digital communication is rising among the young. According to the Pew Internet & American Life Project, 85 percent of those aged twelve to seventeen at least occasionally write text messages, instant messages, or comments on social networking sites (Lenhart et al.). In 2001, the most conservative estimate based on Pew numbers showed that American youths spent, at a minimum, nearly three million hours per day on instant messaging services (Lenhart and Lewis 20). These numbers are now exploding thanks to texting, which was "the dominant daily mode of communication" for teens in 2012 (Lenhart), and messaging on popular social networking sites such as Facebook and Tumblr.

In the interest of establishing the existence of a messaging language, I analyzed 11,341 lines of text from IM conversations

Writer accepts part of critics' argument; transition to next point

For a web source with no page numbers, only author names appear in parentheses

Writer's field research described

between youths in my target demographic: U.S. residents aged twelve to seventeen. Young messagers voluntarily sent me chat logs, but they were unaware of the exact nature of my research. Once all of the logs had been gathered, I went through them, recording the number of times messaging language was used in place of conventional words and phrases. Then I generated graphs to display how often these replacements were used.

> During the course of my study, I identified four types of messaging language: phonetic replacements, acronyms, abbreviations, and inanities. An example of phonetic replacement is using *ur* for *you are*. Another popular type of messaging language is the acronym; for a majority of the people in my study, the most common acronym was *lol*, a construction that means *laughing out loud*. Abbreviations are also common in messaging, but I discovered that typical IM abbreviations, such as *etc.*, are not new to the English language. Finally, I found a class of words that I call "inanities." These words include completely new words or expressions, combinations of several slang categories, or simply nonsensical variations of other words. My favorite from this category is *lolz*, an inanity that translates directly to *lol* yet includes a terminating *z* for no obvious reason.

> In the chat transcripts that I analyzed, the best display of typical messaging lingo came from the conversations between two thirteen-year-old Texan girls, who are avid IM users. Figure 2 is a graph showing how often they used certain phonetic replacements and abbreviations. On the *y*-axis, frequency of replacement is plotted, a calculation that compares the number of times a word or phrase is used in messaging language with the total number of times that it is communicated in any form. On the *x*-axis, specific messaging words and phrases are listed.

Findings of field research presented

Figure introduced and explained

My research shows that the Texan girls use the first ten phonetic replacements or abbreviations at least 50 percent of the time in their normal messaging writing. For example, every time one of them writes *see*, there is a parallel time when *c* is used in its place. In light of this finding, it appears that the popular messaging culture contains at least some elements of its own language. It also seems that much of this language is new: no formal dictionary yet identifies the most common messaging words and phrases. Only in the heyday of the telegraph or on the rolls of a stenographer would you find a similar situation, but these "languages" were never a popular medium of youth communication. Texting and instant messaging, however, are very popular among young people and continue to generate attention and debate in academic circles.

Discussion of findings presented in Figure 2

My research shows that messaging is certainly widespread, and it does seem to have its own particular vocabulary, yet these two factors alone do not mean it has a damaging influence on youth literacy. As noted earlier, however, some people claim that

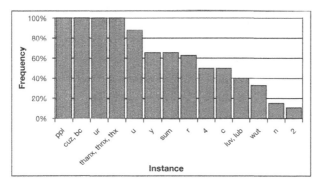

Fig. 2. Usage of phonetic replacements and abbreviations in messaging.

Figure labeled and titled

Writer returns to opposition argument

For author of web source named in signal phrase, no parenthetical citation needed

Transition to support of thesis and refutation of critics

the new technology is a threat to the English language. In an article provocatively titled "Texting Makes U Stupid," historian Niall Ferguson argues, "The good news is that today's teenagers are avid readers and prolific writers. The bad news is that what they are reading and writing are text messages." He goes on to accuse texting of causing the United States to "[fall] behind more literate societies."

The critics of messaging are numerous. But if we look to the field of linguistics, a central concept — metalinguistics — challenges these criticisms and leads to a more reasonable conclusion — that messaging has no negative impact on a student's development of or proficiency with traditional literacy.

Scholars of metalinguistics offer support for the claim that messaging is not damaging to those who use it. As noted earlier, one of the most prominent components of messaging language is phonetic replacement, in which a word such as *everyone* becomes *every1*. This type of wordplay has a special importance in the development of an advanced literacy, and

Linguistic authority cited in support of thesis

Author of print source named in signal phrase, so parenthetical citation includes only page number

for good reason. According to David Crystal, an internationally recognized scholar of linguistics at the University of Wales, as young children develop and learn how words string together to express ideas, they go through many phases of language play. The singsong rhymes and nonsensical chants of preschoolers are vital to learning language, and a healthy appetite for wordplay leads to a better command of language later in life (182).

As justification for his view of the connection between language play and advanced literacy, Crystal presents an argument for metalinguistic awareness. According to Crystal, *metalinguistics* refers to the ability to "step back" and use words to analyze how language works:

> If we are good at stepping back, at thinking in a more
> abstract way about what we hear and what we say, then
> we are more likely to be good at acquiring those skills
> which depend on just such a stepping back in order to be
> successful — and this means, chiefly, reading and writing. . . .
> [T]he greater our ability to play with language, . . . the
> more advanced will be our command of language as a whole.
> (Crystal 181)

    If we accept the findings of linguists such as Crystal that
metalinguistic awareness leads to increased literacy, then it seems
reasonable to argue that the phonetic language of messaging can
also lead to increased metalinguistic awareness and, therefore,
increases in overall literacy. As messagers develop proficiency
with a variety of phonetic replacements and other types of texting
and messaging words, they should increase their subconscious
knowledge of metalinguistics.

    Metalinguistics also involves our ability to write in a variety
of distinct styles and tones. Yet in the debate over messaging and
literacy, many critics assume that either messaging or academic
literacy will eventually win out in a person and that the two
modes cannot exist side by side. This assumption is, however,
false. Human beings ordinarily develop a large range of language
abilities, from the formal to the relaxed and from the mainstream
to the subcultural. Mark Twain, for example, had an understanding
of local speech that he employed when writing dialogue for
Huckleberry Finn. Yet few people would argue that Twain's
knowledge of this form of English had a negative impact on his
ability to write in standard English.

    However, just as Mark Twain used dialects carefully in
dialogue, writers must pay careful attention to the kind of language

Margin annotations:

Block format for a quotation of more than four lines

Ellipses and brackets indicate omissions and changes in quotation

Writer links Crystal's views to thesis

Another refutation of critics' assumptions

Example from well-known work of literature used as support

they use in any setting. Composition specialist Andrea A. Lunsford backs up this idea in a blog post:

> [W]here English is concerned, there is never one solitary right way to proceed: everything depends on the rhetorical situation and the intended purpose.

Email correspondence cited in support of claim

The analytical ability that is necessary for writers to choose an appropriate tone and style in their writing is, of course, metalinguistic in nature because it involves the comparison of two or more language systems. Thus, youths who grasp multiple languages will have a greater natural understanding of metalinguistics. More specifically, young people who possess both messaging and traditional skills stand to be better off than their peers who have been trained only in traditional or conventional systems. Far from being hurt by their online pastime, instant messagers can be aided in standard writing by their experience with messaging language.

Writer synthesizes evidence for claim

The fact remains, however, that youth literacy seems to be declining. What, if not messaging, is the main cause of this phenomenon? According to the College Board, which collects data on several questions from its test takers, course work in English composition classes has decreased by 14 percent between 1992 and 2002 (Carnahan and Coletti 11). The possibility of messaging causing a decline in literacy seems inadequate when statistics on English education for US youths provide other evidence of the possible causes. Simply put, students in the United States are not getting as much practice in academic writing as they used to. Rather than blaming texting and messaging language alone for the decline in literacy and test scores, we must also look toward our schools' lack of focus on the teaching of standard English skills.

Transition to final point

Alternative explanation for decline in literacy

My findings indicate that the use of messaging poses virtually no threat to the development or maintenance of formal language skills among American youths aged twelve to seventeen. Diverse language skills tend to increase a person's metalinguistic awareness and, thereby, his or her ability to use language effectively to achieve a desired purpose in a particular situation. The current decline in youth literacy is not due to the rise of texting and messaging. Rather, fewer young students seem to be receiving an adequate education in the use of conventional English. Unfortunately, it may always be fashionable to blame new tools for old problems, but in the case of messaging, that blame is not warranted. Although messaging may expose literacy problems, it does not create them.

Transition to conclusion

Concluding paragraph sums up argument and reiterates thesis

Craig 10

Heading
centered

Report

Print book

Article from
database

Print
newspaper
article

Downloaded
file

Online report

Subsequent
lines of each
entry indented

Blog post

Online news-
paper article

Graph source

Works Cited

Carnahan, Kristin, and Chiara Coletti. *Ten-Year Trend in SAT Scores*
    Indicates Increased Emphasis on Math Is Yielding Results: Reading
    and Writing Are Causes for Concern. College Board, 2002.

Crystal, David. *Language Play.* U of Chicago P, 1998.

Ferguson, Niall. "Texting Makes U Stupid." *Newsweek,* vol. 158,
    no. 12, 19 Sept. 2011, p. 11. *EBSCOhost,* connection
    .ebscohost.com/c/articles/65454341/texting-makes-u-stupid.

Leibowitz, Wendy R. "Technology Transforms Writing and the
    Teaching of Writing." *Chronicle of Higher Education,* 26 Nov.
    1999, pp. A67-A68.

Lenhart, Amanda. *Teens, Smartphones, & Texting.* Pew Research
    Center, 19 Mar. 2012, www.pewinternet.org/files/old-media//
    Files/Reports/2012/PIP_Teens_Smartphones_and_Texting.pdf.

Lenhart, Amanda, et al. *Writing, Technology & Teens.* Pew Research
    Center, 24 Apr. 2008, www.pewinternet.org/2008/04/24/
    writing-technology-and-teens/.

Lenhart, Amanda, and Oliver Lewis. *Teenage Life Online: The Rise of*
    the Instant-Message Generation and the Internet's Impact on
    Friendships and Family Relationships. Pew Research Center,
    21 June 2001, www.pewinternet.org/2001/06/20/the-rise-of
    -the-instant-message-generation/.

Lunsford, Andrea A. "Are You a 'Comma Queen'?" *Bedford Bits,* 9 Apr.
    2015, community.macmillan.com/community/the-english
    -community/bedford-bits/blog/2015/04/09/are-you-a-comma
    -queen.

McCarroll, Christina. "Teens Ready to Prove Text-Messaging Skills
    Can Score SAT Points." *Christian Science Monitor,* 11 Mar.
    2005, www.csmonitor.com/2005/0311/p01s02-ussc.html.

"SAT Trends 2011." *Collegeboard.org,* 14 Sept. 2011, research
    .collegeboard.org/programs/sat/data/archived/cb-seniors
    -2011/tables.

The Basics of APA Style

Chapters 61–64 discuss the basic formats prescribed by the American Psychological Association (APA), guidelines that are widely used in the social sciences. For further reference, consult the *Publication Manual of the American Psychological Association,* Sixth Edition (2010).

61a Think about what readers need from you.

Why does academic work call for very careful citation practices when writing for the general public may not? The answer to that question is pretty easy: readers of your academic work (your instructor, other students, perhaps even researchers and professionals in your field) expect to get certain information from source citations:

- Source citations demonstrate that while you may not yet be a recognized expert on the topic, you've nevertheless done your homework, and you are a part of the conversation surrounding it. You include sources that you find credible and that provide evidence and good reasons to back up your claims, as well as sources that you need to respond to or refute (see 14a). Careful citation shows your readers what you know, where you stand, and what you think is important.

- Source citations show that you understand the need to give credit when you make use of someone else's intellectual property. Especially in academic writing, when it's better to be safe than sorry, include a citation for any source you think you might need to cite. (See Chapter 15 for details.)

- Source citations give explicit directions to guide readers who want to look for themselves at the works you're using.

The guidelines for APA style help you with this last purpose, giving you instructions on exactly what information to include in your citation and how to format that information.

61b   Identify the type of source you are using.

Before you can decide how to cite your source following APA guidelines, you need to determine what kind of source you're using. This task can be surprisingly difficult. Citing a print book may seem relatively easy (though dizzying complications can arise—such as if the book has an editor or a translator, multiple editions, or chapters written by different people, to name a few possibilities). But citing digital sources may be especially mystifying. How, for instance, can you tell a website from a database you access online? What if your digital source reuses material from another source? Who publishes a digital text? Taking a step-by-step approach can help you solve such puzzles.

Print and digital sources

If your source has printed pages—a book or a newspaper, for instance—and you read the print version, you should look at the Directory to APA Style on pp. 532–33 for information on citing a print source. If the print source is a regularly issued journal, magazine, or newspaper (look for a date or seasonal information such as "Spring" on the cover or first page), consider it a periodical rather than a book.

If you access the digital version of a magazine or newspaper article, or if you read a book on an e-reader device such as a Kindle, then you should cite your source not as a print text but as a digital one. A digital version of a source may include updates or corrections that the print version lacks, so APA guidelines require you to indicate your mode of access and to cite print and digital sources differently.

Magazine and journal sources

APA style treats magazines and journals slightly differently. To determine whether a print source is a magazine (a popular source) or a journal (a scholarly source), see 13a.

Web and database sources

You need a subscription to look through most databases, so individual researchers almost always gain access to articles in databases through the computer system of a school or community library that pays to subscribe. The easiest way to tell whether a source comes from a database, then, is that its information is *not* generally available for free to anyone with an Internet connection. Many databases are digital collections of articles that originally appeared in edited print periodicals, ensuring that an authority has vouched for the accuracy of the information. Such sources often have more credibility than much of what is available for free on the web.

61c Plan and connect your citations.

APA citations appear in two connected parts of your text—a brief in-text citation in the body of your written text and a full citation in the list of references, to which the in-text citation directs readers. The most straightforward in-text citations include the author's name, the publication year, and the page number, but many variations on this basic format are discussed in Chapter 62.

In the text of her research essay (see 19c), Tawnya Redding includes a paraphrase of material from an online journal that she accessed through the publisher's website. She cites the authors' names and the year of publication in a parenthetical reference, pointing readers to the entry for "Baker, F., & Bor, W. (2008)" in her references list, shown below.

MOOD MUSIC   9

References

Baker, F., & Bor, W. (2008). Can music preference indicate mental
      health status in young people? *Australasian Psychiatry, 16*(4),
      284–288. Retrieved from http://www3.interscience.wiley.com/
      journal/118565538/home

types of music can alter the mood of at-risk youth in a negative
way. This view of the correlation between music and suicide risk
is supported by a meta-analysis done by Baker and Bor (2008), in
which the authors assert that most studies reject the notion that
music is a causal factor and suggest that music preference is more

and adolescent suicidal risk. *Journal of Youth and Adolescence,*
      30(3), 321–332.
Lai, Y. (1999). Effects of music listening on depressed women in

61d   Include notes as needed.

APA style allows you to use content notes, either at the bottom of the page or on a separate page at the end of the text, to expand or supplement your text. Indicate such notes in the text by superscript numerals (^{1}). Double-space all entries. Indent the first line of each note five spaces, but begin subsequent lines at the left margin.

SUPERSCRIPT NUMBER IN TEXT

The age of the children involved in the study was an important factor in the selection of items for the questionnaire.[1]

FOOTNOTE

[1] Marjorie Youngston Forman and William Cole of the Child Study Team provided great assistance in identifying appropriate items for the questionnaire.

61e   Format APA manuscripts appropriately.

The following formatting guidelines are adapted from the APA recommendations for preparing manuscripts for publication in journals. However, check with your instructor before preparing the final draft of a print text.

- *Title page.* If your instructor wants you to include a running head, place it flush left on the first line. Write the words *Running head*, a colon, and a short version of the title (fifty characters or fewer, including spaces) using all capital letters. On the same line, flush with the right margin, type the number *1*.

  Center the title and include your name and school affiliation. An author's note at the bottom of the page can give the course name and contact information, if desired.

- *Margins and spacing.* Leave margins of one inch at the top and bottom and on both sides of the page. Do not justify the right margin. Double-space the entire text, including any headings, set-off quotations (15b), content notes, and the list of references. Indent one-half inch for the first line of a paragraph and all lines of a quotation over forty words long.

- *Short title and page numbers.* Place the short title in the upper left corner of each page. Place the page number in the upper right corner of each page, in the same position as on the title page.

- *Long quotations.* To set off a long quotation (more than forty words), indent it one-half inch from the left margin. Do not use quotation marks. Place the page reference in parentheses one space after the final punctuation.

- *Abstract.* If your instructor asks for an abstract, the abstract should go immediately after the title page, with the word *Abstract* centered an inch from the top of the page. Double-space the text. In most cases, a one-paragraph abstract of 150–250 words will be sufficient to introduce readers to your topic and provide a brief summary of your major thesis and supporting points.

- *Headings.* Headings are used within the text of many APA-style projects. In a text with only one or two levels of headings, use boldface type; center the main headings, and position the subheadings flush with the left margin. Capitalize all major words; however, do not capitalize articles, short prepositions, and coordinating conjunctions unless they are the first word or follow a colon.

- *Visuals.* Tables should be labeled *Table*, numbered, and captioned. All other visuals (such as charts, graphs, photographs, and drawings) should be labeled *Figure*, numbered, and captioned with a description and the source information. Remember to refer to each visual in your text, stating how it contributes to the point(s) you are making. Tables and figures should generally appear near the relevant text; check with your instructor or see 13e for guidelines on the placement of visuals.

APA Style for In-Text Citations 62

An in-text citation in APA style always indicates which source on the references page the writer is referring to, and it explains in what year the material was published; for quoted material, the in-text citation also indicates where in the source the quotation can be found.

Note that APA style generally calls for using the past tense or present perfect tense for signal verbs: *Baker (2003) showed* or *Baker (2003) has shown*. Use the present tense only to discuss results (*the experiment demonstrates*) or widely accepted information (*researchers agree*).

DIRECTORY TO APA STYLE

In-text citations

1. Basic format for a quotation, *526*
2. Basic format for a paraphrase or summary, *527*
3. Two authors, *527*
4. Three to five authors, *527*
5. Six or more authors, *527*
6. Corporate or group author, *528*
7. Unknown author, *528*
8. Two or more authors with the same last name, *528*
9. Two or more works by an author in a single year, *528*
10. Two or more sources in one parenthetical reference, *528*
11. Source reported in another source, *528*
12. Personal communication, *529*
13. Digital source, *529*
14. Entire website, *529*
15. Table or figure reproduced in the text, *530*

1. BASIC FORMAT FOR A QUOTATION

Generally, use the author's name in a signal phrase to introduce the cited material, and then place the date, in parentheses, immediately following the author's name. If the source includes page numbers, the page number, preceded by *p.*, should appear in parentheses following the quotation.

> Gitlin (2001) pointed out that "political critics, convinced that the media are rigged against them, are often blind to other substantial reasons why their causes are unpersuasive" (p. 141).

If the author is not named in a signal phrase, place the author's name, the year, and the page number in parentheses after the quotation: (Gitlin, 2001, p. 141). For a long, set-off quotation (more than forty words), place the page reference in parentheses one space after the final word in the quotation.

For quotations from works without page numbers, you may use paragraph numbers, if the source includes them, preceded by the abbreviation *para.*

> Driver (2007) has noticed "an increasing focus on the role of land" in policy debates over the past decade (para. 1).

2. BASIC FORMAT FOR A PARAPHRASE OR SUMMARY

Include the author's last name and the year as in model 1, but omit the page or paragraph number unless the reader will need it to find the material in a long work.

> Gitlin (2001) has argued that critics sometimes overestimate the influence of the media on modern life.

3. TWO AUTHORS

Use both names in all citations. Use *and* in a signal phrase, but use an ampersand (&) in parentheses.

> Babcock and Laschever (2003) have suggested that many women do not negotiate their salaries and pay raises as vigorously as their male counterparts do.

> A recent study has suggested that many women do not negotiate their salaries and pay raises as vigorously as their male counterparts do (Babcock & Laschever, 2003).

4. THREE TO FIVE AUTHORS

List all the authors' names for the first reference.

> Safer, Voccola, Hurd, and Goodwin (2003) reached somewhat different conclusions by designing a study that was less dependent on subjective judgment than were previous studies.

In subsequent references, use just the first author's name followed by *et al.*

> Based on the results, Safer et al. (2003) determined that the apes took significant steps toward self-expression.

5. SIX OR MORE AUTHORS

Use only the first author's name and *et al.* in every citation.

> As Soleim et al. (2002) demonstrated, advertising holds the potential for manipulating "free-willed" consumers.

6. CORPORATE OR GROUP AUTHOR

If the name of the organization or corporation is long, spell it out the first time you use it, followed by an abbreviation in brackets. In later references, use the abbreviation only.

> FIRST CITATION   (Centers for Disease Control and Prevention [CDC], 2006)
>
> LATER CITATIONS   (CDC, 2006)

7. UNKNOWN AUTHOR

Use the title or its first few words in a signal phrase or in parentheses. A book's title is italicized, as in the following example; an article's title is placed in quotation marks.

> The employment profiles for this time period substantiated this trend (*Federal Employment*, 2001).

8. TWO OR MORE AUTHORS WITH THE SAME LAST NAME

Include the authors' initials in each citation.

> S. Bartolomeo (2000) conducted the groundbreaking study on teenage childbearing.

9. TWO OR MORE WORKS BY AN AUTHOR IN A SINGLE YEAR

Assign lowercase letters (*a*, *b*, and so on) alphabetically by title, and include the letters after the year.

> Gordon (2004b) examined this trend in more detail.

10. TWO OR MORE SOURCES IN ONE PARENTHETICAL REFERENCE

List any sources by different authors in alphabetical order by the authors' last names, separated by semicolons: (Cardone, 1998; Lai, 2002). List works by the same author in chronological order, separated by commas: (Lai, 2000, 2002).

11. SOURCE REPORTED IN ANOTHER SOURCE

Use the phrase *as cited in* to indicate that you are reporting information from a secondary source. Name the original source in a signal phrase, but list the secondary source in your list of references.

> Amartya Sen developed the influential concept that land reform was necessary for "promoting opportunity" among the poor (as cited in Driver, 2007, para. 2).

12. PERSONAL COMMUNICATION

Cite personal letters, email messages, electronic postings, telephone conversations, or interviews as shown. Do not include personal communications in the reference list.

R. Tobin (personal communication, November 4, 2014) supported his claims about music therapy with new evidence.

13. DIGITAL SOURCE

Cite a web or electronic document (including social media) as you would a print source, using the author's name and date.

Link and Phelan (2005) argued for broader interventions in public health that would be accessible to anyone, regardless of individual wealth.

The APA recommends the following for electronic sources without names, dates, or page numbers:

AUTHOR UNKNOWN

Use a shortened form of the title in a signal phrase or in parentheses (see model 7). If an organization is the author, see model 6.

DATE UNKNOWN

Use the abbreviation *n.d.* (for "no date") in place of the year: (*Hopkins, n.d.*).

NO PAGE NUMBERS

Many works found online or in electronic databases lack stable page numbers. (Use the page numbers for an electronic work in a format, such as PDF, that has stable pagination.) If paragraph numbers are included in such a source, use the abbreviation *para.*: (*Giambetti, 2014, para. 7*). If no paragraph numbers are included but the source includes headings, give the heading and identify the paragraph in the section:

Jacobs and Johnson (2007) have argued that "the South African media is still highly concentrated and not very diverse in terms of race and class" (South African Media after Apartheid, para. 3).

14. ENTIRE WEBSITE

If you are citing an entire website, not simply a page or document from a site, list the URL in parentheses in the text of your writing project. Do not include it in the list of references.

15. TABLE OR FIGURE REPRODUCED IN THE TEXT

Number figures (illustrations, graphs, charts, and photographs) and tables separately.

For a table, place the label (*Table 1*) and an informative heading (*Hartman's Key Personality Traits*) above the table; below, provide information about its source.

Table 1
Hartman's Key Personality Traits

Trait category	Color			
	Red	Blue	White	Yellow
Motive	Power	Intimacy	Peace	Fun
Strengths	Loyal to tasks	Loyal to people	Tolerant	Positive
Limitations	Arrogant	Self-righteous	Timid	Uncommitted

Note: Adapted from *The Hartman Personality Profile*, by N. Hayden. Retrieved February 24, 2013, from http://students.cs.byu.edu/~nhayden/Code/index.php

For a figure, place the label (*Figure 3*) and a caption indicating the source below the image. If you do not cite the source of the table or figure elsewhere in your text, you do not need to include the source in your list of references.

63 APA Style for a List of References

A list of references is an alphabetical list of the sources you have referred to in your essay. (If your instructor asks you to list everything you have read, not just the sources you cite, call the list *Bibliography*.) Begin the references list on a separate page or slide after the text of your project and any notes, under the centered heading *References* (not italicized or in quotation marks).

- Do not indent the first line of each entry, but indent subsequent lines for the entry one-half inch. (This makes the author names easy to scan.) Double-space the entire list.

- List sources alphabetically by authors' last names or by the title for any works without an author. For titles beginning with the article *A*, *An*, or *The*, don't count the article when alphabetizing the entries.

- List the author's last name first, followed by a comma and initials. For more than one author, use an ampersand (&) before the name of the last author, and separate the names with commas.

- Italicize titles of books and long works. Do not italicize titles of articles and other short works, and do not enclose them in quotation marks.

- For titles of books and articles, capitalize only the first word of the title and subtitle and any proper nouns or proper adjectives. For titles of periodicals, capitalize all major words.

QUICK HELP

Citing Sources That Don't Match Any Model Exactly

What should you do if your source doesn't match the model exactly? Suppose, for instance, that your source is a translation of a republished book with an editor.

- Identify a basic model to follow. If you decide that your source looks most like a republished book, start with a citation that looks like model 18.

- Look for models that show the additional elements in your source. For this example, you would need to add elements of model 13 (for the translation) and model 8 (for the editor).

- Add new elements from other models to your basic model in the order indicated.

- If you aren't sure how to arrange the pieces to create a combination model, ask your instructor.

    To cite a source for which you cannot find a model, collect as much information as you can find about the creator, title, sponsor, date, and so on, with the goal of helping your readers find the source for themselves. Then look at the models in this section to see which one most closely matches the type of source you are using. If possible, seek your instructor's advice to find the best model.

References

Guidelines for author listings

1. One author, *534*
2. Multiple authors, *534*
3. Organization or group author, *534*
4. Unknown author, *534*
5. Author using a pseudonym (pen name) or screen name, *534*
6. Two or more works by the same author, *534*
7. Two or more works by the same author in the same year, *535*
8. Editor, *535*
9. Author and editor, *535*

Print books

10. Basic format for a book, *535*
    SOURCE MAP, *536–37*
11. Entire anthology or collection, *535*
12. Work in an anthology or collection, *538*
13. Translator, *538*
14. Book in a language other than English, *538*
15. Edition other than the first, *538*
16. One volume of a multivolume work, *538*
17. More than one volume of a multivolume work, *538*
18. Republished book (more recent version of an older book), *538*
19. Introduction, preface, foreword, or afterword, *539*
20. Government publication, *539*
21. Book with a title within the title, *539*
22. Article in a reference book, *539*

Articles and short works in print periodicals

23. Article in a print journal, *539*
24. Article in a print magazine, *539*
    SOURCE MAP, *540–41*
25. Article in a print newspaper, *542*
26. Editorial or unsigned article in a print publication, *542*
27. Letter to the editor in a print publication, *542*
28. Review in a print publication, *542*
29. Interview in a print publication, *542*

Digital written-word sources

30. Work from an online database, *542*
    SOURCE MAP, *544–45*
31. Article from a journal on the web, *543*
32. Article from a magazine on the web, *546*
33. Article from a newspaper on the web, *546*
34. Abstract for a journal article online, *546*
35. Comment on an online article, *546*
36. Digital book (online or e-reader), *546*
37. Online editorial or letter to the editor, *547*
38. Online review, *547*
39. Interview published online, *547*
40. Entry in an online reference work or wiki, *547*
41. Report or document from a web site, *547*
    SOURCE MAP, *548–49*
42. Section of a web document, *550*
43. Entire website, *550*
44. Government source online, *550*
45. Online report from a private organization, *550*
46. Blog post, *550*
47. Blog comment, *551*

DIRECTORY TO APA STYLE

References, continued

Visual, audio, multimedia, and live sources

48. Film (theatrical, DVD, or other format), *551*
49. Video or audio on the web, *551*
50. Transcript of video or audio file, *551*
51. Television episode broadcast, *551*
52. Television series, *552*
53. Television episode on the web, *552*
54. Podcast (downloaded file), *552*
55. Sound recording, *552*
56. Video game, *552*
57. Computer software or app, *552*
58. Lecture or speech (live), *553*
59. Lecture or speech viewed on the web, *553*
60. Data set or graphic representation of data, *553*
61. Presentation slides, *553*
62. Work of art or photograph, *553*
63. Map, *553*
64. Advertisement, *553*

Academic sources (including online versions)

65. Published proceedings of a conference, *554*
66. Paper presented at a meeting or symposium, unpublished, *554*
67. Poster session, *554*
68. Dissertation, *554*

Personal communications and social media

69. Tweet, *554*
70. Posting on a public social networking site, *555*
71. Email, private message, or post on a social networking site, *555*

Guidelines for author listings

The list of references is arranged alphabetically. The in-text citations in your writing point readers toward particular sources in the list (see Chapter 62).

NAME CITED IN SIGNAL PHRASE IN TEXT

Driver (2007) has noted . . .

NAME IN PARENTHETICAL CITATION IN TEXT

. . . (Driver, 2007).

BEGINNING OF ENTRY IN LIST OF REFERENCES

Driver, T. (2007).

Models 1–9 explain how to arrange author and editor names. The information that follows the name of the author depends on the type of work you are citing—a print book (models 10–22), a print periodical (models 23–29), a digital written-word source (models 30–47), a media or live source (models 48–64), an academic source (models 65–68), or a personal communication (models 69–71).

1. ONE AUTHOR

Give the last name, a comma, the initial(s), and the date in parentheses.

> Zimbardo, P. G. (2007). *The Lucifer effect: Understanding how good people turn evil.* New York, NY: Random House.

2. MULTIPLE AUTHORS

List up to seven authors, last name first, with commas separating authors' names and an ampersand (&) before the last author's name.

> Miller, S. J., O'Hea, E. L., Lerner, J. B., Moon, S., & Foran-Tuller, K. A. (2011).

For a work with more than seven authors, list the first six, then an ellipsis (. . .), and then the final author's name.

> Lahmann, C., Henrich, G., Henningsen, P., Baessler, A., Fischer, M., Loew, T., . . . Pieh, C. (2011).

3. ORGANIZATION OR GROUP AUTHOR

> Resources for Rehabilitation. (2003).

4. UNKNOWN AUTHOR

Begin with the work's title. Italicize book titles, but do not italicize article titles or enclose them in quotation marks. Capitalize only the first word of the title and subtitle (if any) and proper nouns or proper adjectives.

> *Safe youth, safe schools.* (2009).

5. AUTHOR USING A PSEUDONYM (PEN NAME) OR SCREEN NAME

Give the author's real name, if known, and give the pen or screen name in brackets. If the real name is unknown, use only the screen name.

> Psych Babbler. (2013, August 4). Blogging under a pseudonym [Web log post]. Retrieved from http://www.overacuppacoffee.com/blogging -under-a-pseudonym/

6. TWO OR MORE WORKS BY THE SAME AUTHOR

List works by the same author in chronological order. Repeat the author's name in each entry.

> Goodall, J. (1999).

> Goodall, J. (2002).

7. TWO OR MORE WORKS BY THE SAME AUTHOR IN THE SAME YEAR

If the works appeared in the same year, list them alphabetically by title, and assign lowercase letters (*a, b,* etc.) after the dates.

Shermer, M. (2002a). On estimating the lifetime of civilizations. *Scientific American, 287*(2), 33.

Shermer, M. (2002b). Readers who question evolution. *Scientific American, 287*(1), 37.

8. EDITOR

If the source has an editor but no author, alphabetize the entry under the editor's last name.

Mishra, P. (Ed.). (2005). *India in mind.* New York, NY: Random House-Vintage.

9. AUTHOR AND EDITOR

To cite a work with both an author and an editor, place the editor's name, with a comma and the abbreviation *Ed.,* in parentheses after the title.

Austin, J. (1995). *The province of jurisprudence determined.* (W. E. Rumble, Ed.). Cambridge, England: Cambridge University Press.

Print books

10. BASIC FORMAT FOR A BOOK

Begin with the author name(s). (See models 1–9.) Then include the publication year, title and subtitle, city of publication, country or state abbreviation, and publisher. The source map on pp. 536–37 shows where to find this information in a typical book.

Levick, S. E. (2003). *Clone being: Exploring the psychological and social dimensions.* Lanham, MD: Rowman & Littlefield.

11. ENTIRE ANTHOLOGY OR COLLECTION

Begin with the editor's name, and use the label *Ed.* or *Eds.*

Rudd, E., & Descartes, L. (Eds.). (2008). *The changing landscape of work and family in the American middle class: Reports from the field.* Lanham, MD: Lexington.

APA SOURCE MAP: Books

Take information from the book's title page and copyright page (on the reverse side of the title page), not from the book's cover or a library catalog.

1 **Author.** List all authors' last names first, and use only initials for first and middle names. For more about citing authors, see models 1–9.

2 **Publication year.** Enclose the year of publication in parentheses.

3 **Title.** Italicize the title and any subtitle. Capitalize only the first word of the title and subtitle and any proper nouns or proper adjectives.

4 **City and state of publication, and publisher.** List the city of publication and the country or state abbreviation, a colon, and the publisher's name, dropping any *Inc.*, *Co.*, or *Publishers*.

A citation for the book on p. 537 would look like this:

Tsutsui, W. (2004). *Godzilla on my mind: Fifty years of the king of monsters.*
New York, NY: Palgrave Macmillan.

② Publication Year

2004

GODZILLA ON MY MIND.
Copyright © William Tsutsui, 2004.

First published 2004 by
PALGRAVE MACMILLAN™
175 Fifth Avenue, New York, N.Y. 10010 and
Houndmills, Basingstoke, Hampshire, England RG21 6XS.
Companies and representatives throughout the world.

PALGRAVE MACMILLAN is the global academic imprint of
the Palgrave Macmillan division of St. Martin's Press, LLC and of
Palgrave Macmillan Ltd. Macmillan® is a registered trademark in
the United States, United Kingdom and other countries. Palgrave
is a registered trademark in the European Union and other
countries.

ISBN 1-4039-6474-2

Library of Congress Cataloging-in-Publication Data
Tsutsui, William
Godzilla on my mind : fifty years of the king of monsters / William
Tsutsui.
    p.   cm.
  Includes bibliographical references and index.
  ISBN 1-4039-6474-2
  1. Godzilla films—History and criticism. I. Title.

PN1995.9.G63T78   2004
791.43'651—dc22

A catalogue reco[...]
Library.

Design by Letra [...]

10 9 8 7 6 [...]

Printed in the U[...]

④ City and State of Publication

New York, N.Y.

③ Title

GODZILLA®
ON MY MIND

*

③ Subtitle

*Fifty Years of the
King of Monsters*

WILLIAM TSUTSUI ●——① Author

palgrave
macmillan

④ Publisher

12. WORK IN AN ANTHOLOGY OR COLLECTION

Give the name of the work's author first. List editors after the work's title, and include page numbers after the collection's title.

> Pash, D. M. (2008). Gay family values: Gay co-father families in straight communities. In E. Rudd & L. Descartes (Eds.), *The changing landscape of work and family in the American middle class: Reports from the field* (pp. 159–187). Lanham, MD: Lexington.

13. TRANSLATOR

After the title, give the translator's name and the abbreviation *Trans.* in parentheses.

> Al-Farabi, A. N. (1998). *On the perfect state* (R. Walzer, Trans.). Chicago, IL: Kazi.

14. BOOK IN A LANGUAGE OTHER THAN ENGLISH

Include the English translation (in brackets) after the title.

> Andre, C. (2004). *Psychologie de la peur* [The psychology of fear]. Paris, France: Odile Jacob.

15. EDITION OTHER THAN THE FIRST

> Moore, G. S. (2002). *Living with the earth: Concepts in environmental health science* (2nd ed.). New York, NY: Lewis.

16. ONE VOLUME OF A MULTIVOLUME WORK

List the volume in parentheses after the title.

> Barnes, J. (Ed.). (1995). *Complete works of Aristotle* (Vol. 2). Princeton, NJ: Princeton University Press.

17. MORE THAN ONE VOLUME OF A MULTIVOLUME WORK

List the complete span of volumes in parentheses after the title.

> Barnes, J. (Ed.). (1995). *Complete works of Aristotle* (Vols. 1–2). Princeton, NJ: Princeton University Press.

18. REPUBLISHED BOOK (MORE RECENT VERSION OF AN OLDER BOOK)

> Piaget, J. (1952). *The language and thought of the child.* London, England: Routledge & Kegan Paul. (Original work published 1932)

19. INTRODUCTION, PREFACE, FOREWORD, OR AFTERWORD

Klosterman, C. (2007). Introduction. In P. Shirley, *Can I keep my jersey?: 11 teams, 5 countries, and 4 years in my life as a basketball vagabond* (pp. v–vii). New York, NY: Villard-Random House.

20. GOVERNMENT PUBLICATION

Office of the Federal Register. (2003). *The United States government manual 2003/2004.* Washington, DC: U.S. Government Printing Office.

21. BOOK WITH A TITLE WITHIN THE TITLE

Do not italicize or enclose in quotation marks a title within a book title.

Klarman, M. J. (2007). Brown v. Board of Education *and the civil rights movement.* New York, NY: Oxford University Press.

22. ARTICLE IN A REFERENCE BOOK

Dean, C. (1994). Jaws and teeth. In *The Cambridge encyclopedia of human evolution* (pp. 56–59). Cambridge, England: Cambridge University Press.

If no author is listed, begin with the title.

Articles and short works in print periodicals

Begin with the author name(s). (See models 1–9.) Then include the publication date (year only for journals, and year, month, and day for all other periodicals); the article title; the periodical title; the volume number and issue number, if any; and the page numbers. The source map on pp. 540–41 shows where to find this information in a sample periodical.

23. ARTICLE IN A PRINT JOURNAL

Include the issue number (in parentheses and not italicized) after the volume number (italicized).

Hall, R. E. (2000). Marriage as vehicle of racism among women of color. *Psychology: A Journal of Human Behavior, 37*(2), 29–40.

24. ARTICLE IN A PRINT MAGAZINE

Include the month (as well as the day, if given).

Solomon, A. (2014, March 17). The reckoning. *The New Yorker, 90*(4), 36–45.

1 **Author.** List all authors' last names first, and use only initials for first and middle names. For more about citing authors, see models 1–9.

2 **Publication date.** Enclose the date in parentheses. For journals, use only the year. For magazines and newspapers, use the year, a comma, the month (spelled out), and the day, if given.

3 **Article title.** Do not italicize or enclose article titles in quotation marks. Capitalize only the first word of the article title and subtitle and any proper nouns or proper adjectives.

4 **Periodical title.** Italicize the periodical title (and subtitle, if any), and capitalize all major words. Follow the periodical title with a comma.

5 **Volume and issue numbers.** Give the volume number (italicized) and, without a space in between, the issue number (if given) in parentheses. Follow with a comma.

6 **Page numbers.** Give the inclusive page numbers of the article. For newspapers only, include the abbreviation *p.* ("page") or *pp.* ("pages") before the page numbers. End the citation with a period.

A citation for the periodical article on p. 541 would look like this:

Etzioni, A. (2006). Leaving race behind: Our growing Hispanic population creates a golden opportunity. *The American Scholar, 75*(2), 20–30.

The AMERICAN
SCHOLAR

●──④ **Periodical Title**

Spring 2006 | Vol. 75, No. 2 ●──⑤   **Volume and Issue Numbers**

② **Publication Date**

ROBERT WILSON
Editor

JEAN STIPICEVIC
Managing Editor

SANDRA COSTICH

The AMERICAN
SCHOLAR

③ **Article Title**

Leaving Race Behind

Our growing Hispanic population creates a golden opportunity

AMITAI ETZIONI   ●──① **Author**

Some years ago the United States government asked me what my race was. I was reluctant to respond because my 50 years of practicing sociology—and some powerful personal experiences—have underscored for me what we all know to one degree or another, that racial divisions bedevil America, just as they do many other societies across the world. Not wanting to encourage these divisions, I refused to check off one of the specific racial options on the U.S. Census form and instead marked a box labeled "Other." I later found out that the federal government did not accept such an attempt to de-emphasize race, by me or by some 6.75 million other Americans who tried it. Instead the government assigned me to a racial category, one it chose for me. Learning this made me conjure up what I admit is a far-fetched association. I was in this place once before. When I was a Jewish child in Nazi Germany in the early 1930s, many Jews who saw themselves as good Germans wanted to "pass" as Aryans. But the Nazi regime would have none of it. Never mind, they told these Jews, *we determine* who is Jewish and who is not. A similar practice prevailed in the Old South, where if you had one drop of African blood you were a Negro, disregarding all other facts and considerations, including how you saw yourself.

You might suppose that in the years since my little Census-form protest

~ Amitai Etzioni is University Professor at George Washington University and the author of *The Monochrome Society*.

20 ●── ⑥ **Page Numbers**

25. ARTICLE IN A PRINT NEWSPAPER

Use *p.* or *pp.* with the page numbers.

Fackler, M. (2014, April 9). Japan's foreign minister says apologies to wartime
victims will be upheld. *The New York Times,* p. A6.

26. EDITORIAL OR UNSIGNED ARTICLE IN A PRINT PUBLICATION

Add an identifying label such as *[Editorial]*.

The tyranny of the glass boxes [Editorial]. (2014, April 22). *The New York
Times,* p. A24.

27. LETTER TO THE EDITOR IN A PRINT PUBLICATION

Add an identifying label.

MacEwan, V. (2014, January). [Letter to the editor]. *The Believer, 12*(1), 4.

28. REVIEW IN A PRINT PUBLICATION

Include the author and title of the review, if given. In brackets, give
the type of work, the title, and the author (for a book) or year (for a
motion picture).

Lane, A. (2014, March 17). Double trouble [Review of the motion picture
Enemy, 2014]. *The New Yorker, 90*(4), 78–79.

29. INTERVIEW IN A PRINT PUBLICATION

Blume, J. (2014, January). Judy Blume in conversation with Lena Dunham
[Interview by Dunham]. *The Believer, 12*(1), 39–48.

Digital written-word sources

Updated guidelines for citing digital resources are maintained at the
APA's website (www.apa.org).

30. WORK FROM AN ONLINE DATABASE

Provide the author, date, title, and publication information as you
would for a print document. Include both the volume and issue
numbers for all journal articles. If the article has a digital object identifier (DOI), include it. If there is no DOI, write *Retrieved from* and the
URL of the journal's home page (not the URL of the database). The

source map on pp. 544–45 shows where to find this information for a typical article from a database.

> Hazleden, R. (2003, December). Love yourself: The relationship of the self with itself in popular self-help texts. *Journal of Sociology, 39*(4), 413–428. Retrieved from http://jos.sagepub.com

> Morley, N. J., Ball, L. J., & Ormerod, T. C. (2006). How the detection of insurance fraud succeeds and fails. *Psychology, Crime, & Law, 12*(2), 163–180. doi:10.1080/10683160512331316325

31. ARTICLE FROM A JOURNAL ON THE WEB

Give information as for an article in a print journal (see model 23). If the article has a DOI (digital object identifier), include it. If there is no DOI, include the URL for the journal's home page or for the article, if it is difficult to find from the home page.

> Cleary, J. M., & Crafti, N. (2007). Basic need satisfaction, emotional eating, and dietary restraint as risk factors for recurrent overeating in a community sample. *E-Journal of Applied Psychology, 2*(3), 27–39. Retrieved from http://ojs.lib.swin.edu.au/index.php/ejap/article/view/90/116

QUICK HELP

Citing Digital Sources

When citing sources accessed online or from an electronic database, include as many of the following elements as you can find:

- **Author.** Give the author's name, if available.
- **Publication date.** Include the date of electronic publication or of the latest update, if available. When no publication date is available, use *n.d.* ("no date").
- **Title.** If the source is not from a larger work, italicize the title.
- **Print publication information.** For articles from online journals, magazines, or reference databases, give the publication title and other publishing information as you would for a print periodical (see models 23–29).
- **Retrieval information.** For a work from a database, do the following: if the article has a DOI (digital object identifier), include that number after the publication information; do not include the name of the database. If there is no DOI, write *Retrieved from* followed by the URL for the journal's home page (not the database URL). For a work found on a website, write *Retrieved from* and include the URL. If the work seems likely to be updated, include the retrieval date. If the URL is longer than one line, break it only before a punctuation mark; do not break *http://*.

1 **Author.** Include the author's name as you would for a print source. List all authors' last names first, and use initials for first and middle names. For more about citing authors, see models 1–9.

2 **Publication date.** Enclose the date in parentheses. For journals, use only the year. For magazines and newspapers, use the year, a comma, the month, and the day, if given.

3 **Article title.** Capitalize only the first word of the article title and the subtitle and any proper nouns or proper adjectives.

4 **Periodical title.** Italicize the periodical title.

5 **Volume and issue numbers.** For journals and magazines, give the volume number (italicized) and the issue number (in parentheses).

6 **Page numbers.** For journals only, give inclusive page numbers.

7 **Retrieval information.** If the article has a DOI (digital object identifier), include that number after the publication information; do not include the name of the database. If there is no DOI, write *Retrieved from* followed by the URL of the journal's home page (not the database URL).

A citation for the article on p. 545 would look like this:

Knobloch-Westerwick, S., & Crane, J. (2012). A losing battle: Effects of prolonged exposure to thin-ideal images on dieting and body satisfaction. *Communication Research, 39*(1), 79–102. doi:10.1177/0093650211400596

④ Periodical Title

③ Article Title

⑥ Page Numbers

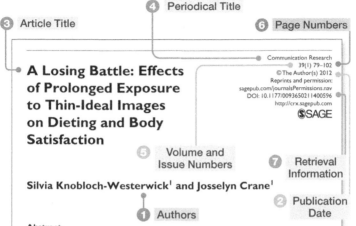

Communication Research
39(1) 79–102
© The Author(s) 2012
Reprints and permission:
sagepub.com/journalsPermissions.nav
DOI: 10.1177/0093650211400596
http://crx.sagepub.com
⑤SAGE

A Losing Battle: Effects of Prolonged Exposure to Thin-Ideal Images on Dieting and Body Satisfaction

⑤ Volume and Issue Numbers

⑦ Retrieval Information

Silvia Knobloch-Westerwick[1] and Josselyn Crane[1]

② Publication Date

① Authors

Abstract

The present study examined prolonged exposure effects of thin-ideal media messages. College-aged females participated in seven online sessions over 10 days including a baseline measures session, five daily measures, and a posttest. Two experimental groups viewed magazine pages with thin-ideal imagery. One of those groups was induced to engage in social comparisons with the thin-ideal models. The control group viewed messages with body-neutral images of women. Prolonged exposure to thin-ideal messages led to greater body satisfaction. This finding was attributed to the fact that the experimental groups reported more dieting behaviors. A mediation analysis showed that the impact of thin-ideal message exposure on body satisfaction was mediated by dieting.

Keywords

body dissatisfaction, body image, dieting, prolonged exposure, social comparison

Idealized body images in the media have been linked to unrealistic body shape aspirations and body dissatisfaction (see meta-analysis by Grabe, Ward, & Hyde, 2008), which, in turn, have been linked to numerous pathological problems, including depression, obesity, dieting, and eating disorders (e.g., Johnson & Wardle, 2005; Neumark-Sztainer, Paxton, Hannan, Haines, & Story, 2006; Ricciardelli & McCabe, 2001). However, another meta-analysis by Holmstrom (2004) found that the longer the media exposure, the *better* the individuals felt about their body. This inconsistency indicates that the factors and processes at work have not yet been fully understood and captured by the research at hand and deserve further investigation. Social comparison theory is the theoretical framework that has guided much

[1]The Ohio State University

Corresponding Author:
Silvia Knobloch-Westerwick, The Ohio State University, 154 N Oval Mall, Columbus, OH 43210
Email: knobloch-westerwick.1@osu.edu

32. ARTICLE FROM A MAGAZINE ON THE WEB

Give information as for an article from a print magazine (see model 24). If the article has a DOI (digital object identifier), include it. If there is no DOI, include the URL for the magazine's home page.

> Galchen, R. (2015, April 13). Weather underground. *The New Yorker, (91)*8,
>
>   34–40. Retrieved from http://www.newyorker.com/

33. ARTICLE FROM A NEWSPAPER ON THE WEB

Include information as for a print newspaper article (see model 25). Add the URL of the searchable website.

> Barringer, F. (2008, February 7). In many communities, it's not easy going
>
>   green. *The New York Times.* Retrieved from http://www.nytimes.com/

34. ABSTRACT FOR A JOURNAL ARTICLE ONLINE

Include a label.

> Gudjonsson, G. H., & Young, S. (2010). Does confabulation in memory
>
>   predict suggestibility beyond IQ and memory? [Abstract]. *Personality &*
>
>   *Individual Differences, 49*(1), 65–67. doi:10.1016/j.paid.2010.03.014

35. COMMENT ON AN ONLINE ARTICLE

Give the writer's real name (if known) or screen name. If both are given, follow the real name with the screen name in brackets. Use *Re:* before the title of the article, and add the label *Comment* in brackets.

> The Lone Ranger. (2014, April 22). Re: The American middle class is no longer
>
>   the world's richest [Comment]. *The New York Times.* Retrieved from
>
>   http://www.nytimes.com/

36. DIGITAL BOOK (ONLINE OR E-READER)

For a book you read online, give the URL for the home page of the site after the book title.

> Stossel, S. (2013). *My age of anxiety: Fear, hope, dread, and the search for*
>
>   *peace of mind.* Retrieved from http://books.google.com/

If you downloaded the book to an e-reader such as a Kindle or Nook, give the version after the title. Include the DOI, if given, or the URL of the home page for the site from which you downloaded the file.

> Schaap, R. (2013). *Drinking with men: A memoir* [Nook version]. Retrieved
>
>   from http://www.barnesandnoble.com/

37. ONLINE EDITORIAL OR LETTER TO THE EDITOR

Include the author's name (if given) and the title (if any). For an editorial, give the label *[Editorial]*. For a letter, give the label *[Letter to the editor]*.

> Shorter drug sentences [Editorial]. (2014, April 10). *The New York Times.*
>
> Retrieved from http://www.nytimes.com/

> Starr, E. (2014, April 4). Local reporting thrives in high schools [Letter
>
> to the editor]. *The Washington Post.* Retrieved from http://www
>
> .washingtonpost.com/

38. ONLINE REVIEW

Cite an online review as you would a print review (see model 28), and end with a retrieval statement.

> Miller, L. (2014, April 20). How the American office worker wound up in a box
>
> [Review of the book *Cubed,* by N. Saval]. *Salon.* Retrieved from http://
>
> www.salon.com/

39. INTERVIEW PUBLISHED ONLINE

> Ladd, A. (2014, February 25). What ends: An interview with Andrew Ladd
>
> [Interview by J. Gallagher]. Retrieved from http://www.looksandbooks
>
> .com/

40. ENTRY IN AN ONLINE REFERENCE WORK OR WIKI

Begin with the title unless the author is named. (A wiki, which is collectively edited, will not include an author.)

> Gunpowder plot. (2014). In *Wikipedia.* Retrieved April 10, 2014, from http://
>
> www.wikipedia.org/

41. REPORT OR DOCUMENT FROM A WEB SITE

List all of the following that are available: the author's name; the publication date (or *n.d.* if no date is given); the title of the document, italicized; and the URL. If the publisher is identified and is not the same as the author, list the publisher in the retrieval statement. The source map on pp. 548–49 shows where to find this information for a report from a website.

> Institute of Medicine of the National Academies. (2011, August 25). *Adverse*
>
> *effects of vaccines: Evidence and causality.* Retrieved from http://www.iom
>
> .edu/Reports/2011/Adverse-Effects-of-Vaccines-Evidence-and-Causality.aspx

1 **Author.** If one is given, include the author's name (see models 1–9). List last names first, and use only initials for first names. The site's sponsor may be the author. If no author is identified, begin the citation with the title of the document.

2 **Publication date.** Enclose the date of publication or latest update in parentheses. Use *n.d.* ("no date") when no publication date is available.

3 **Title of work.** Italicize the title. Capitalize only the first word of the title and subtitle and any proper nouns or proper adjectives.

4 **Retrieval information.** Write *Retrieved from* and include the URL. For a report from an organization's website, identify the organization in the retrieval statement. If the work seems likely to be updated, include the retrieval date. If you need to break a long URL in the retrieval statement, do so before a punctuation mark.

A citation for the web document on p. 549 would look like this:

Parker, K., & Wang, W. (2013, March 14). *Modern parenthood: Roles of moms and dads converge as they balance work and family.* Retrieved from the Pew Research Center website: http://www.pewsocialtrends .org/2013/03/14/modern-parenthood-roles-of-moms-and-dads -converge-as-they-balance-work-and-family/

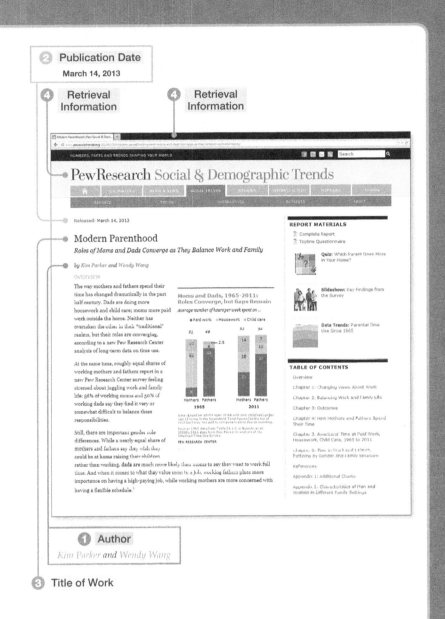

2 **Publication Date**

March 14, 2013

4 Retrieval Information

4 Retrieval Information

Released: March 14, 2013

Modern Parenthood

Roles of Moms and Dads Converge as They Balance Work and Family

by Kim Parker and Wendy Wang

OVERVIEW

The way mothers and fathers spend their time has changed dramatically in the past half century. Dads are doing more housework and child care; moms more paid work outside the home. Neither has overtaken the other in their "traditional" realms, but their roles are converging, according to a new Pew Research Center analysis of long-term data on time use.

At the same time, roughly equal shares of working mothers and fathers report in a new Pew Research Center survey feeling stressed about juggling work and family life: 56% of working moms and 50% of working dads say they find it very or somewhat difficult to balance these responsibilities.

Still, there are important gender role differences. While a nearly equal share of mothers and fathers say they wish they could be at home raising their children rather than working, dads are much more likely than moms to say they want to work full time. And when it comes to what they value most in a job, working fathers place more importance on having a high-paying job, while working mothers are more concerned with having a flexible schedule.[1]

Moms and Dads, 1965-2011: Roles Converge, but Gaps Remain

Average number of hours per week spent on ...

Paid work Housework Child care

REPORT MATERIALS

- Complete Report
- Topline Questionnaire

Quiz: Which Parent Does More in Your Home?

Slideshow: Key Findings from the Survey

Data Trends: Parental Time Use Since 1965

TABLE OF CONTENTS

Overview

Chapter 1: Changing Views About Work

Chapter 2: Balancing Work and Family Life

Chapter 3: Outcomes

Chapter 4: How Mothers and Fathers Spend Their Time

Chapter 5: Americans' Time at Paid Work, Housework, Child Care, 1965 to 2011

Chapter 6: Time in Work and Leisure, Patterns by Gender and Family Structure

References

Appendix 1: Additional Charts

Appendix 2: Characteristics of Men and Women in Different Family Settings

1 **Author**

Kim Parker and Wendy Wang

3 **Title of Work**

42. SECTION OF A WEB DOCUMENT

Cite as you would a chapter in a book (see model 12).

> Fox, S., & Rainie, L. (2014, February 27). Part 1: How the Internet has woven itself into American life. In *The web at 25 in the U.S.* Retrieved from Pew Research Center website: http://www.pewinternet.org/2014/02/27 /part-1-how-the-internet-has-woven-itself-into-american-life/

43. ENTIRE WEBSITE

Do not cite an entire website in your list of references. Give the URL in parentheses when you mention the site in the body of your writing project.

44. GOVERNMENT SOURCE ONLINE

If the document is numbered, give the number in parentheses.

> U.S. Census Bureau. (2013, September). *Income, poverty, and health insurance coverage in the United States: 2012* (Report No. P60-245). Retrieved from http://www.census.gov/prod/2013pubs/p60-245.pdf

45. ONLINE REPORT FROM A PRIVATE ORGANIZATION

If the publisher and author are the same, start with the publisher. If they are different, identify the publisher in the retrieval statement.

> Southern Poverty Law Center. (2013, February). *Easy money, impossible debt: How predatory lending traps Alabama's poor.* Retrieved from http:// www.splcenter.org/sites/default/files/downloads/publication/Payday _Lending_Report_web.pdf

46. BLOG POST

Give the author's real name (if known) or screen name; the date of the post (or *n.d.* if no date is given); the title, followed by the label *Blog post* in brackets; and the URL.

> Black, D. (2014, April 22). Wealthy white people from good backgrounds are never involved in crime [Blog post]. Retrieved from http://www .eschatonblog.com/2014/04/wealthy-white-people-from-good.html

47. BLOG COMMENT

Follow model 46 for a blog post, but put *Re:* before the title of the article commented on, and use the label *Blog comment* in brackets.

> JennOfArk. (2014, April 16). Re: Friends in high places [Blog comment].
>
> Retrieved from http://alicublog.blogspot.com/2014/04/friends-in-high
> -places.html

Visual, audio, multimedia, and live sources

48. FILM (THEATRICAL, DVD, OR OTHER FORMAT)

Begin with the director, the producer, and other relevant contributors.

> Bigelow, K. (Director, Producer), Boal, M. (Producer), & Ellison, M. (Producer).
>
> (2012). *Zero dark thirty* [Motion picture]. United States: Annapurna.

If you watched the film in another medium, such as on a DVD or Blu-ray disc, indicate the medium in brackets. If the DVD or Blu-ray and the film were not released in the same year, put *Original release* and the year in parentheses at the end of the entry.

> Hitchcock, A. (Director, Producer). (2010). *Psycho* [Blu-ray disc]. United
>
> States: Universal. (Original release 1960.)

49. VIDEO OR AUDIO ON THE WEB

Use the label *Audio file* or *Video file* in brackets after the title. If the video or audio is a segment or episode of a show rather than a stand-alone file, identify the show, as in the first model below.

> Buckner, T. (2013, May 7). *Last laugh* [Audio file]. In *The moth*. Retrieved
>
> from http://www.themoth.org/

> Klusman, P. (2008, February 13). *An engineer's guide to cats* [Video file].
>
> Retrieved from http://www.youtube.com/watch?v5=mHXBL6bzAR4

50. TRANSCRIPT OF VIDEO OR AUDIO FILE

> Glass, I. (2014, March 28). *Bad baby* [Transcript of audio file no. 521]. In *This
>
> American life*. Retrieved from http://www.thisamericanlife.org

51. TELEVISION EPISODE BROADCAST

> Weiner, M. (Writer), & Hornbacher, S. (Director). (2014, April 13). Time zones
>
> [Television series episode]. In M. Weiner (Executive producer), *Mad men*.
>
> New York, NY: AMC.

52. TELEVISION SERIES

> Gilligan, V. (Executive producer). (2008–2013). *Breaking bad* [Television series]. New York, NY: AMC.

53. TELEVISION EPISODE ON THE WEB

> Weiner, M. (Writer), & Hornbacher, S. (Director). (2014, April 13). Time zones [Television series episode]. In M. Weiner (Executive producer), *Mad men*. Retrieved from http://www.amctv.com/

54. PODCAST (DOWNLOADED FILE)

For an episode of a podcast series, follow model 53. For a standalone podcast, follow model 41 for a document from the web. Include an identifying label in brackets.

> Britt, M. A. (Writer & Producer). (2013, December 13). Ep. 211: Is a little deception okay? Paid crowds and native advertising [Audio podcast]. In M. A. Britt (Producer), *The psych files*. Retrieved from http://www.thepsychfiles.com/

> Spack, N. (2014, April 16). *How I help transgender teens become who they want to be* [Video podcast]. Retrieved from http://www.ted.com/

55. SOUND RECORDING

> The Avalanches. (2001). Frontier psychiatrist. On *Since I left you* [CD]. Los Angeles, CA: Elektra/Asylum Records.

56. VIDEO GAME

Begin with the game's creator, if possible. Follow with the label *[Video game]*. If you accessed the game on the web, give the URL; if you played on a game console, identify the type.

> Harmonix. (2012). *Rock band blitz* [Video game]. New York, NY: MTV Games. Xbox 360.

> King. (2014). *Candy crush saga* [Video game]. Retrieved from http://www.candycrushsaga.com/

57. COMPUTER SOFTWARE OR APP

If an individual can be identified as the developer, use that person's name. Otherwise, start with the name of the product and give the version. Use the label *Computer software* or *Mobile application software* in brackets.

> MediaWiki (Version 1.22.0) [Mobile application software]. Retrieved from
> http://www.microsoft.com/web/gallery

58. LECTURE OR SPEECH (LIVE)

> Khan, S. (2014, April 16). *Education reimagined.* Address at the Stanford
> University Ventures Program, Stanford University, Stanford, CA.

59. LECTURE OR SPEECH VIEWED ON THE WEB

Cite as you would a work from a website (model 41).

> Burden, A. (2014, March). *How public spaces make cities work* [Video file].
> Retrieved from http://www.ted.com/

60. DATA SET OR GRAPHIC REPRESENTATION OF DATA

If the graphic appears as part of a larger document, do not italicize the title. Give information about the type of source in brackets.

> U.S. Census Bureau. (2012, December 20). *State-to-state migration for states
> of 8 million or more* [Graph]. Retrieved from http://www.census.gov
> /dataviz/visualizations/028/

61. PRESENTATION SLIDES

> Mader, S. L. (2007, March 27). *The Zen aesthetic* [Presentation slides].
> Retrieved from http://www.slideshare.net/slmader/the-zen-aesthetic

62. WORK OF ART OR PHOTOGRAPH

> Bronzino, A. (1550–1555). *Lodovico Capponi* [Painting]. Frick Collection, New
> York, NY.

> Theotolopoulos, D. (ca. 1570). *Christ driving the money changers from the
> temple* [Painting]. Retrieved from http://www.artsmia.org/

63. MAP

> Australia [Map]. (1999). Retrieved from the University of Texas at Austin
> Perry-Castañeda Library Map Collection website: http://www.lib.utexas
> .edu/maps/australia/australia_pol99.jpg

64. ADVERTISEMENT

> Ameritrade [Advertisement]. (2014, January). *Wired, 22*(1), 47.

Academic sources (including online versions)

65. PUBLISHED PROCEEDINGS OF A CONFERENCE

Robertson, S. P., Vatrapu, R. K., & Medina, R. (2009). YouTube and Facebook: Online video "friends" social networking. In *Conference proceedings: YouTube and the 2008 election cycle* (pp. 159–176). Amherst, MA: University of Massachusetts. Retrieved from http://scholarworks.umass .edu/jitpc2009

66. PAPER PRESENTED AT A MEETING OR SYMPOSIUM, UNPUBLISHED

Cite the month of the meeting if it is available.

Banks, A. (2015, March). *"Ain't no walls behind the sky, baby": Funk, flight, and freedom.* Paper presented at the Conference on College Composition and Communication, Tampa, FL.

67. POSTER SESSION

Barnes Young, L. L. (2003, August). *Cognition, aging, and dementia.* Poster session presented at the 2003 Division 40 APA Convention, Toronto, Ontario, Canada.

68. DISSERTATION

If you retrieved the dissertation from a database, give the database name and the accession number, if one is assigned.

Lengel, L. L. (1968). *The righteous cause: Some religious aspects of Kansas populism.* Retrieved from ProQuest Digital Dissertations. (AAT 6900033)

If you retrieve a dissertation from a website, give the type of dissertation and the institution after the title, and provide a retrieval statement. If you retrieve the dissertation from an institution's own site, omit the institution after the title.

Meeks, M. G. (2006). *Between abolition and reform: First-year writing programs, e-literacies, and institutional change* (Doctoral dissertation). Retrieved from http://dc.lib.unc.edu/etd/

Personal communications and social media

69. TWEET

Include the writer's real name, if known, with the user name (if different) in brackets. If you don't know the real name, give just the user name. Include the entire tweet as the title, followed by the label *Tweet* in brackets.

Waldman, K. [xwaldie]. (2014, April 24). The psychology of unfriending
    someone on Facebook: slate.com/blogs/future_t . . . [Tweet]. Retrieved
    from https://twitter.com/xwaldie/status/459336732232912896

70. POSTING ON A PUBLIC SOCIAL NETWORKING SITE

When citing a posting on a public Facebook page or another social networking site that is visible to anyone, include the writer's name as it appears in the post. Give a few words from the post, and add an identifying label. Include the date you retrieved the post and the URL for the public page. Do not include a page on the list of references if your readers will not be able to access the source; instead, cite it as a personal communication in the text (see model 12 on p. 529).

American Psychological Association. (2014, April 24). Why do many people do
    their best thinking while walking? [Facebook post]. Retrieved April 24,
    2014, from https://www.facebook.com/AmericanPsychologicalAssociation

71. EMAIL, PRIVATE MESSAGE, OR POST ON A SOCIAL NETWORKING SITE

Email messages, letters, and any personal messages or privacy-protected postings on Facebook and other social media sites are not included in the list of references because the APA stresses that all sources in your list of references should be retrievable by your readers. (See model 12 on p. 529 for information on citing personal communication in your text.)

A Student Research Essay, APA Style  **64**

Student Writer

Martha Bell

On the following pages is a paper by Martha Bell that conforms to the APA guidelines described in this chapter. Her project also appears with an activity at **macmillanhighered.com/everyday6e**.

Running head: POST-LYME MYSTERY   1

Running head
(fifty characters
or fewer)
appears flush
left on first line
of title page

Page number
appears flush
right on first
line of every
page

Title, name,   The Mystery of Post-Lyme Disease Syndrome
and affiliation   Martha Bell
centered and   Eastern Mennonite University
double-spaced

Author's note   **Author Note:** This paper was prepared for College Writing 130C,
lists specific   **taught by Professor Eads.**
information
about course
(and can
include contact
information)

Annotations indicate effective choices or APA-style formatting.

Student Writing
APA

Abstract

Lyme disease, prevalent in parts of the United States, is a preventable illness spread by tick bites. Lyme disease is considered treatable with a course of antibiotics in the early stages of infection. In some cases, however, symptoms of Lyme disease persist in individuals who have completed antibiotic treatment. The causes of post-Lyme disease syndrome, sometimes called "chronic Lyme disease," are unknown, and treatment of those suffering post-Lyme disease syndrome is controversial, with some physicians arguing for long-term antibiotic treatment and others convinced that such treatments are harmful to patients. There is a need for more research with a focus on developing the technology to perform replicable studies and eventually an effective treatment algorithm for post-Lyme disease syndrome.

Running head appears in all capital letters flush left on each page

Heading centered

No indentation for abstract

Double-spaced text throughout

Full title
centered

Paragraphs
indented

Background
information
supplied

Boldface
headings
help organize
review

Reference
to work with
six or more
authors uses
et al.

First reference
to organization
gives abbre-
viation for later
references

The Mystery of Post-Lyme Disease Syndrome

The Centers for Disease Control and Prevention (CDC) estimates a total of 300,000 cases of Lyme disease annually. Many medical professionals believe Lyme disease can be cured in a matter of weeks with a simple antibiotic treatment. In some cases, however, patients develop post-Lyme disease syndrome, sometimes called "chronic Lyme disease," exhibiting persistent symptoms of Lyme after initial treatment is completed. The scientific community, divided over the causes of post-Lyme disease syndrome, cannot agree on the best treatment for the syndrome. Although Lyme disease is preventable, people are still vulnerable to infection; consequently, there is a need for more research and collaboration with a focus on developing the technology to perform replicable studies, which may subsequently lead to an effective treatment algorithm for post-Lyme disease syndrome.

Prevention

Ixodes ticks, also known as blacklegged and deer ticks, are infected with the bacterium *Borrelia burgdorferi*, responsible for Lyme disease (Hawker et al., 2012). Since being bitten by an infected tick is the only known way of contracting Lyme disease, evading Ixodes ticks is an effective measure. According to M'ikanatha, Lynfield, Van Beneden, and de Valk (2013), "Lyme disease is acquired peridomestically and the risk is highest in residential settings abutting areas with forests, meadows, and high prevalence of deer" (p. 168). While adult ticks are more active in the cooler months, developing Ixodes ticks, called nymphs, feed the most during the spring and summer months (Centers for Disease Control and Prevention [CDC], 2011b). Therefore, avoiding areas such as meadows and grasslands in the spring and summer seasons aids in preventing Lyme disease.

Using permethrin repellent on clothes and 20 to 30 percent DEET insect repellent on the skin also keeps ticks away (U.S. Department of Health and Human Services [HHS], 2012). Other measures include wearing light-colored clothing to make ticks more visible, wearing long sleeves and long pants, tucking shirts into pants and pants into socks, and taping closed open areas of clothing when spending time outdoors in areas where ticks are prevalent (Hawker et al., 2012; HHS, 2012). Additionally, individuals should keep yards and houses clean to avert mammals, such as deer and rodents, that carry Ixodes ticks, and should check pets for ticks (HHS, 2012).

More than one reference included in citation

Though all of these measures greatly reduce the chance of receiving a tick bite, they are not foolproof. The bacterium *B. burgdorferi* takes approximately 36 to 48 hours to become infectious after the tick has bitten an individual (Hawker et al., 2012). A bull's-eye rash called erythema migrans is the only unique symptom of Lyme disease (HHS, 2012). It appears 3 to 32 days after infection (Hawker et al., 2012). According to one study, only 70 to 80 percent of Lyme disease victims develop erythema migrans; therefore, other symptoms must be assessed (Steere & Sikand, 2003). Other characteristics of Lyme disease include fevers, headaches, stiff neck, swollen lymph nodes, body aches, fatigue, facial palsy, polyarthritis, aseptic meningitis, peripheral root lesions, radiculopathy, and myocarditis (CDC, 2011a; Hawker et al., 2012; HHS, 2012).

On average, it takes a few weeks for infected individuals to produce antibodies against *B. burgdorferi* (HHS, 2012). Consequently, most cases of Lyme disease have better outcomes and recovery rates when antibiotics are administered quickly (Steere & Sikand, 2003). Administered in the beginning stages of

Lyme disease, antibiotics help speed recovery and prevent more serious symptoms, such as heart and nervous system problems, from developing (HHS, 2012).

Erythema migrans is not always present, and other symptoms of Lyme disease are similar to other illnesses. Therefore, Lyme disease may be misdiagnosed and untreated. Raphael B. Stricker (2007), a doctor at the University of California at San Francisco, explained that "in the absence of typical features of Lyme disease, patients may go on to develop a syndrome with multiple nonspecific symptoms that affect various organ systems, including the joints, muscles, nerves, brain, and heart" (p. 149). Conversely, even when patients receive proper antibiotic treatment for two to four weeks they can continue to experience symptoms.

Parenthetical citation for quotation from print source includes page number

Post-Lyme Disease Syndrome

The majority of Lyme disease patients are cured after multiple weeks of antibiotics; however, 10 to 15 percent of patients acquire relapsing nonspecific symptoms such as fatigue, arthritis, and short-term memory problems that can persist for months or even years (Brody, 2013). When there is no other possible origin of the nonspecific symptoms, and the individual has had proper treatment for Lyme disease, the patient is classified as having post-Lyme disease syndrome (Lantos, 2011). Adriana Marques (2008) of the Laboratory of Clinical Infectious Diseases explains, "The appearance of post-Lyme disease symptoms seems to correlate with disseminated diseases, a greater severity of illness at presentation, and delayed antibiotic therapy; but not with the duration of the initial antibiotic therapy." The medical community is unsure of how to treat the nonspecific symptoms or what causes them (Lantos, 2011).

Possible Sources of Post-Lyme Disease Syndrome

Scientists are unable to identify the exact source of post-Lyme disease syndrome for several reasons. Identifying patients is difficult because of the general nature of the symptoms. Several surveys demonstrate that a relatively high percentage of the overall population reports nonspecific symptoms, such as fatigue, chronic pain, or cognitive dysfunction after a tick bite (Lantos, 2011). In addition, researchers struggle to find participants for their studies (Marques, 2008). Study participants must have previous documentation of contracting Lyme disease, which significantly diminishes the testing population (Lantos, 2011).

Scientists and physicians suspect the source of post-Lyme disease syndrome to be multifactorial (Marques, 2008). Plausible causes of reoccurring nonspecific symptoms include persistent infection of *B. burgdorferi*, other tick-borne infections, a natural healing process after infection, post-infective fatigue syndrome, autoimmune mechanisms, and intercurrent conditions (Marques, 2008). Nevertheless, only a few ideas have been thoroughly explored thus far by the scientific community. The majority of scientists believe remaining damage to tissue and the immune system from the infection causes post-Lyme disease syndrome; however, some believe persistent infection of the bacteria is the source (CDC, 2014).

Despite complications, a majority of the medical community considers persistent symptoms to be a result of residual damage to the tissues and the immune system that occurred during the infection. These "auto-immune" reactions, which the body uses against foreign elements, occur in infections similar to Lyme disease such as Campylobacter, Chlamydia, and Strep throat (CDC, 2014). Patients report their nonspecific symptoms improving over time after the typical antibiotic treatment (Marques, 2008). Physicians who followed their patients with post-Lyme disease syndrome for extended times also see nonspecific symptoms resolve without further antibiotic treatment (Marques, 2008). Consequently, post-Lyme disease syndrome may be a natural evolution of the body healing after an intense infection.

A smaller portion of the medical community considers persistent infection of the microorganism *B. burgdorferi* as the cause of post-Lyme disease syndrome. Recently published studies performed on animals show signs of ongoing infection of the bacterium. One scientific study infected mice with *B. burgdorferi* and gave them intense treatment of antibiotics that should have wiped out the bacterium (Bockenstedt, Gonzalez, Haberman, & Belperron, 2012). Bockenstedt et al. (2012) observed the mice over a period of time and found "that infectious spirochetes are rapidly eliminated after institution of antibiotics, but inflammatory *B. burgdorferi* antigens persist adjacent to cartilage and in the enthuses" (p. 2652). This is one of the first studies to show continuous effects of the harmful microorganism in post-Lyme disease syndrome. Another recent scientific study was conducted on nonhuman primates, rhesus macaques. Once again the scientists infected the animals with *B. burgdorferi* and then four to six months later administered an antibiotic treatment to half of the monkeys (Embers et al., 2012). Their results also confirmed that *B. burgdorferi* could withstand antibiotic treatment in rhesus macaques and proceed to cause post-Lyme disease syndrome (Embers et al., 2012). Nonetheless, these results showing perpetual infection as the cause of post-Lyme disease syndrome have yet to be replicated in humans.

In contrast, many studies over the years contradict the theory of ongoing infection, though these studies have not been confirmed true in humans. Lantos (2011), an MD Medical Instructor in the Department of Medicine at Duke University School of Medicine, clarifies that "[n]o adequately controlled, hypothesis-driven study using a repeatable method has demonstrated that viable *B. burgdorferi* is found in patients with persistent post-Lyme symptoms any more frequently than in those with favorable outcomes" (p. 790). Most scientific studies trying to prove persistent infection of *B. burgdorferi* have not been replicated because their procedures and techniques are at fault (Marques, 2008). The problem derives from the technology that detects the microorganism (Lantos, 2011). PCR and *B. burgdorferi* culture are commonly used to find evidence of the bacteria in the body; however, both have "low sensitivity in most body fluids from patients with Lyme disease" (Marques, 2008). Even though other methods, such as finding antibodies in immune complexes, changes in C6 antibody levels, and PCR in urine samples, have been tried, none prove helpful (Marques, 2008). Therefore, the persistent infection of *B. burgdorferi* has not yet successfully been proven as the cause of post-Lyme disease syndrome.

Post-Lyme Disease Syndrome Treatment

Since the cause of post-Lyme disease syndrome is controversial, treatment for the infection varies from patient to patient and physician to physician. Treatment is still in the experimental stages, meaning no set treatment algorithm currently exists. Numerous patients rely on long-term antibiotic medication, despite the overwhelming defying scientific evidence against this treatment (CDC, 2014). The research studies that focus on prolonged antibiotic treatment observe no dramatic difference in benefits or recoveries of those who had the treatment and those who did not (Marques, 2008). On the contrary, many long-term antibiotic research studies found that post-Lyme disease syndrome patients develop harmful side effects (Lantos, 2011). These adverse health effects include "catheter-associated venous thromboembolism, catheter-associated septicemia, allergic reactions and ceftriaxone-induced gallbladder toxicity" (Lantos, 2011, p. 792). Therefore, most of the scientific community considers long-term antibiotic treatment for chronic Lyme disease a harmful, risky, and unbeneficial plan.

Most of the scientific community advises against the use of long-term antibiotics because of potential adverse effects. Nevertheless, a small minority of physicians have observed improvements with long-term antibiotics. Because numerous studies show a lack of benefit to long-term antibiotics, these hopeful patients may be experiencing a placebo effect, which occurs when patients improve because they believe they are receiving an effective treatment (Marques, 2008).

Solving the Mystery

Individuals can take various simple preventive measures to avoid contracting Lyme disease. If the infection is contracted, those who seek prompt treatment increase the chance of full recovery and decrease the chance of developing post-Lyme disease syndrome. However, these steps do not guarantee complete avoidance of post-Lyme disease syndrome. Finding the source of post-Lyme disease syndrome will lead to a specific treatment plan that effectively heals patients. Many scientists deem the source of post-Lyme disease syndrome to be a natural autoimmune reaction; conversely, a few other scientists consider persistent infection as the cause. Both theories, however, need better technology to prove their accuracy. Since scientists disagree about the source of post-Lyme disease syndrome, a variety of experimental treatments have arisen. Replicable studies are needed so that an effective treatment for post-Lyme disease syndrome can be found.

Conclusion indicates need for further research

References

Bockenstedt, L., Gonzalez, D., Haberman, A., & Belperron, A. (2012). Spirochete antigens persist near cartilage after murine Lyme borreliosis therapy. *The Journal of Clinical Investigation, 122*(7), 2652–2660. doi:10.1172/JCI58813

Brody, J. (2013, July 8). When Lyme disease lasts and lasts. *The New York Times*. Retrieved from http://nytimes.com/

Centers for Disease Control and Prevention. (2011a, April 12). *Signs and symptoms*. Retrieved from http://www.cdc.gov/lyme/

Centers for Disease Control and Prevention. (2011b, April 12). *Transmission*. Retrieved from http://www.cdc.gov/lyme/

Centers for Disease Control and Prevention. (2014, February 24). *Post-treatment Lyme disease syndrome*. Retrieved from http://www.cdc.gov/lyme/

Embers, M. E., Barthold, S. W., Borda, J. T., Bowers, L., Doyle, L., Hodzic, E., . . . & Philipp, M. T. (2012). Persistence of *Borrelia burgdorferi* in rhesus macaques following antibiotic treatment of disseminated infection. *PLoS ONE, 7*(1). doi:10.1371/journal.pone.0029914

Hawker, J., Begg, N., Blair, L., Reintjes, R., Weinberg, J., & Ekdahl, K. (2012). *Communicable disease control and health protection handbook* (3rd ed.). Retrieved from http://reader.eblib.com.hartzler.emu.edu

Lantos, P. (2011). Chronic Lyme disease: The controversies and the science. *Expert Review of Anti-Infective Therapy, 9*(7), 787–797. doi:10.1586/eri.11.63

Marques, A. (2008). Chronic Lyme disease: An appraisal. *Infectious Disease Clinics of North America, 22*(2), 341–360. doi:10.1016/j.idc.2007.12.011

References begin on a new page

Article from an online newspaper

Two works by the same author in the same year

Work with more than seven authors

Journal article with DOI

Electronic
book

M'ikanatha, N. M., Lynfield, R., Van Beneden, C. A., & de Valk, H.
(2013). *Infectious disease surveillance* (2nd ed.). Retrieved from
http://reader.eblib.com.hartzler.emu.edu

Steere, A., & Sikand, V. (2003). The presenting manifestations
of Lyme disease and the outcomes of treatment. *The
New England Journal of Medicine, 348*(24), 2472–2474.
doi:10.1056/NEJM200306123482423

Stricker, R. (2007). Counterpoint: Long-term antibiotic therapy
improves persistent symptoms associated with Lyme
disease. *Clinical Infectious Diseases, 45*(2), 147–157.
doi:10.1086/518853

U.S. Department of Health and Human Services, National Institutes
of Health, National Institute of Allergy and Infectious
Diseases. (2012, October 9). *A history of Lyme disease,
symptoms, diagnosis, treatment, and prevention.* Retrieved
from http://www.niaid.nih.gov/topics/lymedisease
/understanding/pages/intro.aspx

Acknowledgments

Derek Bok. "Protecting Freedom of Expression at Harvard." First published in *The Boston Globe*, March 25, 1991, p. 15. Reprinted with permission of the author.

Emily Dickinson. "A Little Madness in the Spring." From *The Poems of Emily Dickinson*, edited by Thomas H. Johnson, Cambridge, MA: The Belknap Press of Harvard University Press. Copyright © 1951, 1955, 1979, 1983 by the President and Fellows of Harvard College.

Langston Hughes. "Harlem—A Dream Deferred." From *The Collected Poems of Langston Hughes*, edited by Arnold Rampersad with David Roessel, Associate Editor. Copyright © 1994 by the Estate of Langston Hughes. Used by permission of Alfred A. Knopf, a division of Random House, Inc., and Harold Ober Associates, Ltd.

James Hunter. "Outlaw Classics: The Albums That Kept Nashville Real in the Sixties and Seventies." From *Rolling Stone*, March 9, 2006, p. 95. Copyright © 2006 Rolling Stone LLC. All rights reserved. Used by permission.

Andrea A. Lunsford and Karen J. Lunsford. "Mistakes Are a Fact of Life: A National Comparative Study." From *CCC* 59.4 (2008): 781–806. Used by permission of the National Council of Teachers of English.

Joshua Oppenheimer. Director's Statement, "The Act of Killing." Used by permission of Final Cut for Real.

Revision Symbols

Some instructors use these symbols as a kind of shorthand to guide you in revision. The numbers refer to a chapter number or a section of a chapter.

abb	abbreviation **54a–g**	*para*	paraphrase **14d, 15**
ad	adjective/adverb **42**	*pass*	inappropriate
agr	agreement **40, 41f**		passive **33c, 38g**
awk	awkward	*ref*	unclear pronoun
cap	capitalization **53**		reference **41g**
case	case **41c–d**	*run-on*	run-on (fused)
cliché	cliché **7e, 29d**		sentence **45**
co	coordination **30a**	*sexist*	sexist language **27b, 41f**
coh	coherence **6e**	*shift*	shift **33**
com	incomplete	*slang*	slang **29a**
	comparison **31e**	*sp*	spelling **29f–g**
concl	weak conclusion **6f, 16b**	*sub*	subordination **30b**
cs	comma splice **45**	*sum*	summarize **14d, 15, 18b**
d	diction (word choice) **29**	*t*	tone **7d, 14c, 29a, 29d**
def	define **6c**	*trans*	transition **6e, 35b**
dm	dangling modifier **43c**	*u*	unity **6a**
doc	documentation **57–67**	*vague*	vague statement
emph	emphasis unclear **30**	*verb*	verb form **38a–d**
ex	example needed **6b–c**	*vt*	verb tense **38e–h**
frag	sentence fragment **46**	*wv*	weak verb **38**
fs	fused sentence **45**	*wrdy*	wordy **34**
hyph	hyphen **56**	*ww*	wrong word **1, 7e, 29a–b**
inc	incomplete	*,*	comma **47**
	construction **31**	*;*	semicolon **48**
intro	weak introduction **6f, 16b**	*. ? !*	period, question mark, exclamation point **49**
it	italics (or	*'*	apostrophe **50**
	underlining) **55**	*" "*	quotation marks **51**
jarg	jargon **29a**	*( ) [ ] —*	parentheses, brackets, dash **52a–c**
lc	lowercase letter **53**		
lv	language variety **28**	*: / ...*	colon, slash, ellipsis **52d–f**
mix	mixed construction **31a**		
mm	misplaced modifier **43**	*∧*	insert
ms	manuscript form	*∿*	transpose
no ,	no comma **47j**	*⌒*	close up
num	number **54h–j**	*X*	obvious error
¶	paragraph **6**		
//	faulty parallelism **6e, 32**		

The
Bedford
Researcher

Mike Palmquist
COLORADO STATE UNIVERSITY

Part I
Joining the Conversation

1	Getting Started
2	Exploring and Focusing
>	**3**	**Developing Your Research Question and Proposal**

3

Developing Your Research Question and Proposal

> **Key Questions**

3a. **How can I develop my research question?** 45
Reflect on your issue and disciplinary context
Focus on your role
Focus on an aspect of your issue
Choose and focus your research question
Refine your research question

3b. **How can I create a research proposal?** 57
Identify your topic, issue, and research question
Provide a review of literature
Explain how you'll collect information
Develop a project timeline
Compile a working or annotated bibliography
Clarify and elaborate on your core proposal

Your research question provides the foundation for developing your position — the main point you will make about your issue. It also guides your efforts to develop a research proposal, create a search plan, and collect information.

3a

How can I develop my research question?

A research question directs your efforts to collect, critically read, evaluate, and take notes on your sources. Most research questions are narrowly focused, allowing writers to collect information in time to meet deadlines. Research questions are also subject to revision as writers learn more about an issue. It's best, at this early stage in your project, to think of your research question as a flexible guide.

Developing your research question involves reflecting on your issue and disciplinary context, focusing on your role, focusing on an aspect of your issue, and refining your question.

Step 1: Reflect on Your Issue and Disciplinary Context ? WHAT'S MY PURPOSE?

As you've explored your topic and focused on your issue, you've learned more about the conversation you've decided to join. The sources you've read have helped you gain an understanding of some of the most important information, ideas, and arguments shaping the conversation. You might also have had the opportunity to talk with others about your issue and perhaps even to conduct observations. If you're like most research writers, your initial thoughts about your topic and issue have changed as you've carried out your investigations.

As you begin generating ideas for a research question, ask whether what you've learned about the issue has changed your understanding of your writing situation. Then ask yourself what you'd like to learn next. As you ask these questions, consider how disciplinary or professional contexts might shape the questions you can ask. If you are writing a research report for a biology class, for example, your understanding of the kinds of questions biologists typically ask about issues will come into play. That's true for virtually every discipline and profession, each of which has areas that are of interest to its members and each of which has particular ways of asking questions about those areas of interest (see Table 3.1).

TABLE 3.1 DISCIPLINARY QUESTIONS		
Discipline	**Types of Questions**	**Examples**
Humanities	Interpretive questions about literature, music, philosophy, rhetoric, and the arts	How did the acceptance of Manet's painting style open the door for Impressionism? What similarities does Toni Morrison's character Amy Denver in *Beloved* share with Twain's character Huck Finn?
Social Sciences	Questions about factors that affect human behavior	What is the significance of social networking sites such as Facebook in modern-day protest movements? What factors contribute to a person becoming a mass murderer?
Sciences	"How" and "why" questions about the natural world, including both the environment and living beings	How can we combat the obesity epidemic among school-age children? What are the preventable causes of global warming?
History	"How" and "why" questions about past events	What role did evangelicalism play in the American conservative movement of the twentieth century? Why did fascism ultimately fail in Italy in the 1940s?

Similarly, your understanding of the kinds of genres typically used to communicate within the discipline or profession—such as articles, presentations, and essays—will shape your work on your research question. Some genres, such as books and longer reports, are well suited to broader questions. Others, because of their comparative brevity (think of poster sessions, conference presentations, reports, and essays), are better suited to highly focused research questions.

Step 2: Focus on Your Role   [FRAMING MY ARGUMENT]

Your role as a writer—the manner in which you'll relate to your readers—will have a profound impact on your decisions about your research question. Writers who inform their readers, for example, develop strikingly different questions than those who seek to persuade them to take action. Had featured writer Brandon Tate decided to inform his readers about the impact of hydraulic fracturing on air and water quality, for example, he might have pursued questions such as the following.

What are the effects of fracking on local air and water quality?

How have opponents of fracking characterized its impact on air and water quality?

What have recent scientific research studies indicated about the impact of fracking on air and water quality?

In contrast, had Brandon adopted the role of advocate, his research questions might have resembled the following.

In light of recent findings about the impact of fracking on air and water quality, should Coloradoans enact legislation to ban fracking?

Given scientific evidence that fracking has a negative effect on air and water quality, should the government establish regulations that might reduce or eliminate those effects?

Given scientific evidence that fracking has a negative effect on air and water quality, what steps should Coloradoans take to mitigate its effects?

The roles writers can adopt vary widely (p. 9). Table 3.2 provides a list of some of the most important roles you might adopt and offers examples of the kinds of questions writers adopting a particular role might ask. These questions serve as sentence starters that you can use to generate potential research questions (p. 25).

Step 3: Focus on an Aspect of Your Issue

You can begin to generate potential research questions by using freewriting (p. 22), looping (p. 23), the sentence starters found in Table 3.2 (p. 48), and the question matrix found in the My Research Project activity on p. 50. As you

TABLE 3.2 THE RELATIONSHIP AMONG ROLES AND RESEARCH QUESTIONS

Purpose	Role	General Questions
To Inform	Reporter	What is known—and not known—about _____?
		How might we define _____?
To Create and Share New Knowledge	Inquirer	What causes _____?
		What are the effects of _____?
		What can [cure / repair / prevent] _____?
To Reflect	Observer	What are the implications of _____?
		How can we learn from the example of an individual or group?
		What can we gain from thinking about an idea, a work of art, a work of literature, or a performance?
To Evaluate	Evaluator	What conclusions—merited or not—have writers and readers already made about _____?
		What assumptions are shaping current thinking about _____?
		What are the best choices available for addressing _____?
		What are the relative strengths and weaknesses of _____?
To Analyze	Interpreter	What has occurred in the past that is relevant to _____?
		What causes _____?
		What are the effects of _____?
		Does the data suggest that _____ [is / is the result of] a trend?
		What is likely to happen [to / as a result of] _____?
		In what ways is _____ similar to _____?
		In what ways does _____ differ from _____?
To Solve Problems	Problem Solver	Why is _____ a problem?
		What is the best solution to _____?
		Why should we adopt _____ as a solution to _____?
To Convince (Change Readers' Beliefs or Attitudes), **Persuade** (Cause Readers to Take Action), **or Mediate** (Seek to Establish Common Ground among Readers)	Advocate	What are the origins of this argument?
		What is the status of this argument?
		Who has made the best arguments about _____?
		What do the writers and readers involved in conversation about _____ want to [see happen / avoid happening]?
		What should be done about _____?
		How should _____ be accomplished?
		How can we find common ground about _____?

TUTORIAL

How do I generate research questions consistent with my role?

Each role listed in Table 3.2 is associated with sentence starters you can use to generate potential research questions. Once you've identified your purpose and chosen the role you'll adopt as you work with your readers, you can use these sentence starters to generate potential research questions.

Adopting the role of interpreter, for example, featured writer Lauren Mack might have generated the following research questions about her issue, the problems facing coral reefs.

Interpreter   **What has occurred in the past that is relevant to _____?**
- the potential extinction of many forms of coral?
- efforts by state and local governments to preserve coral reefs?

What causes _____?
- individuals to act in ways that contribute to the demise of coral reefs?
- nonprofit organizations to work to preserve coral reefs?
- government agencies to adopt regulations that might lead to the demise of coral reefs?

What are the effects of _____?
- damaging or destroying coral reefs?
- commercial activity on coral reefs?
- overfishing on coral reefs?

Does the data suggest that _____ [is / is the result of] a trend?
- the die-off of coral reefs?
- individual action to preserve coral reefs?

What is likely to happen [to / as a result of] _____?
- the communities that rely on coral reefs for commercial benefits?
- aquatic species that rely on the ecosystem provided by coral reefs?

In what ways is _____ similar to _____?
- damage to coral reefs similar to the systematic killing of the plains bison in the 1800s?

In what ways does _____ differ from _____?
- the commercial exploitation of coral reefs differ from past exploitation of old growth forests?

generate potential questions, consider both your role and general areas of focus within the issue you've decided to address. The following areas often lead to useful lines of inquiry.

- **Information.** What is known—and not known—about an issue?

- **History.** What has occurred in the past that is relevant to an issue?

- **Assumptions.** What conclusions—merited or not—have writers and readers already made about an issue?

- **Goals.** What do the writers and readers involved in conversation about this issue want to see happen (or not happen)?

- **Outcomes.** What has happened so far? What is likely to happen?

- **Policies.** What are the best procedures for carrying out actions? For making decisions?

With your issue and role in mind, you can generate questions using one or more of these areas as a starting point. In addition, you can narrow the focus of your questions by exploring the intersections between these areas and specific thinking processes, such as examining trends, similarities and differences, and cause/effect relationships.

Step 4: Choose and Focus Your Research Question

Review your potential research questions and select a question that interests you and is appropriate for your research writing situation. You should be confident that you will be able to respond to the question in a substantive and useful way. You should also be confident that your response will be neither too simplistic nor too ambitious to address in an essay. Questions that can be answered with an unelaborated "yes" or "no" response, for example, are not generally pursued in a research writing project. It is also the case, however, that many initial research questions are far too broad to serve as the basis for a focused research project.

My Research Project

Generate a Matrix of Research Questions

Use the table on p. 51 to generate potential research questions. You need not complete every cell in the table and you can create more than one question in each cell. To complete the activity, choose a column, such as "Information," and then generate questions to focus on, for example, defining what is known about the issue, tracing causes and effects, charting trends, and so on.

To generate questions, use freewriting or the sentence starters found on pp. 25–26.

bedfordresearcher.com
My Research Project Activities > Generate a Matrix of Research Questions

↑	**Definition** (Describe specific aspects of the issue.)	**Causes and Effects** (Ask what leads to a specific result.)	**Trends** (Ask about sequences of events.)	**Relationships** (Examine connections between aspects of an issue.)	**Similarities and Differences** (Compare and contrast.)	**Strengths and Weaknesses** (Assess relative merits.)
Information: What is known—and not known—about an issue?						
History: What has occurred in the past that is relevant to an issue?						
Assumptions: What conclusions—merited or not—have writers and readers already made about an issue?						
Goals: What should happen (or not happen)?						
Outcomes: What has happened so far? What is likely to happen?						
Policies: What are the best procedures for carrying out actions? For making decisions?						

In general, a research question that is too broad will lead to answers requiring far more space to answer than most writing assignments allow, while a question that is too narrow will lead to answers that are so specific that they will fail to interest most readers. In both cases, the document that emerges will usually lack depth and fail to make a useful contribution to the conversation.

Too Broad:

How did real estate development on the East Coast of the United States affect the environment during the twentieth century?

Too Narrow:

In what ways has source-point pollution of the Minnesota River affected the profit margins of women-owned metal fabrication companies in the Mankato area?

Balanced Focus:

How can we best address drinking-water problems caused by the dumping of polluted lake water into Florida rivers and estuaries?

Too Broad:

How does public education vary among industrialized nations?

Too Narrow:

Do first-grade teachers prefer Expo or Quill dry-erase markers?

Balanced Focus:

How can the use of tablets improve reading fluency among U.S. fourth-grade students?

Consider how specific question words can help you create a focused research question. If you are interested in conducting an analysis, for example, you might use the words *what, why, when, where, who,* and *how.* If you are interested in informing readers about the goals or outcomes associated with a particular issue, you might use the words *would* or *could.* If the conversation focuses on determining an appropriate course of action, as might be the case if you were adopting the role of an advocate, generate questions using the word *should.* Take a look at the differences in the following questions.

- What are the benefits of hydraulic fracturing?

- Would it be feasible to require oil and gas producers to reduce or eliminate the use of chemicals during hydraulic fracturing?

- Should the federal government pursue legislation to reduce the environmental and health impacts of hydraulic fracturing?

Each question would lead to differences in how to search for sources of information, which sources to use in a project document, what role to adopt as a writer, and how to organize and draft the document.

WORKING TOGETHER

Craft Focused Research Questions

Working with a small group of writers, use question words to focus potential research questions. To prepare for the activity, review your list of potential research questions and identify two or three that interest you most. Then carry out the following activities.

1 Taking turns with other members of the group, share a research question and ask the other members of the group to brainstorm variations on the question that use the question words *who, what, where, when, how, why, would, could,* and *should.* Take notes on the variations.

2 After you have each shared your best research questions, review your notes. Highlight the variations on the questions that will help you best accomplish your purpose and address the needs and interests of your readers.

3 Taking turns, share your conclusions with the group. Ask for reactions and additional suggestions. Take notes.

4 After the activity, review your notes and determine whether you should revise your research question.

Step 5: Refine Your Research Question

Choose the research question that emerged from the research project activity *Craft Focused Research Questions.* Refine your question by referring to shared assumptions and existing conditions, narrowing its scope, and conducting preliminary searches.

Refer to Shared Assumptions and Existing Conditions You can refine your research question by using qualifying words and phrases to narrow its scope, by calling attention to assumptions that have been made by the community of writers and readers who are addressing your issue, or by referring to existing conditions relevant to your issue. Note the difference between the following three versions of featured writer Alexis Alvarez's research question.

Original Question:

What should be done about steroid use by adolescent girls involved in competitive sports?

Alternative 1:

Even though we know that widespread drug testing of all athletes, younger and older, is impossible, what should be done about steroid use by adolescent girls involved in competitive sports?

Alternative 2:

Given the lack of knowledge among athletes and their parents about the health consequences of steroid use, what should be done about steroid use by adolescent girls involved in competitive sports?

As you refine your research question, you might use conditional words and phrases such as the following.

Mix . . .	and Match
Although	we know that . . .
Because	it is uncertain . . .
Even though	it is clear that . . .
Given that	studies indicate . . .
In light of	recent events . . .
Now that	it has been shown . . .
Since	the lack of . . .
While	we cannot . . .

Narrow the Scope of Your Research Question   Early research questions typically suffer from lack of focus. You can narrow the scope of your question by looking for vague words and phrases and replacing them with more specific words or phrases. The process of moving from a broad research question to one that might be addressed effectively in a research essay might produce the following sequence.

Original Research Question:

What is behind the increased popularity of women's sports?

Refined:

What has led to the increased popularity of women's sports in colleges and universities?

Further Refined:

How has Title IX increased opportunities for women athletes in American colleges and universities?

In this example, the writer has narrowed the scope of the research question in two ways. First, the writer has shifted its focus from women's sports in general to women's sports in American colleges and universities. Second, the writer has moved from a general focus on increased popularity of women's sports to a more specific focus on opportunities brought about by Title IX, federal legislation that mandated equal opportunities for women athletes. Table 3.3 shows the featured writers' progress from a general topic to a focused issue to a refined research question.

Conduct Preliminary Searches   One of the best ways to test your research question is to conduct some preliminary searches in a library catalog or database or on the Web. If you locate a vast amount of information in your searches, you might need to revise your question so that it focuses on a more manageable

TUTORIAL

How do I refine my research question?

The first draft of your research question might be too broad, which can make it difficult for you to focus your research efforts. Refine your initial research question so that you can collect information efficiently.

In this example, Brandon Tate refines his research question about the impact of hydraulic fracturing on local air and water quality. He used his research question as he collected and worked with sources, and later, he developed his thesis statement to answer his question.

Preliminary Research Question:
What should we do about hydraulic fracturing?

1 Refer to shared assumptions and existing conditions by using phrases such as *although it is clear that . . .*, *because we cannot . . .*, and *given that studies have shown. . . .*

Given the national commitment to reducing our reliance on foreign oil, what should we do about hydraulic fracturing?

2 Identify vague words and phrases, such as *what should we do about*, and replace them with more specific language.

Given the national commitment to reducing our reliance on foreign oil, what steps can U.S. citizens take to ensure that environmental concerns play an important role in the regulation of hydraulic fracturing?

3 Using these specific terms, conduct preliminary searches in your library catalog, databases, and on the Web. If you get too many results, narrow your focus even further. (Here, Brandon narrows his target audience from U.S. citizens to Colorado citizens and focuses on passing a statewide referendum.)

Given the national commitment to reducing our reliance on foreign oil, what steps can Colorado citizens take to pass a statewide referendum regulating hydraulic fracturing?

aspect of the issue. In contrast, if you find almost nothing in your search, you might need to expand the scope of your research question.

TABLE 3.3 THE FEATURED WRITERS' RESEARCH QUESTIONS

Featured Writer	Topic	Issue	Initial Research Question	Final Research Question
Alexis Alvarez	Women and competitive sports	Steroid use among adolescent girls involved in competitive sports	What are the effects of competitive sports on adolescent girls?	What should be done about steroid use by adolescent girls involved in competitive sports?
Nicholas Brothers	Private military corporations	Use of private military corporations to support the U.S. war on terror	How important have private military corporations become for the U.S. military?	What roles do private military corporations play in the U.S. military's war on terror?
Elizabeth Leontiev	The war on drugs	Impact of U.S. war on drugs on South American coca farmers	What are the effects of the U.S. war on drugs on South America?	How can we reduce the economic impact of the war on drugs on South American coca farmers?
Lauren Mack	Protecting marine life	The problems facing coral reefs	What are the threats to coral reefs?	Why are coral reefs important, and what can be done to protect them from destruction?
Cori Schmidtbauer	William Shakespeare's dramas	Portia's unconventional role in *The Merchant of Venice*	How are women portrayed in Shakespeare's plays?	How does Portia's character in *The Merchant of Venice* fit the ideal of an Elizabethan woman?
Brandon Tate	Hydraulic fracturing	Impact of fracking on local air and water quality	What do readers need to know to form an educated opinion about hydraulic fracturing?	What do individuals need to know to develop an informed opinion about the controversial issue of hydraulic fracturing?

Josh Woelfle	A cure for cancer	Promising new treatments for cancer	What new treatment options are available for cancer patients?	What makes new cancer treatments potentially superior to traditional treatments such as che- motherapy and radiation?

3b

How can I create a research proposal?

A research proposal—sometimes called a prospectus—is a formal presentation of your plan for your research writing project. A proposal helps you pull together the planning you've done on your project, identify areas where you need additional planning, and assess the progress you've made so far.

Unlike a research plan (p. 30), which is designed primarily to help *you* decide how to collect information, a research proposal is addressed to someone else, usually an instructor, a supervisor, or a funding agency. Although the specific format for research proposals can vary widely across disciplines, a research proposal typically includes the following parts.

- A title page
- An introduction that identifies your topic, issue, and/or research question
- A review of literature
- An explanation of how you will collect information
- A project timeline
- A working bibliography

In addition to these core elements, you can also provide an abstract or executive summary, offer an overview of key challenges, and include a funding request. You can read about how to develop each of these core and optional elements below.

Identify Your Topic, Issue, and Research Question

A title page and introduction offer your readers an overview of the topic and issue you'll address in your project document. Your title page should include the working title of your research writing project, your name and contact information, and the date. Your introduction should identify the topic you've chosen and the issue you've decided to address; state your research question and, if you have created one, your position on the issue (p. 70); describe your purpose; and identify and describe your readers. It should also identify the type of document you'll create and explain how your choice of genre reflects your purpose, your understanding of your readers, and the contexts that will shape your work on your research project.

Provide a Review of Literature

A review of literature presents an overview of the key information, ideas, and arguments in the sources you've collected so far. You should identify the most useful sources you found during your exploration of your topic and explain why you found them useful. Keep in mind, however, that a review of literature goes beyond the simple list of sources that are typically found in a working bibliography by offering a discussion of important approaches to your issue. That is, a review of literature focuses not so much on individual sources as on groups of sources and the shared ideas or positions taken by groups of sources. Focusing on general approaches to an issue, as opposed to the individual positions adopted in particular sources, can help you understand the major ideas that are being considered in the conversation you are planning to join. By understanding existing approaches to an issue, you can determine whether you agree with any of those approaches or whether you want to introduce a completely new approach. In turn, this will help you develop your own individual position on the issue.

For an example that illustrates how key approaches to an issue can be discussed, see featured writer Nicholas Brothers's review of literature on p. 61.

Explain How You'll Collect Information

Your research proposal should help your reader understand how you will collect information. Your plan should identify:

- the types of sources you intend to collect (such as books, journal articles, or opinion columns). Read about types of sources on p. 32.
- the types of search tools (such as library catalogs, databases, and Web search sites) and research methods (such as browsing library shelves, consulting librarians, or conducting surveys) you want to use. You can learn about search tools in Chapter 9, library research in Chapter 10, and field research in Chapter 11.
- the types of strategies (such as simple and advanced database searches or field research) that you intend to use in your searches (pp. 146-54).
- the schedule you will follow as you carry out your searches (p. 59).

i **INFORMATION LITERACY**   Your research question will influence your decisions about how you will collect information. For example, you can use your research question — and, if you've developed one, your position on your issue (p. 70) — to help identify keywords and phrases that might be used in database, catalog, and Web searches.

Develop a Project Timeline

A project timeline will give your reader an indication of the range of days, weeks, or months over which you will be completing your research and writing your document. Your timeline can range from a general description of the number of days or weeks you'll devote to your project to a detailed list of key project activities and the amount of time devoted to completing them. If you are working on a group project, a project timeline can be especially useful, since it will require discussion of individual responsibilities for completing tasks and deadlines for completing them.

Compile a Working or Annotated Bibliography

A working bibliography lists the sources you've collected so far. Sometimes you will be asked to create an annotated bibliography, which contains a brief description of each source. Your working or annotated bibliography should conform to the documentation system (such as MLA, APA, *Chicago*, or CSE) specified by your instructor, supervisor, or funding agency. For more information on bibliographies, see p. 119.

Clarify and Elaborate on Your Core Proposal

Depending on your purpose, your reader, and the scope of your research writing project, you can choose to include several optional elements.

- An abstract or executive summary provides a brief summary — usually fifty to two hundred words — of your project. It should allow your reader to gain a general understanding of your project and your plans for completing it. Writers who wish to provide additional information, such as explanations of their personal interest in an issue, can provide an introduction, as Nicholas Brothers does in his research proposal (p. 60).

- An overview of key challenges allows you to share your thoughts about potential problems you'll need to address as you work on your project. This section of your research proposal might discuss difficulties you're likely to encounter, such as locating or collecting specific types of sources, gaining enough knowledge about an issue to develop a credible position, or finding enough respondents for a survey. It also provides an opportunity for your instructor, supervisor, or potential funder to respond by suggesting strategies for meeting specific challenges.

- A funding request and rationale provides a budget that identifies costs for key project activities, such as conducting your search, reviewing the sources you collect, writing and designing the document, and publishing or distributing the document.

Writing a formal research proposal allows you to reflect on the work you've done so far and get feedback on your plans to carry out your project. Perhaps more important, it requires you to make decisions about the best strategies for completing your project.

Brothers 1

Nicholas Brothers

English 108: College Writing and Research

Dawn Terrick

September 17, 2013

Research Proposal: Private Military
Corporations and the War on Terror

Introduction: For my research project, I would like to explore the
world of the modern private military corporation (PMC). Mercenaries
have been used throughout history by countries all over the world.
With few exceptions, they have suffered a poor reputation; seen as
unprofessional and unreliable, they went unused by many first-world
nations in the age of standing professional armies. Yet, in recent
years, PMCs have morphed into corporate entities and gained new
respect. But is this respect deserved? Throughout the Afghanistan and
Iraq conflicts, the United States' use of private military corporations
has increased to what I consider startling levels.

While I will strive to be as objective as possible when
conducting my research, my prior personal interest in this issue has
always put me at odds with the supporters of PMCs. Fundamentally, I
believe that overreliance on contractors is a danger to national and
international security. However, it is entirely possible that, with
further study, I will gain a new appreciation for PMCs and their
personnel.

Position statement is clear and concise.

My purpose is ultimately to build an argument about the United
States' continued use of PMCs. To present my position on the issue, I
will need to inform my readers about the history of PMCs and analyze
the corporations' evolving role in our country's military engagements.
My readers are my class peers (from many different backgrounds and
studying different subjects) and my instructor. Although there is a
wide range of scholarship and reportage on this topic, I believe
the general public remains unaware of the pervasiveness of these
corporations. It's my hope that upon reading my paper, the layperson
will have a better understanding of how and why PMCs are involved
in the wars in Iraq and Afghanistan. I will be creating an academic
essay and a brief presentation to convey my research and argument
to my readers. The print format of the essay will allow readers to
follow my logic at their own pace and reread sections of the essay
as needed, and it will also provide them an easy way to look up the
sources I use if they want to explore the topic further — which I hope
they will. The presentation will allow me to explain a complicated
issue in a more conversational format and answer any questions.

Discussion of purpose addresses the writer's intent and the readers' needs.

Brothers 2

I plan to begin my paper with background information — mostly recent history unless I find something compelling from the distant past that I feel readers must know to better understand the present. I would like to explore the practical and moral costs of using PMCs. In doing so, I will likely focus on specific companies and incidents during the "War on Terror" years.

Research Question: What roles do private military corporations play in the U.S. military's war on terror?

> The research question is open-ended but focuses on a specific time and place.

Review of Literature: The book that originally piqued my interest in this topic was Jeremy Scahill's *Blackwater: The Rise of the World's Most Powerful Mercenary Army*, which depicts PMCs as very dangerous entities. Articles I've come across in publications such as *Salon.com* and *Mother Jones* also strongly criticize PMCs. On the complete opposite end of the spectrum are the corporate Web sites of the PMCs, which of course paint their contractors in only the most positive light. I found a more evenhanded approach to the topic in P. W. Singer's *Corporate Warriors: The Rise of the Privatized Military Industry*, which provides a solid overview of the history of PMCs and explains their structure and functions.

> The literature review helps Nicholas think about his sources' different positions.

Search Plan and Relevant Sources: I will need to continue to seek out a range of perspectives on PMCs as I develop my own argument. I plan to conduct some field research by interviewing people who have firsthand experience with or expertise on PMCs. My brother, Michael Brothers, is in the military and might agree to an interview, and I plan to look at the research interests of the political science professors at Missouri Western to see if anyone might be able to provide me with insight on the wars from an academic perspective.

I have already located three books on the subject through the library's catalog, and by reading through the citations and sources used by the authors of these books, I have identified several other books that I might explore. In addition, I have used simple keyword and advanced searches on EBSCOhost, LexisNexis, and *NYTimes.com* to find several magazine, newspaper, and scholarly journal articles that provide contrasting viewpoints on the use of PMCs. They range from first-person accounts of PMC operations to academic articles analyzing the history and current use of PMCs.

I'd also like to take a look at some official government reports and read the actual language of some of the laws that surround PMCs. The Department of Defense Web site as well as senators' and representatives' Web sites might be good places to start.

> Nicholas identifies both a general search idea and a specific plan to carry out the search.

Brothers 3

Once my first draft is complete, I might conduct another round of research to help answer any new questions or expand on new supporting points that I've developed.

Project Timeline: I have a little more than one month to complete this project. I already have several solid sources and plan to have my first assignment (the background paper based on what I know so far) completed one week from today. The next week, I'll conduct my interviews and write an interview paper based on my conversations. From there, I will combine the background paper and the interview paper, synthesizing these two drafts along with any new sources I've found. I will receive feedback on my first draft from my classmates and instructor. Then, I'll conduct any additional research needed and revise the draft by the due date of Oct. 20th. After the final draft is submitted, I'll create a reverse outline and summarize my paper's most important points for a brief in-class presentation the following week.

> A general project timeline indicates the time devoted to each stage of the process.

Key Challenges: Finding knowledgeable first-hand sources will be the main problem I will encounter, but I have some candidates in mind in helping me to understand the perceptions of U.S. military personnel, the history of mercenaries, and the political ramifications of their present-day use by the United States. I will contact them soon to inquire about their willingness and availability. I feel that I have already amassed a good deal of research material and plans, but I am wary that my sources so far might be geared toward my inherent bias toward the subject. I would like to make sure I have real opposing views to explore and not just straw men; this is a goal I will continually have to work toward.

> Writing down key challenges helps Nicholas avoid potential problems.

Time is another challenge. I have to conduct field research quickly and synthesize the results of the interview paper with the rest of my research in a short amount of time to create a first draft. I'm also concerned about focusing my topic enough for the paper to make sense — there are a lot of issues related to my topic that are intriguing, from the history of mercenaries to the legal status of PMCs and their lack of culpability for their crimes. Limiting the scope of my project could be difficult given the many aspects of the topic that seem worth addressing.

Brothers 4

Working Bibliography

Scahill, Jeremy. *Blackwater: The Rise of the World's Most Powerful Mercenary Army*. 2nd ed. New York: Nation Books, 2007. Print.

This book details the history of the private military corporation formerly known as Blackwater, with a focus on its controversial operations in Iraq and Afghanistan. Scahill is a reporter for *The Nation* and has reported extensively on Blackwater. I will use this book throughout my research project, as Blackwater (now Xe Services) remains one of the most powerful, visible, and divisive PMCs in the world.

Singer, P. W. *Corporate Warriors: The Rise of the Privatized Military Industry*. 2nd ed. Ithaca: Cornell UP, 2008. Print.

This scholarly look at the issue takes a balanced view: Singer is able to see the opportunities that PMCs provide while casting a critical eye at the potentials for abuse. I believe this will be an essential resource due to its balanced viewpoint and thoroughness.

Smith, Eugene B. "The New Condottieri and US Policy: The Privatization of Conflict and Its Implications." *Parameters: US Army War College* 32.4 (2002): 104. *Academic Search Premier*. EBSCO. Web. 11 Feb. 2010.

Written before the invasion of Iraq, this academic article briefly outlines the history of the privatization of warfare and concludes that the United States should employ PMCs due to their track record. At the time of this article's writing, Eugene B. Smith was a lieutenant colonel in the United States Army and served in the United States Central Command area of operations. This article might be useful in understanding the mindset of the military command that has increasingly employed private contractors in the last decade.

The working bibliography summarizes sources and evaluates their usefulness.

Joining the Conversation

My Research Project

Create a Research Proposal

Use the following activity to create a formal research proposal.

1. Provide the working title for your project.

2. Describe your issue.

3. Describe your purpose for working on this project.

4. Describe your readers' needs, interests, knowledge, experiences, values, and beliefs.

5. State your research question.

6. Briefly review key findings about your issue from the sources you found as you explored your topic.

7. Indicate how you'll locate additional information, ideas, and arguments about your issue.

8. Include your project timeline.

9. Include your working bibliography.

10. Discuss the key challenges you face (optional).

11. Identify specific funding requests (optional).

bedfordresearcher.com
My Research Project Activities > Create a Research Proposal

> **QUICK REFERENCE**

Developing Your Research Question and Proposal

☑ Reflect on your issue and disciplinary or professional context. (p. 46)

☑ Consider how your role will shape your research question. (p. 47)

☑ Focus on specific aspects of your issue. (p. 47)

☑ Choose and focus your research question. (p. 50)

☑ Refine your research question. (p. 53)

☑ Develop a research proposal. (p. 57)

Part II
Working with Sources

4	Reading Critically and Actively
5	Evaluating Sources
6	Taking Notes
7	**Managing Information**
8	Avoiding Plagiarism

7

Managing Information

Key Questions

7a. How can I save and organize the information I find?   113
Decide how to save and organize print information
Decide how to save and organize digital information

7b. How can I use a bibliography to organize information?   119
Create a working bibliography
Create an annotated bibliography

Even with a narrowly defined research question, it's likely that your searches will produce a large number of relevant sources. To use those sources most effectively, decide how to save, organize, and keep track of your sources. Doing so will help you work with your sources more easily as you plan and draft your document.

7a

How can I save and organize the information I find?

As you begin to collect information, spend some time reflecting on how you will save and keep track of it.

Decide How to Save and Organize Print Information

During your research project, you'll accumulate a great deal of print information, such as:

- your written notes (in a notebook, on loose pieces of paper, on Post-It Notes, and so on)
- printouts from Web pages and databases
- articles sent through a library's interlibrary loan service
- printed word processing documents, such as various drafts of your research question and position statement

- books, magazines, newspapers, brochures, pamphlets, and government documents
- photocopies of articles, book chapters, and other documents
- letters, printed email messages, survey results, and so on

Rather than letting all this information build up in messy piles on your desk or stuffing it into folders in your backpack, create a filing system to keep track of your print documents. Filing systems can range from well-organized piles of paper labeled with Post-It Notes to three-ring binders to file cabinets filled with neatly labeled files and folders.

Regardless of the approach you take, keep the following principles in mind.

- **Make it easy to locate your print materials.** Decide whether you want to group material by topic, by date, by pro versus con, by type of material (Web pages, photocopies, original documents, field sources, and so on), or by author.

- **Stick with your organizing scheme.** You'll find it difficult to locate materials if you use different approaches at different points in your research project.

- **Always include complete publication information.** If a source doesn't contain publication information, write it on the document yourself. You'll need it later. Publication information includes author, title, publisher, place and date of publication, and—for a Web source—sponsoring organization and URL.

- **Record the date.** Indicating dates when you recorded information can help you reconstruct what you might have been doing while you took the notes. Dates are also essential for documenting Web sources and other sources obtained online.

- **Write a brief note on each of your print materials.** Indicate how it might contribute to your project.

Decide How to Save and Organize Digital Information ⓘ INFORMATION LITERACY

As you save digital information, keep it organized. The simplest organizational strategy is to save your work in a single folder (see Figure 7.1). As you save your work, use descriptive file names. Rather than naming a file "Notes 1," for instance, name it "Interview Notes from John Garcia, April 22." Keep in mind that the single-folder approach might not work well for larger projects. At some point, the sheer number of files in the folder makes it difficult to find a single file easily. Rather than scrolling through several screens of files, you might find it more efficient to create multiple folders to hold related files (see Figure 7.2). ▦

Downloading Toward the end of your research writing project, particularly when you are drafting your document, you might find yourself wishing that you'd saved all of your digital sources on a hard drive, flash drive, or a network-based

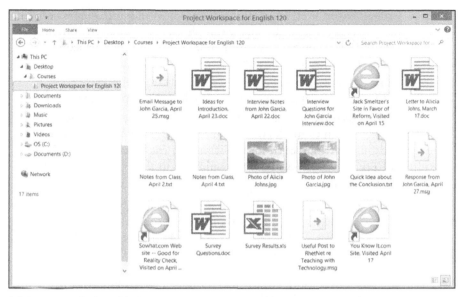

FIGURE 7.1 A Project Workspace Using a Single Folder

service such as DropBox, iCloud, or SkyDrive. Downloading sources allows you to open them in a Web browser or word processor at a later time (see Figure 7.3).

How you save your sources will vary according to the type of digital source you're viewing.

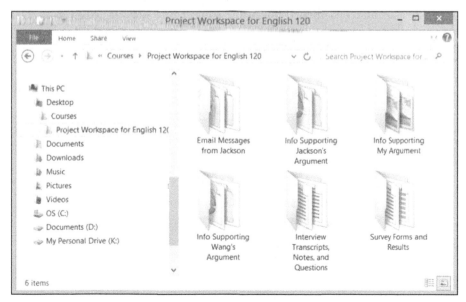

FIGURE 7.2 A Project Workspace Using Multiple Folders

- To download entire Web pages, right-click (for Windows), command-click (for Mac), or press and hold a finger (on phones and tablets) on the page and choose the Save or Save as command. Or use the options icon or menu to save the page (see Figure 7.3).

- To download images and other media materials from the Web, click or press and hold on the item you want and select the appropriate command.

- To download records from a database, check the online help pages. Most databases allow you to mark and save records returned by a search. To download full-text sources from databases, you can open and save the file (often a PDF file or a text file) or download it in the same way you would download an image.

Remember that downloading a source does not automatically record the URL or the date on which you viewed the source for the first time. Be sure to record that information in your research log, in your working bibliography (p. 119), or in a document in the folder where you've saved your files.

Copying and Pasting   You can save text from relevant sources as notes in a word processing document. Be sure to keep track of source information, such as the URL and the date you viewed a source, so that you can return to it if necessary and cite it appropriately.

Using Email   You can email yourself messages containing digital documents you've found in your research. Some databases, such as those from EBSCO and OCLC/FirstSearch, allow you to email the text of selected records directly from the database (see Figure 7.4). You can also use email as a form of file folder by sending messages to yourself that include copies of documents in the form of pasted text or attached files. If you use a subject line such as "My Comp 110 Research Project," you can sort your messages by subject line and easily view all of the information you've collected or you can simply search for messages containing the phrase *research project*.

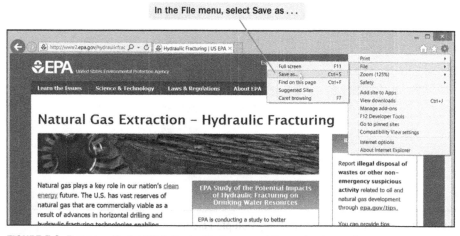

FIGURE 7.3 **Downloading a Web Page** [Environmental Protection Agency.]

E-mail Manager

Back

Articles

Number of items to be e-mailed: 8

E-mail from: ephost@epnet.com

E-mail to: nicholas.brothers@statecollege.edu

Separate each e-mail address with a semicolon.

Subject: Sources for Research Assignment

Comments: Sources from Academic Search Premiere, search on "private military corporations"

Format: ● Rich Text ○ Plain Text

☐ **Remove these items from folder after e-mailing**
For information on e-mailing Linked Full Text, see online help. For information on using Citation Formats, see online citation help

Include when sending:

☑ HTML Full Text (when available)
☑ PDF as separate attachment (when available)
○ **Standard Field Format**
　Detailed Citation and Abstract ☑
● **Citation Format**
　Chicago/Turabian: Humanities ☑
○ **Customized Field Format**

Send

FIGURE 7.4 Sending Email from a Database [Courtesy of EBSCO.]

Taking Photos, Making Recordings, and Saving Notes If you have a smart-phone or a tablet, you can record conversations with others, record voice memos that contain ideas about your project, save video, take photos of sources you find in the periodical room (p. 173), and surf the Web to locate sources. Most phone and tablet operating systems provide access to "apps" (or applications), often at no or low cost, that allow you to collect and organize information in the same way you would on a laptop or desktop computer (see Figure 7.5).

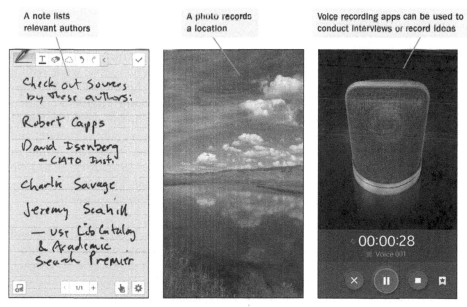

A note lists relevant authors

A photo records a location

Voice recording apps can be used to conduct interviews or record ideas

FIGURE 7.5 Saving Digital Information with Apps

As you save information with these tools, keep your work well organized. Use descriptive names, save work in folders or albums, and add information about where and when you found the information. Be sure to talk with other writers about the apps they've found useful and, if they're free, try them out yourself.

Saving Bookmarks and Favorites in Your Browser   You can use a Bookmarks or Favorites list in your Web browser to keep track of your sources. Be aware that there are drawbacks to relying on a Bookmarks or Favorites list as a place to "store" your sources. First, pages on the Web can and do change. If you suspect that the page you want to mark might change before you complete your research writing project, download or print it so that you won't lose its content. Second, some Web pages are generated by database programs. In such cases, you might not be able to return to the page using a Bookmarks or Favorites list. A URL like the following usually indicates that a Web page is generated by a database program.

http://firstsearch.oclc.org/FUNC/QUERY:%7Fnext=NEXTCMD%7F%22/
FUNC/SRCH_RSULTS%22%7FentityListType=0%7Fentitycntr=1%7Fentity
ItemCount=0%7F%3Asessionid=1265726%7F4%7F/fsres4.txt

Although this long string of characters starts out looking like a normal URL, the majority of the characters are used by the database program to determine which records to display on a page. In many cases, the URL works only while you are conducting your search. If you add such a URL to your Bookmarks or Favorites list, there's a good chance it won't work later. To avoid this problem, consider downloading Web pages (p. 116) or using Web capture and clipping tools (p. 118).

Keep in mind that Bookmarks and Favorites lists can become disorganized. To avoid this problem, put related items into folders, and give the items on your list descriptive names.

Web Clipping and Content Curation Tools   You can also use Web-based tools to save content from online sources. Web clipping tools, which work with your browser as toolbars or "add-ons" (a term used for programs that work within browsers), can be used to copy all or part of a Web page. Leading, free Web capture tools include Diigo (**diigo.com**) and Zotero (**zotero.org**). Content curation tools allow you to create collections of sources and share them—individually or as a group. Scoop.it (**scoop.it**), for example, allows you to save, annotate, and easily revisit Web sites, blogs, and other online content (see Figure 7.6). Although these tools were created largely for commercial purpose (in particular, to help users market products and services), they offer useful tools for writers. Leading, free content curation tools include Listly (**list.ly**) and Paper.li (**paper.li**).

Using Bibliography Tools   Use online bibliography tools such as The Bedford Bibliographer at bedfordstmartins.com/bibliographer to save bibliographic information about each of your sources, write a brief note or annotation about each source, evaluate each source, and save text from digital sources. You can also create a bibliography formatted in MLA, APA, *Chicago*, or CSE style. Read more about bibliographies on the following page.

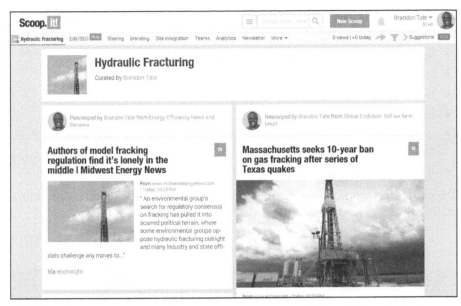

FIGURE 7.6 Scoop.it Allows Writers to Collect, Organize, and Share Online Sources
[Scoop.it! EnergyWire. Peter Andrews/Reuters.]

Backing Up Your Files   Whatever strategies you use to save and organize digital materials, replacing lost information takes time and effort. Avoid the risk of lost information by taking the time to make copies of your digital files and downloads, email messages, saved Web pages and clippings, and Bookmarks or Favorites list.

7b

How can I use a bibliography to organize information?

A bibliography is a list of sources with complete publication information, usually formatted according to the rules of a documentation system such as those created by the Modern Language Association (see Chapter 23), the American Psychological Association (see Chapter 24), or the Council of Science Editors (see Chapter 26), or found in books such as the *Chicago Manual of Style* (see Chapter 25). As you take notes on your sources, use a working bibliography or an annotated bibliography to keep track of the sources you've consulted.

Create a Working Bibliography

A working bibliography is a running list of the sources you've explored and plan to use as you work on your research writing project. Publication information is provided for each source. The organization of your working bibliography can vary according to your needs and preferences. You can organize your sources in any of the following ways.

- in the order in which you collected your sources
- in categories
- by author
- by publication title
- according to how the information, ideas, and arguments in the source align with your position on your issue
- according to an outline of your project document

The entries in a working bibliography should include as much publication information about a source as you can gather (see Table 7.1).

TABLE 7.1 INFORMATION YOU SHOULD LIST IN A WORKING BIBLIOGRAPHY	
Type of Source	**Information You Should List**
All Sources	Author(s) Title Publication year Medium consulted
Book	Editor(s) of book (if applicable) Publication city Publisher Series and series editor (if applicable) Translator (if applicable) Volume (if applicable) Edition (if applicable)
Chapter in an Edited Book	Publication city Publisher Editor(s) of book Book title Page numbers
Journal, Magazine, or Newspaper Article	Journal title Volume number or date Issue number or date Page numbers
Web Page, Blog Entry or Reply, Discussion Forum Post, Email Message, or Chat Transcript	URL Access date (the date you read the source) Sponsoring organization (if listed)
Field Research	Title (usually a description of the source, such as "Personal Interview with Jessica Lynn Richards" or "Observation of June Allison's Class at Tavelli Elementary School") Date (usually the date on which the field research was conducted)

Your working bibliography will change significantly as you work on your research writing project. As you explore your topic and choose an issue, collect sources, read them critically, evaluate them, and take notes, you will add potentially useful sources and delete sources that are no longer relevant. Eventually, your working bibliography will become one of the following.

- a *works cited* or *reference list*—a formal list of the sources you have referred to in a document

- a *bibliography* or *works consulted list*—a formal list of the sources that contributed to your thinking about an issue, even if those sources were not referred to explicitly in the text of the document

Keeping your working bibliography up-to-date is a critical part of your research writing process. It helps you keep track of your sources and increases the likelihood that you will cite all the sources you use in your document—an important contribution to your efforts to avoid plagiarism (see Chapter 8). Bibliography tools allow you to create, organize, and update a working bibliography formatted in styles such as MLA or APA.

The first five sources from Elizabeth Leontiev's working bibliography are found in Figure 7.7.

Entries follow MLA style
(p. 338).

"US Weighs Cost of Plan Colombia." *BBC News*, 5 July 2005, news.bbc
.co.uk/2/hi/4627185.stm.

Forero, Juan. "Coca Advocate Wins Election for President in Bolivia."
The New York Times, 19 Dec. 2005, www.nytimes.com/2005/12/
19/world/americas/coca-advocate-wins-election-for-president-in
-bolivia.html.

Gordon, Gretchen. "The United States, Bolivia, and the Political
Economy of Coca." *Multinational Monitor*, vol. 27, no. 1, Jan./Feb.
2006, www.multinationalmonitor.org/mm2006/012006/gordon
.html.

Harman, Danna. "In Bolivia, a Setback for US Anti-Coca Drive."
The Christian Science Monitor, 22 Dec. 2005, www.csmonitor
.com/2005/1222/p04s02-woam.html.

United States, Office of National Drug Control Policy. *Coca in the
Andes*, www.whitehouse.gov/ondcp/targeting-cocaine-at-the
-source. Accessed 29 May 2010.

Use access date when no publication date is given.

FIGURE 7.7 Part of Elizabeth Leontiev's Working Bibliography

Working with Sources

Create an Annotated Bibliography [FRAMING MY ARGUMENT]

An annotated bibliography provides a brief note about each of the sources you've listed, in addition to its complete citation information. These notes, or annotations, are typically no longer than two or three sentences. The content, focus, and length of your annotations will reflect both your purposes for creating an annotated bibliography and the needs and interests of your readers (see Table 7.2).

TABLE 7.2 PURPOSES AND FEATURES OF ANNOTATED BIBLIOGRAPHIES				
	Your Readers			
	Yourself	**An Instructor**	**A Writing Group**	**External Audience**
Purpose	Keep track of sources; plan your document	Show progress on a project; serve as an intermediate assignment	Show how a source might be useful for a group project	Share information about important sources addressing an issue
Features				
Include complete source citation, using proper formatting.	✔	✔	✔	✔
Summarize the source, noting significant findings and key information.	✔	✔	✔	✔
Evaluate the source, including how it is relevant and background information on the author and publisher.	✔	✔	✔	✔
Compare sources.	✔			
Identify passages containing useful information, ideas, and arguments.	✔		✔	
Reflect on how the source could be used in a project document.	✔	✔	✔	
Note how readers might react to information, ideas, and arguments in the document.	✔			
Respond to the source with your own reaction or analysis.	✔			
Create polished, well-crafted sentences.		✔	✔	✔

The following examples show how the same source might be annotated for different readers.

For Yourself:

This Web page discusses everything about the hydraulic fracturing process and is one of very few sources that gives specific numbers for the amount of water being used in fracking. I will use this information in the section on the disadvantages of fracking.

For an Instructor:

This Web page provides a great deal of information about the hydraulic fracturing process. It is one of few sources I've found that gives specific numbers about the amount of water being used in fracking. I will use this information to explore some of the environmental and economic disadvantages of fracking.

For Classmates in a Writing Group:

This Web page discusses everything about the hydraulic fracturing process and is one of very few sources that give specific numbers for the amount of water being used in fracking. We can use this site to get a good understanding of the disadvantages (environmental and economic) of fracking.

For an External Audience, such as Visitors to a Web site:

The Explore Shale Web page provides an easy-to-understand overview of hydraulic fracking. Its graphical images allow visitors to see how the process works. It also provides details about the hydraulic fracturing process, including the amount of water being used in fracking.

My Research Project

Create a Working or Annotated Bibliography

Create a bibliography to keep track of your sources as you work on your research writing project. Your bibliography should include complete citation information for the sources you are considering for use in your project. You may also include annotations that contain source descriptions, source evaluations, reflections on the source, and plans for using the source in your project.

You can create a bibliography in print form (such as in a notebook) or in digital form (for example, in a word processing file). You can also use bibliography tools, which allow you to create entries for new sources, annotate sources, evaluate sources, copy and save some or all of the text from a source, and display your working bibliography in various citation styles (see Part V).

bedfordresearcher.com
My Research Project Activities > Create a Working or Annotated Bibliography

Costello, B. (2004, July 4). Too late? Survey suggests millions of kids could be juicing. *New York Post.* Retrieved from http://www.nypost.com

> Entries follow APA style (p. 368).

This article discusses steroid and other performance-enhancing drugs used by eighth- through twelfth-grade boys and girls and provides a number of relevant statistics. I'll use this source to support statements about steroid use among young female athletes.

Davies, D., & Armstrong, M. (1989). *Psychological factors in competitive sport.* New York, NY: Falmer Press.

> Annotations provide brief summaries of the purpose and content of the sources.

This book addresses various psychological factors in sports including learning, motivation, anxiety, stress, and performance. I'll use it to support my discussion of why sports can have negative effects on girls.

DeNoon, D. (2004, August 4). *Steroid use: Hitting closer to home.* Retrieved from http://webmd.com/fitness-exercise/features/steroid-use-hitting-closer-to-home

> Annotations are intended for Alexis and her teacher. They indicate how and where Alexis will use the sources in her document.

This Web page provides information about increasing steroid use in America as well as the latest statistical figures regarding this use. I'll use it for statistical evidence and to drive home the point that this problem needs to be addressed.

Dexheimer, E. (2004, May 13). Nothing to lose: The Colorado Impact teaches girls about life — then hoops. *Denver Westword.* Retrieved from http://www.westword.com

Article about a different way of coaching club basketball focusing mainly on the Colorado Impact club and their policies on practice and community service. I'll use it to provide the basketball coach's viewpoint of club basketball and the effects of it on parents, athletes, etc.

FIGURE 7.8 Part of Alexis Alvarez's Annotated Bibliography, Written for Herself and Her Teacher

An annotated bibliography is a useful tool even if it's not something you'll be expected to submit for a grade or share with other readers. By turning your working bibliography into an annotated bibliography, you can remind yourself of important information, ideas, and arguments in your sources; record your reflections, evaluations, and analyses of each source; note your responses to your sources; and record your ideas about how the source might be used to advance your position on your issue.

> **QUICK REFERENCE**

Managing Information

☑ Decide how you will save and organize print information. (p. 113)

☑ Decide how you will save and organize digital information. (p. 114)

☑ Create a working bibliography. (p. 119)

☑ Depending on your purpose and audience, create an annotated bibliography. (p. 122)

Working with Sources

12 Developing Your Thesis Statement

13 Developing and Organizing Your Argument

14 Drafting

15 **Using Sources Effectively**

16 Designing Documents

17 Revising and Editing

18 Presenting Your Work

15

Using Sources Effectively

> **Key Questions**

15a. How can I use sources to accomplish my purposes as a writer? 258
Introduce an idea or argument
Contrast ideas or arguments
Provide evidence for your argument
Align your argument with an authority
Define a concept, illustrate a process, or clarify a statement
Set a mood
Provide an example
Amplify or qualify a point

15b. How can I integrate sources into my draft? 262
Identify your sources
Quote strategically
Paraphrase information, ideas, and arguments
Summarize
Present numerical information
Use images, audio, video, and animations

15c. How should I document my sources? 271
Choose a documentation system
Provide in-text references and publication information

15d. How can I ensure I've avoided unintentional plagiarism? 273
Quote, paraphrase, and summarize accurately and appropriately
Distinguish between your ideas and ideas in your sources
Check for unattributed sources in your document

As you draft your document, remember the range of strategies you can use to support your points, convey your ideas, and illustrate positions taken by other authors. This chapter discusses how you can use source information to meet the needs of your writing situation and addresses the primary techniques for

257

integrating source information into your document: quotation, paraphrase, and summary. It also looks at techniques for working with numeric information, images, audio, video, and animations.

Much of the information in this chapter is based on MLA style, which is commonly used in the humanities. See Chapter 20 for more on MLA style and Chapters 21–23 for guidelines on APA, *Chicago*, and CSE styles.

15a

How can I use sources to accomplish my purposes as a writer?

Your sources can help you introduce ideas, contrast the ideas of other authors with your own, provide evidence for your points, align yourself with an authority, define concepts, illustrate processes, clarify statements, set a mood, provide an example, and qualify or amplify a point. You can present information from sources in several ways.

- as a quotation, paraphrase, or summary
- as numerical information
- as illustrations such as images, audio, video, and animations

As you draft your document, consider how your use of sources can lead your readers to view your issue in terms that are most favorable to your purposes. By selecting source information carefully, you can make your point more directly than you might want to using your own words. Calling opponents of a proposal "inflexible" and "pig-headed," for example, might signal your biases too strongly. Quoting someone who uses those terms, however, allows you to get the point across without undermining an otherwise even and balanced tone.

The following are some of the most effective ways to use information, ideas, and arguments from sources to contribute to a written conversation about an issue.

Introduce an Idea or Argument   [FRAMING MY ARGUMENT]

You can use a quotation, paraphrase, or summary to introduce an idea or argument to your readers. As you choose a quotation, paraphrase, or summary, keep in mind that it will call your readers' attention to particular aspects of your argument.

Consider how the following quotation, for instance, leads readers to view a public debate about education reform as a battle between reformers and an entrenched teachers union.

> "The teachers union has balked at even the most reasonable proposals for school reform," said Mary Sweeney, press secretary for Save Our Schools, which has

sponsored a referendum on the November ballot calling for funding for their voucher plan. "We believe
the November election will send a wake-up call about
the need to rethink their obstructionist behaviors."

> Phrases such as "balked at even the most reasonable proposals" and "their obstructionist behaviors" place the blame for the problem on the teachers union.

If Sweeney and supporters of Referendum D are
successful, the educational landscape in . . .

In contrast, note how the following quotation frames the debate as a question of
how best to spend scarce education funds.

"In the past decade, state and local funding of public
education in real dollars has declined by 7.2 percent,"
said Jeffrey Allister, state chair of the governor's Special Commission on Education Reform. "Referendum
D, if passed, would further erode that funding by
shifting state dollars to private schools." As the state

> Phrases such as "funding of public education in real dollars has declined" and "further erode that funding" call attention to the financial challenges faced by schools.

considers the merits of Referendum D, which would institute the first statewide
voucher program in the United States, opponents of the measure have . . .

Contrast Ideas or Arguments

When you want to indicate that disagreement exists on an issue, you can use
source information to illustrate the nature and intensity of the disagreements.
The following example uses partial quotations (p. 264) to highlight differences in
proposed solutions to a problem.

> Solutions to the state's higher education funding shortfall range from traditional
> approaches, such as raising taxes, to more radical solutions, among them privatiz-
> ing state colleges and universities. Advocates of increased taxes, such as Vincent
> Richards of the Higher Education Coalition, argue that declines in state funding
> of higher education "must be reversed immediately or we will find ourselves in a
> situation where we are closing rural community colleges and only the wealthiest
> among us will have access to the best education" (A4). Those in favor of privatiz-
> ing higher education suggest, however, that free market approaches will ultimately
> bring about "a fairer situation in which the poor, many of whom have no interest
> in higher education, are no longer asked to subsidize higher and higher faculty
> salaries and larger football stadiums" (Pieters 23).

Base your choices about how to contrast ideas and arguments on the clarity and
conciseness of your sources and on the effects you hope to achieve. If you want
to express complex ideas as concisely as possible, you might use paraphrase and
summary. If you want to convey the emotional qualities of an author's position
on an issue, use quotations.

Provide Evidence for Your Argument

Arguments that consist of a series of unsupported assertions amount to little
more than a request for a reader's trust. Even when the writer is eminently trustworthy, most readers find such arguments easy to dismiss. In contrast, providing
evidence to support your assertions increases the likelihood that your readers will
accept your argument. Note the differences between the following passages.

Unsupported Assertion:

Given a choice between two products of comparable quality, reputation, and cost, American consumers are far more likely to purchase goods that use environmentally friendly packaging. Encouraging the use of such packaging is a good idea for America.

> No evidence is provided to support the writer's assertion.

Supported Assertion:

Given a choice between two products of comparable quality, reputation, and cost, American consumers are far more likely to purchase goods that use environmentally friendly packaging. A recent study by the High Plains Research Institute found that the shelf life of several biodegradable plastics not only exceeded the shelf life of the products they were used to package, but also cost less to produce (Chen and Lohann 33). In addition, a study by the Consumer Products Institute found that, when made aware that products were packaged in environmentally friendly materials, consumers were more likely to buy those products.

> Summaries of the results of two studies provide evidence for the assertion made in the first sentence.

Similarly, visual sources can lend support to an assertion. For example, an assertion about the unintended consequences of military action might be accompanied by a photograph of a war-torn street or a wounded child.

Align Your Argument with an Authority

Aligning an argument with an authority—such as a subject matter expert, a scientist, a politician, or a religious figure—allows you to borrow someone else's credibility and status. Start by making an assertion and follow it with supporting information from a source, such as a quotation, paraphrase, or source summary.

> Although voice recognition appears to be a promising technology, challenges associated with vocabulary, homonyms, and accents have slowed its widespread implementation. "The computer right now can do a very good job of voice recognition," said Bill Gates, co-founder and former chairman of Microsoft Corporation. "It certainly will re-define the way we think of the machines when we have that voice input" (Gates, par. 42).

Define a Concept, Illustrate a Process, or Clarify a Statement

Writers commonly turn to information from sources when that information is clearer and more concise than what they might write themselves. You might define a concept by quoting or paraphrasing a dictionary or an encyclopedia, or use an illustration to help readers understand a complex process, such as the steps involved in cellular respiration.

Writers also use information from sources to clarify their statements. A writer might amplify a statement by providing examples from sources or qualify a statement by noting that it applies only to specific situations and then use a quotation or paraphrase from a source to back that up.

> Studies have found connections between weight loss and coffee intake. This doesn't mean that drinking a couple of cups of coffee each day leads to weight loss. However, three recent studies reported that individuals who increased their coffee

intake from fewer than three cups to more than eight cups of coffee per day experienced weight losses of up to 7 percent over a two month period (Chang, Johnson and Salazar, Neiman). "It may be that increased caffeine intake led to a higher metabolic level, which in turn led to weight loss," noted John Chang, a senior researcher at the Centers for Disease Control. "Or it might be that drinking so much coffee depressed participants' appetites" (232).

Set a Mood

You can also choose quotations and illustrations with an eye toward establishing an overall mood for your readers. The emotional impact of images of a celebration at a sporting event, an expression of grief at a funeral, or a calming mountain vista can lead your readers to react in specific ways to your document. Similarly, a striking quote, such as "The screams of pain coming out of that room will stay with me as long as I live," can evoke a specific mood among your readers.

Provide an Example

It's often better to *show* with an example than to *tell* with a general description. Examples provide concrete evidence in your document. Note how the writer of the following passage used an example from a well-known film to illustrate a point about her family's relationship with food.

> And the obsession with eating! My grandmother feeds us constantly. My dad and I always laugh at that scene in *Goodfellas* where the mobsters show up at two in the morning after killing someone, and one mobster's mother whips up a full pasta meal for them. We know that my grandmother would do the same thing: "Are you hungry? Here, sit, eat!" Grandma holds interventions over pasta. If she is unhappy with something someone in the family is doing, she invites everyone over for pasta and we hash it out together.

Amplify or Qualify a Point

You can use amplification to expand the scope of a point. Consider how information from a source is used in the following example to broaden a discussion of the dangers football players face when they add bulk.

> NFL offensive linemen who weigh less than 300 pounds are often described as "undersized," so it's no surprise that young football players are getting the message that bigger is better—and bulking up. A recent study of high school linemen in Iowa showed that 45% were overweight and 9% were severely obese, while only 18% of other young males were overweight; even more troubling, a study in Michigan revealed that among football players from ages 9 to 14, 45% could be considered overweight or obese (as cited in Longman, 2007).

Qualifications, in contrast, allow you to narrow the scope of a statement, reducing the possibility that your readers might misunderstand your meaning. Note how the writer made it clear that deaths related to weight gain are a rare occurrence in football.

> Although such fatalities are unusual, a growing number of doctors believe that use of dietary supplements increases the risk of heat stroke among football players.

15b

How can I integrate sources into my draft?

You can integrate information, ideas, and arguments from sources into your draft by quoting, paraphrasing, summarizing, presenting numerical information, and using illustrations. As you do so, make a point of distinguishing your ideas and information from those found in your sources.

Identify Your Sources

You should identify the sources of information in your document for several reasons. First, doing so fulfills your obligation to document your sources. Second, it allows you (and your readers) to recognize the boundaries between your ideas and those borrowed from sources. Third, it can help you strengthen your document by calling attention to the qualifications or experiences of the person whose ideas you are incorporating.

Use Attributions and In-Text Citations   Whenever you quote, paraphrase, or summarize, distinguish between your ideas and information obtained through your sources by using attributions—brief comments such as "according to" or "as the author points out"—to alert your readers that the point is not your own.

Writers who use MLA or APA documentation format also provide citations—or acknowledgments of source information—within the text of their document to indicate where borrowed material ends. These citations, in turn, refer readers to a list of works cited or a list of references at the end of the document.

Note the following examples, which use attributions and in-text citations.

> **MLA Style:**
> Pamela Coke argues, "Education reform is the best solution for fixing our public schools" (22).
>
> *Attributions identify the author of the quotations.*
>
> "Education reform is the best solution for fixing our public schools" (Coke 22).
>
> *MLA-style In-text citations include the author's name and exact page reference.*
>
> **APA Style:**
> Pamela Coke (2008) has argued, "Education reform is the best solution for fixing our public schools" (p. 22).
>
> *APA-style In-text citations include the author's name, publication date, and exact page reference.*
>
> "Education reform is the best solution for fixing our public schools" (Coke, 2008, p. 22).

As you acknowledge material you've borrowed from sources, you'll want to vary the wording of your attributions. As you do, be aware of the way that the verbs in attributions can convey important shades of meaning—for example, the difference between writing that someone "alleged" something and someone "confirmed" something. The form your attributions take will depend on your use of citation style. MLA recommends present tense ("the author points out"), while

APA recommends past tense ("the author pointed out") or present perfect tense ("the author has explained").

Some Common Attributions

according to	claimed	expressed	reported
acknowledged	commented	inquired	said
affirmed	confirmed	interpreted	stated
alleged	declared	mused	suggested
asked	denied	noted	thought
asserted	described	observed	wondered
assumed	disputed	pointed out	wrote
believed	emphasized	remarked	

You can learn more about in-text citations and the MLA, APA, *Chicago*, and CSE documentation systems in Part V.

Provide a Context   Skilled writers know the importance of providing a context for the source information they include in their documents. It's not enough to simply put text within two quotation marks and move on. Such "orphan quotations"—quotations dropped into a paragraph without any introduction—are confusing. Worse, paraphrases and summaries inserted without context can easily be mistaken for the writer's own work, leading to accusations of plagiarism.

To provide a clear context for your source information, establish why the quotation, paraphrase, or summary is reliable by identifying the source's credentials. In addition, indicate how it relates to your main idea and what it contributes to the point you are making. If you don't, readers will wonder why it's there.

However, Wechsler et al. (2003) of the Harvard School of Public Health analyzed trends at schools using social norms marketing and revealed that the campaigns did not necessarily decrease student drinking; in some cases, schools even reported higher alcohol consumption, according to seven criteria that measured whether students drank, how much, and how often. As the researchers explained, "individual students' drinking behaviors align more closely to the drinking behaviors of their immediate social group rather than to the overall student population at a given school" (pars. 30–33).

> Attribution identifies the source as experts.

> Writer follows APA style; parenthetical citation identifies the paragraph numbers where the quotation was found.

Quote Strategically

A well-chosen quotation can have a powerful impact on your readers' perception of your argument and on the overall quality of your document. Quotations can also add a sense of immediacy by bringing in the voice of someone who has been affected by an issue or can lend a sense of authority to your argument by conveying the words of an expert. Quotations can range in form from brief, partial quotations to extended, block quotations. As you integrate quotations into your

IV Creating Your Document

document, remember that you might need to modify them to suit your purpose and fit the flow of your sentences. When you do, be careful to punctuate them properly.

Use Partial, Complete, and Block Quotations   Quotations can be parts of sentences (partial), whole sentences (complete), or long passages (block). When you choose one type of quotation over another, consider the length and complexity of the passage as well as the obligation to convey ideas and information fairly.

Partial Quotations can be a single word, phrase, or most of a sentence. They are often used to convey a well-turned phrase or to complete a sentence using important words from a source, as in the following example.

> Nadine K. Maxwell, a guidance services coordinator in Fairfax, Virginia, says that students' chances of being admitted can be greater if they apply early, although this varies from school to school and year to year and "may depend upon the applicant pool at the school where they are applying" (32).

Quotation marks indicate the borrowed phrase.

Source information, including the number of the page containing the quotation, is clearly identified.

Complete Quotations are typically one or more complete sentences and are most often used when the meaning of the passage cannot be conveyed adequately by a few well-chosen words, as in the following example.

> I smiled when I read Elizabeth Gilbert's memoir *Eat, Pray, Love*. She writes, "The Neapolitan women in particular are such a gang of tough-voiced, loud-mouthed, generous, nosy dames, all bossy and annoyed and right up in your face just trying to friggin' *help* you for chrissake, you dope—*why they gotta do everything around here?*" (78).

Since the source of the quotation is identified in an attribution ("Elizabeth Gilbert's memoir . . ."), only the page number appears in the citation at the end of the sentence.

Block Quotations are extended quotations (usually more than four typed lines) that are set off in a block from the rest of the text. In general, use a colon to introduce the quotation, indent the entire quotation one inch from the left margin, and include source information according to the documentation system you are using (such as MLA, APA, *Chicago,* or CSE). Since the blocked text indicates to your readers that you are quoting directly, you do not need to include quotation marks.

> In the article "In the Best Interest of America, Affirmative Action in Higher Education Is a Must," William H. Gray III states:

> High school achievement and test scores are considered to be very important criteria in the admissions process by most of the four-year public degree-granting colleges and universities. Nonetheless, high school grades and test scores are not the only factors considered by colleges and universities in the admissions process. Other factors that influence college admissions decisions include high

Quotation marks are not used to surround block quotations.

school rank, being an athlete, alumni connections, extracurricular activities, special talents, and other personal characteristics of applicants. (par. 5)

In block quotations, the citation information is placed after the period.

A paragraph number is provided for an online source.

Modify Quotations Appropriately   You can modify quotations to fit your draft. It is acceptable, for example, to delete unnecessary words or to change the tense of a word in a partial quotation so that it fits your sentence. For example, if you wanted to change the tense of a verb in a partial quotation so that it fits the sentence, you would use brackets to indicate the change.

Original Quotation:
"They treated us like family and refused to accept a tip."

Quotation Modified Using Brackets:
It's a place where the staff treats you "like family and [refuses] to accept a tip," said travel writer Melissa Ancomi.

Brackets indicate a word that has been changed.

Keep in mind, however, that research writers have an obligation to quote sources accurately and fairly. You should indicate when you have added or deleted words, and you should not modify quotations in a way that distorts their meaning.

The most useful strategies you can use to modify quotations include using ellipsis marks (. . .) to indicate deleted words, using brackets [ ] to clarify meaning, and using "sic" to note errors in a source. You can learn more about modifying quotations using these strategies on pp. 101–03.

Punctuate Quotations Correctly   The rules for punctuating quotations are as follows.

- Use double quotation marks (" ") around partial or complete quotations. Do not use quotation marks for block quotations.
- Use single quotation marks (' ') to indicate quoted material within a quotation.

  "The hotel manager told us to 'make ourselves at home.' "

- Place commas and periods inside quotation marks.
- Place question marks and exclamation points outside quotation marks if the punctuation pertains to the entire sentence rather than the quotation. In the following example, the original quotation is not a question, so the question mark should be placed after the quotation mark.

  But what can be gained from following the committee's recommendation that the state should "avoid, without exceptions, any proposed tax hike"?

- Place question marks and exclamation points inside quotation marks if the punctuation pertains to the quotation itself.

  Dawn Smith asked an important question: "Do college students understand the importance of avoiding running up credit card debt?"

- Place colons and semicolons outside quotation marks.

  > Many young consumers consider themselves "free at last"; all too often, however, they find that freedom has its costs.

- When citation information is provided after a quotation, place the punctuation mark (comma, period, semicolon, colon, or question mark) after the parenthetical citation.

  > "Preliminary reports have been consistent," Yates notes. "Without immediate changes to current practices, we will deplete known supplies by mid-century" (335).

- At the end of a block quotation, place the final punctuation before the parenthetical citation.

- Use three spaced periods (an ellipsis mark) to indicate an omission within a sentence.

  > According to critic Joe Robinson, Americans are overworked: "Ask Americans how things are really going and you'll hear stories of . . . fifty- and sixty-hour weeks with no letup in sight" (467).

- Place a period before the ellipsis mark to indicate an omission at the end of a sentence:

  > The most recent information indicates, says Chen, that "we can expect a significant increase in costs by the end of the decade. . . . Those costs, however, should ramp up slowly" (35).

CHECKLIST FOR INTEGRATING QUOTATIONS INTO A DOCUMENT

✔ Identify the source of the quotation.

✔ Punctuate the quotation appropriately.

✔ Use ellipsis marks, brackets, and "sic" as necessary.

✔ Check each quotation against the source to be sure you aren't introducing errors or misrepresenting the source.

✔ Use transitions and attributions to integrate the quotation effectively into your document.

✔ Ensure that the source is cited in your works cited or references list.

Paraphrase Information, Ideas, and Arguments

A paraphrase is a restatement, in your own words, of a passage from a source. Unlike summaries, which are shorter than the text being summarized, paraphrases are about as long as the text on which they are based. Paraphrases can be used to illustrate or support a point you make in your document or to illustrate another author's argument about an issue.

TUTORIAL

How do I integrate a quotation into my draft?

After you select a passage to quote, you'll need to acknowledge the source, punctuate the quotation properly, and provide a context for the information. This example uses MLA style; be sure to follow the guidelines for the documentation style you are using.

Original Passage

1 Locate the passage you want to quote and identify the text you want to include in the quotation.

One clear warning from both resilience theory and practical experience is that prevention is better than cure. The empirical evidence is unambiguous: the trajectory of reef condition is declining globally; because once a reef is degraded it usually stays that way (but see below). Interventions need to focus (a) on reversing interacting slow drivers, particularly overfishing, pollution and greenhouse gas emissions, to avoid transgressing thresholds leading to phase-shifts, and (b) on promoting processes like coral recruitment and herbivory that maintain the coral-dominated states of healthy reefs.

Source: Hughes, Terry P., et al. "Rising to the Challenge of Sustaining Coral Reef Resilience." *Trends in Ecology and Evolution*, vol. 25, no. 11, November 2010, pp. 619–80.

2 Add quotation marks or, if the quotation is long, set the text in a block (p. 264). If you modify the passage, use ellipsis marks and brackets appropriately (p. 265).

"One clear warning . . . is that prevention is better than cure. . . . Interventions need to focus (a) on reversing interacting slow drivers . . . and (b) on promoting processes like coral recruitment and herbivory that maintain the coral-dominated states of healthy reefs."

3 Identify the source of the quotation and the location, such as the page number. Give the author's qualifications in an author tag if you haven't already done so for this source in your document.

In their article "Rising to the Challenge of Sustaining Coral Reef Resilience," Terry P. Hughes et al. note, "One clear warning . . . is that prevention is better than cure. . . . Interventions need to focus (a) on reversing interacting slow drivers . . . and (b) on promoting processes like coral recruitment and herbivory that maintain the coral-dominated states of healthy reefs" (638).

4 Avoid "orphan quotations" by providing a context for your quotation. Introduce the quotation and indicate how it relates to your argument.

It is not enough to try to rehabilitate damaged reefs. In their article "Rising to the Challenge of Sustaining Coral Reefs," Terry P. Hughes et al. note, "One clear warning . . . is that prevention is better than cure. . . . Interventions need to focus (a) on reversing interacting slow drivers . . . and (b) on promoting processes like coral recruitment and herbivory that maintain the coral-dominated states of healthy reefs" (638). Sustaining coral reefs involves protecting existing coral in healthy reef environments.

IV Creating Your Document

Your notes are likely to include a number of paraphrases of information, ideas, and arguments from your sources. (See Chapter 6 to learn how to write a paraphrase.) To integrate these paraphrases into your document, begin by making sure your paraphrase is an accurate and fair representation of the source. Reread the source to double-check the accuracy and fairness of your paraphrase, and then revise the paraphrase so that it fits the context and tone of your document. Use attributions to ensure a smooth transition from your ideas to the ideas found in the source.

In the following example, note how Alexis Alvarez lets her readers know where her statement ends and where the support for her statement, in the form of a paraphrase, begins.

Competitive sports also teach athletes how to cope with failure — Alexis's idea.
as well as success. In the best of situations, as Sieghart (2004)
noted, athletes are able to assess their achievements realistically, The source of paraphrase is cited per APA style.
letting neither winning nor losing consume their reality.

An attribution marks transition from Alexis's idea to source ideas.

CHECKLIST FOR INTEGRATING PARAPHRASES INTO A DOCUMENT

☑ Identify the source of the paraphrased material.

☑ Compare the original passage with your paraphrase. Make sure that you have conveyed the meaning of the passage but that the wording and sentence structure differ from those in the original passage.

☑ Use transitions and attributions to integrate the paraphrase smoothly into your document.

☑ Ensure that the source is cited in your works cited or references list.

Summarize

A summary is a concise statement, written in your own words, of information found in a source. (See below to learn about summarizing entire sources and lengthy passages within a source.) When you integrate a summary into your draft, review the source to make sure your summary is an accurate and fair representation of the ideas in the original source. Be careful, as well, to identify the source and include a citation. You can summarize an entire source, parts of a particular source, or a group of sources to support your argument.

Summarize an Entire Source   Research writers frequently summarize an entire work. In some cases, the summary might occupy one or more paragraphs or be integrated into a discussion contained in one or more paragraphs. In other cases, the summary might be as brief as a single sentence.

Alexis Alvarez summarized a report issued by the Centers for Disease Control and Prevention in her research essay about steroid use by adolescent girls involved in competitive sports.

In May 2004, the Centers for Disease Control and Prevention (CDC) published its latest figures on self-reported drug use among young people in grades 9 through 12. The CDC study, "Youth Risk Behavior Surveillance—December 2003," found that 6.1% of its survey participants reported using steroids at least once, up from 2.2% in 1993. The report also showed that use of steroids appears to be increasing among younger girls: While only 3.3% of 12th-grade girls reported using steroids, 7.3% of 9th-grade girls reported using them. Moreover, girls might be starting to use steroids at a higher rate than boys. The CDC study indicated that 9th-grade girls had reported slightly higher rates of steroid use than boys (7.3% and 6.9% respectively), while 10th-, 11th-, and 12th-grade girls all reported lower use than boys.

> The author, title, and publication date are identified in the text, so parenthetical citation is not required for either MLA or APA style.

> The main point of the report.

> Additional information from the report.

In contrast, Alexis offered a much briefer, "nutshell" summary of a related source.

A 2003 article in *Drug Week* stated that girls who participate in sports more than eight hours a week are at considerable risk for taking many illicit drugs: The higher the level at which athletes compete, the higher their risk for substance abuse ("Sporting Activities").

Summarize Specific Ideas and Information from a Source   You can also use summaries to convey key information or ideas from a source. In his research essay, Nicholas Brothers summarized a section of a book about private military corporations.

A look at definitions in Singer's *Corporate Warriors* reveals that PMCs and traditional mercenaries differ in several key ways. Perhaps the most important difference is that a private military corporation is just that: a legal corporate entity[10] (as opposed to the illegal adventurer or rag-tag squad evoked by the word "mercenary"). Another significant distinction is that PMCs offer a wide range of services ... while mercenaries can rarely do more than engage in combat.

> The summary is introduced with the author and specific source of the ideas.

> Per *Chicago* style, a citation appears as a numbered footnote.

Summarize a Group of Sources   In addition to summarizing a single source, research writers often summarize groups of sources. It's not unusual, for instance, to encounter in research documents phrases such as "Numerous authors have argued . . ." or "The research in this area seems to indicate that. . . ." Such collective summaries allow you to establish a point briefly and with authority. They are effective particularly at the beginning of a document, when you are establishing a foundation for your argument, and can serve as a transitional device when you move from one major section of the document to another.

When you are summarizing a group of sources, separate the citations with a semicolon. MLA guidelines require including author and page information, as in the following example.

Several critics have argued that the Hemingway code hero is not always male (Graulich 217; Sherman 78; Watters 33).

APA guidelines require including author and date information, as in the following example.

> The benefits of early detection of breast cancer have been well documented (Page, 2007; Richards, 2007; Vincent, 2008).

CHECKLIST FOR INTEGRATING SUMMARIES INTO A DOCUMENT

✔ Identify the source you are summarizing.

✔ Ensure that you have summarized the source in your own words. Make sure that you do not merely string together a series of close paraphrases of key passages.

✔ Use transitions and attributions to integrate the summary smoothly into your document.

✔ Ensure that the source is cited in your works cited or references list.

Present Numerical Information

If it suits the issue you are addressing, you might use numerical information, such as statistics, in your document. You can present this information within sentences, or you might use tables, charts, or graphs, as Brandon Tate did on his Web site about hydraulic fracturing (see Figure 15.1). Keep in mind that you still need to accurately and fairly present the numerical information in your document and clearly identify the source of the information, just as you would for textual information. For more information about using tables, charts, and graphs, see pp. 285–86.

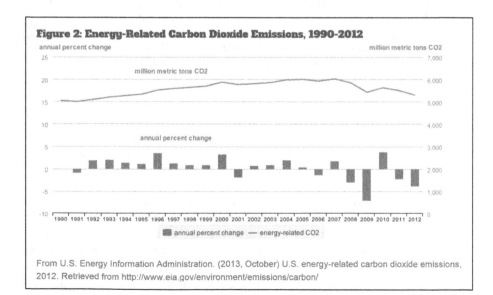

Figure 2: Energy-Related Carbon Dioxide Emissions, 1990-2012

From U.S. Energy Information Administration. (2013, October) U.S. energy-related carbon dioxide emissions, 2012. Retrieved from http://www.eia.gov/environment/emissions/carbon/

FIGURE 15.1 Chart on Brandon Tate's Web Site

Use Images, Audio, Video, and Animations

Including images in your print document and images, audio, video, or animation files in your electronic document can enhance its effectiveness. Use caution, however, when taking images and audio, video, or animations from other sources. Simply copying a photograph into your document might be a form of plagiarism. The same is true of audio, video, and animations files.

Lauren Mack carefully documented the sources of the images, audio clips, and video clips she used in her multimodal research essay. Since she was writing an academic essay—rather than a document intended for publication and wide distribution—she did not seek permission to use the images, audio, and video that she had found in other sources. (In contrast, the publisher of this book sought and received permission to publish those materials.)

ⓘ **INFORMATION LITERACY** If you are creating a digital document, such as a Web page or a multimedia presentation, use the following approach to integrating digital illustrations.

- Make a link between your document and a document that contains an image, sound clip, or video clip—rather than simply copying the image and placing it in your document.

- If it isn't possible or appropriate to create a link to another document, you should contact the owner of the image, sound clip, or video clip for permission to use it.

- If you cannot contact the owner, review the fair use guidelines discussed on p. 131 for guidance about using the material.

As you've done for the other sources you cite in your document, make sure you fairly present images, audio, or video and identify their author or creator. ▪

15c

How should I document my sources?

You should cite your sources within the text of your document as well as provide complete publication information for each source you've used. Fully documenting your sources in this way can help you achieve your purpose as a writer, such as establishing your authority and persuading your readers. Documenting your sources also helps you avoid plagiarism, gives credit to others who have written about an issue, and creates a record of their work that your readers can follow and build upon.

Choose a Documentation System

The documentation systems most commonly used in academic disciplines are the following.

- MLA This style, from the Modern Language Association (MLA), is used primarily in the humanities—English, philosophy, linguistics, world languages, and so on. See Chapter 20.

- **APA** This style, from the American Psychological Association, is used mainly in the social sciences — psychology, sociology, anthropology, political science, economics, education, and so on. See Chapter 21.

- *Chicago* Developed by the University of Chicago Press, this style is used primarily in history, journalism, and the humanities. See Chapter 22.

- **CSE** This style, from the Council of Science Editors (formerly the Council of Biology Editors), is used mainly in the physical and life sciences — chemistry, geology, biology, botany, and so on — and in mathematics. See Chapter 23.

Your choice of documentation system will be guided by the discipline or field within which you are writing and by any requirements associated with your research writing project. If your project has been assigned to you, ask the person who assigned it or someone who has written a similar document which documentation system you should use. If you are working on a project for a writing class, your instructor will most likely tell you which documentation system to follow.

Your choice will also be guided by the genre you have chosen for your document. For example, while academic essays and articles appearing in scholarly journals typically use a documentation system such as MLA or APA, newspaper and magazine articles often do not; instead, they identify sources in the main text of the document rather than in a works cited or references list. If you write a digital document that cites other online sources, you might simply link to those sources.

Provide In-Text References and Publication Information

The specific format of your in-text citations will depend on the documentation system you use. If you use MLA or APA style, you'll cite — or formally acknowledge — information in the text using parentheses and add a list of sources to the end of your document. Key publication information is usually provided in a works cited list (MLA and CSE), reference list (APA), or bibliography (*Chicago*). This list appears at the end of the document and includes the following information about each source.

- author(s) and/or editor(s)
- title
- publication date
- publisher and city of publication (for books)
- periodical name, volume, issue, and page numbers (for articles)
- URL and access date (for online publications)

Each documentation system creates an association between citations in the text of a document and the works cited or reference page. See Part V for documentation models.

15d

How can I ensure I've avoided unintentional plagiarism?

Because plagiarized material will often differ in style, tone, and word choice from the rest of your document, your readers are likely to notice these differences and wonder whether you've plagiarized the material—or, if not, why you've written a document that has so many stylistic inconsistencies. If your readers react negatively, it's unlikely that your document will be successful.

You can avoid unintentional plagiarism by quoting, paraphrasing, and summarizing accurately and appropriately; distinguishing between your ideas and ideas in your sources; and checking for unattributed sources in your document.

Quote, Paraphrase, and Summarize Accurately and Appropriately

Unintentional plagiarism usually occurs when a writer takes poor notes and then uses the information from those notes in a document. As you draft, do the following.

- Look for notes that differ from your usual style of writing. More often than not, if a note doesn't sound like your own writing, it isn't.

- Place quotation marks around any direct quotations, use ellipsis marks and brackets appropriately (see pp. 264–66), and identify the source and the page or paragraph number of the quotation.

- Make sure that paraphrases differ significantly in word choice and sentence structure from the passage being paraphrased, and identify the source and page or paragraph number from which you took the paraphrase.

- Make sure that summaries are not just a series of passages or close paraphrases copied from the source.

bedfordresearcher.com
Tutorials > Do I Need to
Cite That?

Distinguish Between Your Ideas and Ideas in Your Sources

Failing to distinguish between your ideas and ideas drawn from your sources can lead readers to think other writers' ideas are yours. Examine how the writer of the following passage might have failed to distinguish his ideas from those of Joel Levine and Lawrence May, authors of a source used in the essay.

Failing to Credit Ideas to a Source:
According to Joel Levine and Lawrence May, authors of *Getting In*, entrance exams are an extremely important part of a student's college application and carry a great deal of weight. In fact, a college entrance examination is one of the two most significant factors in getting into college. The other, unsurprisingly, is high school grades.

Because the second and third sentences fail to identify Levine and May as the source of the information about the second important factor affecting admissions decisions—high school grades—the passage implies that the writer of the research essay is the source of that information.

In contrast, the writer actually included the following passage in the essay.

Giving Credit to the Source:
According to Joel Levine and Lawrence May, authors of *Getting In*, entrance exams are an extremely important part of a student's college application and carry a great deal of weight. In fact, they claim that a college entrance examination is "one of the two most significant factors" in getting into college (the other, unsurprisingly, being high school grades).

> The attribution, "they claim," credits Levine and May as the source of the information.
>
> Quotation marks are used to indicate a partial quotation.

To distinguish between your ideas and those obtained through your sources, use attributions—words or phrases that alert your readers to the source of the ideas or information you are using. As you take notes and draft your document, use the name of an author or the title of the source you're drawing from each time you introduce ideas from a source.

Examples of Attributions
According to Scott McPherson ...
Jill Bedard writes ...
Tom Huckin reports ...
Kate Kiefer observes ...
Bob Phelps suggests ...
In the words of Pamela Coke ...
As Ellen Page tells it ...
Reid Vincent indicates ...
Jessica Richards calls our attention to ...

Check for Unattributed Sources in Your Document

You should include a complete citation for each source you refer to in your document. The citation should appear in the text of the document (as an in-text citation, footnote, or endnote) or in a works cited list, reference list, or bibliography.

In the following MLA-style examples, the writer includes parenthetical citations that refer readers to a list of works cited at the end of the document. Note that MLA style allows for a combination of attributions and parenthetical information to refer to sources.

Reid Vincent argues, "We must explore emerging energy technologies before we reach a peak oil crisis" (322).

"We must explore emerging energy technologies before we reach a peak oil crisis" (Vincent 322).

> MLA-style in-text citations include the author's name and exact page reference.

> **QUICK REFERENCE**

Using Sources Effectively

☑ Use source information to accomplish your purpose. (p. 258)

☑ Integrate quotations appropriately. (p. 262)

☑ Integrate paraphrases appropriately. (p. 266)

☑ Integrate summaries appropriately. (p. 268)

☑ Integrate numerical information appropriately. (p. 270)

☑ Integrate images, audio, video, and animations appropriately. (p. 271)

☑ Choose a documentation system. (p. 271)

☑ Provide in-text references and a works cited or reference list. (p. 272)

☑ Check for unintentional plagiarism by checking your quotations, paraphrases, and summaries; checking for unattributed sources; and distinguish between your work and information, ideas, and arguments from your sources. (p. 273)

IV Creating Your Document